BECOMING A
TRUSTED
BUSINESS
ADVISOR

How to Add Value, Improve Client Loyalty, and Increase Profits

by William L. Reeb, CPA, CITP and
Dominic Cingoranelli, CPA, CMC

D1592024

AICPA® PCPS
Private Companies Practice Section

Notice to Readers

Becoming a Trusted Business Advisor: How to Add Value, Improve Client Loyalty, and Increase Profits does not represent an official position of the American Institute of Certified Public Accountants, and it is distributed with the understanding that the author and publisher are not rendering, legal, accounting, or other professional services in the publication. If legal advice or other expert assistance is required, the services of a competent professional should be sought.

Copyright © 2010 by
American Institute of Certified Public Accountants, Inc.
New York, NY 10036-8775

All rights reserved. For information about the procedure for requesting permission to make copies of any part of this work, please visit www.copyright.com or call (978) 750-8400.

1 2 3 4 5 6 7 8 9 0 CS 1 9 8 7 6 5 4 3 2 1 0

ISBN: 978-0-87051-902-4

Acquisitions Editors: Martin Censor, Erin Valentine
Developmental Editor: David Cohen
Project Manager: M. Donovan Scott
Book Design: Tom Caley and David McCradden

About the Authors

William L. Reeb, CPA, CITP

Bill has been consulting for three decades to all sizes of businesses, from Mom and Pop operations to Fortune 100 companies, primarily in the areas of organization, automation, and revenue generation. He decided to add the credentials of CPA behind his advisory work and became a CPA in 1986. Prior to his life as a CPA, he worked in sales for IBM back in the late 70's. As an entrepreneur, Bill has founded eight small businesses in the retail, software development, and services sectors, including his recently launched consulting firm, Succession Institute, LLC.

As an award-winning public speaker, Bill lectures throughout the United States and Canada to thousands of executives and CPAs each year. In addition, he has been featured on numerous video-taped and live television programs. As an award-winning author, Bill is published internationally with hundreds of articles and columns to his credit. He currently authors a bimonthly column called "In the Bill-iverse," which, at the time of this printing, is distributed by 15 state CPA societies as part of their practice management e-newsletter. Besides being published by various magazines, journals, and newspapers, this book is the fourth edition of books Bill has written on delivering advisory and consulting services. The third edition was called *Start Consulting: How to Walk the Talk*, published by AICPA in the United States and by the Certified General Accountants (CGA) in Canada. Bill has another new book published in 2010 on Succession, **Securing the Future: Taking Succession to the Next Level**, which is a sequel to his first book, *Securing the Future: Building a Succession Plan for Your Firm*, which was originally published in July of 2005 by the AICPA Private Companies Practice Section (PCPS). Finally, Bill coauthored the Succession Resource Center Web site materials for PCPS in 2009.

Bill is an active volunteer within his profession and has served in many leadership roles in the AICPA including current member of its Board of Directors, and a current commissioner of the National Accreditation Commission. He also has served in numerous other roles including as a member of the AICPA Council several times, a member of Strategic Planning, and chair of the Consulting Services Committees. On a local level, Bill has been a member of the Executive Board, Strategic Planning, and has chaired several technology committees for the Texas Society of CPAs. Additionally, he has been honored by being named as a CPA ambassador, was presented the *Pathfinder Award*, and has served as the Texas Vision Delegate. *Accounting Today* has recognized his efforts by listing him as one of the *Top 100 Most Influential CPAs*, *CPA Magazine* has named him as one of the *Top 100 Most Influential Practitioners*, and *Inside Public Accounting* listed him several times as one of the most recommended CPA firm consultants, and has recognized him as one of the Top 10 most recommended CPA firm consultants in 2008.

Dominic Cingoranelli, CPA, CMC

Dom has been consulting for three decades to a variety of organizations, from professional services firms to nonprofits, construction companies, and Fortune 500 companies. He has been a CPA for thirty-five years and started his own firm in 1976. He ran an office of a local CPA firm located in a rural area of Colorado until 2008 when he joined Bill Reeb to create the Succession Institute, LLC. During his career in public accounting, Dom had the privilege of working with a variety of small and midsize business owners, and he truly lived the role of most trusted business advisor in his interactions with these clients. His work also includes assisting project managers with partnering and conflict resolution on large, complex construction projects of over $300 million. In addition to being a CPA, Dom is a Certified Management Consultant, and he earned his MBA with honors from Regis University.

He speaks frequently on management and consulting topics and has made presentations at AICPA conferences, state societies of CPAs and CPA firm association conferences, as well as the Annual Conference of the Institute of Management Consultants—USA (IMC-USA). Dom has created continuing professional education (CPE) offerings on matters ranging from strategic planning to partnering on construction projects, to professional firm practice management and a background primer for CPAs on the business issues of the construction industry. In addition to his CPE courses, Dom has been published in the *Journal of Accountancy, The CPA Journal, The Practicing CPA, CPA Insider, CPA Management Consultant, Constructor, Broker*, and other state, regional, and national media. Many of his position papers can be downloaded from the Succession Institute Web site at www.successioninstitute.com. Dom has been quoted in the *Dow Jones Wealth Manager, CPA Insider, the Journal of Accountancy*, and the *Construction Company Strategist*, and he has participated in national webcasts of the Institute of Management and Administration and the AICPA on CPA firm management and succession planning. Besides coauthoring the revisions to this book, Dom coauthored another new book a on succession management, **Securing the Future: Taking Succession to the Next Level**. He also coauthored the Succession Resource Center Web site materials for PCPS in 2008 and the PCPS Trusted Business Advisor Web site in 2009.

Dom has served in a variety of leadership positions for nonprofit and professional organizations. He chaired the Management Consulting Services Committee for the Colorado Society of CPAs and served on a variety of AICPA committees, with his most recent position being that of chair of the Consulting Services Executive Committee. He also has assisted as a panel member for interviews of candidates for the CMC designation at the IMC-USA. Outside of accounting, Dom has been active in the heavy construction industry, having received the Associate Member of the Year Award in 2007 from the Colorado Contractors Association. He is a past chair of the Associate Member Council (Board of Directors) and member of the Contractor Board of Directors of the Colorado Contractors Association.

Acknowledgments

We would like to thank our partner, Michaelle Cameron, PhD, who helped us think through and organize this information. She offered significant insight throughout the materials, which we believe made a significant impact in the final manuscript. And, as you see in the technical acknowledgments, Michaelle was the contributing author for the marketing material as well.

We would also like to thank the AICPA publications team who helped fine-tune this book, particularly Martin Censor, David Cohen, and Erin Valentine. Their common-sense approach to editing made what can often become a tedious, time-consuming process a true pleasure.

Finally, we wish to thank Mark Koziel and the Private Companies Practice Section. Their support of the Most Trusted Business Advisor concept has been invaluable.

Technical Acknowledgments

We would like to thank:

- *Larry McGinnes*, Senior Associate, Communispond, Inc., for his assistance in the area of presentation skills.
- *Michaelle Cameron, Ph.D.*, Associate Professor of Marketing, Saint Edward's University, Austin, Texas, for guidance throughout the book and as a contributing author for chapters 11 and 12.

Contents

Section 1: The CPA as Most Trusted Business Advisor

Chapter 1: Becoming Your Clients' Most Trusted Business Advisor 3
Overview...4
Frequently Asked Questions About the MTBA Role 5
Organization of This Text.................10
It's Time 12

Chapter 2: The Changing Profession 13
The World Continues to Change.......14
The Profession Is Continuing to Be Reshaped 14
The Commoditization of Traditional Services.................16
Unbundling Services....................18
Moving to the Future 19
The AICPA's Position on Advisory and Consulting Services..................20
What About Attest Clients? 22
Incorporating the MTBA Framework Into Your Daily Routine 23
Who Should Become an MTBA? 24
The Minimum Transition Requirement for Moving to MTBA Status.........................39

Chapter 3: Making the Transition to Most Trusted Business Advisor: How and Why 41
The Essence of the Most Trusted Business Advisor Framework 42
Obstacles or Opportunities.................42

Our Answers to the Questions and Objections.......................................43
Fees and Pricing Issues 43
Positioning Issues.........................44
Workload Issues............................45
Addressing These Issues.....................47
Compensation Systems 47
Clients and Fees............................47
Stop Giving Away Work 50
Technology 51
Managerial Leadership 51
The General Contractor Model.....................................52
More on the Opportunities of an MTBA...53
Revenue Growth 53
Account Control 56
The MTBA Framework Is a Logical Role for CPAs............57
The Market Has Changed...........57
Organizational Opportunities......58
To Answer the Question 59

Chapter 4: The General Contractor Model..61
Using the General Contractor Model 62
The Role of MTBA 62
The General Contractor Role 63
GC Case Study............................63
Skills Required for the GC Role 65
Will People Pay Me to Function as a GC?...................................66
Case Study.................................67
Important Nuances of the GC Approach 68
Being a GC Means More Than Just Referring Someone 68

Bill for Your Time 69

Build Your Subcontractor
Network 69

Benefits of a Strong Subcontractor
Network 70

Your True Value as MTBA
and GC....................................70

Your Need to Stay Involved as
MTBA and GC 70

Your Role as GC in Dealing
With Subcontractors 70

Final Thoughts on the GC Model......71

Section 2: The MTBA Framework

Chapter 5: Developing Your Self Skills

Skills...75

Treating the Symptoms 76

What is Your Emotional I.Q.? 77

Taking Down the Barriers.................79

Self-Esteem: The Greatest Obstruction
to More Effective Communication ..80

Communicating With Your
Friends 81

Self-Esteem: Awareness Goes a Long
Way 83

Failure: A Sign of Real Growth 84

Your Attitude Makes a Big
Difference 87

Recapping Some Potentially
New Ideas 89

Before You Move On.......................90

Chapter 6: Refining the Most Important MTBA Tool: Communications

Communications 93

Communication Foundation 96

Making a Good First Impression 96

Interpreting Nonverbal Messages........97

Ask Questions...................................103

Take Notes and Refer to Them
Often..103

Ask Only One Question at a
Time...105

Ask Open-Ended Questions 105

Probing and Follow-Up
Questions.............................107

Don't Forget to Use the Global
Functions as Your Questioning
Checklist.......................................108

Avoid the Impulse to Announce
Quick Solutions 113

Your Job Isn't to Have Answers.......115

Listen Actively 117

Clarification and Paraphrasing for
Understanding..............................121

Does Gender Make a Difference?.....121

In Conclusion 122

Before You Move On......................122

Chapter 7: Advanced Communication Skills: Working as a Facilitative Advisor Instead of as a Technical Expert

Expert 135

Show Me the Money!—
Quantification 136

The Omnipotent Advisor: A
Relationship You Can't Count on
Having as Well as a Risk You Can't
Afford 139

If This Is So Straightforward, Then
Why the Opposition? 141

Perspective is the Key 142

Different Approaches Are Necessary for
the Advisory (MTBA) and Expert
Advice Roles.................................143

The Hierarchy of Sources 145

Before You Move On......................147

Chapter 8: Delivering Value-Added Services

Services...151

Cash, Capacity, and Capability.........152

The Balancing Act 156

How Do You Find the Right
Balance? 157

A Simple Format...............................158

What If the Client Doesn't Want to
Do the Leg Work!........................159

The End Result 159
Estimating the Project: Pricing
   Approaches 159
Commissions and Contingent Fees:
   Where Do They Fit in? 165
Before We Move On 166

**Chapter 9: Advanced Advisory
Skills and Practices: Conducting
Effective Sales Calls With Clients
and Prospects** 173
Where We've Come From 174
Going Even Further 174
   The Structured Discovery Call .. 175
   The Structured Sales Call 175
   The Structured Consulting or
      Advisory Call 175
Uncovering Relevant Information ... 176
   The Structured Discovery Call .. 179
The Sales Process 186
   Feature, Benefit, Result 187
   The Structured Sales Call 188
   The Closing Phase of the Sales
      Call 197
Service Delivery 205
   The Structured Consulting or
      Advisory Call 205
The Number One Failing 212
Before We Move On 213
   The Discovery Call Role Play .. 213
   Paper Closing Exercise 215
   Sales Call (Information Gathering
      or Branch) Exercise 215
   Self-Assessment 216

**Section 3: Administrative and
Organizational Issues**

**Chapter 10: Billing and Engagement
Considerations** 231
Tracking Your Time for Billing
   Purposes 232

Time and Charges Approach 232
Project Billing Approach 236
Value Billing Approach 237
Frequency of Billing 239
Survey Information You Might Find
   Interesting in This Context 240
Gaining an Edge on Being Paid for
   Your Involvement 244
   The Value of Advisory Fees Is
      More Subjective 245
   Sometimes When Senior
      Management Asks You What
      the Problem Is, You Have to
      Tell Them That They Are the
      Problem 246
   Project Deadlines Are Internally
      Generated 246
   Client Commitment Is
      Imperative 246
Retainers Aren't a Panacea 247
   Asking for a Retainer 248
   How Much Retainer Should
      You Ask for? 250
   Summary Regarding
      Retainers 250
Proposals 251
   Typical Proposal Structure 253
   Attachments 256
Engagement Letters 256

**Section 4: Identifying and
Marketing Your Services**

**Chapter 11: Two Approaches to
Providing Advisory and Consulting
Services** 265
Understand to Whom the Service Is
   Targeted 267
Building Your Fortress' Wall of
   Services 271
   Building the Wall Profitably 273
   In the Real World 275

Building the Empire........................275
    Determining the Most Appropriate
      Services: The Notion of
      Synergy..............................277
We're Doing Both and It Seems to Be
    Working Fine.............................282
    Don't Get Complacent.............284
    Stay on Top of Your Marketing
      Focus.................................284
A Summary of the Differences.........285
It's Time to Make the
    Determination............................287
Before We Move On.....................287

**Chapter 12: Marketing Your Firm
and Your Services** 293
Developing a Marketing Strategy.....295
Developing Your Marketing Plan....296
    Understand Your Market..........296
    Understand What You Are
      Selling................................297
    Determine Your Objectives......298
    Fine Tune Your Target
      Audience 299
    Fine Tune Your Message..........305
    The Role of Exposure..............306
    Choose Which Exposure Vehicles
      Are Best for Your
      Organization.........................307
    Monitor the Results..................326
Don't Let Marketing Get Out of
    Hand..327
Manage Your Marketing Time........328
Marketing Must Be Planned.............329
Everyone Has to Be Accountable to
    Someone for Marketing to
    Work..329
Customer Relationship
    Management 331
Where Your Firm Is in Its Life Cycle
    Matters Too 332
Before You Move On.....................333

Section 5: Putting It All Together

**Chapter 13: Facilitating Your Clients'
Meetings** 355
Our Role in Meeting Facilitation.....356
    Stay Neutral—Do Not Take
      Sides 356
    Manage the Process 357
    Help the Group Stick to Its
      Guidelines............................357
    Help Stay on Track and Keep
      Moving Along 358
    Ensure All Are Heard 358
    Provide Concepts and Comments
      When Useful 358
    Suggest Procedures 359
    The Bottom Line About Our
      Role 359
Types of Meetings..........................360
    Problem Definition Meetings....360
    Decision Analysis Meetings.......361
    Implementation Planning
      Meetings..............................362
Process Facilitation: Facilitating Your
    Clients' Meetings 364
    Gaining a Shared Understanding
      of Objectives, Agenda, and
      Approach 366
    Expectations and Concerns.......366
    Keeping Everyone Focused on the
      Matters at Hand 367
    Processes to Help Your Group Be
      Productive 367
    Dealing With Difficult
      Behavior 369
Meeting Management 371
    Utilizing the Minimum Decision
      Resource to Make Decisions:
      Who Should Be Making the
      Decision? 373
    The Bottom Line.....................376
    The Right People, the Right

Number, and the Right
Climate 376
Effective Group Presentation
Techniques 377
Control Your Eyes 378
Be Aware of Your Posture 379
Use Gestures to Give Emphasis
and Avoid Appearing Stiff 379
Project Your Voice 379
Clear Your Visual Aids 380
Using PowerPoint or Other
Presentation Packages 380
Look, Then Turn and Speak 381

Silence Is Powerful 381
Handling Questions 382
Practice Creates a Path to
Comfort 384
Before We Move On 385

Conclusion 389

**Appendix A: Sample Timed
Agenda** 393

**Appendix B: Food for Thought for
CPAs Regarding Facilitating
Client Meetings** 395

Section 1

The CPA as Most Trusted Business Advisor

Becoming Your Clients' Most Trusted Business Advisor

"Consult your friend on all things, especially on those which respect yourself. His counsel may then be useful where your own self-love might impair your judgment."

~ SENECA

Overview

Almost without exception, CPAs truly are their clients' most trusted business advisors. CPAs are the people clients trust with the keys to their kingdoms, who know what's going really well for their clients, and who know where the skeletons are buried. In our own experience, we've had clients share information with us that they didn't even want their significant others to know, much less the outside world. Being a most trusted business advisor is a big responsibility, but one that is rewarding and can really make a difference in your clients' lives and in your practice.

Most CPAs already provide advisory or consulting services. Some have gone to the extra effort of formalizing this area. And a few are even strategically shifting the image of their firms from that of traditional accounting to advisory practices with accounting expertise.

This book was written to assist those CPAs who want to fulfill or enhance their role as the most trusted business advisor to their clients. What we're going to cover in this text applies whether your firm is providing formal advisory services or not, and whether your firm has a separate advisory department or not. This book most likely applies to you, no matter what the nature of your practice is! Functioning as your clients' most trusted business advisor (MTBA) is NOT simply about calling in your consulting partner (if you have one), or framing up a formal management consulting project for a client. It is a much broader and more pervasive concept.

 Keep In Mind

In our opinion, functioning as your clients' MTBA is something every CPA in public practice should be doing, regardless of their own area of professional specialization or the nature of their practice.

Although you will learn more about this as you cover the material in this text, suffice it to say for now that, unless you can quickly rattle off the top of your head your top clients' key strategic concerns, opportunities, and initiatives for the next year or two, you are not fully functioning as their MTBA at this time. Tax planning, accounting, and reporting concerns don't count when you are going through this mental exercise. You most likely already are their most trusted *financial* advisor, but unless you can answer the question in broader, more strategic terms, you are not yet their most trusted *business* advisor.

This book will provide you with tips, techniques, and food for thought as you journey down the path toward MTBA status. For CPAs with minimal advisory experience, this text will review the fundamental issues relative to acting as the MTBA on a step-by-step basis. For those who already are successfully delivering on their MTBA role or who also may be performing many advisory or consulting services, our material offers a back-to-the-basics review. This review will not only help you pinpoint possible weaknesses but facilitate the creation of new ideas for improving your offerings and your practice.

Regardless of where you are in your overall practice development, by the time you finish working through this publication, you should be able to construct a pathway that will enhance your ability to live up to our profession's MTBA mantra. This means that you will be making time to regularly have the critical conversations with your clients that are endemic to living up to this role. This commitment will then lead to your being able to easily identify services that will add value to your clients' organizations. However, we ask for your indulgence in reading this book. *Some* of the concepts we introduce are like abstract pieces to a puzzle. By themselves, each of the concepts may not seem to reveal a discernible picture or hold up under much scrutiny. But once all the pieces of the puzzle have been detailed and are in place, the picture should be clear and provide a structure and foundation from which to function as your clients' MTBA. With this in mind, we thought we would start by covering some commonly asked questions that we get when we work with CPAs across the country who are trying to make this transition.

Frequently Asked Questions About the MTBA Role

What I really think I need to do is develop more technical expertise in order to be an MTBA to my clients. As well, I feel I need to be able to deliver these services at a very competitive price. How will this help?

We have a two-part answer to this question. First, you will find that you already have most, if not all, of the skill, knowledge, background, and experience you need to help your clients as their MTBA. And when you don't have all of the particular technical expertise you might need for an issue or a project, we can assure you that you won't have a problem finding a subcontractor professional to fill in the gaps for you—which we will cover in more depth in chapter 4. Second, although it is assumed by the vast majority of CPAs that technical expertise is critical to functioning as the MTBA, two Institute of Management and Administration (IOMA) publications (IOMA publishes two reports for the accounting profession: AOMAR [Accounting Office Management and Administration Report] and PR [Partner Report for CPA Firm Owners]) from a few years back lead to a different conclusion. They basically concluded that "clients assume their CPAs' technical competence as a given," and that "technical excellence is rarely discernible by clients." These findings certainly match with our experience. On the price side, an IOMA survey called the *CPA Firm Client Satisfaction Survey*, conducted in the fall of 2008, surmised that although fees were quite important to clients, they were not the driver of change that so many CPAs believe they are. For example, 54.7 percent of respondents agreed that "fees are just about right for what we receive" from the CPA firm. And 28 percent indicated that "fees are on the high side, but it is worth paying more for the value we are getting." This is the positioning that we advocate firms strive to achieve. Prices are high, but worth it! Only 14.7 percent of those responding agreed with this statement: "fees are on the high side, and this is a reason that we are considering changing firms." A mere 2.7 percent felt that "fees are on the high side, and we are definitely planning to switch firms because of this." So, less than 3 percent of the clients definitely are going to change CPA firms because of price, but you have to ask the question, is even this small group in the process of change because of price, or more likely, because of the lack of perceived value they are receiving for the dollars being paid?

So if technical expertise and price are not the formidable hurdles slowing the expansion of the MTBA role for CPAs, what is? We believe it is the unconscious bundling of what we term the *Most Trusted Business Advisor Framework* (MTBA Framework) and *niche expertise*. In the article, "Body of Knowledge" by F. Anne Drozd, printed in *CA Magazine*, which is published by the Canadian Institute of Chartered Accountants in Toronto, Canada, the author lists seven key skills all advisors should have:

• Ability to learn quickly
• Proficiency in asking questions
• Ability to patiently listen and observe
• Possession of people skills
• Adeptness at analyzing information/situations and drawing conclusions
• Creativity
• Competence as a communicator

These skills are the essence of the MTBA Framework. Let's assume that your firm develops a 22-step program outlining the delivery of a new niche service called "The Small Business Checkup." Let's further assume that it can be profitably delivered for $5,000. It is our contention that although a niche expertise such as this one is invaluable, it is only useful as long as the CPAs in your organization are comfortable and competent in the following:

• Identifying which clients have a need that this service could benefit
• Convincing those clients of the value of having this service performed
• Communicating and persuading management to take appropriate action
• Taking on the role of the change agent facilitating this transition
• Establishing an environment that is conducive to creatively resolving conflicts and overcoming obstacles

Almost all CPAs do this to some degree on a regular basis. And for that reason, this capability may sound simple, straightforward, and common. However, few CPAs have fine-tuned the skill set required (those skills identified as the MTBA Framework) needed to do this well. Because of the significance of these skills, this text is focused primarily on building the MTBA Framework. It is our experience that almost every CPA firm is loaded with niche expertise of one kind or another that are underutilized and underdelivered. (Yes, we're referring to the underutilized and underdelivered technical competence that everyone seems to be so worried about developing more of.) By better understanding and embracing the MTBA Framework, firms quickly can raise the utilization and delivery of their current levels of competence. It's like software and technology: although there is an almost infinite number of new programs we can add to our current systems, the most effective approach is usually to make sure we are fully utilizing the tools we already have. By simply learning what your clients need and must have to thrive and survive, as well as identifying opportunities to help them meet those needs, you quickly can leverage the tools you already have in your toolkit. This higher utilization of existing expertise, in turn, augments existing revenues while simultaneously improving client satisfaction and building incredible client loyalty.

> I am not looking for today's quick fix to a stagnating or declining revenue problem. I am searching for a long-term solution. Why do you think the MTBA role and Framework fit that description?

We believe that functioning as our clients' MTBAs is much more fundamental to our profession's future than just being some quick fix as an additional revenue source. Paraphrased, the 2008 IOMA *CPA Firm Client Satisfaction Survey* concluded that clients are fairly loyal to their CPA firms. They report staying with their current CPA firm an average of 12.8 years!

The following is a sampling of comments from the survey, which identify some reasons why clients stay:

- "Great service. Knows our business well. Gives good advice!"
- "We are a family-owned company, as they are, and we've grown together over the years. They understand our business."
- "Familiar with our business operations and are able to do our work quickly and accurately without interrupting business operations."
- "Good relationship between ownership and CPA firm. Ownership trusts the advice received from the firm, and has a history of solid results."
- "They do a good job servicing our needs, communicate well with us year-round, and are reasonably priced."
- "Good consistency of service delivery. Professional staff with very low turnover."

The following are some reasons clients leave their firms and look for new ones:

- "Our previous firm seemed to have grown so much that they did not provide us with good communication that affects our business. Their fee structure also increased significantly."
- "Switched from previous firm due to a lack of interest/assistance with our business growth/success. We became nothing more than another billing account."
- "We were tired of a 'one size fits all' audit approach and were getting no real business value from our other firm. We also felt we were paying too much for the service."
- "Changed from Big 4 firm 5 years ago in order to save money and gain access to a locally-based firm."

In surveys from IOMA on this topic in past years, they have logged additional client complaints like the following:

- I'm looking for "services that spark new ideas or can save additional dollars."
- I want "customized advice, not 'boilerplate' recommendations."
- "Providing guidance and direction for the future," is the kind of help we need, "not just a slap for prior transgressions."
- My CPA needs to have an "interest in our business—not just our tax returns or financial statements."
- I want a better balance between "advice based on perceived opportunities versus fixing problems."
- My advisor should have "the presence to answer questions in a manner that can be understood by the lay person, and not be afraid to say 'I don't know, but I'll find out.'" (Our emphasis added.)

The message is simple. Clients are saying, "I want to work with a CPA firm who cares about me—the whole me (personal and business)!"

Although relationships with partners and staff are important in making this connection, a revealing and surprising response from the survey was that 82.2 percent said they would stay with the current CPA firm if the lead partner retired or became unavailable. This statistic clearly states to us that if a CPA is providing value by acting in the MTBA role and caring about the client as a whole that they will be loyal to the firm even beyond the current relationship manager.

A survey by Bay Street Group LLC, Rick Telberg, Principal, conducted at the end of 2006 called, "What Clients Really Want," arrived at some interesting conclusions. The main finding to us was the size of the gaps between "what CPAs think their clients think," and "what their clients actually think." Here are several examples that caught our eye.

When asked the question, "Would you recommend your CPA firm to a friend?," 45 percent of the clients said that they would NOT make that recommendation (or 55 percent said they would). When the CPA was asked about the percentage of their clients that would recommend them, 35 percent said "nearly every client—over 80 percent." Another 45 percent said that most of their clients would recommend them—60 percent to -80 percent. If you take a conservative average of those two findings, about 80 percent of the firms thought that about 79 percent of their clients would recommend them, compared to only 55 percent of the clients agreeing with that.

Another telling question that demonstrates our lack of understanding of our clients from this survey was, "Why would you change CPA firms?" At 80 percent, the number one reason why a client would leave their CPA was "poor service, attentiveness." Only 34 percent of CPAs chose "poor service, attentiveness" as a reason for clients to leave. At 51 percent, the number one reason why CPAs felt their clients would leave them was because of "price, fees, affordability." To support this even further, 35 percent of the clients said they would change CPAs because the CPA "was not proactive enough," whereas only 19 percent of the CPAs thought this was important.

This survey, which you can get online for free by registering with Bay Street Group's Web site, shows huge misconceptions about what is important to our clients. This, to us, is just another indication that we need to do a better job of staying in touch with our clients and living up to our MTBA role.

These surveys are just a few of many that have been conducted over the past 20 years that have revealed basically the same message: clients are looking for more than accounting from their CPA firm.

And when they can't find the assistance and care that they want and need, clients are going to go elsewhere, often to other CPA firms. The MTBA role is *not* just another revenue source—it's the client-demanded future of our profession. Clients want it, and they are willing to pay you for it!

> I like what I'm reading at this point, but I am already too busy to keep up with existing client work—how on earth can I do any more?

We often hear this question (or objection) to the whole notion of functioning as a client's most trusted business advisor. For too long now, many CPAs have been working too many hours, struggling with delegation to staff, (perhaps with even being able to keep staff), and creating enough profits to allow them to provide other services their clients sorely need. Unfortunately, many CPAs have been functioning as "order takers," answering the phone when the clients call with questions, rather than proactively taking an interest in their clients' businesses and helping their clients find ways to get better, faster, and stronger. If any of these symptoms sound familiar, don't be discouraged. You can take some very practical steps right now to change things. In chapter 3, we will address the steps you must take in order to free up your time to function at your highest level—that of MTBA.

> What should I expect if I read this?

Many firms are ignoring the changing demands of their clients. And of those that have responded to the changing demands, some unfortunately are providing MTBA services unprofitably, in a manner prone to litigation, and in a way that provides less than optimal value. This text can help avoid pitfalls and make improvements in each of these areas.

We make no promises or guarantees that the ideas and approaches in this text will work for you. However, you do, at a minimum, have the opportunity to see what works well for us and for other firms with which we have counseled. By using this information as a starting point for reorganizing and planning your firm's MTBA evolution strategy, you should be better able to consistently deliver services which are *both* valuable to your clients and profitable to your organization.

Organization of This Text

This book is broken into sections and chapters. The sections are as follows:

- "The CPA as Most Trusted Business Advisor"
- "The MTBA Framework"
- "Administrative and Organizational Issues"
- "Identifying and Marketing Your Services"
- "Pulling It All Together"

We organized the material in this manner because we are attempting to "skill build or skill enhance." Therefore, we have laid out this text, for the most part, to build on the skills in the same order that you would use them in practice. For example, because it's not customary to prepare an engagement letter before you know what the engagement is all about, we cover the skills necessary to define the engagement before we worry about administering it. Another example is that we cover the skills necessary to identify services the client is interested in before we discuss how to motivate the client to hire you. With this in mind, the following shows the way the book breaks down, some of the main focal points of each section, and the plan that this text follows to create an entire advisory methodology.

The first section, "The CPA as Most Trusted Business Advisor," focuses on the concept of the MTBA and why it is so important to fulfill that role for your clients. It contains four chapters: "Becoming Your Clients' Most Trusted Business Advisor," "The Changing Profession and the MTBA," "Making the Transition to MTBA: How and Why," and "Using the General Contractor Model." These chapters lay the groundwork regarding why being the MTBA is not just providing another service but a new way of doing business. These chapters also cover why some strategies have been more successful than others and how you can begin freeing up time to implement the MTBA framework at your firm.

"The MTBA Framework" section includes five chapters: "Developing Your Self-Skills," "Refining the Most Important MTBA Tool: Communications," "Advanced Communication Skills: Working as a Facilitative Advisor Instead of as a Technical Expert," "Delivering Value-Added Services," and "Advanced Advisory Skills and Practices: Conducting Effective Sales Calls With Clients and Prospects." The first two chapters, "Developing Your Self-Skills" and "Refining the Most Important MTBA Tool: Communications," deal predominantly with self-awareness, communication, persuasion and listening skills. Without an in-depth understanding of how we act and react, as well as how to facilitate change, it will be difficult for us to ever get into a position to show very many clients what we can do. Additionally, we cover how CPAs can have a dialogue with a key client to identify what really matters to that client in just a few minutes.

The third chapter within "The MTBA Framework," "Advanced Communication Skills: Working As a Facilitative Advisor," covers quantification—how you help your client determine the value of addressing what matters at his or her business, and it provides critical advice on staying in your facilitative role rather than the traditional expert role we are used to operating within. The fourth chapter in this section, "Delivering Value-Added Services,"

The CPA as Most Trusted Business Advisor

Chapters: 1–4

- Why Use the MTBA Approach
- Definition of MTBA Approach
- Advisory Services Versus Niches
- Providing Differentiated Services
- Making the Transition

- Organizational Implementation
- Global Services
- Implementation Strategies
- The Evolution of the Profession

The MTBA Framework

Chapters: 5–9

- Developing Your Self Skills
- Improving Communication Techniques
- Consulting Techniques
- Unbundling Services and Phases
- Advanced Skills—Sales Calls

- Evolving Investigative Questioning
- Learning to Facilitate the Client's Solution
- Pricing Techniques
- Structured Advisory Calls

Administration and Organizational Issues

Chapter: 10

- Billing Issues
- Retainers and Collection Issues

- Being Paid for Your Involvement
- Engagement Considerations

Identifying and Marketing Your Services

Chapters: 11 and 12

- Building the Fortress
- Building the Empire
- The Marketing Plan
- The Message

- Determining the Most Appropriate Services
- Exposure Alternatives
- Client Service Plans

Pulling It All Together

Chapter: 13

- Meeting Facilitation
- Types of Meetings
- Meeting Management

- Our Role as Facilitator
- Facilitation Techniques
- Presentation Skills

not only covers some critical techniques about how to deliver advisory services, but it also includes direction regarding estimating projects. The last chapter in this section is "Advanced Advisory Skills and Practices: Conducting Effective Sales Calls With Clients and Prospects," which covers three different call types: the Discovery Call, the Sales Call, and the Advisory or Consulting Call. This chapter hones in on how to conduct each of these interactions effectively.

After you have been hired to perform advisory services, a variety of "Administrative and Organizational Issues" come into play. Hence, we created a section to cover them. The chapter in this section covers "Billing and Engagement Considerations," including methods and frequency of billing and the use engagement letters and proposals.

By this time, the book has taken you through skills and techniques which augment selling, delivering, billing, and collecting for advisory or consulting services. It's time now to focus on marketing. Building the best mouse trap doesn't mean anyone will buy it. That's where marketing comes in, so we created a section called "Identifying and Marketing Your Services." This section includes the chapter "Growing Your Business," which helps you determine what services your firm should be offering and why. The second chapter, "Marketing Your Firm and Your Services," not only reviews the most commonly used exposure vehicles, but it also covers how to create a marketing plan as well.

Finally, we introduce one of the most important sections of all: "Pulling It All Together." The chapter, "Facilitating Your Clients' Meetings," takes you through a simple format for running small, informal meetings for your client management teams and gives you tips and techniques for successful meeting management and facilitation.

It's Time

With all of this in mind, it's time to get started. We ask that you be patient and read through the entire text. Much of this material will seem to be common knowledge and, at times, insignificant. But note this: although this review of the basics and the subtleties of this text might not jump off the page as important, by incorporating these ideas and techniques into your skill set toolbox, you will find yourself in a new world with seemingly unlimited opportunities and the competence and confidence to deliver a higher level of value to the clients you serve. We hope you enjoy reading this as much as we did writing it!

The Changing Profession

"Nothing endures but change."

~ HERACLITUS

The World Continues to Change

You've all read, heard, seen, and felt it before, so we're not going to belabor this point, but the world *is* changing. And the changes that have occurred and will occur continue to redefine the business landscape. Some broad categories of change that continue to play a prominent role in the future of the profession and of our clients' businesses include the following:

- *Technology*. In the section immediately following, we cover how technology is driving change in the way we deal with the information value chain. From PDAs and smartphones to VOIP (voice-over-Internet-protocol) and telecommuting, as well as a variety of other factors, you can expect continuing changes that will affect your business.
- *Demographics*. Boomers are at or approaching retirement age. How are you teaming up with those client relationships so that when your regime and their regimes change, you have a connection? What are you doing to enrich the sense of professional accomplishment of the younger generation working for or with you?
- *Market forces*. As you'll see under our discussion of specialization and the "General Contractor" model, the way you help your clients meet their needs has to change.
- *Regulatory and legislative*. What can we say about this that hasn't already been said, often with a peppering of expletives that have to be deleted for general consumption?

We need to get used to the idea that the "good old days" (if they ever were that good) are gone and they're not coming back. Life is more complex. We all (including our clients) have higher levels of expectations for services and goods we receive in exchange for value paid. The younger generation, for the most part, will *not* be spending their lives at the office or on client projects. It's not going to happen. Work-life balance is a concept that is here to stay, unless there is another great depression, which might allow employers to demand unreasonable expectations of the fortunate few that have jobs. The world continues to change, and our profession is changing with it. But there are steps you can take to better deal with these changes. And we're going to cover some of these steps as they relate to creating stronger client relationships and finding ways to better meet your clients' needs.

The Profession Is Continuing to Be Reshaped

The AICPA and State Society Vision Project looked into the future of the profession and formalized the way it was, and would likely continue to be, reshaped. Consider the AICPA's core purpose statement for the CPA profession:

"CPAs...Making sense of a changing and complex world"

By definition, a vision statement expresses just how good something could be in the future. Consider the vision statement for the CPA profession describing where the profession is headed:

> CPAs are the trusted professionals who enable people and organizations to shape their future. Combining insight with integrity, CPAs deliver value by:
> - Communicating the total picture with clarity and objectivity,
> - Translating complex information into critical knowledge,
> - Anticipating and creating opportunities, and
> - Designing pathways that transform Vision into reality.

We absolutely believe in this vision as exemplified in a 1996 article written by Bill Reeb and Michaelle Cameron, "The Evolution of the CPA," which was published in the AICPA's *Journal of Accountancy*. Reeb's and Cameron's article referred to four personality profiles each CPA needs to be prepared to emulate. Those profiles were artist, educator, visionary, and leader. By constantly changing roles, you will be better able to deliver the value outlined in the previous vision statement.

Now, back to the vision. We like to overlay the AICPA vision on a graphic we refer to as the "Information Value Chain" (figure 2-1) to better illustrate what it means to CPAs and what services we provide.

In the past, our professionals predominantly helped clients accumulate data or put their financial data into an informational format. According to a recent Kennedy Research Group survey, this space showed the marketplace paying about $100 per hour for this type of work. The problem is (1) not only was this "data-to-information" space one of the lowest paying services they reviewed but, (2) technology continues to disintermediate that service away from us. In other words, as software continues to evolve each year, it seems to automatically do more and more of this "data-to-information" transition for the uninitiated. So, given this trend, it certainly makes sense that this is not the space to hang your business future. In that same survey, Kennedy showed that people working in the "information-to-knowledge" space charged about $250 per hour for their time. Those that spent time anticipating opportunities or working in the knowledge space charged, on average, $450 per hour. And

Figure 2-1: **Information Value Chain**

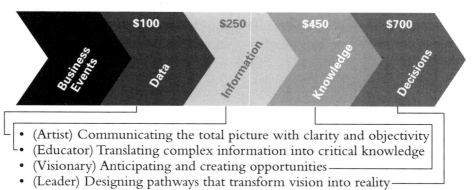

- (Artist) Communicating the total picture with clarity and objectivity
- (Educator) Translating complex information into critical knowledge
- (Visionary) Anticipating and creating opportunities
- (Leader) Designing pathways that transform vision into reality

finally, those that spent their time in the decision space (transforming vision into reality) were realizing an average of $700 per hour.

Now the point here is not whether these rates have changed or apply to your specific area, but that the higher up the information chain your services move, the greater the perceived value to the client. The lowest perceived value is at the information level, which, historically, is what many of our traditional CPA services have been built to provide. The highest value is dealing with strategy, which is where CPAs operate when they're functioning as clients' most trusted business advisors (MTBAs).

The Commoditization of Traditional Services

While historically serving as the backbone of the CPA industry, traditional services (taxes, audits, financial statements) unfortunately have become commodities to many in the eyes of the public. Simply stated, this means that the general public often views the traditional services CPAs perform, such as tax preparation, as being pretty much the same, regardless of the CPA's personal experience or knowledge, or both (more on this in a minute). So, what happens to a commodity when it is left to stand on its own merits? When quality is considered a constant, then price predictably will become the most important buying criterion.

Even after the changes caused by the Enron and WorldCom scandals, many firms continue to be confronted with this issue in the audit marketplace, where severe price discounting battles have been fought. To be fair, audit prices have increased, but only because the profession has to spend more time satisfying increasingly rigorous audit standards. Meanwhile, many firms are now feeling this same fee pressure in areas like financial statement and tax return preparation.

So why have so many traditional CPA services become commodities? The main reason is that our profession has done a great job of selling the value of a CPA's education, training, and skills. A long time ago, our profession focused on creating a distinction between the CPA and everyone else that worked in accounting. Because this was done very successfully, the marketplace now recognizes that those three initials behind someone's name in the accounting field is an added value. But because our professionals dramatically have expanded the scope of services we offer (both in public and industry) in the last 20 years, we are finding the quality "public relations program" started 50 years ago is plaguing us. Why? Because during the fight to create a distinction between a CPA and a non-CPA, we perpetuated the idea that all CPAs have the same skill set. This resulted in the idea that a CPA is a CPA is a CPA. This image went beyond the work performed, and a unique accountant stereotype emerged. Just ask anyone you meet on the street to describe a CPA. This stereotype of CPAs, where we all think alike, act alike, and have the same skills, is now part of the problem. Our marketplace tends to judge us as a profession rather than individually. As a result, the public often generalizes that the traditional services a CPA delivers (that is, audits, financial statements, and tax returns) are the same, regardless of who actually performs the work.

Why Should I Move Beyond Accounting Per Se?

Clients have become more sophisticated over the years. With the advent of the Internet, more and more information can be obtained online easily by just about anyone. More people are connected to share information—one client of your firm has more and easier access to a client of another firm, to compare notes, share their experiences, and learn how that client gets his or her problems addressed.

In interviews conducted by CPA2Biz with CEOs of three small to medium-size organizations, picked randomly for the Trusted Business Advisor Workshops, the message came across loud and clear: clients expect more from their CPAs than simply providing historical accounting information. When you consider the facts, this should come as no surprise. Not only do clients expect it, but many demand it.

 Keep In Mind

If you are not providing advisory assistance—helping your clients in a consultative and facilitative fashion—they will find someone else to help them.

This is a primary reason why the Most Trusted Business Advisor Framework is so important to our profession. The MTBA role is the value-added component that converts a commodity into a unique offering. It helps differentiate one CPA's product from another based on that individual's experience and knowledge. It's really just a logical extension of what you are already doing. You already know the client and, in general, what is going on with them financially. By taking this knowledge to the next level and increasing your understanding of his or her challenges and opportunities and strategies for dealing with them, you make yourself an indispensable management resource.

To put this into perspective, consider how a local hardware store succeeds in selling a Black and Decker® power tool for $40, when a discount chain will sell it for $30. The answer is the additional advice and personal service that comes with the drill. At the hardware store, a salesperson will be available to answer your questions about the product and make suggestions that might help you better utilize the tool in an upcoming project. If you need a special drill bit, the salesperson most likely will be able to recommend the best bit for the job. On the other hand, at the discount store, you'll be lucky to find a warm body to talk to, much less someone who actually could help you make a more informed decision.

This same analogy regarding differentiation also holds true in our profession. With some patience and a little accounting knowledge, anyone can prepare a financial statement or tax return. And due to the abundance of quality computer software, these products are getting easier to produce. This flood of "me too" product offerings can be combated by creating unique new offerings which combine a commodity product (like a financial statement) with advice based on your personal knowledge and experience.

The MTBA Framework is the forum which allows you to deliver that advice, thereby differentiating your product from those of your competitors. For example, a financial statement is merely a compliance report until the information is analyzed, synthesized, and presented in a manner that management can easily understand and use. Therefore, many firms no longer just offer a financial statement alone. They bundle this product with quarterly meetings to discuss results and future plans, making this commodity service a unique offering. Those CPAs who are not working as an MTBA with every client are delivering services which are destined to become price-sensitive commodities. On the other hand, those who are delivering on their MTBA role will not only protect their existing client base, but will be able to grow profitably and have fun while they do so. In our view, this is pretty much a no-brainer!

Unbundling Services

Don't preach to me, I am already advising my clients!

Even if you are regularly advising your clients, if this service is not highlighted and properly identified, it could prove to be of little value to your firm. The American consumer has grown accustomed to being able to choose between goods in a stripped-down, bare-bones package and those bursting with extras. Although our profession will provide this delineation of services, it seems common practice to confuse the consumer by referring to both the bundled and unbundled versions identically. For example, let's say one of your clients calls you several times during the year with tax questions regarding the financial impact of various decisions they are considering. If you are like many CPAs around the country, you will record that time and bill it when you deliver the tax return. The bill received by the client will often read only, "Tax Return Preparation." So here's a case when tax consulting services were appropriately delivered, but because they were not labeled as such, the client incorrectly will assume that "Tax Return Preparation" includes quality advice throughout the year as part of the package.

This practice of bundling our services and generically referring to the work performed trains our clients to believe that "Our advice is free because we make our living selling paper products." This creates an impression that few CPAs would deem positive. The damage this misunderstanding causes becomes apparent when a competitor offers to do your clients' tax returns at half of what you have been charging. Based on this savings, or the feeling that they have been taken advantage of by you, or both, a few of your clients might decide to change CPAs. What these "ship-jumping" clients are likely to find is that the tax return is less expensive, but the overall bill will remain about the same. It's just that the new CPA charges separately for advice. However, it's too late, several clients are lost, and they are not likely to switch again until another significant issue arises (even if they realize they didn't make the best decision, they will not want to admit as much, nor will they want to put themselves through the strain of yet another change in professional relationships.) In this circumstance, the clients didn't change providers due to poor performance, but rather because quality services were delivered that the client was motivated to take for granted.

The solution, once again, is utilizing the MTBA Framework. It provides you with an approach that allows you to differentiate your personal knowledge and experience from that of your competitors'. As your clients' MTBA, your discussions with them will provide a forum to entertain and address questions such as "How to?," "How does this apply?," or "What can be done?" In other words, your discussions often will focus on the future, and with your client, you will brainstorm together to attempt to predict outcomes or best approaches to situations or decisions that your client needs to be making today.

In this respect, our formal definition of the role of the MTBA might be: That decision-making part of any project, task, or function that must be undertaken without sufficient information to predict a final outcome with any certainty.

Our less formal definition is that you are most likely operating in an advisory role anytime you are guessing. The only way you can *know* the answer to a client's problem or situation is if you are reviewing history and making an expert interpretation of the facts and data. And if you *think* you know the answer to your client's problem or situation, you are referring to the future.

When you embrace the role of being your clients' MTBA, you are helping them make better guesses about what might need to be done to better leverage the future, rather than just rehashing and scolding your clients for what has happened in the past. Moving to an MTBA approach will provide a natural transition that occurs when the question, "What has happened?" is replaced by, "Based on what has happened, what changes should we consider to best position our organization for the future?" As advisors, we should always be reflecting on the past as a part of the process of helping our clients create a better future. Figure 2-2 shows this concept graphically.

Moving to the Future

A simple step to help you move your services from reviewing the client's past into something more unique is to add a future-focused conversation at the end of every compliance service. For example, the next time you prepare a tax return, make sure you end up talking about tax, retirement, estate, or financial planning as part of that engagement. If you perform bookkeeping services, no statement should be delivered without spending time with the client reviewing the meaning behind the numbers. This additional time should be classified as advisory or consulting time, and it should be itemized and billed accordingly because it creates a distinction between the commodity (the financial statements), and the value-added advice given, which requires your special skills and experience. The result is a distinctive service that gives you a competitive edge, both for building client loyalty and generating new business.

But functioning as the MTBA doesn't stop there. MTBA is an approach that should be woven into the operational fabric of your firm. Everyone should always be thinking about

Figure 2-2: **Consulting Transition Timeline**

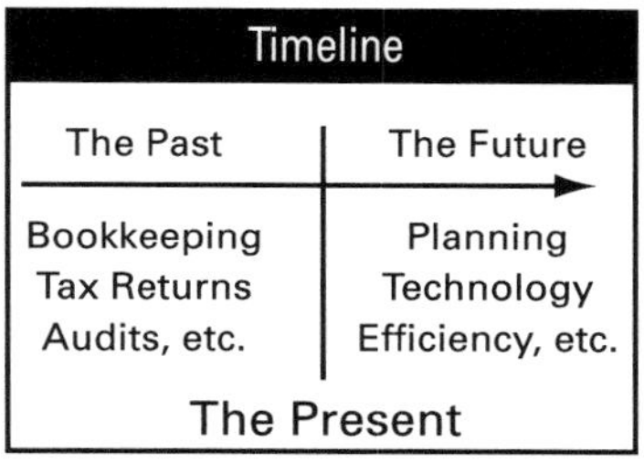

Timeline	
The Past	The Future
Bookkeeping Tax Returns Audits, etc.	Planning Technology Efficiency, etc.
The Present	

the clients—what are their challenges, what are their opportunities, how could they achieve even more, and so on. Partners, directors, and managers should be spending time routinely with their top clients to learn about their challenges, opportunities, and strategic initiatives. MTBA is not a spectator sport—you need to call clients and set up times to talk with them, go out and visit them, ask questions, and be a good listener. And we need to make this point clear:

 Keep In Mind

MTBA is NOT about selling; it's about having discussions with your clients to understand what they should to be doing to be even more successful.

The AICPA's Position on Advisory and Consulting Services

Now, because we've shared our thoughts on advisory services with you, it's only fair to include the AICPA's position on this broad area called "consulting services." Based on Statement of Standards for Consulting Services (SSCS) No. 1, *Consulting Services: Definitions and Standards*, (AICPA, *Professional Standards*, vol. 2, CS sec. 100), CPAs provide businesses with professional advisory or consulting services characterized by the following qualities:

• Two-party relationship.
• Disciplined objective.
• Objectivity is needed.
• Independence rules do not apply.
• No known third-party reliance

The advisory or consulting services would comprise the following services:

• Diagnosing
• Strategizing
• Constructing
• Implementing
• Operating

These services would be applied in the following arenas:

• Management services
• Transactional services
• Operational services

Why the extreme difference between the two definitions? Very simply, SSCS No. 1's definition has a much broader objective than ours. First, it creates a distinction between consulting or advisory services (a two-party relationship) and assurance services (a three-party relationship), which is an important issue when it comes to standards, workpaper requirements, and liability issues, to name a few. As you know, in a two-party relationship (the CPA advisor and management), CPAs are not hired to make representations to the public—they are retained to help management. Obviously, as soon as another party becomes reliant on the information provided by the CPAs, such as the public, a bank, the Securities and Exchange Commission, and so forth, and especially if those third parties are presuming independence on the part of the CPA's work, then the relationship becomes one of assurance rather than consulting.

Second, SSCS No. 1's definition has to consider the work performed by small, large, regional, national, and international CPA firms for clients ranging from the "Mom and Pop" shops through the Fortune 100. This takes in a scope of work in which some 42,000+ CPA firms around the country will never have (nor probably want) an opportunity to be involved. For example, very few of us will ever be asked to provide a million dollars worth of services over a week's period of time with three weeks' notice. Yet SSCS No. 1 has to cover these types of services, which are not only projects our firm doesn't want, but projects that we couldn't do.

Third, SSCS No. 1's definition includes the advisory function we highlight in this book in concert with an almost inexhaustible, ever-expanding list of nontraditional services or consulting packages. Although our definition says it much differently, it primarily focuses on the first half of the SSCS No.1 definition. In the "comprises the following services" section of the SSCS No.1 definition, by the time you get down to "constructing" and beyond, because we tend to work with small to medium-sized businesses, this work most often falls to the client. Occasionally it will fall to a specialist, using a subcontractor professional or other third party , or an alliance with another organization.

The point we are trying to make is we agree with the AICPA's broader definition of *consulting and advisory services*. We were actually part of the committee that developed this definition. We recognize the need for each of these phases during the implementation of a project. But simply put, for smaller to medium-sized businesses, the most valuable service the advisor has to offer is helping the owners diagnose, strategize, and put together an implementation plan for the client's personnel to follow. For large organizations, advisors will often give away the diagnosis and strategy components because their real interest is in supplying the humanpower it takes to construct, implement, and operate the solution. The good news is there is something in here for everyone. The big difference between our two definitions is that we maintain that the MTBA Framework, for most clients, has to become the flagship service that forms the foundation of our evolving profession. This not only allows us to maintain and enhance the status of our CPA initials, but to indeed live up to our status as the most trusted business advisors.

This profession survival message is directed towards expanding the relationships with your clients as their most trusted, valued business advisor. This advisor, by our definition, is someone who can spark new ideas, deliver customized advice, provide guidance and direction for the future, show a genuine interest in the client's business, provide advice based on perceived opportunities, and so forth. These services are two-party in nature and have no expectation of independence. Rather, the advisor is contributing an objective viewpoint from outside the organization. This is the value-added service component that we believe every CPA should be trained to deliver. Make no mistake about it: in our opinion, our profession's success in no way depends on whether your firm can install a computer network or perform a business valuation. These are merely two examples of literally hundreds of nontraditional services that your firm may or may not consider offering. So, for the sake of minimizing confusion, for the remainder of this text, unless we specify otherwise, when we refer to *advisory or consulting services*, think about acting as your clients' MTBA, not the endless list of potential nontraditional services and formalized consulting packages.

What About Attest Clients?

Some firms have become almost singularly focused on the audit and other attest services for clients and, as we all know, there are strict rules about maintaining your independence when delivering these services. Because of this, some CPAs eschew incorporating an advisory component into their attest services, opting instead to keep those services pure and focused on meeting the compliance rules. We don't believe that the MTBA Framework and attest services need this clear division as a wall between the two because it likely will result in a less effective and more commoditized offering. Recently, we had a discussion similar to this with AICPA audit guru Chuck Landes, and his words to us were paraphrased, "The auditor should know and understand the strategy of the organization they are serving as well as be part of these kinds of conversations. Without this knowledge and inclusion, it would be very easy for the auditor to either overlook or turn a blind-eye towards important, changing areas of the business." Clearly, no one is suggesting that the auditor act as part of the management team because this would be a clear violation of the independence rules. But there is great distance between acting in the role of management versus being a sounding board or facilitating discussions with your clients regarding matters that are important to their organizations.

For some, that "great distance" we mentioned previously is perceived as being filled with dangerous shades of grey. And if that is the way you feel, then for your attest service clients, walk a very clear line of only providing compliance work with independence as your leading differentiator. However, of all of the firms we have talked to and work with, we have encountered very few that ONLY provide attest services. So, if you are like most firms and deliver both attest and other services, and if you decide you want to build an unscalable wall between attest and those other services, then that is a decision only you should make, and we totally support it! But for your nonattest service clients, please don't hide behind the independence rules just because the MTBA Framework is different from what you are used to or currently is uncomfortable for you or the people within your firm. At the end of the day, every CPA firm we work with prides themselves on delivering outstanding client service. If you believe this about your firm as well, then we ask you, "How can you be

Figure 2-3: **Moving Away From Traditional CPA Services Using the MTBA Framework**

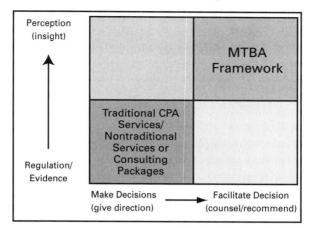

providing outstanding client service to your nonattest clients if you don't even know what keeps them awake at night?"

The MTBA Framework is about filling the role of being a high-level sounding board and sharing your insights with your clients. As you can see in figure 2-3, the extremes run from facilitating and offering your perceptions to directing based on regulation and evidence, with everything in between. Our traditional services tend to fall in the darker blue box on the bottom left with the CPA making decisions based on regulation or evidence. This role as an expert is rooted in the deepest part of our comfort zone as we follow specific sets of steps in order to deliver answers to finite questions.

The focus of this book and the Trusted Business Advisor workshops is predominantly on the upper right hand quadrant, with CPAs calling on their facilitative skills and providing objective insight for clients to consider in their decision making. It's about following a process to help your clients identify what is important to them, talking through their perceived options with them, and helping them come up with a strategy to move forward in a direction consistent with their goals. This process can be used regardless of your role and the services you currently provide to your clients. The MTBA Framework does not limit what you can do but rather expands it. However, the key is to always know which quadrant and which direction you are moving into because each area you operate within will have some do's and don'ts to follow to maximize your effectiveness and limit your liability.

Incorporating the MTBA Framework Into Your Daily Routine

How hard is it to incorporate the MTBA Framework into your daily routine? In theory, it is very simple. This is because we are discussing a change in philosophy more than a change in capability. However, everyone's habits need to be reexamined to ensure that those performing the work are motivated to look beyond the client's past and present and into their future. Second, as professionals, we have to learn to become more comfortable and, at the same time, more humble when it comes to "guessing" what a client's future might hold. Remember, in the MTBA space, we are not bound up in regulatory rules and evidence but rather by creativity and imagination. Our opinions about what might work or fail are just that: opinions (not fact or crystal ball enlightenment). Here's how this might break down for many firms:

> The managing partners of many firms are typically not only marketing oriented, but future-focused, compared to the rest of the firm's personnel. This is partly due to their job description requiring this perspective. Therefore, it stands to reason that these CPAs, because of what they do for their own firms, are more apt to enter into strategic level discussions with their clients. Including the managing partner, we've found (through our experience working with CPA firms across the country) that it is common for approximately 20 percent to 33 percent of the partners or managers within any CPA organization to have a comfort level switching between services constrained by facts, procedures, and regulations to those services laden with ambiguity and guesswork. However, despite one's preferences, each partner or manager of a CPA firm is likely to have a specific client or two that force him or her into this more ambiguous "I know you don't have a crystal ball, but help me think through what some actions are that I might consider taking today to best position my organization (or me [*the client*]) for the future" role. Usually, the more mature the accountant, the more probable, and the more often this role request is made by the client.

The point is everyone can, and likely does, perform some high level advisory work, albeit some more naturally than others. The trick is to get everyone to perform this service instinctively whenever possible. This transition is a logical place to encounter stumbling blocks. The good news is the "MTBA Framework" section of this book will go a long way toward helping you identify how to go about facilitating this change.

Who Should Become an MTBA?

Regarding who should develop MTBA skills within your firm, as you have probably already guessed, this is one area where our philosophy differs from the practiced norm. To most firms around the country, providing advisory or consulting assistance is considered a unique skill limited to a group of specialized people delivering niche services within a nontraditional department (figure 2-4). In these organizations, "consulting and advisory services" is really just the catch-all phrase describing a variety of what we call "consulting packages." The focus is not on the "advisory" function of consulting but rather on delivering nontraditional niche services or industry specialties like business valuations, forensic investigations, litigation support, wealth management, technology, construction, manufacturing, and banking, just to name a few (they span both services and industry niches).

Figure 2-4: **Traditional Firm Structure**

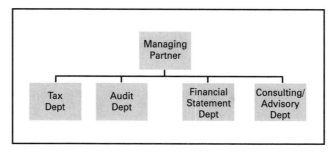

Figure 2-5: **Consulting-Centric Firm Structure**

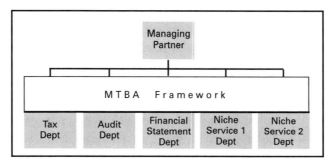

As we mentioned earlier, we feel the best place to start adding value is from an advisory perspective. As you can see in figure 2-5 and compare it to figure 2-4, we believe strongly that every department or service, (or both, for that matter) should have an advisory component added to it. This means that every high-level member of every department (partners and managers at a minimum) should incorporate business advisory assistance for clients into the current work being performed. One reason is the benefit derived by both you and your clients from spending just a little more time together to help them determine how to best utilize whatever information is being delivered. The other is to develop deeper relationships with your key clients as you help them achieve their business goals and objectives. Certainly, the more experience (we are not talking about expertise, but broad life and business experience) one has, the greater latitude available in the advice to be offered. But remember, living up to our MTBA status, simplistically speaking, is embracing a philosophy which requires us to constantly think through or discuss with our clients the following types of questions as part of almost every service we provide:

- What can we do to improve our situation based on what we now know?
- What actions can we take to positively leverage where we are?
- How can we use what we have learned to help us achieve our goals?

This approach to working with your clients is the

- easiest to implement approach with the fastest return on investment.
- least risky.

- greatest value-add to the client.
- easiest to get paid a premium to do.
- most effective in transforming the culture of the firm.
- yet, the least likely to be found at many CPA firms, including your competitors.

If this is such a good strategy, why is it the least likely to be found?

It is the least likely philosophy to be found because the largest CPA firms have successfully implemented a departmental or consulting package strategy for formal consulting, even to the point of splitting off from the CPA firm itself. And many smaller firms use their approach as a model. However, if you look closely, most of the larger firms would be more appropriately named Smith Nontraditional Services rather than Smith Advisors or Consultants. The terms *advisory* or *consulting* services used by most CPA organizations do not refer to a holistic approach for providing business advice. They do not refer to services focused on finding out "what keeps the business owners awake at night" and then helping them resolve those issues.

Instead, they refer to a variety of nontraditional services or consulting packages that are being offered, like system development, programming, reengineering, and literally hundreds more. This translates into mass specialization because large firms have the luxury of allowing generalists to become specialists purely due to volume of work. For example, instead of just having a tax department, these organizations are likely to have a tax division with tax departments for the United States, Canadian, Pacific Rim, European, and North American Free Trade Agreement markets. This depth of knowledge becomes a competitive strength large firms can and should highlight and sell. And as long as demand is adequate, expansion through consulting packages (or nontraditional niche services) suits their already-in-place management and organizational structure.

We call the approach large firms use the "Swiss cheese approach" to consulting package delivery. Here's why.

Assume the picture to the left represents a block of cheese. Also assume that this block of cheese pictorially represents the total potential demand for nontraditional services from a CPA firm's client base. Large firms jump right to the high dollar project opportunities by picking various nontraditional services, developing the required expertise and methodology, and offering them. As the demand for one nontraditional service dwindles or a new niche service grows, resources are shifted to poke new holes or deliver new services to the untapped and underserved opportunities which exist in the current client base. After periods of opportunistic service delivery, total potential demand begins to resemble a piece of Swiss cheese as the firm continually creates new consulting packages to satisfy the changing demands within its client base and drive profits to the firm.

Once again, if your client base is large enough, then continually poking holes in the overabundance of client demand (constantly going after the low-hanging fruit) can be a wonderfully profitable strategy. That's why the job description of the consultant in these larger organizations is often defined by the word *travel*. When consulting packages are launched, in order to maintain an acceptable volume of billable hours, a consultant has to work throughout the country (with all of the offices) in order to build a large enough demand base to consume the available expertise. As demand rises, more consultants with specialized knowledge are hired or shifted from other work, thereby either allowing the organization to respond to bigger and bigger projects or reducing the geographic area each consultant needs to cover, or both.

However, when smaller firms attempt this same strategy, because of their more limited client base size, a full-time CPA with narrow niche specialty skills quickly can become underutilized. This converts to idle, unbillable time, which translates to expensive overhead and marginal profits (if at all), and often, abandoned specialties. The problem, especially for small to medium-sized CPA firms, is that while the firm focused its limited time and resources on building a new niche specialty consulting package, it was overlooking an important client service that was in high, continuous demand. Although we absolutely believe in offering consulting packages, we don't believe they should be developed at the expense or nullification of the MTBA Framework (advisory services). Our order is to always leverage the MTBA Framework, and then some of that work will morph naturally into logical consulting packages for the firm to offer. It just makes sense: building a business around taking a holistic view to understand what keeps <u>all</u> of your top clients awake at night is a much better strategy than picking a unique service that will only be of interest to a small portion of your top clients and launching a package to serve them.

Logically, the creation of a variety of consulting packages works well for any size firm if there is enough volume. But don't confuse consulting packages or nontraditional services with the focus of delivering on your MTBA status. Offering consulting packages is especially lucrative for large firms because they often act more like staffing organizations. When you are selling huge projects, advice is not the key to making money—being hired to do the detailed work in the trenches is what they are after. When you are looking for relationships that generate annually a minimum of $100,000 of revenue or projects that range from several hundred thousand into the millions of dollars, the real profit on the work is not from the advice given but from implementation assistance. Often the clients served by large CPA firms have very highly paid, high profile people driving strategy and advice. These clients turn to the large CPA firms looking for ways to turn the identified vision into reality. Or put another way, they are looking to outsource the implementation to an organization that can instantly put hordes of feet on the ground to get the work done.

The larger the client organization, the more visionary and specialized skills are available through normal channels such as advisory boards, directors, key stockholders, and internal management talent. Therefore, when Fortune 1,000-sized companies outsource help, they are often looking for specialized specialists. By the time the consultant group is being hired, the discussions are not about why or when, but how, how much, and how long. For example, consider that a decision has been made to implement an Oracle system to provide better information to management. The client company is not bringing in experts to discuss the pros and cons of change—they are looking for an expert team with a proven track record installing Oracle systems within companies in the client's industry. As we stated earlier in this chapter, with larger clients, it is rarely about the diagnosing and strategizing, but rather about the constructing, implementing, or operating.

Unfortunately or fortunately, most small and middle-market firms are not responding, and cannot respond, to projects that require instant hordes of available human-power. Firms of this size typically work close to capacity with recurring work, with excess capacity constituting a few untapped workers here and there. They don't have 30–50 people ready for the next nontraditional, nonrecurring project. Generally, the smaller the CPA firm, the more boutique in nature it's organization, and the more hands-on the partner's approach. Partners and managers are not only the main contacts but also the main workers on many of their clients' projects. This is partly due to the clients' levels of sophistication. For example, the smaller the client-organization, the more likely outside, objective, management-level, forest-through-the-trees advice is seen as a mission critical service. That's why it is such a great match for smaller businesses (under $100 million in sales, if you're looking for a quick size guideline) to work with small to medium-sized accounting firms where the contact person and the service provider is the same individual. Or at a minimum, the same contact person is involved regardless of the project being performed, which allows the CPA to provide consistency and better advocate on the client's behalf since he or she can easily act as a kind of "General Contractor" over all of the projects offered.

To summarize, the smaller the client organization, the more advice, vision, and project oversight will open doors. The larger the client-organization, the more specialized and plentiful the CPA firm labor force, and the easier it is for the CPA firm to get the client's attention. The great news is that small, regional, national, and international CPA firms deliver different products and services to different marketplaces. Although it seems at times we compete with each other, in reality, each segment of firms is well suited for solving different problems for different target clients. Therefore, for the most part, we tend to compete for business with those of a similar size or a slight step up or down in size from our own firms. With this in mind, recognize that according to the Private Companies Practice Section of the AICPA, of the more than 42,000 firms represented by AICPA membership, over 40,000 have 10 or fewer professionals. This book is focused on serving the 40,000 or so firms that predominantly are working directly with the business owners who are looking for diagnostic and strategic advisors to help them navigate through some difficult waters. And to be competitive in this marketplace, it makes both dollars and sense for your organization to focus on improving everyone's ability to deliver high-level, customized advisory services by acting as your clients' most trusted business advisors.

So far, both the MTBA Framework (Advisory Services) and Consulting Packages (Nontraditional Services) have been mentioned several times in the same paragraph; can you further clarify their dividing line?

Although a distinction exists between the MTBA Framework and Consulting Packages, the dividing point can be a little gray and messy. Figure 2-6 takes the MTBA framework a step further to include these consulting packages. The extremes are easy to see (upper right quadrant back of the cube [MTBA Framework at its most unstructured] and the lower left front of the cube [Consulting Packages, Nontraditional Services or Traditional CPA Services]. For the area in the front portion of the lower right quadrant of the cube, this would represent a service that follows a specific methodology but uses facilitative skills (because of the formal methodological approach, these services, although facilitative in nature, will tend to be consulting packages or those formalized as consulting packages). For example, conducting a strategic planning session for your client would fit into this service area—highly structured but facilitative in nature. As another example, consider the area in the upper left quadrant in the back part of the cube. It demonstrates a service that is just the opposite because it is very unstructured. In this situation, because the advisor is kind of feeling his or her way through the project, making the decisions intuitively about what to do next, the service will look like and tend to rely heavily on the MTBA Framework. For example, this might be a service offered where the client says, "I know we have a huge morale problem, but I am not sure what is at the root of it. Would you please investigate and tell me what you find?"

Here is a situation where the advisor most likely is not considered a "morale expert," but rather as someone the client can trust to handle such a delicate matter. This type of service

Figure 2-6: **The MTBA Framework and Structured vs. Unstructured Consulting**

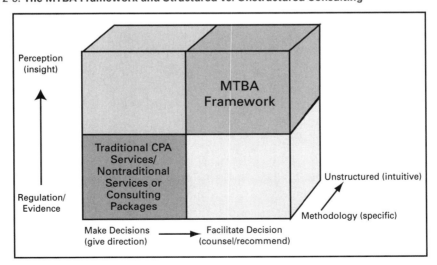

might eventually morph into one in the future that the firm holds out to the market as a consulting package. This assumes, however, that there is consistent demand for this service, and the CPA develops a specific approach and defined process for arriving at a solution. Consulting packages often emerge from advisory services following the processes within the MTBA Framework as the

- volume of work increases;
- depth of knowledge required to perform the work intensifies;
- work itself begins to become more standardized and formalized because you find yourself following a specific methodology and set of procedures; , and
- work strays further and further from a business advisory capacity.

Now let's take another look at figure 2-6. The simplest explanation for this mental model is that the more unstructured the work, the more it relies on insight and perception. The more you rely on your facilitation skills to find the solutions, the more you will rely on the processes we include in the MTBA Framework. On the other hand, the more that the work is driven by regulation and evidence, the more it follows specific methodology. The more the CPA looks to expert sources for decisions, then the more that service has morphed into a traditional or nontraditional service (or consulting package). The reason why we are spending so much time talking about all of this—and why it matters—is because our profession commonly works in the front portion of the cube (we are the most comfortable in the dark blue areas, but we will often also venture into services that fall into the light blue areas within all of the quadrants). As a profession, we are comfortable facilitating (client deciding) when we are following methodology, and the work is based in regulation and evidence (like tax planning). We are also very comfortable making the decisions at each step along the way and then providing our opinion when that insight is steeped in structure (like audit opinions). And even in the top right-hand portion of the graphic, many can find comfort if they can operate in the very front of the cube when their facilitation and opinions are grounded by strong methodology (like an internal control assessment). However, the more we move away from structure, the more uncomfortable we get. Structure is the bedrock of our comfort zone. The purpose of this book is to help you shed your discomfort with unstructured work, minimize your insecurity about providing insight without regulation and evidence, and gain comfort in helping the client arrive at their own answers rather than you providing them. The MTBA Framework is a loose set of processes that will help you navigate through unstructured work and assist the client in discovering some new possibilities, solutions, and opportunities.

The bottom line is this: the more quickly you can pinpoint where the service you are offering falls in the preceding graphic, the easier it is to manage your own tendencies while delivering the service in a profitable manner, at minimal risk, and at the greatest value to the client. Let's consider the following scenario and then break out each service:

You are working with a $10 million business. The original services this company hired you for were financial statements and tax return preparation. Because your client's business is continuing to grow at a fairly fast pace, the CEO tells you that they need a more formalized direction for their future. To that end, the CEO asks you to help them develop a 5-year business strategy and associated goals. After facilitating a 2-day retreat, your client requests that you meet with the management team monthly for the next 6 months to help them stay focused on achieving the goals they established. Three months into the process, after defining expectations with one particular goal—to establish a formal budgeting process— the client turns to you for implementation help. In this case, the client wants you, their CPA firm, to help them develop next year's budget for the company while establishing a process for this annual project that they can replicate internally during successive years. During the next few months, while you are still facilitating their monthly goal update meetings, your staff also is working in the trenches with the client to create the first draft of next year's budget. A year later, while the client's personnel are working through the budget process on their own, they request that a member of your staff sit in on a 2-hour weekly meeting for a month to provide advice and counsel as they work through their first internally-generated budget. And the story continues to evolve with new projects and new requests.

This example describes the natural evolution and expansion of services a CPA is likely to encounter while working in an advisory and consulting package capacity with his or her business clients. This natural evolution is referred to in the marketing textbooks as *service extension*. As trusted business advisors deliver one service, logical extensions of that service are easily identified, sold, and then delivered. With all of this in mind, here is how we would categorize each service:

- *Tax return and financial statements traditional services*. These services would reside in the front part of the lower left-hand corner of the cube.
- *Retreat facilitation*. Although this would be within the MTBA Framework, it would likely be a service that would be represented in the front portion of the upper-right quadrant because of the strong methodology the facilitator would follow.
- *Monthly meetings to stay on track*. MTBA Framework or Advisory Services and would likely be in the top right-hand quadrant towards the back of the cube. The reason for this placement is because the CPA is attending the meetings to provide objective commentary, respond to conversations and issues as they arise, facilitate solutions when a disconnect occurs, and keep the project moving forward (provide a feeling of structure when there isn't any)
- *Preparation of the first budget*. We would say that this service, because it is the first time the budget is created, would be pinpointed about dead center in the middle of the cube. Why? Because the CPAs will be making a number of the decisions but will have to rely a great deal on their facilitation skills to determine reasonable draft budget ranges. Although they will be working from a strong base in the evidence portion of regulation, they will have to share their opinions to make sure their approach is on track. And because this is the first time around for the budgetary process, the work will be far less structured. This is classic work that can morph into a consulting package after doing a number of similar projects for different clients.

- *Creation of the budgetary processes.* After the budget is complete and the work shifts to documenting and establishing a future process, the work moves from the middle of the cube more towards the middle front of the bottom left quadrant because the CPA is creating the methodology from the steps just taken, and the process will be framed within accounting regulation and principles.
- *Staff facilitation of budget preparation.* As with the partner's meetings, this service also would be found within the MTBA Framework or Advisory Services quadrant and be pinpointed towards the back of the cube for the same reasons as were identified previously.

As you can see, even with projects that seemingly fall into our traditional services area (that is, the CPA makes decisions based on regulation and evidence within a clearly structured approach), it doesn't take much (like the loss of structure, the requirement for facilitation, or the demand for us to opine) to shift that project into a space where the MTBA Framework becomes an important implementation tool.

So how does providing services using the MTBA Framework metamorphose into consulting packages?

Here's how that might happen:

> After you finish facilitating the goal management meetings and establishing a strong budgeting process, the client is excited. She tells several of her CEO peers about how your work improved her organization. Before you know it, you have several more clients, some of them new, asking you for the same assistance. Because your time is limited, you have trouble taking care of your current client work and squeezing in all of this new demand for your time. So, as a solution to a wonderful problem you are encountering, you start writing down exactly what you did, in the order that you did it, and the key decisions you made at each step along the way so that you can involve others to do the work. As time goes on, occasionally you overhear other partners in your firm talking to their clients about how they can benefit from this "goal management and budgeting" assistance. Clients continue to respond with interest. You begin to consider having someone specialize in this service in order to meet demand, to ensure that adequate focus is placed on expanding it into new markets, and to use it to create a differentiation between you and your competitors. The point is that as the work becomes standardized, a consulting package emerges from an MTBA service, and people are trained to follow a specific methodology so that the firm can consistently deliver a highly valued new client service.

In this example, what started out as an on-site, tailored advisory service requiring a great deal of MTBA skills (skills that we believe every high-level person in your firm should have) eventually morphed into a full-blown consulting package. How can we tell? Because the

- work volume relative to this service increased;
- service was standardized and documented so others could perform it as well; and

- work has moved far away from the "make-it-up-as-you-go" (unstructured) business advisory function to a service that is steeped in methodology, bound by regulation and evidence (documentation), and performed by people with expertise doing the same things over and over again.

The fact that the goal management and budgeting service becomes a consulting package doesn't mean that no one can do the work anymore except those who specialize in this service. However, if there is bandwidth available from that group, they should be the first to take on the work because their process approach will allow them to more efficiently market, manage the implementation of, and control the service's profitability. Think of it this way: some of the services we deliver using the MTBA Framework will cultivate consulting packages. And consulting packages are just a broad category for nontraditional services.

As we have said before, we are attempting to delineate the distinction between advisory services (using the MTBA Framework) and consulting packages early because, depending on which you are trying to implement, your road to success is different. The good news is that both can be very profitable for your organization. We will address how to best chart your course throughout this text in a logical step-by-step fashion.

You've stated that everyone in a CPA organization should be capable of delivering advisory services. Which areas of a client's business does that include?

A clue about where to start should be to consider broad categories of needs with which all businesses constantly struggle. These categories include the following:

- Planning
- Personnel (motivation and performance, retention)
- Operational (processes, procedures, efficiency)
- Governance
- Technology
- Marketing (target markets, distribution model, contact strategy)
- Management and specialization (the right skills in the key jobs)
- Profitability
- Accounting and finance
- Products and services
- Information management
- Succession management

Because every business needs services that help them improve their capabilities in each of the areas previously listed, we call them "global business functions" (GBFs). From our perspective, the MTBA Framework revolves around the delivery of services around these GBFs. And we believe that every business advisor within your firm should be able to, at a moment's notice, talk to any client about any of these areas. We maintain that a business advisor's basic tool kit should include the following:

- An ability to communicate with the client regarding each of these functional areas
- An understanding of some of the common improvements and refinements that organizations are making in these functional areas
- Typical malfunctions and inefficiencies encountered in these areas
- Your firm's general approach to enhancing performance in these areas
- An ability to manage others who might assist in performing projects

Note that specialized knowledge regarding GBFs is not a required tool for the MTBA, but a general knowledge is. For example, knowing that

- cost control is only one vehicle for helping businesses become more profitable. Each CPA should be equally ready and comfortable talking about ways to increase revenues, discussing typical advertising approaches, and reviewing pricing and compensation models in order to better stimulate sales.
- implementation of plans is one of the most common failings of small business owners. They get so busy responding to the crisis of the moment or trying to leverage a short-term opportunity that they lose sight of the little steps they need to be taking every week to position themselves for the future they dream of living. It is our job as the MTBA to help our clients keep their desired future in clear view by having regular conversations with them about the progress they are making toward their chosen destination.
- developing others is not a strength of the typical entrepreneur. Entrepreneurs are usually self-starting, self-reliant risk-takers who survive and prosper through their sheer force of will. When they hire people, they normally are looking to find others who are motivated to drive themselves. They typically only hire people when their personal bandwidth is at full capacity and their backs are against the wall, so training is rarely part of the package. As companies grow and prosper, they need the MTBA to help them build a foundation of structure, training, and standard operating procedure so that the labor force is better prepared and more skilled to do their jobs.

And the stories go on.

The point here is that when a CPA walks into the client's office, he or she mentally should examine each area on the GBF list looking for ways to improve the operation. The answers to these mental questions may call for further discussion with the client, specific focus on a problem, or acquisition of specialists to access specific technical information or approaches. But that is all in a day's work for the MTBA. There is more on this in the chapter, "Refining the Most Important MTBA Tool: Communications."

OK ... I buy off on the idea that our firm needs to build better advisory capability throughout the firm. However, isn't there still room for some specialized services?

Absolutely! However, before you offer any new service, you need to answer two questions: Who is the service targeted to serve and why it is important for you to serve that market? We have developed a methodology to help you in this analysis that uses the terms *fortress* and *empire*. The chapter, "Growing Your Business," focuses on issues that should drive the decision regarding whether or not to specialize as well as which specializations might be most appropriate.

If we focus on building the better advisory capability you are describing, will we lose out in the long term to those who put their emphasis into a couple of specialty areas?

We believe just the opposite will be true; those who focus on building better advisory skills will have much greater control over their own destiny than those firms concentrating in a few niche specialty areas. This is especially true for the 40,000+ firms around the country with less than 10 professionals. But before we defend our position, we want to tell you a story, our version of the evolution of the medical profession. We believe the practice of medicine serves as a good benchmark for the kind of changes our profession is likely to undergo.

Until about 70 years ago, most doctors entered the marketplace expecting to practice family medicine (often referred to as *general practitioners* or *GPs*). As the practice of medicine continued to become more involved, complicated, and just as important, doctors turned to specialization for relief. Specialization created a wealth of opportunity as new services began popping up everywhere due to clearer lines being drawn regarding expertise. This helped insulate doctors because their scope of work was narrowed dramatically. And due to the litigious environment of medicine, GPs were glad to refer their patients to these specialists anytime there was the slightest indication of a problem. Specialists had a great situation. Not only did they enjoy a steady stream of patients from other doctors' referrals, their more highly specialized skills and training allowed them to demand greater fees.

It seems hard to believe now, but specialization was supported by many doctors yet fiercely contested by many others. Even in the early 1900s, those who held themselves out as "specialists" were considered "quacks" by their own industry. Those favoring specialization believed that it was in the public's best interest to clarify the fact that all doctors didn't have the same skills. Those doctors that had developed niche expertise were frustrated by a system that didn't recognize their unique capabilities. Many other doctors felt it would be disastrous to the profession to start restricting one's service latitude by creating a variety of designations. These doctors knew that once the door for specialty designations opened, they would multiply exponentially. And once this occurred, just by virtue of not having a designation in a specific area where a doctor wanted to practice, put him or her at a competitive and litigious disadvantage. Well, we all know how this story evolved. Board certified specializations were adopted and have become commonplace today. Those who had spent significant time working in a highly specialized niche area were the first to raise their new differentiation banner.

Specialization also provided an interesting twist. Although the most experienced doctors tended to specialize at first, specialization turned out to be an even greater windfall for new doctors. It provided them with a greater chance to compete and find employment opportunities. For example, years ago, significant opportunity could be found by associating with one of the few big medical practices that existed in every major metropolitan area. However, with a steady stream of new doctors constantly emerging from the educational system, the marketplace for the good jobs became more and more competitive. So new doctors started becoming even more highly specialized; they became specialists in a specialty field so to speak. For instance, it wasn't that long ago when a GP would have X-rays done and then attempt the diagnosis. But along came practitioners who did nothing but read X-rays (radiologists). Today, doctors don't just become radiologists, they become neuroradiologists, pediatric radiologists, nuclear radiologists, and so forth. What's odd is that the early adopters of the specialization, radiology, are now GPs in the specialty field of radiology.

Today, insurance companies are restricting access to many of the specialists as a cost control measure and also are capping the money they will pay for these unique services. Insurance companies are requiring patients to first seek assistance from GPs, and if the GP feels involvement from a specialist is appropriate, a referral is made. Because GPs have become the gatekeepers for most services rendered within the medical profession, there is growing demand for more general practitioners. Why has this job become more attractive? Because GPs are the people with account control. They determine what other services should be called upon. And although GPs can recommend specific practitioners, unless the recommended specialist is on the client's insurance company's constantly changing approved list, they will never see the referred patient.

Although this was a long story, much of it is applicable to our profession and the changes it is likely to undergo. The scope of work that CPAs profess to perform is so vast (with many of those services being exceptionally complex, detailed, and constantly evolving), no human could maintain the bandwidth of knowledge required to be competent in all of these areas. This diverse similarity within our profession promotes an increasingly litigious environment. When you consider all of this, as well as the ever-increasing competition within our profession, specialization quickly rises to the top as an alternative, providing some relief in the battle for survival.

Just as with the medical profession, our profession has been wrestling with specialization. However, accreditations appear to be here to stay because the AICPA now offers four credentials to their members. They are in the fields of financial planning (PFS), business valuation (ABV), technology (CITP), and the most recent, forensics (CFF). Because Bill serves as a commissioner for the National Accreditation Commission, the body that oversees the credentialing process, we believe it is safe to say that CPAs can expect continued expansion of specialized services in our profession with specialty designations growing to support these changes. As each designation is released, just by virtue of not having a designation in a specific area in which a CPA wants to practice puts him or her at a competitive and litigious disadvantage. Specialization will create tremendous opportunity for new CPAs entering the profession because they will become more and more highly specialized in order to attract the interest of existing successful organizations. Once again, just like the medical profession, the more specialized firms become, the more dependent they will be on their alliances and referrals from mainstream CPA firms (general practitioners acting as MTBAs). And as more and more specialty designations are created, general practitioner CPAs more commonly will refer or subcontract with highly specialized CPAs for their unique services.

If we put this into a pictorial perspective, it might look like figure 2-7. The outside circle represents market demand for the countless number of services our profession offers. The next ring represents our first point of involvement, which should be as the GP or

Figure 2-7: **Market Demand Summary for CPA Specialization**

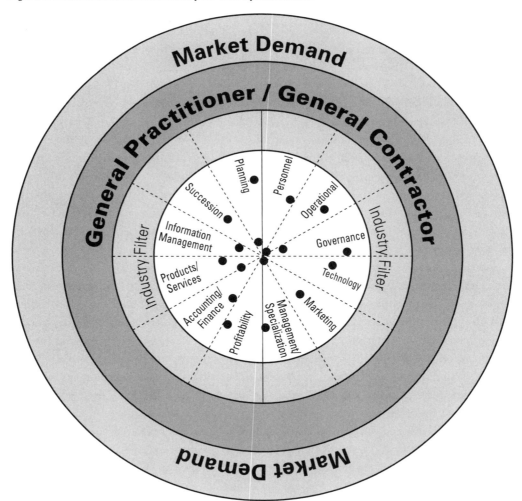

the general contractor (GC), or better put, as the MTBA. In this space, it is our job to first figure out what the client needs or wants. Then, we need to assess the level of resources required and justifiable to assist the client. In other words, if we are a GC, the first thing we need to understand is what does the house that the client wants to build look like given the resources they can spend to build it. Inside the GP ring is an industry filter. Although it is often not required, those who specialize in an industry can make a more compelling argument to a new client that they might be a better resource for helping the client achieve success because of their unique industry experience. In our opinion, in most cases, the first professional a small business should hire should be a GP or a niche-experienced GP (a GP with an industry filter) because you don't hire the plumbers to install the bathroom before you have designed the house.

Next come the GBFs. As you can see, they span through the industry filter as well as the GP rings. Just as we previously discussed, the GP (or GC) needs to have an understanding of each of the GBF areas in order to be prepared to assist the client by doing the proper diagnosis about where the "pain" or "opportunity" might lie. It is up to the GP to help the client bring the necessary resources together to resolve or leverage their current situation. For firms with industry concentrations, the whole model would shift so that all of the GBFs would be viewed or tailored to respond to the needs of that specific industry. So, for example, if your firm has a construction specialty, the GP would have industry knowledge, and the planning GBF would be better titled planning for contractors GBF, and so on.

Finally, you will note the little circles located throughout the GBFs. These are consulting packages or traditional services (the Swiss cheese example we described earlier). In other words, if the client needs tax assistance, you have a defined service with a methodology ready to help them. If they need their business valued, you might have a defined service ready to offer to take care of that need as well. Depending on the size and resources of the firm, more packaged services will be available to provide the necessary assistance. Migrating inside and outside the boundaries of the GBFs as well as outside of the packaged offerings (the circles) are many unstructured services that require the utilization of the MTBA Framework that a firm can offer, as well as service areas that firms can go to their professional network to fill.

Although there are many points we are trying to make with this graphic, the most important one to us is that of control. Whoever is the GP (GC or MTBA) should be controlling the account because they know it is their job to constantly assess their clients' individual and business health. When a problem arises, the GP is in the driver's seat to refer work to his or her own firm when the firm can deliver the packaged service or skill set required. In this picture, the CPA-GP maintains the closest ear to the management teams and, therefore, is the key to business opportunity. Although specialization may be more lucrative for some in the short term than maintaining a general advisory role, the more highly specialized the practice in terms of specific offerings, the more dependent it will become on the GP's referral. So if your firm decides tomorrow to become an audit only firm (or decides to specialize in any group of subcontractor services—the circles in the middle), which is great and probably very lucrative, recognize that your firm just shifted from a business environment of serving its own clients to one of servicing the clients of other CPA firms. Why? Because in our opinion, over time, every sophisticated client will eventually demand that a professional, whether that be a CPA, lawyer, insurance agent, and so forth, fill the GP or GC role for their company.

As with the case of the GP in the medical profession, over time the CPA-GP will be the critical position to hold for long-term business opportunity. Whoever is the CPA General Contractor—the person with the primary relationship with the client—he or she will become the business services gatekeeper. And as gatekeepers, one of the most critical skills required to defend this position will be an ability to help organizations facilitate change, which not only has to be a foundation skill for our profession but is a fundamental component in the skill set of the MTBA Framework.

To be clear, we are not suggesting that you shouldn't develop industry specialties if your practice, your interests, and your market support them. You can still be a GP or GC for your clients in any specialized industry niches you might serve (such as medical practices, auto dealers, contractors, lawyers, and so forth). And as their practices grow, with professional standards continuing to multiply, many firms will likely need to pick a few industries to focus on in order to be profitable and be good at what they do.

The Minimum Transition Requirement for Moving to MTBA Status

In order to make the transition to an MTBA-focused accounting firm, at a minimum you need to have the following:

- Management commitment
- A belief that functioning as an MTBA is required to stay in step with the profession
- An understanding that your maximum return on investment will be earned only when everyone within the firm incorporates a future-focused or advisory mindset toward the client work they perform
- The patience to sow advisory service seeds throughout the client base and harvest those which experience exceptional interest or growth into consulting packages

Although this transition demands a great investment of your firm's time and energy, the rewards far outweigh the costs. Utilizing the MTBA Framework provides you with a value-added service delivery mechanism and a marketing platform to ensure your clients can differentiate you from all of the others. It forces everyone within the firm to not only analyze where your clients have been, but more importantly, where they are going. The MTBA Framework creates loyalty because it is apparent that both you and your clients have a common goal—their future. It enhances client satisfaction because your umbrella of services is more encompassing. And what results from all of this is as follows

- Greater client retention
- Increased revenues per client
- More professional satisfaction in the work you and your people are doing
- A rock solid foundation positioning you and your firm for the future.

Making the Transition to Most Trusted Business Advisor: How and Why

"Obstacles cannot crush me. Every obstacle yields to stern resolve."

~ LEONARDO DA VINCI

The Essence of the Most Trusted Business Advisor Framework

We are encouraging you to have everyone in your firm step up to the plate and be counted as, and indeed live up to, the most trusted business advisor (MTBA) role your clients have bestowed upon you. We are *not* suggesting that you just run right out and start developing consulting packages to try to sell. We're not even suggesting that you try to sell anything. We are suggesting that you spend more time with your top clients, learning what they need in their businesses to achieve their goals. Be interested, be helpful, be a good listener, and work with them to help them be better. It's that simple. Having said that, we do find CPAs who are frustrated with, or anxious about, taking on more of an advisory role with their clients.

Obstacles or Opportunities?

Everywhere you go, you can find CPAs frustrated with the business of advising or consulting with clients. And everywhere you turn, another reason why you shouldn't bother embracing the MTBA Framework is expressed. Here are some comments that might ring a familiar bell:

- Fees and pricing issues:
  - My small business clients can't afford to pay for any advisory assistance or consulting. Even though we provide the service, it's just never been profitable. So we try to give a little free advice now and then, hoping we'll be remembered when there is more fat in the client's budget.
  - Many of our small-business clients occasionally call and ask us a few questions. We don't bother recording the time because it doesn't amount to much.
  - We give away our advisory or consulting time throughout the year and adjust our year-end tax fees accordingly.

- Positioning issues:
  - Our clients don't think of us for help in solving business problems. We are their accountants. They have a very narrow view of what we can offer.

- Workload issues:
  - I have a small firm, and I don't have the luxury of being able to offer numerous niche services outside of traditional accounting.
  - Between tax returns, financial statements, and audits, we don't have time to worry about the few extra bucks we can make from being advisors or doing consulting. We're always struggling to keep up as it is. Besides, we make a decent living doing exactly what we're doing.

These are just a few of the remarks we've heard too many times. Unfortunately, many reasons exist about why the implementation of MTBA services and the realization of increased revenues has fallen short of expectations. The first and foremost is CPAs haven't had to deliver MTBA services to remain viable or profitable. Most have been busy enough just sitting in the office and taking orders when the phone rings. So if we don't have to, why take the risk? Consulting per se is not a sure thing, as exemplified by the fact that many firms have already tried, failed, and abandoned their consulting service expansion; albeit most of those firms used a consulting package approach rather than the MTBA Framework approach. Because success is not automatic, why bother at all? Well, here are a few issues to consider.

Our Answers to the Questions and Objections

Fees and Pricing Issues

What Clients Really Want (and Will Pay for)

Some CPAs are hesitant to bill clients for what they do at times. We've already covered the Accounting Office Management and Administration Reports that show that most clients believe that their CPAs' fees are fair, and that most also want more than assistance with a look in the rearview mirror from their CPAs. Interviews of small to midsize clients by CPA2Biz for its Trusted Business Advisor workshops also showed that clients want forward-looking assistance, and that they are willing to pay for it. Remember—it's about adding value, and most reasonable people will pay for value received. But the value has to be what they perceive, not what you perceive. So, if your value pitch is that "We have everything in our office checked three times before it goes out, and we get clean peer review reports every time," after the yawning is over, your client may respond with, "So, what's your point?" Standing alongside your client to help them noodle through their tough issues is what is most valuable to them and, typically, they will let you know this is the case. So don't let your self-imposed fees-and-pricing fear get in your way.

Rates and Fees

Many firms are not pricing their work where they should be. Their rates are too low, and even if their nominal rates are in the ballpark, they are writing down their production to the point that their effective, realized rates are too low. Fees and rates that are too low are usually the result of one or more of the following causes:

- The firm owner or owners price the work at rates that will provide them with an adequate enough living for their personal goals, and the rates are not adjusted to keep up with market rates.
- Some CPAs are afraid if they charge what they'd like to charge, their clients will leave them, so they don't raise their fees or rates as they should.

- Some clients are unreasonable and brow-beat the CPAs into discounts they really shouldn't be given.
- Due to poor project management and communication with clients, appropriate expectations aren't set upfront before starting work, and then scope creep is accepted without a quid pro quo in the form of a discussion resulting in a change order and appropriate pricing.
- Partners are rewarded based on the amount of revenue they manage, so they sell work at lower rates than they should to build up their managed revenue.
- As mentioned earlier, the wrong people are doing the work (the partners, instead of lower level people), so the partners will bill at lower amounts than they should to reflect the lower level of work they decided to personally do.
- Because of a lack of good delegation and supervision practices, staff members work without the proper amount of direction, and they end up spinning their wheels or having to redo the work, or both, once someone straightens it all out.

These themes vary, but this short list covers the majority of the more common causes that we see and hear for rates and fees that are too low. Why do we care about what you're charging your clients? Because if you charged them what you should, you'd probably have a few less clients to deal with; you would generate at least as much, if not more, in revenue and bottom line income; and you could easily find the time to be working in the MTBA mode and taking better care of your clients (instead of finding ways to put it off).

Positioning Issues

How do your clients and your referral sources see you: as a good CPA, as a good CPA who is a good business advisor, or as a good business advisor who is also a good CPA? We are dealing with client perceptions again, and their perceptions are their reality about who you and your people are. Branding and positioning are big topics—ones that are worthy of a lot more space than we can provide here. The following are some issues you should deal with as a firm to get your positioning where you want it to be in your clients' eyes:

- What is your firm's mission and vision?
- What is your overall strategy in your market(s)?
- What are your key offerings to clients, and why should they matter to the clients?
- What is your target client profile?
- What are you doing to communicate regularly and repeatedly with your partners and staff about what you do for clients and how you are positioned as MTBAs?
- What are you doing to communicate with your clients regularly and repeatedly about what you can do for them?
  - Having one-on-one discussions with clients and referral sources to see what's going on in their lives and talk about what your firm is doing to help others in an advisory capacity

— Sending your clients white papers or other firm-prepared missives highlighting areas you work in and are passionate about
— Maintaining an up-to-date Web site that showcases your capabilities as advisors and accountants
— Using printed handouts to emphasize your position and capabilities as advisors
— Speaking at service clubs and other venues whenever you can get the chance on topics about which you are passionate (including taxes and audits, but especially in other areas as well because that demonstrates your uniqueness in the marketplace)

When it comes to positioning your firm, or more aptly, repositioning it, don't underestimate the effort required to do it properly. You cannot overcommunicate. In fact, you likely will find that after many, many touches (various contacts or communications with your clients) about a specific skill or capability your firm has, your client will still say during a conversation with you, "I didn't know you could do that!" Why? Because they are busy running their own lives, and it is very hard to get their attention long enough to tell them about ours. We have a saying about communication, and it goes like this: "When you reach the point that if you have to share a message one more time, you feel like you will throw-up because you have covered it so often, you are probably, finally starting to reach that group."

Workload Issues

When we talk to CPAs about adopting the MTBA approach, the biggest barrier perceived by practitioners is focused around workload issues. Many CPAs truly believe that they are just too busy to expand their services and spend the time required on MTBA efforts. We respond to this with the old adage that "You make time for what is really important to you." This book is our attempt to provide additional visibility about the importance of developing the MTBA aspects of your business. Until you see this as critical to your future success, although this transition might always be on your to-do list, it will be too low in priority or urgency to ever gain any real traction. And even if this issue is already high on your to-do list, which is why you might have bought our book in the first place, workload is a legitimate obstacle that you have to be willing to address. But before we cover what you can do about workload issues, let's review what most likely causes them in the first place.

The Upside Down Pyramid

Many firms today are struggling with the phenomenon we refer to as the *Upside Down Pyramid*, illustrated as figure 3-1.

Figure 3-1: **The Upside Down Pyramid Workflow Process**

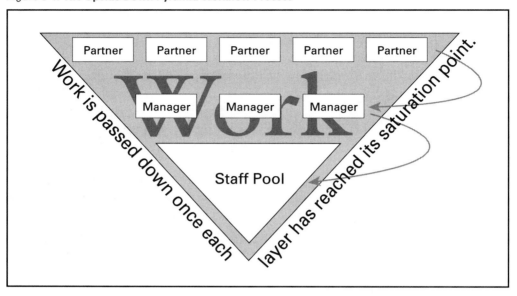

What's happening here is that the partners are not delegating work as they should. They hold on to it for as long as they can and try to do as much as they can themselves before they pass it on to the managers or seniors. Why? Common responses we hear are, "It is just as quick and easy to do it myself," "My people can't do this work by themselves, so I would have to teach them, which would take me longer if I involve them," and "We are under a deadline and don't have the luxury of getting others involved and teaching them as we go."

The managers or seniors learn by watching the partners, so they, in turn, glom onto work and hoard it rather than pushing it down to their people, until they absolutely have to push something down. They use excuses like, "There is no one that I can push this work down to," and "I get paid for my billable time so if I push it down, I might not have as much billable work to do," or "For me to push this work down, I would have to spend time training and coaching my people, which will make me personally less chargeable. So, while I will make the people that work for me better, I will get beat up in the form of bonuses and other actions to punish me because my individual performance numbers will be down."

Normally when either the partners or the managers finally do push something down, their "delegation" looks more like abdication or "dumping" (they just drop the work on someone's desk and walk away because the partners' and managers' desks already are overloaded with work with near-term deadlines). Consequently, management regularly misses great opportunities to properly develop their people, and a huge skill gap emerges because of underdevelopment between the partners or managers, or both, and the next level of people. Typical symptoms we've seen under the Upside Down Pyramid include the following:

- Partners, and perhaps managers, working inordinately long hours (up to 2,600 or more hours per year, even up to and in excess of 3,000 hours per year in extreme cases).

- Even though partners and managers are overcommitted, staff members often are looking for work to do.
- Partners and managers don't trust the remaining staff to work on their projects because the staff "doesn't have the necessary experience."
- When clients call for new work, partners try to talk them out of it or put it off. For example, if a client tells the partner that the bank or surety wants an audit, the partner might try to talk them and the third party into accepting a lower level of service because the partner already is overwhelmed with work.
- At some point, with the highest level people working a level or two below where they should be, there's going to be a problem with realization.

We could go on, but you probably get the picture and may have seen something similar at some point in your career. This problem is a chronic situation in our profession. And to make matters worse, firms that are behind the power curve in technology utilization only exacerbate this problem because they are not as efficient as they otherwise could be.

Addressing These Issues

Compensation Systems

Part of the reason why CPA firms struggle with the challenges we've listed so far in this chapter is that the owners and managers are being compensated based on personal production, charge hours, and books of business. They are not being compensated based on their support of the firm's overall strategy (if there even is one), nor are they being rewarded based on how well they delegate to, and supervise, their people. People generally go where the money is, and if the money is in personal production metrics, that's where your people will spend their time and efforts. If you want to change the behaviors, you need to change the compensation system. If you want your top people to pass work down and develop others so that they can free up capacity, you have to reward that behavior instead of punishing them for it. If you want your partners and your people to begin functioning as MTBAs, what are you doing to be sure they get rewarded for doing so and punished for finding every excuse to blow it off?

Clients and Fees

Our first piece of advice to you, which we previously mentioned, is if you want to make time to be an MTBA, raise your rates. Even in questionable economic times, raise your rates. This alone will free up some time, and we've not seen a situation where the loss of fees from clients who left was greater than the increased fees from those who stayed. Next, run off marginal clients. Get rid of those who complain, abuse the staff, and are always slow to pay.—They're sucking the life out of you and your people.

Over the years, many firms have grown and developed according to some previous strategy, or none at all, resulting in having some clients who really may not belong in the firm's current business model, strategy, and future. Additionally, some clients have evolved or changed in ways that may make them less desirable as clients today than they were a few years ago. For that matter, for one reason or another, some clients you currently have should never really have been clients in the first place. For all of these reasons and more, firms need to take a hard look at their present clients and at their client acceptance and retention policies and clean house.

We use a simple system for classifying clients. Our sample client definitions are as follows:

- *A-clients.* An A-client is one of 15 percent to 20 percent of the clients that make up 70 percent to 80 percent of the firm's revenues. If you sorted your clients by revenues for last year (clients representing relationships, not just one entity), you would identify quickly those clients that generated substantial fees for your firm. An A-client is one that you are probably adequately serving, one that will continually have new projects for you to do, and one that generates sizable revenues for your firm.
- *B-clients.* A B-client is one that right now, you most likely are underserving but who has an opportunity to generate sizable revenues for your firm. For example, you might have a business client for whom you only do tax returns. However, based on what you know of the business (for example, they are $5 million in size or have 100 employees), you easily could provide them thousands of more dollars in needed services each year.
- *C-clients.* A C-client is a client that does not have much additional service opportunity other than what you already do, and the revenues generated are small. However, they are good clients, do not have complex situations, pay you on time, pay average or better fees, and are pleasant to work with. The best description of this group of clients is they are your typical individual tax return-only clients. Don't confuse the C rating with school and assume they need to become B-clients to make the grade. A firm can have all C-clients and do very well.
- *D-clients.* A D-client could seemingly fall into any of the preceding classifications. However, these clients present at least one of a number of possible problems. They most likely are unprofitable to the firm as a result of poor rates, realization, or utilization. They also might be hard to work with because they are abrasive, late payers, never timely so they always create scheduling problems, always want special accommodations, require services that are too difficult to provide (for example, this client is the one governmental audit you perform, which is very inefficient work for you), or only pay your last bill as an incentive for you to start their next project. None of these issues alone automatically classifies someone as a D-client. For example, you might have someone that always pays you late (but they do pay), and you always charge them premium fees for their work to make up for their business approach, which makes him or her an acceptable client. Or someone may constantly negotiate every fee but, nevertheless, involves you in big projects that are profitable to your firm. Generally speaking, most firms quickly know who falls into their definition of the D category. At the end of the day, you do not want any D-clients. This means that your objective is to either find a way to convert them into C-clients or better or introduce them to your fiercest competitor. In the latter instance, you have positioned these clients to waste your competitor's resources instead of yours.

Once again, a CPA firm having only C-clients is not a bad thing. In this situation, the firm's client base could be described as a cluster of small clients who pay timely and are fun to work with but who have little potential to provide additional business. In this case, you would make sure these clients are reminded regularly of your various services through media like postcards, newsletters, seminars, and so forth. In this way, they are positioned to refer you to others because they likely will not have many additional needs themselves. On the other hand, regarding your A and B-clients, you need to have regularly scheduled personal contact with them to make sure you understand their priorities (and not just their financial priorities).

The fundamental questions that you need to be able to answer with facts, not conjecture, are as follows:

1. Do your clients know what your firm can do to help them?
2. For your A and B-clients, do you know what is keeping them awake at night (that is, the concerns and opportunities they are trying to address at this time)? Note that, an important part of this process is for you to uncover issues regardless of whether or not you are able to resolve them. For issues that you cannot address, give your clients referrals to professionals who can give assistance. It always surprises us how many firms expect professionals to refer business to them but do not reciprocate. Providing a referral for a needed service not only helps the client, it makes the client want to talk to you about all of their issues because they want the benefit of your network. Moreover, giving referrals stimulates futures referrals back to you.
3. Do your clients know what your firm's total service capability is so that they are armed and ready to refer you to friends, associates, and family?

As we previously mentioned, for A and high B-clients, the answers to preceding questions 1 and 2 should be identified through regularly scheduled contact. By posing question 3 to your A and B-clients and questions 1 and 3 to your C-clients, you should get an affirmative answer and referral sources as a result of your firm's marketing campaign.

Now we want to take a moment to make a special point regarding question 2. You are in danger of losing A or high B-clients if the partner or manager in charge of these accounts cannot at least articulate each client's priorities. Because if you don't know what they are focusing on, how can you say you are taking care of them? On the other hand, if a client is classified as a D, then the person in charge of that relationship needs to develop a strategy to convert them a C-client or better. That strategy could be as simple as the following:

• Let's say you have a client at about 65 percent of standard rates. Your strategy might be to bill them at 85 percent of standard rates this year, 95 percent next year, and then keep them at that level or higher or they will not be able to remain a client, or
  — we will transition this client to one of our senior staff members to manage and bill because the client's needs are better suited to the senior's experience level and billing rate, which also will fix the realization issue.

Alternatively, the strategy could be as drastic as the following:

- Assuming a client that only pays the last job off at the start of the next project, the partner needs to inform this client that the account must be paid current and kept that way, or the client needs to find another accountant.

We don't normally believe in firing clients. Occasions do arise when firing the client is the absolute right action, especially if you don't trust the client or the client mistreats your personnel. But most of the time, the appropriate change is to make both the partner and the client accountable to sustaining a profitable relationship.

If the client wants the relationship to be one-sided (in other words, profitable only to him or her), then adjust the policies and billings to the right level, and let the client decide whether they want to stay or go. Don't be surprised how many of our D-clients have become that way because we created an operating environment that steered them in that direction. If you have a few clients who are sucking the life out of you and your people, you need to deal with them. Raising fees and rates often will be just what you need to create a little more quality time with your A and B-clients, not to mention be more profitable overall.

One last thing about D-clients. Our experience is that about half convert to C-clients or higher, the other half go away. We tend to think that if we hold the line on converting our D-clients to be profitable again that they all will leave us. Remember, your clients know and trust you. They might not be happy about paying you more money, but when they look at their market alternatives, many of them realize that you are just adjusting your rates to charge them a fair fee—the same kind of fee everyone would bill them for a similar quality and response level of service.

Stop Giving Away Work

You need to record all of your time and show your total time and fees. You may end up discounting some of it, but you'll never bill it if you don't account for it in the first place. Have you been brow-beating your staff about why they can't meet the impossible budget you set for the work when you sold it at less than your standard rates? If you have, you can bet that they're "eating" time as well. You can count on this fact too: when you focus on realization, people stop recording their time. You can't improve your business with bad information. So make sure all of the time is recorded, verify what that job really takes, and then deal with the whole problem (whether your people are adequately trained to do the work efficiently or whether you are charging too little for the job, or a combination of both). Regardless, you need to know how much total time you are devoting to individual clients and their projects if you want to be able to improve your profitability and make time to be an MTBA. We know this may be hard to believe, but in this day and age, some CPAs don't have the data to perform this kind of analysis. There is no reason not to have it given the technology available at this time—but more on that later.

Stop giving away work, time is your most scarce resource—don't give it away. Your clients value what you do for them. Even during economic downturns, many CPAs have more work than they can handle comfortably, leading to a shortage of time to perform as MTBAs. Yet they price work at less than standard rates. Our profession owns the franchise on attest services, yet we continue to bid for audits at less than market rates. Stop giving away work and devote that time at full rates to your best clients as their MTBA.

Technology

Technology has vastly improved the way we work and has created significant efficiencies for CPAs who use it as they should. Yet we continue to find CPAs who don't want to invest in technology and are not up to date on it. Even with the advances in paperless accounting packages, many firms still have not embraced the concept and, therefore, haven't availed themselves of the time savings and efficiencies it will create after the two- to three-year implementation period required. Believe it or not, some CPAs still are not using electronic spreadsheets in their practices. Technology allows you to leverage your time. Use technology whenever possible and pass on the costs to clients—use the leverage that technology provides, whether it's paperless systems or more integrated software—to make you and your people more efficient, thereby allowing you more time to function as an MTBA.

And while we're talking about passing on costs to clients, let's talk about the cost of technology. Technology is not free to us. Keeping up with it easily can run 3 percent to 5 percent of net revenues every year, yet we still find firms who are not recovering that cost in the way that they bill. This is tantamount to a heavy contractor not charging an owner for the use of its million dollar scraper on a job. You need to add a technology charge to your work-in-progress (WIP) for everything you do. If your response is, "Why add a technology charge if I am not even billing full rates for my time yet?" then the answer is simple. We are no different than a homebuilder. We need to look at our job costs (billable time) from two perspectives. First, we are doing the analysis of costs to give us an idea of what to bill this time around (were there change orders, additional new issues not in scope, and so forth?). Second, we want to use the data to provide us insight into what we should be selling this type of work for in the future. Loading the right charges into WIP may not make any difference with the current bill, but it should make a significant difference in the conversations you will have with the client (and the partner or manager, or both, in charge of that client) between now and the next billing cycle or project.

Managerial Leadership

Be a Better Manager

Your people watch what you actually do, rather than what you say or what you have framed and hanging on the wall in the office. If you really believe that using the MTBA approach is what your firm needs to survive and thrive, then you need to take action and be an exemplar for others. If necessary, get some training and coaching in effective leadership, delegation, and supervision. Make yourself uncomfortable learning to be a better managerial leader and then help your partners and people learn how to be better leaders, better project managers, and better professionals. It's not going to happen by itself. Delegate—hand off lower level work—you can't be an MTBA if you just sit in the office doing grunt work and waiting for the phone to ring.

Develop Your People

Train your people. You won't turn the inverted pyramid over until you have trained your people and allowed them to grow professionally. They represent your firm's most significant resource. Create a plan for "people development" and follow it. Yes, this will take time, but it also will result in your time being freed up to do higher level work, like being your clients' MTBA.

If you are a solo practitioner, hire part-time help if you have no one working for you. Stop viewing people as a cost—they represent a way to leverage your time, freeing you up for higher level work and allowing you to generate higher fees as a result. People in our business are our inventory and our profit centers, not cost centers. Can you imagine a retail store trying to make money with no excess inventory? For us to grow and be profitable, we have to free up capacity at the top, which means we need to be constantly developing at the bottom.

Strategy

Develop your firm's overall strategy and approach to meeting market needs and being MT-BAs and communicate with everyone inside the firm as well as clients and referral sources outside the firm regularly and frequently. Take some small steps, set short-term goals, and then build from there to get some momentum going. This will take time, but if you delay, it's only going to take time later on. The sooner you start, the sooner you can begin reaping the benefits of your more focused efforts. Stop procrastinating or waiting for just the right moment or stalling this effort until the economy is better or delaying for that time when you finally have all of the "right" people. The time is now to chart a new course and be vigilant about navigating towards your new destination.

The General Contractor Model

Another way to alleviate some pressure is to operate under what we refer to as the "General Contractor" model, which we mentioned briefly earlier. This model allows you to maintain the primary relationship with your clients and stay in the driver's seat when it comes to meeting their needs. Under it, you use a network of other professionals, including your own, some who are CPAs and some who are not, to help clients with their challenges and opportunities. The point should be clear by now that clients don't expect one person (their CPA) to have all the answers—they just want to know that you can help them find the answers they need through using your network or other means. If every time a client needs something done you believe that you have to do it all, you will be less inclined to jump on it and help create successes. Living up to this expectation is simply too overwhelming a task. The General Contractor model helps avoid those problems. We will cover this model in more detail in the following chapter.

More on the Opportunities of an MTBA

So far we've covered some of the reasons people give for not pursuing MTBA status. Now, let's go to the "rest of the story" as the late, great Paul Harvey would have said.

Revenue Growth

Traditionally, the typical CPA practice has concentrated on taxes, financial statement preparation, and audit services. Each of these areas has seen price resistance or profit-margin pressure during the past 10–15 years, although Sarbanes-Oxley breathed a bit of new life into audit services after Enron and WorldCom. CPAs have been unloading write-up work for years due to its low profit margin. Even if you have been shrewd enough to have developed a profitable way to deliver this service, the proliferation of computer hardware and software is moving this function back into the client's office, and for small businesses, into the home.

Further affecting the profitability of tax and financial statement preparation services is the growth of non-CPA providers, such as American Express Tax and Business Services, CBiz, H&R Block, and thousands of local competitors. Marketing textbooks would describe the current state of our financial marketplace as "mature," which translates to

- numerous competitors;
- slow to flat growth of the market;
- niche marketers who target narrow, well-defined, underserved segments of the market;
- a basically undifferentiated product with stylistic rather than functional nuances;
- new business for one firm is often the result of lost business from another;
- falling prices; and
- shrinking profit margins.

Look this up in any text book. Our profession is not undergoing a unique phenomenon; we are just simply experiencing a stage in the well-known model of the product/service life cycle. History clearly gives us insight about what is likely to happen next. More advertising dollars will be spent attempting to entice the consumer, special offers or promotional pricing (discounting), or both, will be used to attract new business, and marginal competitors will begin dropping out of the marketplace. Each time a competitor changes the game, like a major player in a market discounting audit fees, the bar is reset, and everyone has to react and decide whether they are going to play or not.

If this weren't doom-and-gloom enough, consider the entry of players like IBM, AT&T, EDS, Hewlett-Packard, and many others, which clearly have entered the market on the advice side of our business. If you think these organizations will stop at delivering high-level management assistance, you're kidding yourself. These companies want what you have, something you take minimal advantage of. It's called account control. Account control gives them easy access to management's ear. You can bet these corporations will push deeper and deeper into your clients' organizations with services similar to yours until there is no meat left on the bone. Years of business experience has taught them that it is far more profitable to sell additional complementary products and services (product and service extension) to an existing customer than to find a new one.

Now that we have written graffiti all over the picture of the future of tax and financial statement preparation services, let's discuss the viability of audits. First, the procedures and requirements constantly are becoming more stringent. When you add this to the skyrocketing liability insurance premiums and peer review costs associated with auditing, you'll find that this revenue source also has lost some of its appeal. It is at this point that we hear the argument, "While audits have lost some of their appeal, at least they are not under siege by outsiders like tax and bookkeeping services. This is one place CPAs need to make their stand. Assurance services are our only protected area."

By the way, we believe that to some extent, assurance services, like audits, will continue to be protected. However, what most CPAs fail to see is that the traditional audit is falling out of favor. The information contained in these examinations is not only too old, but too slow in arriving for review. Most of the decisions pertaining to this information have long since been made with the results already known by the time the reports are available. To make matters worse, electronic transaction flow is evolving in such a way and pace that it makes this reporting seem even more inadequate.

Traditional services like financial statement preparation and audits take the approach of creating a snapshot of a business's financial condition at a specific point in time. Although this approach is still viable today, the problem is time compression. In today's fast paced economic climate, information indicating that a company was financially sound six months ago does not provide a lot of insight about whether to lend or invest in that organization today. This creates a tremendous need for more timely information. In response to that need, many of our world's businesses already submit summary data on a daily or weekly basis to analysts, investors, banks, and so forth. Assuming this trend continues in the future, which is almost a given at this point, as more organizations adopt continual reporting of a company's progress, CPAs will have to learn to work with moving, not stagnant, information. This could not be more evident than by the growing global adoption of tools like XBRL (eXtensible Business Reporting Language, which is a royalty-free, international information format designed specifically for business information). The use of XBRL will provide major benefits in the preparation, analysis, and communication of business information through cost savings, greater efficiency, and improved reliability and timeliness to all those involved in supplying or using financial data.

Catapulting the ability for companies to deliver more timely information and, therefore, the need to assure its reliability, is the acceptance of "cloud computing." For example, CPA2Biz now has a Web portal offering for AICPA members to help them leverage the power of today's technology. Intaact, one of the oldest accounting services players in the cloud computing world, and CPA2Biz have codeveloped a new version of Intacct's financial management and accounting application, which has been designed specifically for CPA firms and their small to medium-sized business clients. It includes unique content from the AICPA, customizable dashboards for easy metric and performance monitoring, and much more. Financial applications like this, coupled with businesses on–demand accounts payable software from Bill.com and HR resources from Paychex is just the beginning of what this new future holds. The point is not that long ago, CPAs typically put their clients' financial statements together by inputting the data from paper receipts and checkbooks. Today many of our clients provide that same data to us already captured in an electronic format. As you can see from options like CPA2Biz's Web portal accounting solutions, some CPAs already have taken a giant leap forward by utilizing systems that can monitor their clients business performance on a daily basis with exception reporting through dashboards (like alerting the CPA that specific performance metrics have changed beyond an expected range).

All of these changes are creating an intense demand to be able to validate the reliability of the data capturing and communication systems, not the data itself. Unfortunately, the audit as we now know it does not remotely address this dilemma. However, you can expect new services to emerge that the CPA professional is uniquely qualified to deliver, but it likely won't be protected by our current audit franchise.

Given the changes taking place, it is not surprising that an AICPA Special Committee on Assurance Services proposed years ago that the financial audit will, at some point in the future, be replaced by a broader information audit. No one knows exactly when this will sweep the financial marketplace, but those that look to audits for assurance, like banks, the Securities and Exchange Commission, and investors are not satisfied with the out-of-date, narrowly focused, historical review of a company's health.

In a recent edition of *The CPA Letter*, the Special Committee on Assurance Services stated

> To seize future opportunities, CPAs must recognize consumers' information needs and the changes in their demands. New services must be designed to meet decision makers' vital needs.
>
> In the future, CPAs will likely find that:
>
> - The power to decide information content will shift from producers of information (such as preparers and auditors) to consumers (managers, investors, creditors and other decision makers).
> - Information technology advances will both enable and drive change in decision-makers' needs and the services CPAs provide.
> - There will be many providers of information for decision making. CPAs will have to compete to furnish many new services in a non-regulated, market-driven environment very different from the current market.
>
> To ensure a brighter economic future, CPAs must:
>
> - Capitalize on their strengths to expand their service offerings and
> - Design services that are based on what users need.

What this says to us is that our one protected area will still be protected; it's just that there could easily be an erosion of buyers for that protected service. Keep in mind that the demand for many of our traditional services is not consumer-driven; the demand is compliance-driven. And when those demanding compliance change their product/service requirements, like banks requiring an information audit rather than a financial audit, for example, then overnight, the demand for some of our traditional services could decline rapidly.

Given all of this, holding on to traditional accounting as your flagship service seems to be shortsighted. We are not saying that you should stop performing the services on which our reputation has been built. On the contrary, traditional services help you hang on to your current clients and also help bring in new clients. However, we are saying that the future, as well as critical additional revenue sources, lie in the expansion or augmentation of our core services.

Account Control

Another reason to embrace the MTBA approach is to protect your client base. This is critical to your firm's future survival. Why? Because it is a lot easier, not to mention more profitable, to sell additional services to your current clients than it is to attract new ones. Because many MTBAs deliver one service, logical extensions of that service easily are identified, sold, and then delivered (service extension). Our accidental application of marketing theory is one of the main reasons why CPAs have been able to grow, thrive, and dramatically increase their personal incomes given a relative stagnation of fees from traditional services like tax, financial statement, and audit services. Our profession has experienced a vast expansion of services horizontally. During the past 15 years, CPAs have been fairly creative in augmenting existing services, as well as offering new ones to existing clients. This has not only increased our average revenue per client but enhanced loyalty as well. Service extension is most successful when you have account control. Account control occurs when you have easy access to management's ear, and management considers you to be a trusted advisor to the organization. Consider this common scenario:

> You are having lunch with a good client and he says to you, "I feel like my company is drifting. While we are certainly making good money, it seems all we ever have time to do is put out fires that are burning out of control." You then respond with a really sophisticated marketing statement like, "Several of our clients have felt the strain of exponential growth like yours. What we have done that has really seemed to help is to organize and facilitate a two-day executive retreat. This not only puts the fires into perspective, but brings into full focus the priorities everyone should be working toward." The client responds, "That sounds like something that we would be interested in. Let me talk to the rest of the team and get back to you."

This would be a classic example of service extension. Because we are trusted advisors of management, we have the opportunity and access to suggest our involvement and quickly consummate a new engagement with virtually no resistance. Although the client could still want the same service, without such an existing relationship and involvement, the client might consider a number of other resources in the marketplace, which would then make the hiring decision a much more prolonged and price-competitive process.

As previously mentioned, service extension occurs more frequently for those who have account control. Unfortunately, the world is full of predators who want the account control that you already have. Many of those predators are other CPA firms. Account control is why our service extension strategy has been so successful. If we fail to protect our client base and lose account control, we will be relegated to delivering only those services that others deem too unprofitable.

The MTBA Framework Is a Logical Role for CPAs

Another reason to augment your offerings is the idea that who is in a better position to offer general business guidance than the CPA? We regularly examine our clients' financial situation and have a fundamental understanding of their business activities. Logically, the next step is to take a more active role in helping them become more profitable, which inevitably leads to success for the CPA.

Also be aware that other professionals covet our title of MTBA. We were at a management consultants' convention not too long ago where the term *trusted business advisor* was used by multiple speakers in discussing the role that management consultants can have with small to medium-sized clients. If our profession does not seize the opportunities presented, we will find other parties playing in our sandbox with our clients. The good news is that you can protect your sandbox by employing the MTBA Framework and approach if you start now.

The most difficult part of making this transition is shifting your image from the technical expert with the answers to a person who can facilitate the answers and contribute good ideas. It requires a change in perspective, from one of a purely historical view, to one which considers the past in order to better anticipate the future. How to make this transformation is a major focus in many of the remaining chapters in this book.

The Market Has Changed

Our experience is that today's client is more educated and inquisitive than ever before. This sophistication has created a new breed of client that is demanding more than a tax return and a balance sheet. They expect more than a financial advisor: they are looking for a business advisor.

If We Don't Satisfy the Need, They'll Find Someone Who Will

This is best exemplified by the fact that over half of our profession now works outside public accounting. And where you used to only find a CPA controller-type position being filled in a $50 million company, today you are likely to find a CPA controller in most $5 million dollar organizations. If trends continue as they have, by early in the 21st century, any company with more than $1,000,000 in sales is a candidate for an in-house CPA professional. Therefore, it is our contention that a transition is well underway.

 Keep In Mind

The nonpublic CPA (industry CPA) likely will become the single biggest purchaser of public accounting services.

What baffles us is how the profession can continue to ignore the significance of this phenomenon. When you look at the typical CPA firm, they hold out their various levels of assurance services as their most significant offering. So what's wrong with this picture when public practitioners continue to sell the same services we always have even though

- the person in the future that is most likely to hire you is also a CPA;
- you are trying to convince the client to buy services he or she is already performing internally;
- the company is small or financially strong enough to not have an independent compliance requirement;
- the industry professional desperately is looking for assistance helping them perform their jobs, yet accounting is becoming a smaller and smaller part of that job;
- management teams are more and more interested in all information, not just financial information; and
- management teams constantly are pushing compliance reporting to the bottom of their priority list.

To put this into a more personal perspective, do you, as a public accountant, hire an outside CPA firm to help you with your financial statements? Of course not! Typically, when CPA firms hire professional services, they hire people to help

- complete projects that require more time than they have available, or
- perform tasks or functions for which they do not have the skills, or both.

These same criteria should be used to determine the kind of services you could and should be offering to our future marketplace, nonpublic CPAs. This is really simple—just look at the preceding list and stop trying to sell your CPA controllers what they don't want, and start selling them what they actively are looking for. Not long ago, we were talking with the then current chair of the AICPA when she commented on this topic. Paraphrased she said, "If my CPA is not smart enough to talk to me about my whole business, then why would I consider hiring them to help me in areas they have never shown any interest in?"

It is perceived by many of our industry counterparts that a great number of our public practitioners are too narrowly, too historically, and too nontechnologically focused to be a significant value-add in helping them perform their jobs. Quite simply, the market has changed. If we continue to ignore the need for us to live up to our MTBA reputation and disregard the requirement to expand the kind of conversations we should be having with our clients, the most significant future purchaser of our services (the industry CPA) will likely stop looking to us for assistance outside of a narrow band of compliance and assurance services.

Organizational Opportunities

Business advisory work can be more enjoyable, demanding, exciting (and at times, more frustrating) than traditional compliance work. This intensity often acts as a catalyst to revive and rejuvenate the interest and focus of disenchanted management and staff.

So if you, as a firm, want to attract and retain talented CPAs, you need to be able to offer opportunities and new challenges. The MTBA approach does just that. The additional revenue potential not only provides room for new talent in-house but creates management positions as well. This expansion, in turn, secures a retirement funding source. Retirement then creates additional openings.

To Answer the Question

To answer the question "Why bother with the MTBA approach" we offer the following:

Those who maintain a traditional CPA practice will continue to do well in the short-term but will struggle in the future.

You can expect the public accountants' services and rates to be increasingly challenged by non-CPAs. The demand for services will shift from an historically focused service to a future-focused one. The growth of CPAs working in industry will call for a change in service offerings. In order to create differentiation, specialization within our profession likely will flourish as has already begun. Our competitive edge lies in fine tuning those areas that best utilize our unique training and experience. MTBA is a perfect fit.

Exercise 3-1

Action Plans: Making Time for MTBA Services

Based on the materials covered in this chapter, please take a few moments to think about your practice and what you can do to begin making more time to function as your clients' most trusted business advisor (MTBA). Then, using the form below, make note of any areas you plan to work on as well as a timeframe to reassess your progress. This form is provided solely as a tool for your use in improving your practice.

Name: _____

The following are activities I intend to undertake:

- _____ By when: _____
- _____ By when: _____
- _____ By when: _____
- _____ By when: _____
- _____ By when: _____
- _____ By when: _____
- _____ By when: _____
- _____ By when: _____
- _____ By when: _____
- _____ By when: _____
- _____ By when: _____
- _____ By when: _____
- _____ By when: _____
- _____ By when: _____
- _____ By when: _____

The General Contractor Model

"To manage a system effectively, you might focus on the interactions of the parts rather than their behavior taken separately."

~ RUSSELL L. ACKOFF

Using the General Contractor Model

Most CPAs take a great deal of pride being their clients' most trusted business advisor (MTBA). So what does this mean? We characterize this as, "Our professionals want to be their clients' first point of contact when they encounter a business problem, and for many, even a life problem." CPAs are commonly the first point of contact for their clients regarding financial issues, but if this was truly our objective, then our profession's mantra would be "most trusted tax or financial advisor" rather than "most trusted business advisor."

The Role of MTBA

There are two major components to the MTBA role that we aspire to fulfill. The first is to be an advisor. In order to be an advisor, you need to spend time nurturing your role as your clients' confidant. This translates to partners and managers spending time regularly meeting with, listening to, and trying to understand what keeps their clients awake at night. In other words, what are the concerns and opportunities each client is trying to address at this time? The importance here is not about selling services (which you will); it's not about looking for problems that your services will satisfy (which will happen); but it is about uncovering important issues that need to be addressed, regardless of whether or not you or your firm can personally resolve them. In our opinion, you can't be an advisor if you don't understand both the business and personal goals and needs of each of your clients. Although this nurturing role can be established quickly, it takes time to maintain. Realistically, you can't dedicate this level of resource to all of your clients, so you minimally have to focus on those clients that are the most critical to your firm's success (what we've referred to as the A-clients, or the roughly 20 percent of your clients that make up 80 percent of your firm's revenues).

Many of you will be thinking, "What you are describing is no big deal because we already do it." However, here is a quick test to see if you really are doing it. When you get back to your office, walk down the halls and stop in and ask any partner or manager to quickly list the top five issues of each of their three largest clients that they are trying to address in the next 12–18 months. If all you get is financial-related answers, such as completing a tax return, audit, business valuation, and so forth, then that CPA is living up to the lesser mantra of "most trusted financial advisor." If a partner or manager paints a much more holistic picture of a client's objectives, such as expanding the plant production by 20 percent; changing their sales compensation system; increasing employee retention; improving customer service; and so forth; then congratulate that CPA for living in rare air because in our opinion, they are among less than 5 percent of public practitioners that currently serve their clients at this superior level.

Now that you are aware of what your top clients want to achieve, it's time for us to discuss the second component of being your clients' MTBA, which we believe is best described as filling the general contractor (GC) role.

After working closely with CPA professionals for almost three decades, we can tell you that our technical background often gets in our way when trying to make this transition.

When we think of helping our clients, the first thing that comes to mind is, "Do I have the skills to perform the specific service my client needs?" Although this thinking is foundational to being successful when performing traditional accounting work, it is counter to performing advisory work. Our professional standards clearly state that we either have to "know how to perform the work" or "know enough to supervise it." However, we tend to write off the second option as a no-value service. We tend to overvalue being the one that does the actual work and undervalue supervising it.

The General Contractor Role

Right now, let's take a look at a GC analogy to clarify why it is so perfectly suited to guiding our evolution as advisors. First, would you expect your GC to personally possess all the skills to complete a project for you? Probably not, unless your contractor is also a licensed plumber, electrician, and a skilled framer, roofer, trim carpenter, and more. However, we would expect a GC to listen to our ideas and desires, either utilize or modify an existing plan or create a new one, and then bring in whatever subcontractors are necessary to complete the project. GCs may execute some phases of a project by either performing the work themselves (that is, using their crews to accomplish specific tasks), but they also depend heavily on subcontractors to deliver on many of the skilled jobs. So naturally, a primary responsibility for the GC is finding, scheduling, and managing the resources required to build whatever you have in mind.

GC Case Study

Let's talk through a recent home construction project Bill managed as the GC. Don't worry, once we are done stepping through the gory details, we will tie all of this back to how this project management approach creates an ideal framework for CPAs to follow to fully develop their MTBA capabilities.

Bill's wife, in this situation (the client) wanted their dilapidated boat dock renovated. She thought it would be nice if they could walk on it without falling through, sit on the upper deck without feeling like a gust of wind would topple the upper story into the water, be shaded by a roof from the scalding sun in the summer as well as augmenting the dock with a few additional amenities. So, he went to work putting a plan together. The plan and identified assignments broke down as follows:

1. Permit (Bill)
2. Demolition (Bill)
3. Below deck structural work (carpenters)
4. Prep of the boat stall and lift (Bill)
5. Trash removal (Bill)
6. Materials purchase and staging (Bill)
7. Install lower decking (carpenters)
8. Upper deck leveling (carpenters)

9. Reinforce upper deck (carpenters)
10. Install upper decking (carpenters)
11. Manufacture roof posts, trusses (carpenters)
12. Install roof, cap, and edge trim (carpenters)
13. Wire upper deck for lighting (electricians)
14. Build soffit and cornice (carpenters)
15. Build cabinet and stabilizing wall (carpenters)
16. Install lights, speakers, and switches (electricians)
17. Build the staircase and closet (carpenters)
18. Trash removal (Bill)
19. Paint the boat dock (Bill)
20. Weld and install iron railings (welder)

First, he had to get a permit to allow the renovation. After considering his options, he decided that he could do this himself. So Bill took pictures of the boat dock, sketched the changes his wife wanted to make, filled out the necessary forms, and delivered the paperwork to the Watershed Protection and Development Review Department. After about 20 days and multiple follow-up phone calls, his renovation was approved, conditioned on "no new posts" in the water.

The next step was to rebuild the framework supporting the dock posts. Every year or two, Austin, Texas lowers the water for 20 days so people can perform maintenance on their docks. The permit process had taken a little longer than Bill had hoped, and he only had 10 days left until the water would rise again. He had a carpenter in mind and quickly negotiated with him to stop work on his current job just long enough to reframe the portion of the boat dock structure that would soon be underwater. The carpenters were able to quickly reframe it and once that work was done, they went back to their other project. While they were gone, Bill took advantage of the water being down and installed bumpers and dock edging.

While the carpenters were gone, he also started tearing off the old decking so that his skilled carpenters could focus their time on reframing. After removing the old decking, he then needed to clean up the site to make room for the incoming materials. The remains of his old boat dock were put on a trailer so they could be hauled to the dump.

Once the carpenters were back on site, their immediate focus was to build out both the lower and upper decks. Next was the installation of the roof posts, 16 roof trusts, the metal roof, the ridge cap, and the eve trim.

At this point, we needed to get the electricians on site. It was time to run the wires so that the upper deck had the desired lighting and power outlets. Once the roof area was wired and the light cans installed, the carpenters finished installing the wood cornice and soffit. As you can see, the carpenters Bill hired are very versatile because they not only did framing work (like the structural framing, decking, and trusses), but they also did the roofing as well as the trim work (like the cornice, soffit, and soon to be built closets). They were able to fill the role of several specialty subcontractors, which made his job as the GC much easier.

Next, we called the electricians back in to finish up their work installing lighting fixtures, power outlets, and the speakers.

The stairs were the next challenge because they had to be designed so that they are wider than the current stairs, not as steep, must also help stabilize the boat dock by tying it to the land, built in such a way so they avoid the palm tree, and still integrate back with the entry to the boat dock. Bill originally had designed a nice closet under the staircase, but that had to be abandoned to incorporate the important functionality of stability with a stronger connection of the dock to the land.

Then it was time to paint. Bill had a feeling all along that the project might be pushing the limits of the budget by this time, and he was right. Needless to say, Bill did the painting to stay within budget.

The final subcontractor needed was the welder. His job is to build the railings. However, as complex projects sometimes go, a problem was identified. Wind can be a major problem for boat docks because rivers can generate a wind funnel creating high gusts. Therefore, in order to strengthen and more securely tie the upper deck and the roof together, we either needed to build wall wind braces at every corner of the upper deck or come up with some other solution to secure the dock. Given that one of his wife's requests was to maximize visibility wherever possible rather than add walls, which would reduce visibility dramatically, the team kicked around some ideas and decided on integrating iron wind braces with the railing system.

And once that work was done, it was finally time to relax and enjoy the completed results.

By now many of you may be wondering how this "better homes and gardens do-it-yourself project" description has anything to do with developing your MTBA skills. Let's tie it all together.

Skills Required for the GC Role

As you know, Bill is not a general contractor by trade but a homeowner who was trying to satisfy a family request—turn a dilapidated boat dock into an enjoyable outdoor living space. Even if he would have had the time, he didn't have the skills required to perform the technical work required for each stage of this project. However, he does have the project management skills to plan the project, work with talented people to oversee each phase, keep close tabs on the project to make sure that the envisioned boat dock has some similarity to the completed one, step in and listen to the various alternatives when problems are encountered and give guidance on which solutions to implement. At various times, he also can step in to perform various subcontractor roles. For example, in this project, he did some demolition work pulling the old deck materials off the dock, hauled the old lumber away, did some painting, and so forth.

The project management ability we are describing here is no different than the project management skill set CPAs demonstrate everyday any time we have multiple people involved in the production of a financial statement or audit. We have been acting as the financial subcontractor on our clients' projects for decades, so we already have tons of experience in this role. And just as Bill's carpenters ended up doing the technical work usually required by three or four different subcontractors, CPAs, assuming we have the technical ability, can act in the capacity of multiple subcontractors as well.

For those of you reading this who are sole proprietors, besides the idea that everyone should devote time to building a network of non-CPA professionals (like attorneys, insurance agents, bankers, and so forth.), you also should consider developing a network with other small firms so that you can leverage their skills as subcontractors on your clients' projects.

In our opinion, the GC role is a great model to describe how CPAs should operate as their clients' MTBA. Our first job is to understand the vision of the client—what he or she wants to accomplish. In our example, what are the features and functionality of the boat dock? Our next job is to put a plan together and identify the necessary resources, including bringing in various technical experts if necessary, so that we can assist our clients in successfully accomplishing their objectives. In our boat dock example, this meant that Bill, as GC, needed to identify the various steps required, determine for each phase whether he was going to do the work or hire someone else to do it, estimate the costs, and manage the project through completion.

As CPAs, we don't help our clients build their boat docks but, in staying with that same analogy, we commonly come in and install a closet, build a simple cabinet, or maybe even do something more extensive, like electrical work. But at the end of the day, we all too often abandon the MTBA role by complacently taking on a technical expert role as one of our client's many subcontractors rather than embracing a holistic approach of solving problems. This, in turn, usually forces our clients to figure out how to renovate their boat dock all by themselves.

Will People Pay Me to Function as a GC?

Sometimes we might hear, "Well, since I don't know how to renovate a boat dock, all I can do is be a subcontractor," or "My client won't pay me to do this kind of work, so this approach is a waste of my time." Our response to both of these opinions is "bull." Regarding the first question, most of the people reading this probably have 10 or more years of experience working in the CPA profession and have worked with hundreds of businesses, both successful and marginal. You bring so much street knowledge, education, and practical experience to the table that you are more than ready to take on advisory work.

Regarding your clients being unwilling to pay you: that is simply not true, at least not of your top clients. The truth is that we are more unwilling to bill our clients for this type of work than they are unwilling to pay us. All it takes is one meeting where the client sees how you ask questions he or she hasn't thought of or hears you challenge a solution being offered because it seems off track with the project objectives, and your presence (or bill) will never be questioned again. As a matter of fact, once you act as the GC on your first project with your client, you will find yourself being asked to tag along on a number of unrelated projects just for your objective and thoughtful counsel. Remember this: we know our clients well, much better than some stranger trying to sell them a new product or service. We've worked with our clients for decades, even generations. We often know better than anyone else their comfort with risk, demands regarding quality, personal availability of time, and expectations regarding completion. We are perfectly suited for the role of MTBA especially using the GC role as our model.

 Keep In Mind

We know our clients well, much better than some stranger trying to sell them a new product or service. We often know better than anyone else their comfort with risk, demands regarding quality, personal availability of time, and expectations regarding completion.

Case Study

Let's take a real life business example and walk through the concept with it. Consider that a young doctor is referred to you, and she tells you that she wants to establish her own practice. She has an excellent reputation, is highly trained in her specialty, is already established with a number of loyal patients from her previous employer, but she has virtually no experience in business. The services that naturally come to mind to assist this young doctor are bookkeeping and tax return preparation or, in other words, "working as her financial subcontractor." However, as her advisor, we need to consider her bigger problem, which is establishing her own professional practice. In terms of doing so, some other factors to address with her might include the following:

- Establishing a banking relationship for lines of credit and operational funding
- Business formation—setting up a legal entity for her new business
- Finding a location for her practice and establishing a lease
- Hiring an office administrator to manage patient scheduling, collection, and her normal day to day business matters
- Acquiring technology to help her run her business
- Setting up processes and procedures
- Establishing payroll and human resources support
- Installing an accounting system and other software support tools to help her manage her business
- Acquiring medical equipment to be used in her practice (considering buy versus lease alternatives)
- Establishing her professional practice with one or more insurance providers

Just as Bill did with the boat dock, after you have identified various factors, you can decide whether you or your people are appropriate subcontractors or whether you want to reach out to your professional network for assistance. Sometimes your network won't be broad enough, so you will have to use your network to tap into the networks of your other professional sources.

Now let's walk through the steps of getting our doctor started and see where we end up. You probably already have someone in mind for the banking relationship and a source for payroll and HR support. As for establishing her new legal entity, you might have two or three attorneys that you feel would be a good fit. Regarding technology, you are very confident in the person that helps you with your business, so that one is easy. Also you know the perfect commercial realtor to help her identify several suitable locations to consider. Your doctor has a good idea where she wants to buy her medical equipment as well as insurance providers with whom she wants to associate. However, you feel that before she finalizes any deals, the two of you should meet with one of your well-established doctor clients just to talk through the current plan and get feedback from someone who has experience navigating the road she is about to travel. So, considering our preceding short list, we are down to dealing with just the following issues:

- Hiring an office administrator to manage patient scheduling, collection, and the doctor's normal day-to-day business matters
- Setting up processes and procedures
- Installing an accounting system and other software support tools to help her manage her business

After giving each of them some thought, you have decided that you and your people can assist her in completing all of these tasks. So now, we have taken the boat dock GC approach and tied it to a common client situation. It's funny, when you break "setting up a practice" into smaller steps, it really isn't that complicated, especially when you are bringing in subcontractors (other professionals) to assist with each unique specialty area.

Important Nuances of the GC Approach

Now let's cover some important nuances of the GC approach.

Being a GC Means More Than Just Referring Someone

The first nuance is the difference between *bringing in* subcontractors and *managing* them versus just referring work to someone and walking away. It is our belief that the only time the latter is the best solution is when the work being done by the referred resource is out of the mainstream of issues with which you and your client commonly deal. In our preceding example, although a banker, an attorney, a technologist, and a realtor are all personal referrals, in our opinion, you should treat them like subcontractors and make sure you are involved in at least the introductory meeting, when the project scope is covered, as well as any meetings were solutions are being proposed. Your participation is also necessary at the meeting between the young new doctor and your experienced doctor client.

Bill for Your Time

To be clear, we definitely *are* suggesting that you bill for all of your time involved in planning, identifying resources, managing resources, attending meetings, and so forth. However, we are *not* suggesting that you bill for the work done by the subcontractors. You are not taking ownership of the work of your subcontractors. They don't work for you. You are there to make sure they perform, and if they don't, you will be there to help your client deal with the fallout. All too often we simply refer work to other professionals and walk away until we get another phone call. When we do this, each professional has to learn the client's vision, interpret what their role should be, and decide on appropriate deliverables. In a complex project like starting a new business, it is important that we stay involved throughout each stage to ensure that the completed project turns out as it was envisioned. As an MTBA, we are the common thread keeping all the resources and assets focused on the client's desired outcome throughout all stages of a project. And that adds value.

Build Your Subcontractor Network

Another nuance is the idea of creating and maintaining your subcontractor network. You need to seek out and nurture relationships with professionals and other resources that can be valuable to your clients. Over and over we hear clients say, "My CPA doesn't have to have the answers … I just want him or her to be able to find them or call upon their network for help." These networks require time on your part. Just as it is imperative that you take time to understand the needs of your key clients, you constantly have to schedule time to build relationships with key resources and professionals. Your professional network of subcontractors is an essential part of your service offering as an advisor. Your "inventory" consists of your specialty skills, those skills offered by others within your firm, and your external network; and we all know that managing your inventory is a time-consuming process.

The most common products in an inventory that an advisor likely would be asked to provide for a client would include the following:

- Planning
- Technology
- Human resources
- Legal assistance
- Banking
- Insurance
- Family-owned business issues
- Other expert services

The more sophisticated the client, the more likely that a specialist for each area will be needed. A less sophisticated client, which describes most small businesses, will only require a CPA, along with three or four other professionals, to adequately address these issues, just as we did with the boat dock.

Benefits of a Strong Subcontractor Network

You provide a great benefit to your firm when you establish a quality subcontractor network. Each of these professionals has clients of his or her own, and for each referral you give, you are likely to receive one in return. You need this network as part of your basic inventory to fulfill your role as your client's MTBA, and yet, this same network ends up being a major contributing factor to your firm's future growth and success. As we stated earlier, it always surprises us how many firms expect other professionals to refer business to them, but who do not feel it is part of their responsibility to reciprocate. Providing a referral for a needed service helps the client (they get access to needed skills), helps the firm (referrals–out create more referrals–in), and helps the advisor better manage the project (because of the efficiency and ease of management when working within existing professional relationships).

Your True Value as MTBA and GC

Yet another nuance is in understanding the real value of your role as the client's GC and advisor. Anyone can manage a project that rolls out flawlessly. However, we've never seen a complex project that rolled out that way, so as MTBAs, we earn our money every time we have to reconnect the dots between the plan and reality. Years ago, we were working closely with a highly skilled furniture carpenter, and we asked him how he could build such quality products. His response was, "the real difference between people like me and a novice is that we have learned how to make our mistakes look like they were part of the original plan. We make just as many mistakes, but we have learned how to cover them up or turn them into added features."

That is a key deliverable in your role as the GC. Mistakes, shortcomings, and unanticipated problems are common at every stage in a project. It is not "if" issues will arise, but rather "how they are resolved." Going back to the boat dock example, Bill did not realize to what extent wind bracing would be required, so in order to maximize visibility while providing a strong structure, his project team built iron see-through panels to securely connect the corners of the roof frame to the upper deck. In doing so, they made the "fix" look like it was part of the original plan.

Your Need to Stay Involved as MTBA and GC

Another nuance is that, "Plans always change," and you need to stay involved so that you are up-to-speed and ready to help brainstorm acceptable "plan B" alternatives. Simply put, some things make sense during the planning stages that don't work at the point of implementation. On the boat dock, Bill had planned on building a large closet under the stairs, but because of more important priorities, he could not make this work. So he improvised, creating two closets on the lower deck that gave them more space than originally planned as well as additional wind bracing.

Your Role as GC in Dealing With Subcontractors

This leads us to our final nuance. Because problems are the norm, it follows logically that having to solve them is also the norm. Therefore, it will be common for you to have to negotiate with the subcontractors because problems also typically equate to the need for more money, blame regarding who was responsible, mistrust, conflict, and more. Because you often will find yourself referring work to various subcontractors and because they will want to keep you satisfied so that their referral network remains active, logically, you will have more clout with them to work out compromises or solutions. Even though your sub-contractors are other professionals, it does make a difference from a negotiation standpoint if a client with one project wants a special accommodation versus you—a person who refers business often—wants an accommodation.

The point is the role of the general contractor is to always keep the client's vision of the project in sight to best guide the continual modifications that have to be made. In the end, your job as the MTBA is to be the constant thread throughout the project, weaving those necessary changes into a tapestry that looks like they were always part of the original plan.

Final Thoughts on the GC Model

As CPAs, too many times we simply listen to our clients to hear about services we can offer rather than trying to understanding what they want to accomplish. And when our clients' needs do not sync up with what we want to sell them, we usually smile, change the subject, or give them a phone number of someone to call and then walk away.

What a sad day it is when we, our clients' MTBAs, avoid a topic because we don't feel we are experts in it. If it is important to the client, then it should be important enough to us to help our clients find the resources they need to evaluate their options and make educated choices. Being your clients' MTBA means that you don't walk away from their problems. You help them find resources, act as their advocate, help them evaluate their options, and stay involved. Truly being your clients' MTBA is a badge of honor that our profession is proud to wear. Using the GC model, you should be able to more easily begin reinventing yourself to better live up to our MTBA status.

Exercise 4-1

Action Plans: Using the General Contractor Model

Based on the materials covered in this chapter, please take a few moments to think about your practice and what you can do to begin using the General Contractor Model (or using it more, if you're already using it somewhat) to better function as your clients' MTBA. Then, using the following form, make note of any areas you plan to work on as well as a timeframe to reassess your progress. This form is provided solely as a tool for your use in improving your practice.

Name: _____

The following are activities I intend to undertake:

- _____ By when: _____
- _____ By when: _____
- _____ By when: _____
- _____ By when: _____
- _____ By when: _____
- _____ By when: _____
- _____ By when: _____
- _____ By when: _____
- _____ By when: _____
- _____ By when: _____
- _____ By when: _____
- _____ By when: _____
- _____ By when: _____
- _____ By when: _____
- _____ By when: _____
- _____ By when: _____

Section 2

The MTBA Framework

Developing Your Self Skills

"Everything that irritates us about others can lead us to an understanding of ourselves."

~ CARL JUNG

Although it seems an odd place to start, identifying client opportunities begins with a better understanding of ourselves. In order to identify and service the needs of our clients from a most trusted business advisor (MTBA) perspective, we have to change our role from that of providing answers to one of being an information springboard or idea facilitator.

This requires the highest degree of communication and persuasion expertise. And in order to maximize both of these, we have to first learn what makes us tick; how we react; when, why, and what messages we send; what makes us defensive; and much more. The more we know about ourselves, the better we can control the messages we send and the more accurately we can interpret the messages we receive. This skill enhancement allows us to become significantly more powerful in our ability to get the client to talk openly with us, to listen and learn what motivates the client, and to be able to persuade the client into taking action.

By understanding ourselves and how this affects our ability to communicate and persuade, we can improve six of the seven skills outlined in the MTBA Framework. Our "ability to learn quickly" is enhanced every time we can take down a self-denigration barrier. In other words, what often gets in the way of our listening is that ever-present feeling that we have to continually prove our worth. This causes us to allocate too much brain power towards finding something impressive to say. By repressing our need to impress, it becomes easier to stay focused on the client and "stay in the now," which enhances our ability to learn.

Proficiency in asking questions and the ability to patiently listen and observe are exponentially advanced by becoming more self-confident. This self-confidence often manifests itself by knowing that we don't have to have all the answers and in knowing that we provide value just by listening and helping people formalize their thoughts. As we become better listeners and more aware of the messages we send, our people skills dramatically improve.

Creativity, we think, is directly related to one's comfort in being wrong, which is discussed later in this chapter.

Finally, competence as a communicator is the culmination of all of these skills.

Although the next couple of chapters are called "soft skills" or "topics" by many, they deliver hard, relevant, required information. In the opinion of the authors, these chapters on interpersonal skills have a better chance of immediately affecting your capabilities than any equivalent technical reading you can do. Why? Because as we stated earlier, we think CPAs are the greatest analyzers and implementers in the world. However, without better knowledge of yourself, along with fine-tuned communication and persuasion expertise, your opportunities to help businesses analyze and implement are reduced significantly.

Treating the Symptoms

Since the beginning of the industrial revolution, businesses have been looking for ways to improve productivity, increase efficiency, accelerate profits, and so forth. During the past few decades, many ideas have emerged to promote these efficiencies. Some of these concepts are as follows:

- Management by Objectives
- Situational Leadership®
- Management by Walking Around
- One Minute Management
- Teams and Team Building
- The Quality Movement
- Empowerment

A common theme among these concepts is improving communications. These concepts emphasize working together, getting input from all levels of workers, and stimulating a friendly, cohesive, nonthreatening but accountable work environment. To facilitate this corporate cultural change, workers at all levels have undergone training to learn more about the communication process and the various techniques which improve information flow. The problem is that gaining a better understanding of the technical aspects of communication is helpful, but it only treats the symptom. The cause of communication breakdown, in our opinion, is the lack of understanding in each of us about ourselves. This chapter is written to introduce the idea that your own self-awareness, self-esteem, and feelings of worth are often the diseases that infect and injure your ability to communicate.

What is Your Emotional I.Q.?

In his seminal work on emotional intelligence, Daniel Goleman tells us that we are all being judged not just by how smart we are or by our technical education and experience, but also by how well we interact with others. In today's competitive world, being smart and being educated are just part of the ante to get you into the card game of professional livelihoods. The people in life who ultimately experience the most success, in whatever terms you wish to measure success, are those who have developed a higher level of emotional intelligence or the ability to understand their own emotions and those of others, and how to be smart about emotions. (It's not about being emotional, or being nice all the time, or adding smiley faces to your e-mail, but how well you can manage whatever feelings you are experiencing.)

Research conducted over time on tens of thousands of people shows that the "bull in the china closet" syndrome doesn't give anyone a leg up but, in fact, is a significant impediment to moving up the organizational food chain. We've all seen more than one person who is or was brilliant, an expert in their field, who simply crashed and burned professionally at some point not because they lost their technical edge, but because they were too difficult to work with. By the same token, we've probably seen more than one instance of the person who is not dialed in closely enough to their own emotional state that it results in their jumping to false and costly conclusions about other people and their intentions, with collateral damage to relationships, projects, and businesses.

This is important to CPAs who want to adopt the MTBA approach at their practice because it speaks to the heart of the advisory concept. People do not care how much you know until they know how much you care. They are looking to their MTBAs for caring, responsive, respectful help. Blockheads need not apply! Conducting yourself as the MTBA for your clients requires you to be emotionally smart, to be able to understand

- the emotions you are experiencing
- as much as possible, the emotions the person or people you are dealing with are experiencing
- how your behavior affects others
- how to modify your behavior in order to get the desired results from your interactions with other people.

We usually encounter a couple of questions, or objections phrased as questions, when we discuss emotional intelligence with groups of CPAs. The first is, "Does this mean that I have to go around and be all 'touchy-feely' now?" Our answer to this question is no, you don't have to adopt insincere behaviors or attempt to be touchy-feely if that is not you in the first place. This is about taking the time to get to know yourself better and to better understand how what you say, when, how, and where you say it can have either good consequences or bad consequences. With every act we perform, there is a bundle of consequences—some good and some bad. By being a little smarter in this arena, you can create mostly positive bundles of consequences as you pay more attention to the interpersonal aspects of dealing with others. Often, the greater value lies in your ability to catch yourself before acting or reacting in a way that carries a large bundle of unintended or negative consequences. Recognize that the fruit of life is not delivered in a linear fashion. In other words, if you treat people fairly, with respect (and yes, this means you can still hold people accountable to perform), and in an emotionally intelligent way for 29 of the 30 days in a month, and then you lose control of yourself and blow up for only an hour on the 30th day, the chaos you create is far greater than the 4 percent of the total time that day would reflect mathematically. As a matter of fact, the odds are very high that most of the goodwill you created from exercising excellent self-control all month if not all of it is lost in your one moment of demonstrated anger. It comes down to a simple adage: People won't follow or support someone that they can't trust. And when others can't count on your emotional balance, you are limiting what you can accomplish and, even more so, what your organization can achieve.

The second question we often get is, "This seems to be pretty much common sense—treat people decently, with respect, and you'll be okay—so what's the big deal?" Well, you're partly right—some of it is common sense and perhaps reminiscent of what Mom and Dad probably told us about how to behave when we were kids. The only problem is that common sense, especially when it comes to interpersonal dealings among technical professionals, is not always real common. It's also one thing to understand intellectually how and why something like this should work. However, it's a totally different issue when it comes to actually remembering to and being able to apply it. Emotional intelligence is not about you never getting mad, never being disappointed, never being cynical about a person's motives, or a million other thoughts that might pass through your head. But rather, regardless of the way you actually feel inside, it is about your being able to respond in an appropriate way for the situation at hand. Emotional intelligence is like a governor (a speed control mechanism) that used to be common on all large commercial vehicles. Its purpose was to make sure that the rig you were driving couldn't accelerate above a certain speed. So no matter how hard you pushed on the gas pedal, at some point, the governor would kick in and limit the top speed you could drive. Emotional intelligence is the governor that always should be processing the thoughts in our head to make sure that regardless of the emotions pulsing through our bodies, our physical actions and interactions are constrained and controlled within appropriate limits. As an MTBA, it pays to hone your emotional intelligence skills. Let's look at what it takes to begin looking inwardly and increasing our self-awareness.

Taking Down the Barriers

The first rule of any self-analysis or self-awareness building processes, at least if you actually want to improve your capabilities, is to shut down your defense systems. By doing so, you allow yourself the opportunity to learn what makes you tick and why. Many people who attempt to analyze themselves, unfortunately, only listen when the discussion revolves around their strengths and then tune out conversations involving their weaknesses. Obviously, this level of denial renders self-analysis useless. Here's a typical chain of six reactions to anything that touches an uncomfortable area: (1) shock, (2) denial, (3) defensiveness, (4) anger, (5) rationalization, and (6) blame.

Let's plug this series of reactions into a conversation with a CPA over improving his or her communication skills.

- Shock:

    CPA: I'm surprised you are even suggesting this to me! I want a checklist of the steps to follow to build an advisory practice, not what I need to do to get to know myself better.
- Denial:

    CPA: And by the way, I actually have excellent communication skills. I tell people what they need to do all of the time.
- Defensiveness:

    CPA: Besides, people pay me for my knowledge, not for being a smooth talker.
- Anger:

    CPA: Just thinking about this touchy-feely stuff is starting to tick me off!
- Rationalization:

    CPA: Why are you trying to convince me anyway? I'm a top performer in my field, and if this was all that important, I wouldn't have been able to achieve such a high level of success.
- Blame

    CPA: My professional educational requirements don't even recognize the need for training in interpersonal skill competencies like communication. How am I supposed to be able to focus on issues like this when I am constantly burdened with standards overload? So until the CPA profession starts doing its job and recognizing that skills like this are necessary in the performance of my work, there's nothing I can do. I'm just a victim of the system.

Unfortunately, this cycle of reaction and these comments are not fabricated just to make a point in this book. They are all too real. Today, without appropriate interpersonal skills, it is getting harder and harder to get yourself into the position of being able to demonstrate your real knowledge. Think of it this way: when you started your career, your success was tied to your ability to learn and accurately complete various technical projects. With each promotion, your job competency requirements shifted a little more toward the soft skill side, whether you actually developed them or not. Now as an MTBA, and as your clients' business General Contractor, although technical skills are still important, they are far overshadowed by the need for you to be able to facilitate solutions rather than just deliver them. So we ask you to sit back, relax, understand that only you expect yourself to be perfect, and let's see if some of the ideas in this text will help you improve your communication abilities.

Self-Esteem: The Greatest Obstruction to More Effective Communication

Self-esteem, in our opinion, is the greatest obstruction to communication today. To emphasize this, consider a CPA asking his client, Bob, the following question:

"So, tell me … what motivated you to invest in the triplex rental unit?"

At a quick glance, the question seems inquisitive, but harmless. The history of this transaction is as follows: the client bought the triplex five years ago, paid $400,000 for the unit, and payments including escrow are $4,100 per month.

In scenario one, let's assume that the real estate market is booming. Therefore, the triplex is now worth $700,000, the rental units average 90 percent occupancy, and the property has a positive cash flow of $1,200 per month. In this case, Bob's response to his CPA's question might be as follows:

"Well, I have been around the real estate business for a long time. When you know what you are doing, you can make some great investments. I bought that property because I could see its potential."

Before we get underway with a discussion of Bob's answer, let's consider scenario number two. In this situation, the real estate market has taken a nosedive. In Bob's locality, real estate typically has declined about 35 percent in value. The triplex is now worth $270,000, the rental units average 60 percent occupancy, and the property has a negative cash flow of $1,000 per month. Under these circumstances, Bob's response might be as follows:

"I don't really know why I made that investment. I guess I was grabbing for the brass ring and missed. Besides, everyone I know is in the same position I am. And those who aren't, well, they either didn't make enough money to buy in to these kind of deals, or they're just cowards for being unwilling to take any risks."

So where are we? A simple question was asked with no inference about the quality of the decision. Yet the quality of the decision creates a stigma of success or failure that often guides the friendliness or hostility of the response. So using this example, where is the most common bottleneck in communication? It often is dominated by the egos or the self-esteem of those attempting to communicate. Problems occur any time people perceive their self-esteem to be threatened. Once threatened, the barriers go up, and the protection systems are armed.

In the second scenario, although Bob started out somewhat humbly with his comments, he clearly was threatened. This was apparent because his response justified his decision, established himself as someone special, and concluded with an attack on those more fortunate. The meaning of what he said was something like this:

> I know I made a mistake, but so did everyone else. By the way, this mistake could only be made by successful people like me. Otherwise, you couldn't have bought rental property in the first place. And those who are successful like me, but didn't get hurt by the real estate market, well, they are cowards and not worthy of my consideration.

It is understandable why most people become defensive and protective of a poor decision, especially when you consider America's view of failure. But why do defense systems engage even when decisions are outstanding?

In the scenario where Bob clearly made an excellent decision, when you analyze his response, a threat was still perceived. Why do we say that? Because Bob made some ego-inflating comments. Comments like, "when you know what you're doing" and "because I could see its potential" were not made for the CPA's benefit but made as verbal inflators to Bob's ego to remind himself that he is somebody special. The fact that the inflator statements were stated to the CPA indicates a likelihood that Bob was uncomfortable with himself about something. He might have felt threatened because he was visiting his CPA. He could have been experiencing some self-doubt due to some unrelated event that happened earlier. Literally millions of reasons are possible why people suffer from self-doubt. However, regardless of the reason, weak egos can quickly disrupt the communication process, especially when two weak egos collide.

As an example, just think what would have happened if the CPA had responded to Bob with similar ego-inflating comments. If Bob was insecure to start with, then he would soon become even more insecure. This insecurity would most likely manifest itself into additional defensive posturing and create even more barriers, which would impede the communication process.

While these scenarios are contrived and exaggerated, they were created to make a point.

There is a fine line between communication and alienation. Your ability to walk this fine line depends on how well you can manage your own feelings of worth and remain non-threatening to the person or persons with whom you are communicating.

Communicating With Your Friends

Your most effective communication usually is shared with a friend. Why? Because the fundamental principles of friendship (trust, loyalty, caring, and so forth), are all barrier busters. Imagine that your best friend just made the following comment to you:

"You have been out of control from the first day we met! You need to get better organized."

Your response to this statement, depending on how you feel about yourself at that moment, could be almost anything: from a sarcastic rebuttal to a thoughtful consideration of the comment, from ignoring the statement to having hurt feelings. However, because the criticism was made by your best friend, you most likely are going to consider it in a positive light. Why? Because of the "assumed message," which varies depending on who made the comment. For instance, consider the following:

> "You have been out of control from the first day we met! You need to get better organized." (Possible assumed nonspoken message: "But even if you don't, I'll still like you and want to continue sharing time with you."); or

> "You have been out of control from the first day we met! You need to get better organized." (Possible assumed nonspoken message: "The only reason I am making this comment is because I know it will improve the quality of your life, and I care about that.")

These assumed messages of unequivocal acceptance and support minimize the chances that protection systems will be armed. That's why you can say almost anything to a friend without having to worry about the consequences. This nonthreatening environment allows everyone's ego to remain in the background, thereby facilitating a free exchange of information.

Consider for a moment the emotional escalation likely to occur when the out of control statement is made by an acquaintance, rather than a friend. The "assumed message" is no longer cradled with feelings of friendship. Because of this, the comment often will be perceived in the most threatening way possible, and it will foster new meanings. For example:

> "You have been out of control from the first day we met! You need to get better organized." (Possible assumed nonspoken message: "Because of your lack of direction, you always waste my time. And until you get your act together, I do not consider you worthy of my respect.")

Although these examples of both positive and negative assumed messages sound ridiculous, they are not far from the extreme subconscious interpretations people make on a daily basis. Always keep this rule in mind when you are communicating: 9 out of 9.1 times, people will assume the worst possible interpretation of the words spoken.

As another example, consider that your manager made the out of control comment. Here's a person that has power over your livelihood, which you almost can guarantee will lead to the worst possible interpretation of the message. This would likely conjure up this mental, if not verbal, message:

> "How do you expect me to get organized when you continually dump more work in my lap? If you were a better manager, you would be able to schedule my workload more effectively."

The result: a boxing match. Blow number one occurred with the "get organized" statement. The counter punch was "it's your fault for being a poor manager." This situation easily can escalate, creating long-term communication obstructions. However, all of this can be avoided if the message receiver can keep his or her paranoia in check, hold down the defense mechanisms, and respond as if a friend was giving constructive criticism. The point is that most of the time, we let our egos or weak self-esteem guide our responses. When this happens, the barriers restricting the communication process become numerous, difficult to anticipate, and often impossible to overcome.

Self-Esteem: Awareness Goes a Long Way

Clearly, the self-esteem of those involved in a conversation is an obstacle. When you are attempting to communicate with someone, the lower his or her self-esteem, the more your communication has to be filtered heavily to minimize the likelihood of unintentional negative messages. This means that you need to pay special attention to the words and gestures surrounding your conversation so that it is as nonthreatening, supportive, positive, and nonconfrontational as possible given the circumstances.

Otherwise, a threat is likely to be perceived, and the person you are communicating with may go on the attack, or potentially just as bad, fully retreat and withdraw. And you can be sure that any communication is over once a threat is perceived.

Keep In Mind
Communication is over once a threat is perceived.

Remember, weak egos have a voracious appetite. As long as you are feeding them, they will follow you where ever you want to go. The proper care and feeding of egos includes a number of almost silly things, such as minimizing the use of the word "I" in your conversation because it automatically focuses on the wrong person, or making sure that the other person talks about himself or herself, which changes the dynamic because when you make someone the center of attention, he or she usually will feel special.

If, as the MTBA, you attempt to build yourself up during a client interview, you actually may do more harm than good. Consider this example:

MTBA:	[Attempting to impress the prospective client with his expertise] If you are looking for someone to help you streamline your manufacturing process, I'm your guy. I have forgotten more about manufacturing than most people will ever know. It's amazing to me how some people stay in business with the stupid things they do.
Prospective client:	[Thinks to himself] *I've been in manufacturing all of my professional life, and I know I've made a bunch of stupid mistakes. If this guy looks around, he'll see some of them. I don't want him laughing at me or telling his friends he can't believe I'm still in business.* [Then says] I really don't need help with anything. I just agreed to meet with you as a courtesy to a mutual friend of ours.

The prospect feels threatened by the MTBA's ego-building comments. As a result, the prospect puts up his defense mechanisms, communication shuts down, and the MTBA's opportunity to assist this business vanishes.

This sounds like a game you shouldn't have to play, well you're probably right—you shouldn't. But if you want to improve your communication ability, then it is in your best interest to consider and incorporate these kinds of communication fundamentals into your new daily routine.

On the brighter side, there are rewards. People with low self-esteem are easy to manipulate, control, and direct. It's simple. By keeping your ego in check and the spotlight off of yourself and on those around you, instead of egos being an obstacle, they will assist you in achieving your desired outcome. As with any skill you develop, it can be used for evil instead of good. But becoming more aware of your own actions and then better controlling them does allow you to easily manipulate others, hopefully for the benefit of those you are attempting to assist.

On the contrary, low self-esteem is exhibited in many different forms. In fact, very often those you might think of as having very high self-esteem may, in actuality, have quite the opposite. For example, someone who is always "dressed-to-the-nines" with every hair in place may, in fact, have such a low opinion about his or her looks that they are too self-conscious to appear in public in "work-around-the-house" clothes. An even more common occurrence is the person who, in order to cover up for a lack of knowledge or understanding about something, becomes aggressive and overbearing in order to reduce the potential of being challenged. Others may exhibit passive-aggressive behavior because of their low self-esteem. They look for ways to throw off any positive progress and take delight in finding and pointing out mistakes others have made.

So far, we've tried to paint the picture that self-esteem is the single greatest barrier impeding the communication process. As a matter of fact, the way it has been previously presented, it could be considered an almost insurmountable obstacle. Well, the good news is just knowing its impact goes a long way toward overcoming it. In the next chapter, we talk more specifically about the communication process. This information, coupled with an awareness of how our feelings of self-worth create barriers, begins to reveal a framework for becoming a better communicator. It's not easy managing your ego while simultaneously trying to deal with everyone else's. However, in our opinion, personal growth in this area is a necessary part of developing your MTBA skills to their fullest potential.

Failure: A Sign of Real Growth

During communication, as soon as there is a perception that one party is attempting to place blame or fault with another, barriers are hoisted up so fast that information flow is blocked immediately.

As mentioned earlier, Americans seem to have a real problem with the idea of failure. In many corporate cultures, such a negative connotation about making mistakes exists that a considerable amount of manpower is wasted on a daily basis in an attempt to cover-up clues that errors ever existed. Often, just fixing a mistake would require far less effort, but that approach won't suffice for many unless all clues to the inexcusable event also are erased. Our profession has been focused historically on looking for mistakes as auditors—getting things right, not wrong, and doing things by the book, (or the checklist). Because of this, CPAs perhaps have an even higher hurdle to overcome in dealing with their perception of mistakes and failure than the already out-of-line corporate cultures. The perpetuation of the idea that failure or mistakes won't be tolerated is not only an incredible waste of productivity and profitability, but a serious detriment to employee growth and morale as well.

How does this attitude toward failure manifest itself? Well, in business, as with life, we are taught by society that to be considered a worthy and good human being, we must "grab for the brass ring." And clichés like "anything other than first doesn't count" are used to motivate people into obtaining "the right perspective." Unfortunately, comments such as these really damage an individual's ability to learn and grow because the idea of failing is so oppressive that it restricts our willingness to venture into unfamiliar areas. The problem is venturing into unfamiliar areas is how we gain experience and knowledge.

 Keep In Mind

It's funny that being wise is considered admirable, yet the road to wisdom, which is paved with failure, is avoided at all costs.

A successful business man was interviewed and asked, "What has made you so successful?" He replied, "Making good decisions!" "How do you make so many good decisions?" the interviewer rebutted. The businessman answered, "My experience." The interviewer questioned, "How did you gain your experience?" He answered, "From bad decisions."

The reality is that growth occurs when we are allowed to make mistakes and learn from them. Why do we say this? Because when you make a good decision, do you spend time reflecting on why it was correct, and what made you chose that alternative? Most likely, no. What our egos tell us to do is to pat ourselves on the back and reflect on how smart we are. It appears that most of our learning comes from those times when our decision process fails, and we attempt to determine why.

So what is the definition of *failure*? The definitions are as diverse as our world population. To some, it is merely "being caught" doing something wrong. In other words, as long as no one knows about a mistake, it wasn't a mistake. This, at least, limits the likelihood of failing. To many, the definition expands to unrealistic heights. It goes back to the idea previously introduced that anything other than being first or being the best constitutes failure. What a ridiculous framework to try to work within. Can everyone be first if they work hard enough? The answer is an "unequivocal NO." Being first shouldn't even be a consideration. We can't control who is first. All we can do is our best; achievement within our own limits is the definition of success. Consider this true story:

> Little Billy trained in martial arts every week. One day, he approached his martial arts Master and asked permission to miss several months of training. He wanted to concentrate on preparing for an upcoming track meet. During this time, Billy trained hard and felt he was ready for the big race.

The starting gun was fired, and they were off. Billy ran as fast as he ever had but finished inches behind the winner. For days after the event, Billy sat in his room feeling discouraged and beaten.

Not sure how to get Billy motivated again, his mother dragged him to the martial arts studio to see if his instructor could help. When the instructor asked what was wrong, Billy could barely comment through his tears. Once the martial arts Master had heard the whole story, this was his reply:

Instructor: Billy, pretend that the boy who won didn't show up because he hurt his leg the day before the race. Because he wouldn't have been there, you would have been the fastest runner. You would have come in first. Would that make you feel better?

Billy: Yes!

Instructor: (Grinning as he put his arms around Billy) Did you train hard and do your best?

Billy: Nods yes.

Instructor: Remember this. You do not become a true champion because of someone else's failure. You also are not a loser because of someone else's success. A champion is judged for his or her achievements working within his or her abilities.

Unfortunately, many people much older than little Billy find themselves falling into this same trap. Why? Because the final outcome becomes more important than the process. In corporate America, we give more credit to people who stay long hours than those who accomplish a great deal. We bestow rewards on those who merely stay within their known limits rather than those who try and fail because they attempted to extend their limits. We empower our employees so that they will take action, yet we punish them when their decisions are wrong or inconsistent with our own. We have a system that expects consistent superior quality and performance but does not allow the personal growth necessary to achieve that. It is sad, but most of us, at some time, fall into the "little Billy trap" and judge people by how they finish the race, rather than the effort they put forth in relation to their capabilities.

 Keep In Mind

Maintaining a positive attitude towards failure is the foundation of success.

Here's how it works (see figure 5-1). As the successful businessman inferred, failure is part of the learning experience. Learning is essential to personal growth. Personal growth is critical to improving one's self-esteem and feelings of worth. Having a strong self-image is the key to effective communication. Quality communication is the cornerstone of building a team. And teamwork is the greatest strategy for prospering in any environment.

Figure 5-1: **From Failure to Success**

Success
Teamwork
Communication
Self-Esteem
Personal Growth
Learning
Failure

As you can tell, we believe that a positive outlook on failure is an essential component of any long-term success strategy. Failure is often the catalyst for major strides in personal growth and learning. And fear of failure immobilizes many to the point of being unwilling to try anything unless success is almost guaranteed.

So let's put failure in its proper prospective. Did you know that Thomas Edison failed literally thousands of times before his first success, the incandescent lamp? How about this one: Walt Disney went bankrupt and had a mental breakdown before he was able to channel his creative energy profitably. Looking at the baseball scene, back when Babe Ruth held the record for home runs, did you know he also held the record for the most strikeouts? Or Ricky Henderson, who entered the Baseball Hall of Fame recently, in his first year of eligibility, he has both the record for stolen bases and the number of times put out while trying to steal a base.

Are these people failures? Most likely not in anyone's book; yet, they certainly experienced failures. In order to be successful, you have to cover some uncharted ground. This exploration exponentially increases your chances of falling flat on your face. So think of obstacles as opportunities to excel. If you succeed, great; if you fail, well, you most likely learned something, probably stretched your personal limits, and experienced the growth of trying something new. Keep this in mind. As long as you put forth a commendable effort, you have earned the right to be proud of yourself regardless of the outcome because failure is a sign of real growth.

Your Attitude Makes a Big Difference

With all this talk of learning from our mistakes, it's probably a good idea to cover the notion of being optimistic rather than pessimistic as we view what's right, what's wrong, and what mistakes we, or others, have made. Once again, we are not suggesting that you go through life with a Pollyanna–like attitude about everything. We are suggesting, however, that your attitude will make a difference in how successful you are as you go through life trying new things and occasionally making mistakes and learning from them.

Decades of research by social scientists, capped off by Martin Seligman's work in attitudes and outlook, *Learned Optimism* shows that how you view the challenges life throws at you makes a big difference. Once again, just being smart in I.Q. doesn't guarantee success—how you view or filter the day-in and day-out ups and downs of life is a differentiating factor in the ultimate determination of success. This is important to you as an individual, and it's important to you as a manager of others, as well as in your role of MTBA to your clients. You will likely be called on, or see the need, to assist them through challenges and related attitudinal issues, so we thought it might be helpful to review how this works.

The research behind this concept is fascinating to us. One part of it involved reading new stories and quotes for content analysis from coaches and team members of professional sports teams after they won and lost games. What the researchers found was that the explanatory style of the losing team was an indicator of future losses or successes. If the losers chalked it up to just being outplayed or having an off night and took it in stride, they more likely would turn it around at the next game or two than if they explained the loss based on how bad they (the losing team) were, how they could do nothing right, and how they, as a team, were in dire straits. This simple, metaphorical finding from sports illuminated how what we tell ourselves about setbacks influences our future.

Let's put this into a more concrete example for an MTBA. Let's say that you have met with a client, and your meeting with them went south. For whatever reason, the meeting didn't end up as positively as you'd envisioned, you are somewhat dissatisfied with the outcome, and you think the client could be as well. If your explanatory style is to assume that the results of this meeting

- will have a negative impact on your relationship with the client for a long time, or
- are a direct result of your inadequacy to facilitate meetings, which you don't see improving much over time, or both,

then you are using a pessimistic explanatory style that could have harmful consequences. In addition, these types of thoughts will make it very difficult for you to get back on the horse and try to ride again. Getting wrapped up in failure tends to cause us to focus too much on ourselves and lose sight of the bigger objective, which is trying to improve our skills so that we can help our clients get better, faster, and stronger.

On the other hand, if your explanatory style (or in a broader sense, your outlook) is such that you reflect on your client meeting and think, "No, it wasn't my best work, but I can learn from this, it was just one incident, and I know can improve," you quickly will find yourself delivering this service again much more effectively. The odds are that a marginally managed client meeting like we are describing, in reality, will end up having a very positive effect on your career because of the learning process and skill development it will engender. Although you need to take responsibility for the results, you should not beat yourself up over them. You also should take inventory of any other external factors that contributed to the marginal success of this meeting, if you want to fully understand what happened. This optimistic explanatory style can quickly help you make the most of life's "school of hard knocks" learning opportunities. And trust us on this one—we all can, and should, learn a great deal in the school of hard knocks. But it is what we do with what we learn that really matters.

Recapping Some Potentially New Ideas

Interpersonal topics such as the material covered in this chapter, often communicate ideas that are easy to agree with but difficult to implement. Here is a quick recap of some points to ponder:

- We have to change our role from that of providing answers to one of being an information springboard or idea facilitator.
- By understanding ourselves, as well as how this affects our ability to communicate and persuade, we can improve six of the seven skills outlined in the MTBA Framework.
- A leading cause of communication breakdown, in our opinion, is the lack of understanding in each of us about ourselves.
- We need to better understand ourselves and strive to understand others more effectively if we want to have optimum impact as their MTBAs.
- The first rule of self-analysis (at least if you want to improve your capabilities) is to shut down your defense systems. By doing so, you allow yourself the opportunity to learn what makes you tick and why.
- Today, without the appropriate interpersonal skills, it is getting harder and harder to get yourself in the position of being able to demonstrate your real knowledge.
- Self-esteem, in our opinion, is the greatest obstruction to effective communication today.
- Problems occur any time people perceive their self-esteem to be threatened. Once threatened, the barriers go up, and the protection systems become armed.
- Always keep your ears tuned to hear "inflator" statements. They indicate a weak ego needing to be pumped up.
- Your most effective communication usually is shared with a friend because the fundamental principles of friendship (trust, loyalty, caring, and so forth), are all barrier busters.
- "Assumed messages" of unequivocal acceptance and support minimize the chances that protection systems will be armed.
- When you are attempting to communicate with someone, the lower his or her self-esteem, the more heavily your communication has to be filtered.
- Weak egos have a voracious appetite. As long as you are feeding them, they will follow you where ever you want to go.
- During communication, as soon as there is a perception that one party is attempting to place blame or fault with another, barriers are hoisted up so fast that information flow is blocked immediately.
- Growth occurs when we are allowed to make mistakes and learn from them.
- Don't let pessimism ruin your attitude—stay optimistic.
- Most of us, at some time, fall into the "little Billy trap" and judge people (and ourselves) by how they finish the race, rather than the effort they put forth in relation to their capabilities.

Before You Move On

Before you begin reading the next chapter, spend a few moments working through the self-assessment exercise in exercise 5-1. You will be asked to identify skills you plan to improve and activities that will facilitate that improvement. This is a personal exercise, one that is designed to help you create a strategy for personal growth.

Exercise 5-1

Self-Assessment Timeline Relative to Developing My Self-Skills

Based on the materials covered in this chapter, please take a few moments and assess your weaknesses. Then, using the following form, make note of any skills you plan to work on as well as a timeframe to reassess your progress. In addition, if there are activities or exercises, or both, you plan on attempting, jot them down and note your intended completion date. This form is provided solely as a self-improvement tool.

Name: _____

The following are skills I plan to improve:

* _____ By when: _____
* _____ By when: _____
* _____ By when: _____
* _____ By when: _____
* _____ By when: _____
* _____ By when: _____
* _____ By when: _____
* _____ By when: _____

The following are activities I plan to attempt:

* _____ By when: _____
* _____ By when: _____
* _____ By when: _____
* _____ By when: _____
* _____ By when: _____
* _____ By when: _____

Refining the Most Important MTBA Tool: Communication

"The most important thing in communication is hearing what isn't being said."

~ PETER DRUCKER

Effective communication skills are fundamental to the most trusted business advisor (MTBA) Framework. When you utilize good communication techniques, you gain a better understanding of the client's needs and desires; you become more effective at getting your message across; and you develop greater persuasive capabilities. Good communication skills equip you with the ability to more accurately interpret both the words spoken and the feelings expressed by your clients.

However, understanding doesn't occur just because the person delivering the message clearly says what he or she means. It only takes place when the message recipient (1) clearly hears and sees the messages being sent, and (2) interprets them in the way they were intended.

Therefore, communication involves much more than words alone because messages combine both verbal and nonverbal signals. Becoming more aware of these signals is a necessity if you and your organization are going to maximize your proficiency as an MTBA. Yes, we can guess what you are thinking after reading the last chapter and starting this one. We've heard the comments a thousand times: this is not MTBA training, it's sales training. Well, when you're right, you're right! However, this isn't one of those times.

Yes, the skills it takes to provide advisory and consulting services overlap with those required to sell. The difference is that sales training is focused solely on getting in the door and convincing someone to buy. Although it is very difficult to provide advisory services without getting in the door, and convincing the client to buy your services seems to be an important step in the process, MTBA (using our definition) is helping clients better navigate their futures. We may even find that navigating their future involves bringing in someone to help them in specialty areas where we can't. The transition to MTBA requires us to move from more of a fact-based to more of a gut-feel-based type of service. As we've stated so many times before, when it comes to predicting the future, we are not undisputed experts but are merely knowledgeable members of the decision support team. And in this situation, the skills that are in the highest demand are those that help

- identify and prioritize opportunities and challenges.
- define problems separately from the symptoms.
- identify a game plan.
- gain consensus.
- determine the implementation steps.
- manage the variety of personalities involved.
- facilitate change.

In many ways, the job of the MTBA could be described as that of a "business psychiatrist." We get owners to talk about

- their hopes and aspirations.
- what's troubling them.
- where the pain or the next opportunity is for them.
- what they think is causing the problem or presenting the opportunity.
- when the pain occurs, and when the pain is the worst.

- whether there has been anything they've done that makes the pain better or worse or moved them closer to or further away from the opportunity.
- what they feel comfortable doing about the particular challenge or opportunity.
- what might be used as plan B if plan A doesn't work as hoped for.

There is no question that our years of experience and expertise working with businesses are essential to this function. However, we feel strongly that CPAs either already have enough technical skills to do a tremendous amount of MTBA work right now or can fill in the blanks easily with a specialized industry guide or two. In our opinion, and one gaining rapid support in industry, CPAs are the premier business problem solvers and project implementers in the country.

With our detail-focused, system-oriented, procedure-formulating, completion-syndrome, over-achiever approach to problem solving, CPAs are ideal to spearhead an assault against almost any ineffective or inefficient area of a business, as well as taking on potentially high-reward opportunities. That's why businesses around the country are changing the job description of the CPA Controller to one that resembles Vice President or Chief Information Officer, or both. This allows our industry counterparts full rights and privileges to deal with every area of the business rather than limiting them to the accounting area.

Just think about the many problems you have helped your clients solve in areas outside the traditional service boundary. What allowed you to work effectively in these uncharted areas was the client's absolute belief in you. Typically, you didn't sell them, influence them, persuade them, or facilitate change using the skills we have been discussing. You told them what to do, and they listened attentively to their omnipotent advisor. Well, this is a relationship luxury that you can't count on having with a critical mass of your clients, and one you can't afford to have either.

As we said previously, we feel that the technical skills for those interested in further developing their MTBA presence currently exist, are easily attainable, or supplemented through currently existing books, guides, educational programs, and so forth. The part most CPAs have trouble with is all the rest. And "all the rest" is what this book is all about. The interpersonal skills, or *soft skills*, as they are so often referred to, are fundamental to delivering as an MTBA. The good news is with just a little practice, everyone can develop the necessary skills.

We are not saying that CPAs don't possess these skills. That would be ridiculous. Successful firms are successful because the CPAs have been able to communicate with clients in a way that motivated them to action. However, CPAs are not accustomed to selling and delivering services for which they are not considered to be the experts. It's one thing to talk a client into adopting a tax strategy that has a predictable outcome; motivating that same client to restructure his or her distribution channels is far more difficult. So, we wrote this chapter as a primer to the interpersonal skills we have been referring to and to help you develop or improve your MTBA Framework skills. In the next chapter, we will cover the difference between providing expert advice and consultative advice, and why you can't afford to be the omnipotent advisor who tells his or her clients what to do.

Communication Foundation

This section is kind of the psychology behind communication. We would like to point out four fundamental tips that will enhance the success of your efforts. They are as follows:

1. Make your first impression work for you.
2. Be aware of the nonverbal messages you are sending and receiving.
3. Ask questions.
4. Listen actively.

Making a Good First Impression

It is scary to think about the dramatic impact the first few seconds make in an introductory meeting. The concept that people can, and often do, judge a book by its cover unfortunately has validity. By this we mean that people have learned to survive in business (and in life) by making quick judgments based on very little information. So, in about the time it takes to say this isn't fair, you can appease or alienate a potential client without making a sound. This occurs because what we wear, how we look, our size, our demeanor, how we smell, and so forth send messages. We'll cover appropriate clothing styles in a bit, but for now, to start things out on the right foot, consider these five steps everyone in your organization should incorporate into the first few seconds of every contact:

1. Look into your client's eyes.
2. Smile.
3. Verbally acknowledge them, for example "Hi, how are you?"
4. Say their name aloud (if you don't know it, ask for their name, then say it aloud—everyone likes to hear their name).
5. If at all appropriate, reach out and touch, for example, a handshake (avoid both the "wet noodle" and "bone cruncher" handshake styles).

In addition, continually ask yourself the questions, "How would I like to be treated?" and "What would most people expect?" (The second question requires you to think a little bit. Many technical professionals may be fine with less gregarious interaction than others, so it's always worthwhile to put yourself in the other guy's shoes as well.) When this client-centered attitude becomes standard operating procedure, you can rest assured that your clients and prospects will start out with a positive feeling towards your organization. Dr. Karl Krumm, a psychologist friend of ours, put it best when he relayed this comment:

> *"Always keep in mind that everybody needs to feel like they are somebody."*

So when you start out every encounter focusing on treating the client like you want to be treated, or if you think they'd appreciate an even higher level of treatment, treating them accordingly, you send the all important message that he or she is special and important to you and your firm.

There are many messages that are sent and received during the first few seconds of an introductory meeting. Becoming aware of them and learning to appropriately respond are of critical importance. Some of these messages are verbal and some are nonverbal, which leads us to the reason we are covering this next topic.

Interpreting Nonverbal Messages

You can learn as much about what is being said by watching ... as you can by listening.

Dr. Albert Mehrabian (1972), a noted researcher in the area of nonverbal communication, estimated that more than 90 percent of a person's feelings are communicated nonverbally. Another communication researcher, M.L. Knapp (1972), cited a series of studies that indicated that listeners tend to give more weight to vocal cues (like inflection, tone, pitch, and so forth.) than to the words themselves.

We mention these specialists only to add emphasis to the issue that nonverbal messages dramatically affect the meaning of the words we say. So, how can we use this information to our advantage? Well, this isn't as hard as it might seem.

The first step is to recognize the impact of nonverbal messages. By now, you should at least be warming up to the idea. The next hurdle is to become accustomed to constantly interpreting these messages because almost everything we do sends some kind of signal, for example, how you are groomed, dressed, or how you smell reflects what you think of yourself, how much money you make, your level of education, and more.

Unfortunately, quick judgments such as these usually are based on stereotypes. Even though stereotyping is a definite form of discrimination, we all do it in varying degrees.

We know *you* don't do this. So go ahead and tell us that you don't have a clue about the income, political posture, or hobbies of a police officer. Does he or she belong to the National Rifle Association? Are they typically Democrats or Republicans? Regardless of your answers, if you had any opinion at all, you are guilty of stereotyping. Each stereotype carries with it some combination of expectations and perceptions. These then become the ruler by which all comments and gestures are measured. For example, many people still have a perception that CPAs sit in ill-lit rooms wearing little green visors and adding up numbers.

It is human nature to subconsciously group people into predetermined categories. So think about how your client is likely to categorize and interpret the nonverbal messages you are sending, like the way you dress, the formality of your office, the car you drive, and so forth. The key here is not to change to fit a certain image, but rather, to be aware of the messages associated with certain careers, possessions, lifestyles, and the like. This awareness then will allow you to take advantage of the positive impressions and adapt or overcome the negative ones.

For instance, it would not be advisable to drive a Lexus and wear a $1,000 suit to visit a prospective family farm client. As a CPA, you already have to deal with a "city slicker" image. Adding an expensive foreign car and a high-priced suit to your introduction would be disastrous. However, if you visit that same farmer wearing jeans and boots, you're likely to be less intimidating. If wearing jeans and boots is a deviation too far from your style, then consider a sport coat and slacks instead of a suit, and at least take off your coat and remove or loosen your tie.

> **Keep In Mind**
>
> It is human nature to subconsciously group people into predetermined categories. So think about how your client is likely to categorize and interpret the nonverbal messages you are sending, like the way you dress, the formality of your office, the car you drive, and so forth.

This same "formality reduction factor" as described for the agricultural venue is just as applicable in a number of other situations too, such as touring a manufacturing plant floor or a construction site. The reason you need to pay attention to this kind of stuff is because you always want to work towards creating an environment that isn't distracting to your client. In other words, your introduction, clothing, and grooming, should not demand more attention than what you have to say or do. And also keep in mind that people look for similarities when they size one another up. Do you want to create an aura of positive influence by your relative degree of similarity, or do you want to risk creating negative influence through the degree to which you look, act, and sound different?

A general concept to keep in mind regarding first impression nonverbal messages is that it is very difficult to sell more than one idea at a time!

For example, if your job is to better understand what is happening on your client's manufacturing shop floor and you show up in a suit, you are likely to receive heightened resistance. This inappropriately formal attire might give the impression that you are a "suit," someone in management trying to con the plant out of necessary equipment, funds, and so forth. By dressing in a similar fashion to the rest of the workers on the shop floor, you have one less strike against you and, therefore, you are one step closer to achieving the desired results.

For this same reason, women in business (years ago, through books like John Malloy's *Dress for Success*) were alerted to dressing in more conservative clothes. Why? Because if the skirt was worn with a slit half-way up the side, then the wearer was attracting too much attention to her appearance. Considering the concept that it is hard to sell more than one idea at a time, it becomes imperative that we do everything possible to insure that what we have to say or do is not being diminished by other distractions.

The issues we've just discussed relate to the kind of first impression you make. And that's important. But ongoing body language (both your client's and your own), carry even more weight.

By constantly monitoring your client's nonverbal cues, you have the opportunity to adjust and fine tune the communication experience to maximize its effectiveness. Here are some common areas to observe:

- Tone of voice
- Posture
- Eye contact
- Arm and leg position
- Body movement (like a head nod or squirming due to restlessness)
- Facial expressions
- Physical distance between you and your client

As an example, when you are with your clients, pay close attention to eye contact, both yours and theirs. Strong eye contact shows interest, but if it is too strong, it appears as if you are trying to peer inside their soul. Too much eye contact becomes intrusive (and creepy). On the other hand, if you continually are looking away, then you are sending nonverbal messages that are likely to be interpreted negatively, such as a lack of confidence, or even worse, not being truthful. Be aware that during your time with your clients, they are sending back messages through their eye contact (or lack of it) as well.

We've worked with thousands of CPAs across the country, and this simple but important area of eye contact is one (of many) that needs some serious work. In exercise after exercise, CPAs exclude people due to sloppy eye contact. Some CPAs just don't want to look at the person they are talking to; they want to look at the floor, the walls, or the ceiling. Others have no problem maintaining eye contact in a one-on-one conversation. But when another party is added, based on the eye contact allocated from the CPA to the new member, you easily could conclude that he or she (the new member) must not actually be there because there is no obvious recognition of their existence during the conversation. We find that women generally are better than men at balancing their eye contact when multiple people are involved in a conversation. However, regardless of your specific talent level, any inadequacy or sloppiness in this area can create real problems when in group meetings. If you don't maintain eye contact and create rapport with everyone around the table, whoever is left out will likely undermine your involvement once you leave. Why? Because when multiple people come to a meeting and you primarily focus your attention on the client's "alpha dog" or group leader, those who were ignored or overlooked won't want to work with you. As Dr. Krumm said earlier, "you need to make people feel special." And in this case, by not giving the other people in the room your attention or giving them clear signs that you want to hear their thoughts, you not only don't make them feel special, but you inadvertently and unintentionally tell them that you think they are insignificant because of your apparent lack of effort to connect with them. Remember, the top executive in the room may sign the check, but the rest of the people he or she invited to the meeting have the exec's ear and will influence the final decision about whether to work with you.

Keep In Mind

If you don't maintain eye contact and create rapport with everyone around the table, whoever is left out will likely undermine your involvement once you leave. Why? Because when multiple people come to a meeting and you primarily focus your attention on the client's "alpha dog" or group leader, those who were ignored or overlooked won't want to work with you.

Keep in mind that it is up to us to maintain eye contact with everyone in the group, whether that is one person, or many. Why? Because it's part of the job of a good communicator to manage your eye contact to make sure everyone feels included. By doing so, you also send important support messages that you are confident, honest, and sincere.

However, a more important job is for you to monitor your clients' eye contact. If they won't look at you during your conversation, then there may be a problem. Maybe the client is embarrassed about an activity going on in their workplace, or maybe the terminology you are using is too technical. Perhaps something being discussed has created some anxiety or anger in the client, or maybe he or she is just shy. The point is loss of eye contact is normally a signal that a problem exists. It's your job to discover what the problem is and then find a way to make it go away.

Another message to monitor is arm and leg position. If your client's arms and legs are crossed, and he or she is leaning away, this could easily be a signal of resistance. But then again, maybe your client is just cold. Or how about when the client glances at his or her watch, starts drumming on the table, or playing with a pen or pencil? How about the signal you get when the client begins to remove his or her eyeglasses and rub their forehead and eye region? It could be that their glasses have irritated them, or it could be that something else has. During a meeting, you always need to keep part of your mind focused on watching nonverbal cues. It's important to note that, usually, gestures mean something. When you encounter one (or more importantly, a group of them), don't ignore what you've seen: react to it. Stop and say something like, "I could be wrong, but it seems to me that since we started talking about this subject, you've become somewhat agitated. Is this true, or am I misreading the situation?"

We do not profess to be experts in the field of nonverbal communications. Nor do we attempt to dissect every body movement and stamp a meaning on it. However, when two or three messages relay the same thing, it's time to respond to them. Unfortunately many people ignore this strategic and valuable input and, accordingly, find themselves constantly misinterpreting conversational messages, as well as being misinterpreted.

As they say in the TV infomercials, "But wait! There's more!" Yet another issue should be considered. Not only should you monitor the nonverbal messages you and your clients are sending, you also should control your messages. As the need arises, you may want to specifically manufacture some messages to improve the effectiveness of your communication. Here's what we mean:

If you are meeting with a client late in the day and you're tired, you might unintentionally send messages of disinterest (like yawning a number of times or lazily sagging in your chair). Think of the message you are sending, "Thank you, client, for coming in to see me. I'm exhausted and a little distracted, but I'll try to wake up enough to help you. By the way, you get to pay the same rate for my time as if I was fresh and alert." To prevent this misperception, manufacture a quality, caring, attentive nonverbal message by purposefully sitting up and leaning forward in your chair. Get yourself pumped up to meet their expectations.

By now, you might be thinking:

Let me see if I understand you correctly. You're saying that I should become manipulative and phony if I want to improve my communication skills. Well, I don't like it ...and I don't buy it!

In response, we like to think of manufacturing nonverbal messages as simply utilizing one of the tools available that can expedite better communications. This conscious utilization of nonverbal communication doesn't seem any more contrived to us than walking up to someone and shaking their hand. Think about it. Weren't you a little self-conscious and uncomfortable the first couple of times you stuck your hand out, especially when you were very young?

It boils down to the fact that the controlled mixing of verbal and nonverbal messages is just a good communication technique. In order to communicate proficiently, you have to consciously work on it. With practice, you will incorporate many of these nuances naturally. Others will be uncomfortable. But over time, most of the once contrived techniques (such as shaking someone's hand) won't seem contrived at all.

The average communicator can start bridging the gap quickly by consciously tuning into the nonverbal world. We often suggest to clients that they "buddy up" in their firms by working in teams, so they can help one another identify and see the many unspoken messages each is commonly sending. Once you become more aware of messages you are sending or receiving, it becomes easy for you to make subtle or small changes to take advantage of this new information. We all do this now for the more obvious messages. For instance, if you see a dog showing its teeth, you quickly recognize that a close confrontation is not in your best interest. By continuously monitoring the subtle but ever-present nonverbal messages around you, your ability to understand and be understood improves dramatically. The following box outlines the different kinds of typical nonverbal cues and their perceived messages.

Nonverbal Message Summary

Positive Messages

Make eye contact	One of the most important things to do. If you neglect to make eye contact with everyone present in the conversational circle, you lose credibility and trust.

(continued)

Include others in the conversation	Include all people present in the meeting by looking at them, and when appropriate, asking them questions.
Lean forward	When you lean forward in a conversation, you are perceived as demonstrating interest in the topic and the person.
Use, but don't abuse, gestures	Using gestures makes the conversation more animated and higher in energy. Don't overdo them to the point of creating a distraction.
Look professional and well-groomed	Wear clothing appropriate to the area and the occasion. Being a little overdressed is safer than being underdressed.
Nod in agreement	This gesture denotes that you are paying attention and depicts a high level of understanding. Don't always assume, however, that someone nodding at you also is in agreement with what you are saying.
Smile	This simple act quickly can change the dynamics of any conversation.
Sit at right angles or next to your prospect at a table	This encourages the perception of equality and teamwork.
Sit at the head of the table	Sit at the head of the table if you want to convey that you are in charge or want to demonstrate authority.
Mimic the other's motions, attitudes, tone of voice	This is often done unconsciously by the most persuasive of people because it reinforces the idea that "I'm like you," which is a powerful connection technique.

Negative Messages

Excluding people from a conversation	When someone isn't included in a conversation (this pertains to group dialog), like occasional eye contact, a reference to them, or questions when appropriate, you may do more than alienate them, you might create a covert enemy.
Leaning away from the client	This gives the impression of disagreement regarding the subject or lack of interest.
Pointing fingers	If you are going to point, use an open whole hand. A pointed finger is a threatening or scolding gesture.
Fidgeting or playing with an object	Nervous gestures or distractions, such as playing with a pen, take people's attention away from what you're saying.

Sitting across from each other with a desk or table between you in a teamwork situation	The desk is a barrier to building a relationship because it "feels" adversarial or authoritative. However, if this is the message you want to convey, have at it.
Expressionless face	Try to smile, keep your eyes wide open, nod when appropriate, or anything to show that you are interested and attentive.
Standing when others are seated	Stay seated with everyone else unless you are trying to create formality, assume authority, or take over the conversation. Standing up when everyone else is seated is a powerful technique at such times when you are looking to change the dialogue or your role in a conversation.
Crossing your arms	This delivers the nonverbal message that you are closed to whatever idea is being discussed or that you don't believe what the other person is saying.

Ask Questions

Now that you've made a good first impression and are on the lookout for nonverbal messages, you need to get a better understanding of the client's situation. The utilization of good questioning techniques can make a world of difference here.

Good questioning techniques lead to a gold mine of knowledge. This knowledge not only incorporates the facts pertaining to a given situation, it includes the perceptions and the emotions that surround it as well. This understanding is necessary because your clients often are not able to articulate what their difficulty is, just that something is wrong. They commonly just give you symptoms. Other times, clients will describe some ancillary problem because they are too embarrassed to tell you about the real one. That's why you have to look at the whole picture—the words and the emotions—in order to be able to read between the lines. In other words, you're normally hired for two reasons:

- First, to identify the unhealthy condition or potential opportunity
- Second, to help find a cure for the problem or way to seize the opportunity

Here are a couple of ideas that should help you perform a better diagnosis.

Take Notes and Refer to Them Often

A client often will reveal several issues or concerns in a single statement. Written reminders will help you go back and address each one. Also, jot down any seemingly off-the-wall comments you hear. These may lead you to the real problems later.

We use a technique called the "Investigative Tree," illustrated in figure 6-1. The theory is that one question often uncovers many issues and, frequently, all of them need to be addressed. However, in a normal conversation, without taking notes, you end up focusing on only the most familiar of the issues. The rest die a quick death. If you will note the graphic, it looks like an upside down tree. The root or trunk represents the question, and the branches depict significant responses. For example, let's assume you ask your client, "So why did you call this meeting?" He or she might reply:

> "Well, I thought it was time I came in to see what I need to provide you so you could **finish my tax return**. You know, it scares me when I think about my taxes. That's why I avoid working on them. It reminds me that I have done such a **poor job planning for my retirement**. It's not that I don't try, but it seems all of my discretionary income is going towards **saving for my kids' college fund**, which looks like it is going to fall short of what I had hoped. By the way, have you heard anything about this new retirement community being built about 15 miles from here? I was thinking that might be **something for my parents to consider** as it is getting harder and harder for them to get around. Now that I sit back and think about all of this ... it makes sense that I'm such a wreck. **My stress level** has to be off the charts.

Although this is exaggerated for the purpose of this text, it's not far from reality. Here's a case where the CPA asked one simple question, and five important issues were raised that require further investigation. Why? Because as advisors, it's important that we understand what is bothering our clients. By always keeping this communication channel open, opportunities for providing assistance constantly will present themselves.

As a note-taking technique, when you think conceptually about your questions as an upside down tree, it helps you tune in to responses that would create new branches. When you hear a comment or thought that needs more attention, write down a key word to remind you of the newly created branch and circle it. Continue on your current course of questioning and note taking, and when you have reached the end of the current branch you

Figure 6-1: **Investigative Tree**

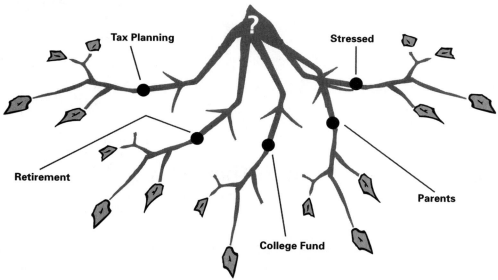

are investigating, stop and review your notes. Find one of the circled words jotted down earlier, and start a new series of questions so that you fully understand that issue as well. By continuously identifying new information branches, you make it much easier to go back later to uncover important ideas or concerns.

Ask Only One Question at a Time

The problem of skipping over important information is obvious in so many conversations. Not only do we overlook valuable information because we forget to go back and pursue it later, but we make the reverse mistake as well. This occurs when we string two or three questions together. If you pay close attention to the questions you ask during the next week or so, don't be shocked at how many times you ask more than one question at a time. The bad news is that because the person you are talking to isn't using our note-taking technique, nine times out of ten, he or she will pick only one of the questions you asked and answer it. This is too bad because often the two or three questions strung together were all significant. In our experience, the questions that are skipped over by the client are then overlooked by the questioner too. Therefore, it's important to use whatever techniques you can to ensure that the questions you ask are answered, and the issues your clients raise are investigated. This focus exponentially increases your chances of helping your clients.

Ask Open-Ended Questions

Open-ended questions force your clients to do the talking. A question that has become a personal favorite of ours that starts conversations with clients is, "So what's been keeping you awake at night lately?" Another standard is, "What do you see as your biggest opportunity in the next six months?" You easily can play off of that later with the same question, except substitute the word *challenge* for *opportunity*. Once you ask whatever open-ended question you are comfortable with to initiate the conversation, let the clients take you where they want to go. Then, play off of each of their answers with more specific questions that help you understand the issues relative to that information branch. This technique stimulates conversation and facilitates a thorough investigation. In the following example, we demonstrate just what we are talking about. Remember that the key here is to use open-ended questions to facilitate topic freedom within the conversation. Then use closed-ended (yes/no, or narrow confirmation type) questions to verify understanding.

The following example demonstrates how to ask open-ended questions and then play off the client's responses:

CPA: So, what's been keeping you awake at night lately?

Client: I'd have to say lately it seems we spend a lot more time focusing on cash flow. As you know, sales have been steadily increasing, but that has the negative effect of incrementally squeezing our cash supply.

Information Branch: Cash flow problem
Information Branch: Steady increase in sales

CPA: You say your business is growing faster than your cash flow. What do you think is causing you to grow so fast?

(continued)

Client: Well, we've introduced a new product, and our customers have been very excited about it.

Information Branch: New product

CPA: Tell me about your product.

Client: It's a portable power tool which allows one repair person to do work that, until now, took two.

CPA: Who uses it?

Client: Anyone that performs field repairs on heavy equipment.

CPA: How big is the marketplace?

Client: Our calculation is that there are at least 12,000 workers who could use our product.

CPA: What geographic area makes up those 12,000 opportunities?

Client: That is just in Texas. But we hope to include California and New York before the end of the year, so the market is even bigger than that. If that turns out okay, then we'll expand throughout the rest of the states. We also have our eye on Europe.

Information Branch: Marketing expansion

CPA: How many of these tools do you need to sell in order to pay the bills, given the first year's planned expansion?

Client: Right now, about 600. But we need to add more manufacturing capacity within the next few years. And with the combination of these facilities and our new sales offices, our overhead will drive that break-even number to about 1,800 within five to six years.

Information Branch: Manufacturing capacity
Information Branch: New sales offices

CPA: What are your sales now?

Client: So far, we are halfway through the year, and our sales and backlog total 500.

CPA: Does this sales volume stress your cash flow?

Client: Well, I guess the answer is "yes" since it currently is out of control. We can easily meet our payables and payroll for the next couple of months, but after that, we'll need more money.

CPA: How much additional money do you need in order to handle your anticipated growth over the next 12 months?

Client: Our management team feels we need to double our lending limit. It currently is $200,000.

Information Branch: Increased lending limit

This conversation easily can continue for hours. The abbreviated scenario is used to illustrate questioning built around the words *who, what, where, when, why,* and *how.* The conversation is not meant to be held up as ideal, but one that follows the client's lead with a combination of open and closed questions to facilitate understanding.

During this conversation, several issues were identified. First, in the very near future the client needs help planning for adequate cash flow around growing sales. This is complicated even further by planned new product expansion into new markets. As well, demand is expected to stress the plant's capacity and sales capability within a few years. All of this equates to a complex set of issues that will require lending limit adjustments and more. In this example, the MTBA has barely scratched the surface regarding questions to ask in order to fully understand each information branch. And it is important to note that the MTBA needs to circle back and pursue each information branch until he or she fully understands the impact that issue might have on the business. But this example makes it easy to see how a question about cash flow can lead to a number of other concerns, just by following the client's lead.

 Keep In Mind

When you are unsure of the next question to ask, take a few moments to think and regroup. Silence is a powerful tool in communication. Using it demonstrates confidence and intensifies the moment. An excellent technique to gain thinking time is to look at your notepad and look for the information branches we discussed earlier. Whether you actually read your notes or not is irrelevant. But because your client assumes that you do, it is easy to steal a few uninterrupted minutes to gather your thoughts.

Probing and Follow-Up Questions

At times, your client will throw out an idea or make an off-the-wall comment like, "They never do what I ask." You need to follow up on this statement to find out who "they" are, determine if "never" is really "not ever" or some low number of times, and what it is he or she is asking them to do. Do not accept broad generalities at face value. Sometimes our clients may have a difficult time articulating just what the issue is, so they start with a broad generalization that we need to have them expand upon. The following includes some questions you could use to probe for more information:

- "Tell me more about that."
- "Can you give me a specific example?"
- "What do you suppose is the cause?"
- Avoid asking "Why did you do that?" Instead ask, "You must have had some good reasons for doing that—would you share your thoughts with me?"

The reason we want to avoid certain kinds of questions is because we are trying to stay away from expressing seemingly accusatory statements or negative overtones. Be careful not to put people on the spot with your questioning (unless the situation calls for that kind of aggressive tactic.) And always try to allow your client a way to save face while providing you with the information you need to help them.

Don't Forget to Use the Global Functions as Your Questioning Checklist

There is one more technique we would like to address pertaining to your investigation. Remember throughout the information gathering process that you are not trying to find just one hot button, you are trying to identify all of them (within reason). Often, the first concern identified is not the primary one; it's just the most comfortable one to talk about.

For example, years ago, a client called us and said he was having trouble managing the growth of his business. After we qualified him over the phone, we set up a meeting at his office. For the first hour or so, we talked about information he needed that he was not getting. He told us about the inadequacies of his accounting system. He introduced us to his sales department personnel and made it clear that they were falling short of expectations. After all of this, with continued diligence in questioning, he finally revealed the reason he called us. He was turning over his entire staff, which consisted of 10 employees, about once a year.

This embarrassed him and was something he initially was not willing to talk about. After about 15 minutes more of venting frustration, our new client asked us to find out why this ridiculous turnover was happening. We were prewarned that his management style probably had a lot to do with it. After days of interviews, observations, and investigation, we met with him and summarized the results of our findings: his employees thought he was a jerk. We addressed that particular problem by hiring a vice president with thick skin and people skills who protected his staff mostly by keeping the owner away from them (often causing the VP to take the bullets from the "jerk" owner in the privacy of his office).

The moral of this story is that most of the time a variety of open issues exist that need to be addressed. Some won't surface immediately because the client is uncomfortable talking about them. Others won't surface in the beginning because the client will attempt to confine his or her concerns to areas in which he or she feels you have expertise. And as we have already mentioned, most clients view our skills far more narrowly than they really are. Therefore, we need to be prepared to bring out issues in a multitude of areas. That's why we came up with using global functions as a springboard for our investigation. Remember from chapter 1 that these areas include the following:

- Planning
- Personnel (motivation and performance, retention)
- Operational (processes, procedures, efficiency)
- Governance
- Technology
- Marketing (target markets, distribution model, contact strategy)
- Management and specialization (the right skills in the key jobs)
- Profitability
- Accounting and finance
- Products and services
- Information management
- Succession management

So what does all of this global function stuff have to do with the investigative process? Simple: use these functional areas as a checklist in the investigative process. Although this next statement sounds bad, it's human nature, not client intelligence that we are referring to: clients rarely remember all of their problems.

A natural response to this statement is, "So if my clients can't remember their problems, how am I supposed to uncover them?" Well, maybe a more appropriate way to say this is that clients rarely remember all of their problems without prompting. This is why the global functions become so important. During the investigative process, you need to page through in your mind each of these functional areas and, where applicable, ask more questions. Here's why:

> In numerous workshops, we have added an uncontrolled element to our role play scenarios: we involve real clients. Although this occurred often, recently we added an extra step to the process. Several days before the workshops that included real clients coming in to work with the CPAs and us, we asked each client to list 10 areas of their business that "kept them awake at night." In addition, we requested that they consider all aspects of their business, not just the accounting area. Finally, each role play (real) client was to send us a copy of their list the day before the workshop, with the items prioritized from 1–10, with 1 being the most critical issue to resolve.
>
> The day of the workshop, the role play clients arrived at their designated times with their copy of the problem list in hand. We asked each of these people to relax and act as naturally as possible given the "fish bowl" in which this exercise was conducted. Our only request was that they put the list away once the meeting began. Remember, these clients made up the list, then prioritized it, faxed it to us, and reviewed it before starting the exercise.
>
> In one role play scenario that comes to mind, two groups performed the same tasks without being able to observe the other. The client was then asked to provide feedback on the success of each MTBA group. Given all of this, you would expect the role play clients (there were several) to be organized, thorough, and provide each role play group with the same information. At least we did! We were wrong, very wrong! The information divulged was different for each group because the clients were responding to the questions being asked. Remember, the one asking the questions, the listener, is controlling the conversation. So, not only were the answers different for each group, so were the priorities. And guess what? No group ever uncovered the predefined top five priorities!

Just to show you how much our questioning and listening skills need to be improved, here is one situation that really hit home with all of us. One MTBA group asked one of the smaller business owners if he had any financial projections to share regarding his business. The business owner responded, "no," that he had never done any projections regarding his business.

At this time in the conversation, the MTBAs were trying to gather information about anticipated volume. The odd thing was that the client had brought with him the performance history and projections of one of his similar sized competitors, which he wanted to emulate. We knew he had brought that with him, so after the exercise, we asked him why he didn't share those numbers with his advisors. The owner replied, "I forgot. Their question was about me providing my company's projection, which I didn't have. And I was so caught up in all the things we were talking about, it skipped my mind."

This is just one example among many. Here was a series of clients who were organized and prepared, at least far more than most we work with because of the formality of the exercise, and yet the information uncovered by the MTBAs differed dramatically. For example, with one interviewer, the client might say that the company's biggest problem was in collecting their receivables. With the next interviewer, the priority might be identified as ineffective automation in sending out statements and delinquency notices. Yet, with a third interviewer, the real issue causing chaos would be identified as the lack of accountability. While all of these statements are likely to be true because all of them are interconnected, making sure you understand the real problem is hard because the client will follow your lead when responding to your line of questions. This latest change in our role play scenarios using real clients working from a premeeting priority list is an option often chosen by firms when we do in-firm workshops. The results are consistent: clients rarely remember all of their problems, and even when they do, the priorities of some of the items would change from their original lists depending on who was interviewing them.

The point of this is by using open-ended questions and following the client's lead, you will uncover a vast amount of information. However, the client is likely to have forgotten a few important issues. And some issues identified might be part of other, much broader problems that haven't been uncovered. So it's a good idea to visit the global function list throughout the investigation in order to maximize your understanding of all of your client's concerns. Just a few of the questions that should come to mind are as follows:

Planning
- Does the client have a plan?
- When was it last updated?
- Does the plan drive the organization, or does the organization drive the plan?
- Does the plan respond to changing market demand?

Personnel
- Does the client have high turnover?
- Do the people seem motivated?
- Do they take care of the customers in a quality manner?
- Is the operation open to litigation due to inconsistent personnel policies or practices?
- Do the employees know what is expected of them?
- Does the company use a competency-based approach to hiring, developing, and counseling employees?
- How well do managers delegate and supervise their people?
- Do people work as a team, or is there constant in-fighting?

Operations
- Does the operation flow smoothly?
- Do steps, paperwork, or functions overlap to the point that duplication of effort is common?

- Are there needless steps, paperwork, or functions being performed?
- How efficient are the operations (measures of output divided by input) compared to industry measures of efficiency, if available?
- What are the efficiency trends over the last two to three years?

Governance
- How is the company organized regarding hierarchy and decision-making?
- Does the board function as a high-level governance body, overseeing the CEO's results, or does it get mired in operational details?
- Does the CEO hold himself or herself and others accountable?
- How are key decisions being made for the company?

Technology
- Is there technology that can be used economically to streamline a function or process?
- Do the people know how to use the technology that is available to them?
- Have legacy systems been kept around unnecessarily, thereby diminishing the effectiveness of new systems that have been implemented?

Marketing
- Is marketing haphazardly handled or adequately planned?
- What is the client's market share?
- What is their targeted market share?
- Has the marketplace been segmented in order to determine the lowest cost and most effective contact strategy?
- Has the customer been identified clearly by the client?
- What motivates that customer to buy?
- How often does the marketing plan facilitate contact with the most likely customers?
- Does the company have clearly defined target markets, customers, clients, and so forth?
- Does the company understand which products, services, and offerings are desired by which segments of its customer base?
- Are the products and services growing or declining in demand?
- What products and services are on the horizon?
- How are the products and services continually enhanced to respond to market changes?
- Are the products and services in the right mix for the customer base?
- What mechanism does the client use to get product and service feedback?
- How well does the client's distribution model serve its customers' and the client's needs? Are there better ways of delivering the offerings?

Profitability
- Is the product mix optimum?
- Is the profitability of each offering being reviewed periodically?

- Are the products priced in a way that leverages the organization's ability (quantity, quality, speed)? Is the gross margin in line with the industry?
- Is the profit margin in line with industry?
- Are adequate funds, motivational commission systems, and customer contact procedures in place to support the sales volume required?
- Do the owners leave enough profit in the company to support debt service and growth, or are they stripping it out each year?
- Does cash flow compare favorably with profitability?

Accounting and Finance
- Does management receive timely, accurate financial statements?
- Can management quickly determine where problems, if any, are beginning in inventory, receivables, and payables?
- Does the company have an adequate system of internal controls?
- Has management reviewed an updated analysis of their cost structure to understand fixed costs, variable costs, break-even, and marginal contribution of revenues?
- Do they have enough funds to adequately support research and development?
- Have they set up credit lines or established lending and investment relationships to support the strategic plan?
- Does the customer have the right kind of resources (both talent and capital) to fulfill the expectations of the company's plan?

Information Management
- Does the customer's information system provide timely, relevant, concise, and accurate information?
- Is there adequate communication within the organization?
- Is the company information protected through daily backup and off-site storage?
- Is there a disaster recovery plan in place?
- Does the reporting system deliver the right information to the right people?
- Does the company report everything, or just on the exceptions they expect people to react to?

Succession Management
- Do all key management positions have a crisis succession plan in place with identified, acting successors in place to fill in?
- Do potential acting successors need additional training and development to step in under a crisis and, if so, what is being done about it?
- What is being done about orderly succession management in terms of
  — ownership and control?
  — management?

We absolutely are *not* suggesting that you ask all of these. We are not even suggesting that you ask most of them. We simply are listing types of questions that might unveil whether there is more we need to discover. Questions like these lead the client into thinking about each area of their business, which then converts into uncovering more opportunities.

A good use of the global functions and supporting questions might come from a common situation, such as you asking the client, "What is keeping you awake at night lately?" Let's say that the client responds with, "Nothing. Everything is going great!" Now, seemingly at a dead end, if you just think through the global function list, you might ask a more specific question to dig into common areas of businesses that tend to suffer to see if the answer changes. You reply, "That's great. So you feel comfortable about your company's 5-year plan?" The client might then respond with, "No, actually we don't have a plan. We have been running around trying to keep up with demand, and that is one thing I think we need to address pretty soon." All of the sudden, a conversation seemingly at a dead end is reinvigorated by diving into one or two of the global function areas and verifying status at a more detailed or direct level.

By the way, if you use the global functions and a question or two in a couple of areas and the answers all come out the same, with the client saying, "no problem," then you are done. This is just a technique to help broaden the conversation; we are not trying to manufacture problems. There is no scarcity of opportunity, so smile, congratulate the client, and move on to talk to another one. Don't worry, time will pass and, in six months, you'll need to go through this same exercise with that same client again because nothing ever stays the same.

Avoid the Impulse to Announce Quick Solutions

One major hurdle most CPAs have trouble overcoming occurs during the implementation of expanded questioning techniques. We call it "premature speculation." In other words, as soon as a client starts telling us his or her concerns, we start the stopwatch. We begin running a race that nobody else knows or cares about. The objective of the race, which only other CPAs seem to be aware of, is to tell our clients how to solve their problems. As soon as we can speculate what the problem is, we change into our "answer person" superhero outfit and solve the life dilemmas of our clients.

All too often, because of our history as technicians, CPAs want to provide quick answers. This may be because we have trained our clients to expect solutions to complex problems in a minimal amount of time. But we need to recognize that the only reason our profession has been able to live up to this expectation is because traditional accounting is repetitive and well-defined by rules. MTBA work is just the opposite.

One of the first rules an MTBA must get used to is that there are very few rules, if any at all. Second, solutions rarely are all right, all wrong, all black, or all white. They usually present themselves in various shades of gray. There could be several "right" answers. To arrive at the best alternative, you have to factor in more than the expected benefits. You also have to consider the disadvantages of each option and the likelihood that the personnel assigned can and will properly implement the solution.

If the solution with the greatest reward is too complicated for company personnel to carry out, then a seemingly less attractive alternative may be the best choice. Following this same logic, if management does not believe in—or is not committed to—a particular solution, then reconsider the other alternatives. Remember, your objective is to help find a solution that works, not just find a solution.

Keep In Mind

Your objective is to help find a solution that works, not just find a solution.

When you consider that an MTBA has to identify the client's problem, understand the pros and cons of possible alternatives, analyze the commitment and experience of the personnel involved, and plan on how to overcome any anticipated hurdles, why would anyone feel compelled to provide instant solutions? We don't know why, but we do know that most CPAs are guilty of this.

Maybe CPAs have an overwhelming urge to demonstrate competence. Unfortunately, more often than not, premature responses produce exactly the opposite results. Consider the interplay between the client and CPA in our previous example. Many interviewers would have stopped the questioning process as soon as they had a nibble on their line. In our scenario, as soon as cash flow was identified as a concern, the typical modus operandi would be for the CPA to deliver a 20-minute monologue on how to control cash. Another soapbox oratory that quickly could follow would be one of slowing expansion.

The problem is that we, too, quickly jump to conclusions about what is really bothering our clients. In the preceding conversation, although cash flow may have been the first issue to be identified, maybe the client has a more immediate desire to deal with the less than adequate lending limit. However, we haven't asked enough questions to really find out yet. A discussion on cash flow or slowing expansion may be reasonable, but at a later time. It's just that we need to be much more patient during the questioning phase of our work. And if you want to introduce a possible solution, rather than just pressing your monologue button, consider converting possible solutions into questions. For instance, consider the following:

CPA: Have you thought about reducing some of your fixed costs by establishing distributorships rather than sales offices?

Client: Well, we've never used distributors. We've always set up our own offices. Do you think using distributors would help us manage our cash-flow crisis?

CPA: A lot of companies have found that to be the case. So we should take a closer look at this possibility and outline its pros and cons. I'll make a note of that, and we'll get back to it later. Now, what factors are motivating you to grow at such a fast pace?

Client: "The demand is there. But more important, we bought the exclusive right to manufacture and sell this product. That right is contingent on our having a presence in at least three states within three years. Also, we need to sell 10,000 total units within five years. If we jump both hurdles, we will have satisfied the terms of the contract and will retain the exclusive rights to this product for the remainder of its patent life."

This sample dialogue reveals two questioning techniques. First, if a direct question is asked, give a short answer (tabling further discussion until later often works well). Then, resume the questioning. This technique allows you to return your focus to the task at hand—the investigation process. By doing a thorough job here, it's easy to understand your client and his or her business. The second point is that when a thought comes to mind that appears to be a solution, make a note, wait for the appropriate time, and present it as a question. If the client likes the idea, you'll look good. If the client already has considered the idea and rejected it, you still look good for asking a logical and relevant question.

Always keep this in mind: the object of this investigative phase is to gather as much information as possible. You have the greatest opportunity to succeed in this quest when you're asking questions, not when you are giving answers. Why? First, your revelation may seem ridiculous in light of some aspect of your client's situation that has yet to be revealed. Second, most of the time, your client will wrestle with a problem for several hours or days before coming to you. When you spit out an answer after 10 minutes of conversation, in a way, you are saying to the client, "Hey, thanks for coming in. However, your problem is so simple and trivial that I don't have to give it a second thought. But don't worry, most of my clients are as stupid as you are." Give your clients the respect they deserve. Make sure you truly understand "what's been keeping them awake at night" before you give your opinions.

Once we feel we have accumulated enough facts, especially if the problem is complex, we give ourselves time to think. We like to allow ourselves at least one night's sleep on the information before proposing alternatives. No one will object to your asking for this time. If the problem were simple, you would never have been called in to solve it in the first place. Once some time has passed and you have had a chance to review the information again, don't be surprised if many new or improved ideas come to mind.

This leads us to our next communication foundation element. Although improving your ability to ask questions is critical to delivering on your MTBA status, this enhanced skill won't have any impact if you don't put significant emphasis on the following communication component.

Your Job Isn't to Have Answers

As an advisor, the client pays you for a variety of reasons: talking to you, bouncing ideas off of you, getting your perspective, helping identify a problem, helping solve a problem, and so forth. But considering all of this, it is still not your job to profess instant solutions.

We know we are repeating ourselves, but as tax accountants, our job is to have answers. We are the undisputed experts. However, when it comes to running someone's business, we merely are trying to fill the role of being valued advisors. And as that advisor, our first job is to ask questions. Our second job is to listen to whatever the client says regarding those questions. Third and fourth respectively, it is our job to ask even more questions and listen even more attentively to the client's responses. At such time that our client has told us everything he or she wants to share, then we move to the fifth step in the MTBA process and ask questions of other key people in the organization. Guess what? This leads us to our sixth step: we need to listen some more.

It may appear that we are toying with you but not as much as you think. We have made a living for almost three decades billing for MTBA services that are based on the premise that our clients not only know what their problems are but how to fix them as well. For example, once a client identifies a problem, our firm members have learned to respond (almost instinctively now) with questions such as the following:

- What has worked in the past?
- What should work but seems to be less effective than anticipated?
- What does your competition do that seems to work?
- What have you thought about doing?
- What do you see as being your biggest downside risk if you stay your present course?

Based on the client's response to these and similar questions, an incredible number of times, two or three good ideas will emerge that can immediately improve their situation. This kind of approach allows us to focus our job around helping our clients articulate, organize, and prioritize their primary objectives. Then, we assist them in identifying, cost justifying, managing, and implementing whatever solutions they choose. Do we suggest ideas? Do we provide answers to many questions? The answer to both questions is "Absolutely." However, that input comes as a natural part of our involvement, with equally valuable ideas and comments being shared by other members of the management team. Most of the time, we contribute more than other group participants. This is not because we are authorities, but rather because we take the time to capitalize on the knowledge workers surrounding us.

Often, this is done on an almost covert basis. For example, if poor accountability regarding the budget appears to be the problem, we would ask questions that lead our clients to that conclusion. We might start with a question like, "Tell me a little bit about the budgetary process?" Then we might follow that with, "What happens if a manager ends the year 20 percent over budget?" When the client responds with, "nothing," then we ask, "Do you think that's an appropriate reaction in light of the corporate objective?" The point is we try to leverage the client's knowledge first. After we have exhausted that resource, we provide whatever information we know or request time to contemplate the information presented and then attempt to identify the next step in the process.

We also believe that one of the best sources for identifying and fixing problems is to talk with the front line people—the guys and gals on the firing line, doing the work in the plant, the field, the office, who are not part of the senior management team. Through one-on-one interviews, surveys, facilitated discussions, focus groups, and so forth, we commonly get to hear, see, and review information to which many of the other management team members are not privy because we are outsiders. A variety of reasons exist for this. One is that many managers don't make themselves very approachable. Another reason for communication breakdown is the manager and employee relationship. Employees are much more likely to criticize processes and management policy with an outsider, especially if they want change to occur. If the areas in question are sensitive or the criticism is likely to be about powerful players in the organization, then you might have to put in an extra layer of anonymity protection through tools like questionnaires if you want to get the real scoop.

Why does this work so well with an outside advisor and not with management? Because employees feel a little safer (that is, more job security) talking with an outsider brought in to help versus speaking directly to management, unless the advisor comes across as <u>not</u> trustworthy (then it works just the same—it fails). Another reason managers don't have access to this critical information is that many just don't pay enough attention to their workers. You will find a kind of status misconception in a multitude of organizations that goes something like this: a $150,000 a year worker is at least three times smarter, with at least three times better ideas, than a $50,000 a year worker.

Well, this simply isn't true. The $50, 000 a year worker most likely won't have the same level of education, won't have as much knowledge or understanding of the business, won't have as much confidence, won't be as good a communicator, and won't be able to package their ideas as well to sell to top management. But make no mistake about it. Plenty of untapped, valuable ideas are waiting to be discovered if you just take the time to listen to this resource.

Keep in mind that it is common for management to identify problems, and reasons for those problems, that are different from those identified by their employees. Sometimes, management is responding more to the symptoms than the actual causes. The actual workers, the people coping with the day-to-day problems, typically are your best source for good solutions. Think of it this way. If you assume that the people working in the trenches have the right solutions, then it often becomes our job to find out how to make their ideas work. It's like finding a diamond in the rough. Plenty of idea gems are buried within the workforce that you have to cut, mold, and polish into workable solutions. This leads us, once again, to the comment that it's not as much our job to have the answers as it is to know how to find or uncover them.

Listen Actively

The last, but certainly not least, of our communication foundation tips is to listen actively. Listening is critical if you want to be effective. If you don't listen, you can't successfully provide MTBA services—it's that important. Listening also is the most difficult of these tips to consistently implement. Why? Because it's normally not the focus of anyone's agenda; people spend almost all of their energy either talking or preparing to talk. For example, why do you think most people can't remember someone's name once they've been introduced? It's simple: we're so busy rehearsing what we're going to say, we don't think about what is being said. To be a good listener, you have to be intent on listening.

 Keep In Mind
To be a good listener, you have to be intent on listening.

We've tested this point for years with thousands of CPAs. For example, after spending 15 minutes discussing the importance of listening, during a workshop, one of us will mention that each participant will have to stand up and give a 3-minute talk on a recent family event. Following this statement, we will make a comment about a personal family experience in which the names of family members and animals are stated. There have been only one or two times when anyone has remembered all of the names mentioned. Most of the time, it takes all the participants working together to be able to come up with all of the names! The reason is that, as soon as everyone is notified of their upcoming speaking event, all listening stops. The participants' minds are focused on identifying what they are going to say.

You may challenge our informal research with the statistic that many people have ranked dying and public speaking with equal disdain, and you may comment that it's no wonder the audiences stop paying attention. Okay, we'll buy that, but the exercise just described is only one example of several. Rehearsing, instead of listening, is one of the behaviors that are barriers to effective, active communication. Let's review a few others while we're on this topic.

Other barriers include the following:

- Filters—on both the sender's part and the listener's part
- Judging others
- Poor listening habits

Each of us is who we are because of genetics, combined with a lifetime of experiences. This lifetime of experiences creates a unique prism regarding how we perceive and interpret our surroundings. These unique perspectives act as filters that we must be aware of when we process what we see, hear, and read as well as when we communicate with others. For example, advisors commonly make assumptions about what the client means based on their (the advisors') filters. Our point here is simple but obvious: when you are acting in the role of MTBA, never assume. Ask for clarification. The fact is that many times your assumptions will be right, but sometimes they will be way off, and you can't afford that level of miscommunication when delivering these kinds of facilitative services.

Judging others can color our receptiveness to what a person is telling us (as well as their receptivity to what we're telling them.) This also can easily trick us as we put both of our feet, squarely in our mouth because we take verbal privileges we shouldn't be taking. Some of the activities that create barriers to effective listening, resulting in misunderstandings or misperceptions include the following:

- *Assumed similarity*. This is when we assume that because we have some similar interests and views, the other person thinks like us on all issues (which they rarely ever do). For example, we assume that because we have a supportive, developmental approach to supervision, that the client does too when we present our ideas on management changes. This causes us to under develop the recommendations, assuming the benefits don't require support given our similar philosophies (ultimately delivering a poor service or unnecessarily confusing the client). Or from a foot in mouth standpoint, because we think our client has a similar political view, you (as the advisor) go off on a rant only to find that your ability to be their confidant has been diminished because the client was offended by a position you took in your rant.

- *Stereotyping.* As discussed earlier, stereotyping occurs when we group people and assume that everyone in a group is similar in some regard and, therefore, we don't verify differences in desires or expectations (once again, diminishing our ability to provide a quality service).

- *The halo effect.* The halo effect occurs when we make judgments based on some single characteristic that overrides the sum total of everything else about the person. The halo can give the person seemingly superhuman abilities or just the opposite. For example, let's say the client is physically unattractive, so the MTBA assumes that they can't be dialed in to what motivates people given that they are frumpy looking. Or consider the flip side, when you make unreasonable assumptions about someone simply because they are physically attractive. You will end up with problems you could have avoided in either of these situations.

And don't roll your eyes when you read that last one. Misconceptions like this happen all the time. By just being aware of these natural tendencies, you can avoid most of the problems they cause when you are listening actively to your clients.

Nearly everyone needs to work on at least some bad listening habits (and it seems that the higher up someone is in the organization, the more bad habits we find). These bad habits include not paying attention, pretending to listen or pay attention when you are not, interrupting, or perhaps listening for disagreement so you can jump in and argue a point. Some people may arguably be listening but not hear part of what someone is saying because it is so contradictory to what they believe. Or they may be listening only for what's expected to be said and missing what actually is said. And as we discussed earlier in this text, feeling attacked can quicklyresult in someone not listening properly. Don't forget the fatigue factor and external distractions either. When you're tired, you need to focus even more on trying to listen effectively, and no matter what you do, if there are enough distractions going on around you, you will not be as effective a listener as you could be. Finally, for some of us boomers, physical impairment of our hearing is an issue, although we may choose to deny it for a while. The fact of the matter is that hearing often diminishes with age, especially if we hadn't used hearing protection as we should have in our younger days. This can create challenges of its own. Here again, just being aware of these factors can be helpful so you can avoid falling prey to them, thereby doing a better job questioning and listening when working with your clients.

When it comes to CPAs having discussions with clients, we often find some patterns of ineffective questioning and listening from another workshop exercise we conduct as well. In one experience that comes to mind, participants typically are broken into groups of three: listeners, talkers, and observers. The observer's job is to make a mark every five seconds on the sheet we provide for a period of five minutes. The mark is charged to whoever is talking at the 5-second interval. Before the clock starts, we make it clear that the objective is for the listeners to spend as much time as possible listening. We also instruct the talkers not to take on a deposition style of responding to the listener's questions; we want them to answer as if they are an interested party to the conversation. We do ask, though, that the talkers stay self-aware enough to ensure they don't ramble on and on and on to a single question. What we are looking for is two things. First, can the listener ask the kind of questions that stimulate conversation? Second, can the listener stay tuned into the talker's responses well enough to continue the conversation?

Based on the results from thousands of participants, we find three common traits. Participants have a tendency to

- ask closed-ended questions (rather than open-ended ones) ,which restrict rather than extend conversations.
- listen for the purpose of identifying areas in which they have expertise rather than just listening to learn.
- change the role from being the listener to the talker as soon as a problem area is uncovered in which the CPA feels competent.

The listeners in our exercises, even with the sole objective of spending time listening, still commonly talk 50 percent or more of the time, often up to 70 percent. After this exercise, frequently listeners breathe a sigh of relief, commenting that they have just experienced the longest five minutes of their lives. Think of it this way, if we talk more than 50 percent of the time when we supposedly are focusing all of our energy on listening, just think how much we talk when we are in our normal conversation mode. We have concluded that for many of our professionals, they don't need a client in the room to perform their monologue conversations. They just need someone available long enough to identify which monologue to launch.

So now that we've reported the idea that nobody likes to listen, notice the hardship that's created in our questioning technique example. Every question, except for the opening one, came from the client's previous answer. So by listening to your client, you not only gain insight into problem areas, but you receive clues for your next question. Even when the topics go beyond your current background, by using our approach, it's rarely noticeable. It allows you to identify your client's areas of concern without requiring a great deal of specialized knowledge. And we find great solace in the fact that what we don't know today we can find out through research, education, or supplement through association tomorrow.

Playing off your client's responses works well because you condition yourself to ask questions and listen, rather than talk. Therefore, you minimize the opportunity of exposing your weak areas. Rarely will you stumble by asking questions, but falling is easy when you're talking. Other ways of saying this are as follows:

- It's better to remain silent and be thought a fool than to speak and remove all doubt.
- It's much harder to ask a dumb question than it is to give a dumb answer.

Clarification and Paraphrasing for Understanding

Being an effective, active listener requires more than merely asking open-ended questions and avoiding barriers to effective listening. It demands that we clearly understand what our clients are telling us, not that we assume or guess the meaning of what they are saying, but that we truly understand what they're trying to tell us. You've probably seen young associates ask a client a question, get a long answer from the client, and then not be able to explain to you what the client's answer was. They didn't understand what the client told them, and they were afraid to ask the client to explain it further. Earlier, we covered some of the typical probing questions you might ask. But what do you do when you just don't get what the client's point is?

Just for the record, we've never been kicked out of a client's office for asking them for clarification. You can say something as simple as, "I heard what you said, but quite frankly, I am not sure I fully understand. Can you expand on your point a little more for me?" Or you can ask, "I'm sorry, I don't see the connection between the two points you just covered—can you clarify your position further?" Or if you have a listening lapse, just tell the client, "I didn't get all of that; can you reiterate what you just said one more time?"

A very powerful tool for active listening is paraphrasing for understanding. After someone tells you something, you can check your understanding by repeating back to the client what you think they said in your own words and then asking them to verify if your interpretation was correct. For example, "What I heard you say just now is that you are frustrated with your operations manager because he has such high employee turnover, and he doesn't seem to be listening to your suggestions or taking action to improve it—is that right?" We are convinced that if you use this tool routinely, your life, both as an advisor as well as in everything you do, will improve dramatically. Paraphrasing allows you to clear up issues and gain shared understanding without being confrontational about it. Use it at work with your staff and colleagues, with your clients, and at home with your family. The value you will realize should be immense.

Does Gender Make a Difference?

Throughout this chapter, we've talked about general communication issues, from recognizing nonverbal signs to asking good questions and actively listening to the answers. We even mentioned that women seem to be instinctively better at maintaining eye contact with a group and interacting with a group than men. So, does either gender have the edge in communication and interpersonal skills? There has been a lot of research and discussion on this topic. Some of the research indicates that, because of the different ways that boys and girls have been raised historically, they end up with different styles of communication and different displays of interpersonal skills. For example, some research indicates that men tend to razz one another as a socially acceptable way of connecting, whereas women find that type of chatter as hostile and attacking. Men are more prone to boast to establish their status, which women more often than not see as arrogance. Similarly, when women seek input and ask questions as their way of connecting, men often view them as showing incompetence by having to ask. And when women won't engage in razzing and bantering, men may see them as humorless. The list goes on and on.

Although we do find some of these generalizations have some validity, we believe that you run the risk of stereotyping people by gender; and as we've said before, stereotyping anybody is never good for them or for you. For example, although the gender specialists will tell us that women are likely to make indirect requests rather than direct requests, we can cite any number of examples of assertive women who are very comfortable being in your face and making direct requests when necessary. On the other hand, although men commonly are chastised for being disconnected with their emotions, we know plenty of sensitive men who are very much in touch with their emotions. So are there gender differences in communication? The answer is most likely "yes," but regardless, good communication skills cut across gender boundaries. So the more we learn to appreciate each individual for his or her uniqueness as a person, the further ahead we will be in developing our communication skills.

In Conclusion

Getting the client to talk, staying focused, learning to ask open-ended questions, taking notes, stealing think time, and employing effective listening habits are very basic ideas. However, just because they are basic doesn't mean they are not important or easy to do. Quite frankly, the basics seem to be the first techniques we forget. Make sure you and your staff revisit these concepts regularly. And don't stop there either. Form role play groups with other members of your firm to refine these concepts and skills. Hire an outside facilitator to work with your people to develop more confidence and expertise in this area. Sit down with one of your closest clients and play the game, "Can I Uncover Your Top Five Concerns" (we have an exercise at the end of "The Structure of the Calls" chapter, which could either be used for in-firm role plays or with a close client). The point is that all of this may sound overwhelming to some. And even if you are comfortable with the concepts, you need to allow yourself a safe, nonthreatening forum to improve your skills. If you make this commitment, your firm's ability to deliver value-added MTBA services increases exponentially. Take it upon yourself to put together a program to help each member of your firm find the MTBA buried inside them.

Before You Move On

We have included two role play exercises (exercises 6-1 and 6-2) to help you diagnose your needs for communication improvements. The first one is a good warm-up exercise in that it is the least threatening. "The Listening Exercise" is meant to highlight whether you tend to talk or get others to talk, as well as whether you rely too heavily on closed-ended questions.

Obviously, the more you can get your clients to talk, the greater the chance you have to find out what might be bothering them. The second exercise, "The Musical Chair Game," is done one person at a time in front of your role play group. Read the rules carefully, and feel free to modify them to suit your organization. The purpose of this exercise is to bring attention to the fact that we miss a significant number of opportunities to uncover areas for which clients have concerns. Not only that, several other issues are uncovered by this exercise that hamper the MTBA investigation, including missing nonverbal messages, sending negative nonverbal messages, eliminating discussion by asking too many closed-ended questions, and asking two or three questions at a time.

Next, we've added a sample script to walk you through an example of how an initial meeting with a client to uncover their concerns might look (exercise 6-3). It is an illustration and not a "checklist" as you might be used to seeing in your work as an expert, so don't rely on this exact script when you meet with your clients. Use your powers of observation, your communication skills, and your knowledge of your client to carry out an effective first meeting.

Finally, and potentially the most important exercise of all, is one of self-assessment (exercise 6-4). Just as in the last chapter, you are asked to identify skills you plan to improve and activities that will facilitate that improvement. Once again, this is a personal exercise. It's easy to skip this step, but don't. The best time to decide whether you want to incorporate any ideas and techniques into your personal MTBA toolkit is right after you finish reading each chapter.

Exercise 6-1

Listening Exercise

This is a listening exercise designed for three or four people. It is simple to do. Get a couple of volunteers from your office, and sit down in a room together to try this. One will take on the role of "listener," another as "talker," and the remaining one or two will act as "observers." The exercise starts with the listener asking the first question. From there, the listener, by listening to the responses of the talker, is to keep the talker talking. Theoretically, the listener should have minimal time recorded by the end of this exercise. To do this, the listener has to ask open-ended questions, note branches in conversations, and pay close attention to the talker. Note: talker, answer the listener's questions and stop talking. Although you are not trying to make it difficult for the listener, you also are not supposed to listen to the first question and then talk for five minutes straight. After the exercise is complete, rotate so that everyone can play each role.

One of the observers will act as a timekeeper. The other observer, if there is one, will watch for non-verbal clues. This sheet is for the timekeeper. Here's how it works. In five-second intervals, sequentially place the abbreviation (Abbv) of the person talking in the next available space below. Common abbreviations might be "L" (for the person on your left) and "R" (for the person on your right), "1" and "2," for the first initial of each person's name, or whatever is easier for the observer to remember. At the end of the five-minute exercise, tally up who was doing all the talking. Silence on the five-second intervals gets charged to the listener, unless it is just a pause in the talker's response.

If there is a second observer, the sheet following this is for you to take notes about nonverbal cues you noticed during the exercise. List both positive and negative attributes that you noticed and, at the end of the exercise, share your findings with the rest of the group.

Listening Exercise

Timer Sheet

Listener name: _____   *Abbv:* _____

Talker name: _____   *Abbv:* _____

_____ _____ _____ _____ _____ _____ _____ _____
_____ _____ _____ _____ _____ _____ _____ _____
_____ _____ _____ _____ _____ _____ _____ _____
_____ _____ _____ _____ _____ _____ _____ _____
_____ _____ _____ _____ _____ _____ _____ _____
_____ _____ _____ _____ _____ _____ _____ _____
_____ _____ _____ _____ _____ _____ _____ _____
_____ _____ _____ _____ _____ _____ _____ _____
_____ _____ _____ _____ _____ _____ _____ _____
_____ _____ _____ _____ _____ _____ _____ _____
_____ _____ _____ _____ _____ _____ _____ _____
_____ _____ _____ _____ _____ _____ _____ _____
_____ _____ _____ _____ _____ _____ _____ _____
_____ _____ _____ _____ _____ _____ _____ _____
_____ _____ _____ _____ _____ _____ _____ _____
_____ _____ _____ _____ _____ _____ _____ _____
_____ _____ _____ _____ _____ _____ _____ _____
_____ _____ _____ _____ _____ _____ _____ _____

Total Time: *Listener:* _____   *# times 5 or > marks in a row:* _____

Talker: _____   *# times 5 or > marks in a row:* _____

Listening Exercise

Listener name: _____

Talker name: _____

Note the nonverbal cues delivered by **both** the listener and the talker. Comment about their style, how they use gestures, what each does with their hands, how they position their bodies, eye contact, confidence in voice, did they include everyone in the conversation, and anything else you see. We're interested in any nonverbal messages being conveyed.

Listener: _____

_____

_____

_____

_____

_____

_____

_____

_____

_____

_____

Talker: _____

_____

_____

_____

_____

_____

_____

_____

_____

_____

Exercise 6-2

Musical Chair Listening Exercise

Rules of the Game

The objective is for the most trusted business advisor (MTBA) to keep the client talking using investigative questioning techniques for a total of 10 minutes. A round is over when either the clock counts down from 10 minutes to 0, or when the MTBA earns his or her third strike. The exercise is played with 3 people, an MTBA, client 1 and client 2. Client 1 is the primary decision maker for the MTBA; however, client 2 is considered by client 1 to be a valuable confidant.

The rotation of the game is as follows: the new player becomes the MTBA, last round's MTBA becomes the current round's client 1, and last round's client 1 becomes the current round's client 2. With each round, a new MTBA is brought into the game, and everyone else in the game rotates to their new position.

As stated above, a round is over when either the clock counts down from 10 minutes to 0, or when the MTBA earns his or her third strike. If you want to extend this game, you can give the MTBA more than 3 strikes before he or she is out (10 minutes almost never passes because 3 strikes are often earned within the first couple of minutes). Finally, although we have listed 5 ways to earn a strike, the main focus really is about the first strike. So you might start off the game only having people watch and listen for the first strike, but as the group gets better, add some of the additional strike definitions to the mix to ramp up the learning. The following are 5 ways for the MTBA to earn a strike:

Strike: If the MTBA doesn't recognize that either client 1 or client 2 has created a branch in the Investigative Tree. In other words, one of the clients makes the following statement, "I called you because I thought it was time we started wrapping up last year's tax return, and because I wanted to talk to you about planning for my retirement." In this case, two important topics are on the table for discussion: the client's tax return and retirement planning. Both ideas need to be recognized by the MTBA. Any time a new problem area or opportunity is introduced or a topic that needs further investigation later is mentioned, the MTBA is to yell, "Branch." If the MTBA does not yell, "Branch" for each issue, he or she earns a strike for each topic missed.

Strike: If the MTBA asks more than one question at a time without correcting himself or herself, a strike is earned.

Strike: Anytime either client sends a nonverbal message that could be meaningful to the conversation, the MTBA is to yell, "Message." If a nonverbal signal is sent that could be meaningful to the conversation and the MTBA ignores it, a strike is earned.

Strike: If a closed-ended question is asked without the MTBA yelling, "Closed" before the question is completed, a strike is earned.

Strike: If the MTBA doesn't make eye contact with client 2 for at least 5 full seconds every 60 seconds, a strike is earned.

Musical Chair Observer Sheet

MTBA: _____

Notes: _____

_____

_____

_____

_____

_____

_____

_____

MTBA: _____

Notes: _____

_____

_____

_____

_____

_____

_____

_____

MTBA: _____

Notes: _____

_____

_____

_____

_____

_____

_____

_____

Exercise 6-3

Advisor Script to Introduce Meeting With Client

First, think about how you can open the conversation.

Think about a few open-ended questions to get the ball rolling. Consider simple questions. Also, remember that your next questions likely are to come from the responses the client just gave you, so listen carefully, take notes if it is appropriate, and follow their lead. You might start off with something like this:

> "Hi! Great to see you again. Thanks for taking the time to have lunch with me. As we discussed on the phone, I just wanted to catch up on how your business was doing and make sure that we have been taking good care of you."

Some natural chit-chat will occur after your opening comment, but at some point, if the transition to a business discussion doesn't occur automatically, you might consider a question such as the following to gently shift the conversation:

- "So, how is business?"
- "Is there anything going on in the business that is keeping you awake at night lately?"
- "Has the economy had an impact on your business?" Depending on the answer, "Why?" or "Why not?"
- "Do you have any upcoming plans that will cause or require significant changes?"

Remember, all you are trying to do is get them to talk in an unguarded manner about their business. If they won't talk, don't fight it. Have a nice lunch, and call on another client. There is no shortage of opportunity, so don't feel like you have to find something to talk about with everyone you talk to. This is a service you are providing. Don't think of this as an exercise to find business but as an obligation that you have to help your clients if they are in need of assistance. And, obviously, the best way you can find out if they need help is to ask them.

Here are some tough questions you might encounter:

- "Why are you asking?" Your response might be as follows:

  "Well, at Cingoranelli and Reeb, we have a wide range of clients and, therefore, services that we offer. Our mission is to help our clients succeed. And we are proud that we have really had an impact with many of our clients. So I am personally touching base with my most important clients (clients always like to know they are important) to make sure that we are (1) doing a good job, and (2) helping you solve or leverage what is most important to you."

- "What is this all about? Are you looking for business?" Your response might be as follows:

  "No, we are not looking for business. We are trying to make sure that we are helping our clients take care of what is most important to them. At Cingoranelli and Reeb, we have a wide range of clients and, therefore, services that we offer. Our mission is to help our clients succeed. And we are proud that we have really had an impact with many of our clients. So I am personally touching base with my most important clients to make sure that we are (1) doing a good job, and (2) helping you solve or leverage what is most important to you."

- "I am glad we are having lunch, but I just want to be upfront that I am not interested in buying anything." Your response might be as follows:

  "I am glad we are having lunch too. And the purpose for this meeting is not for me to sell you something, but to make sure that we are helping our clients take care of what is most important to them. At Cingoranelli and Reeb, we have a wide range of clients and, therefore, services that we offer. Our mission is to help our clients succeed. And we are proud that we have really had an impact with many of our clients. So I am personally touching base with my most important clients to make sure that we are (1) doing a good job, and (2) helping you solve or leverage what is most important to you."

If the client clearly is willing to talk but is thinking about the services you offer in too narrow of a manner, focus the scope of the questioning on some of the Global Function areas and see if that opens up the discussion. Consider some of the following questions:

- *Planning*
    — Do you feel like your business is on track with your organizations' strategic plan?
    — Are you comfortable that your current strategy will guide you where your company needs to be in the next 5 years?

- *Personnel*
    — Do you feel like you have a system of accountability in place that fairly rewards those people that do the lion's share of the work?
    — Do you feel like your employees are adequately motivated and team-players?

- *Operations*
    — Do you feel like your organization (or department) operates as efficiently as it should?
    — Are there areas of inefficiency within your organization that are causing problems either internally or with customers?

- *Governance*
    — Does the board hold the CEO accountable?
    — Does the board focus on strategy and high-level decisions, staying out of day-to-day details?

- *Technology*
    — Do you feel you have gotten the expected return from your technology investment?
    — Are you comfortable that your technological capability is adequate to support this company's goals and objectives?

- *Marketing*
    — Do you have a marketing plan in place that will generate the kind of growth you are expecting in the coming years?
    —Are you comfortable that your marketing approach and capability is adequate to achieve your revenue targets and budgets?
    — Do you feel comfortable that your products (or services) are competitive?
    — Do you feel comfortable that your products (or services) are meeting the needs of your customers?

- *Profitability*
    — Do you feel you are taking home (or making) as much money as you should be given the revenue you are generating?
    — Do you feel like your expenses (both general and cost of good sold) are under good control?

- *Accounting and Finance*
    — Do you have the necessary financing (or capital) to support your current growth levels?
    — Is your cash-flow adequate to support your anticipated growth?

- *Information Management*
  — Do you get information about the status of your company's assets on a timely enough basis?
  — Do you feel like you get the necessary information you need to make the daily business decisions you have to make?

- *Succession Management*
  — Do you have a crisis succession plan in place for all key positions?
  — What have you done about planning for succession at the company—for ownership and control, as well as for management?

Remember, during lunch, your job is to spend no more than 10 minutes talking about this stuff. Fly in at 30,000 feet, identify several issues that your client wants to address, and set up an "on the clock" meeting to drill down into any issues that were a priority. It is your job to help them (and you) identify if and why they need to get you involved now. If they don't need you, that is great because you have fulfilled your MTBA role, at least for now.

Exercise 6-4

Self-Assessment Timeline Relative to Developing My Listening Skills

Name: _____

The following are skills I plan to improve:

- _____ By when: _____
- _____ By when: _____
- _____ By when: _____
- _____ By when: _____
- _____ By when: _____
- _____ By when: _____
- _____ By when: _____
- _____ By when: _____
- _____ By when: _____
- _____ By when: _____

The following are activities I plan to improve:

- _____ By when: _____
- _____ By when: _____
- _____ By when: _____
- _____ By when: _____
- _____ By when: _____
- _____ By when: _____
- _____ By when: _____
- _____ By when: _____
- _____ By when: _____

7

Advanced Communication Skills: Working as a Facilitative Advisor Instead of as a Technical Expert

"Take calculated risks. That is quite different from being rash."

~ GEORGE S. PATTON

Show Me the Money!—Quantification

We've covered how your discussion as a most trusted business advisor (MTBA) can allow you to meet briefly with a key client and learn what his or her top business issues are. Now we want to address what you do with that information. It's one thing to get a laundry list of challenges and opportunities that your client is concerned about. But how do you help the client prioritize them and begin to address them? Usually, that takes place at a second, follow-up meeting with the client, which occurs "on the clock." By that we mean after your first meeting generates the client's list of concerns, you and the client agree to a follow-up meeting to begin working on the list, and that occurs at your normal rates and fees.

To gain the necessary knowledge to help your client in your role as MTBA, your next discussion with your client needs to

- summarize and review your client's concerns identified at the first meeting.
- identify what your client expects to gain, protect, or reduce by addressing these concerns.
- quantify the value of resolving each concern (more coming soon).
- estimate (roughly) the cost associated with fixing each problem area, which includes your fees.
- weigh the expected gain, the likelihood of achieving that gain, and the cost of implementing the needed changes against each other to ensure the end justifies the effort.
- determine whether you have (either internally or access to) the required resources, including both time and skill, to manage or perform, or both, the detailed work relative to this project.

The information required to satisfy these issues can best be gathered by utilizing the communication skills and questioning techniques we have discussed thus far, especially the note-taking technique called the "investigative tree," listening for "branches" as the client talks to you. Remember, throughout this follow-up meeting, we are attempting to gather information, not put our clients on the spot.

In order for your client to allow you, or anyone else, to address his or her concerns, you need to quantify what the successful resolution of these concerns will look like in monetary terms. For example, your client mentioned at the initial meeting that their company has an opportunity to be first or second to market with a new offering that seems to have significant pent-up demand awaiting it. So at this follow-up session, your dialogue on this topic might follow a path such as the following:

MTBA: For this new offering, you mentioned that you might be able to be first or second to market. What would that look like for you in terms of annual revenues?

Client: It could easily be about $500,000 the first year.

MTBA: After the first year of revenues, what do you think your revenues might be for the next couple of years?

Client: We recognize that others will jump on the band wagon, but we think we would be doing about $750,000 per year, conservatively, for the next two years, and possibly even more.

MTBA: With the work you've done so far, what do you think your gross margin would be on those revenues?

Client: We expect the gross margin to be about 40 percent to begin with, and then expect with other entrants coming in, it might drop a bit to about 35 percent.

MTBA: How have you projected your overhead to behave once this rolls out?

Client: We think our overhead would increase about $80,000 per year.

At this point, you would be able to do some simple math and determine that the new initiative, in your client's opinion, could easily generate between $700,000 and $800,000 in gross margin over the first three years and, even if the additional overhead of $80,000 applied to all three years, the client would still be looking at adding $460,000 to $560,000 to their bottom line. "So what?" you may ask. When it becomes this simple and clear to a client that there is significant income at risk or to be made, paying you to help ensure timely responsiveness or delivery usually seems like a no-brainer. But before we did this simple mental quantification exercise, the client might be thinking, "we already have a tight budget and, while we need to get this done, maybe there is a cheaper way we can manage this internally." All of a sudden (and we say this because we have seen the light come on with our clients when we have used this technique, which has been more often than we can count), the client rethinks his or her position. We know this because we have heard them say out loud, "Wow, that is a lot of money, and if bringing you in can make this happen faster and help us get where we need to be sooner, we are not only making more money, but grabbing potential market share and future exclusive rights as well."

By the way, we always try to find at least a 4 to 1 or 5 to 1 benefit ratio (benefit ratio = anticipated client benefit/anticipated fees to pay the advisor). So, in the preceding case, if the client was looking for bottom line increases of around $500,000, and if we thought our work would cost more than $100,000, then we know this is just above the minimum for project acceptance. The fact is that most of the time, when you dig deep enough to understand the real value of action, you find ratios more like 10 to 1 or more. Now we want to be clear here: this ratio we are referring to is about perception, not about reality. Being hired to perform advisory and nontraditional work really can't be about actual results at the time of being hired, but rather about expected results (even though it is common that incentives are placed in projects for actual results attained). So if you find a project that looks like it has a 10 to 1 benefit ratio, then even if your costs are higher than anticipated and the client's gain is lower, everyone still ends up very happy. But when on the front end, the benefit ratio is low (2 to 1 or 3 to 1), and if you still push the client to move forward anyway, it doesn't take much on either side for that ratio to go bad. Although you might make extra money, the client looses a little faith in you and is left with a bad taste in his or her mouth from the project.

We can hear you saying, "Well, that same thing could happen if the benefit ratio was 10 to 1 too!" The answer is you are absolutely right. But the difference is that when the ratio is that positive, you are not pushing the client to bring you in, they are pushing you to clear your calendar. When that kind of project goes bad, then the conversation between you and the client more likely will resemble this: "We sure missed that one. We just didn't conceive of how low the gross margin would drop when the competitors decided to jump into our market." The conversation is more about missing signals than placing blame, which would sounds something like this: "I didn't want to do this in the first place, but you were so adamant that this was the right move for us that I went along with you."

The reason we are covering this is that CPAs frequently tell us that their clients won't pay for help with this type of facilitative work. The reason they won't is because you haven't helped them figure out what they stand to gain or lose if the issue is or isn't addressed properly and timely. Once clients are able to identify economic benefits, they usually are more than willing to pay for effective help.

Do we suggest that you take the fees on a contingency or a specific actual performance basis? We are not suggesting this, and most clients are reasonable enough to not suggest this either and really mean it. Too many variables are involved to guarantee that clients will achieve the results they hope for, with the biggest one being management themselves. For example, overnight, management may decide to move your project from a very high priority to a low one. All of the sudden you can't get people's attention, resources are shut down, organizational focus is lost and so on. Or management simply loses its stomach to complete the project (meaning they are unwilling to make the changes necessary for the project to have the expected impact). These are two common barriers we encounter, and for these reasons and more, when you are being hired to produce specific outcomes as an advisor, it is a fool's game unless you can control all of the variables. Even after 60 years of combined author experience, we still are looking for one of those types of projects where we control *all* of the variables. Finally, you just can't afford the risk of guaranteeing outcomes unless (1) you have performed the work being requested numerous times, with each time delivering positive outcomes within some predictable range, and (2) you are offering a volume-driven service where you have standardized and created extremely efficient processes knowing that if you take on this work ten times, as a group of projects, you can expect a range of positive results. In other words, you might know that statistically speaking, out of 10 identical projects, 2 will provide no revenues for you, but 4 or 5 will likely be profitable, with the remaining projects being exceptionally profitable. So the overall contribution of the 10 projects will more than meet your expected income targets.

Although it is probably unnecessary to say, if you take on work that pays on results, then pin down as well as possible the approach, resources, timeframe, and so forth on both your side and the client's, then when any of the variables change, your reward package does as well. It is critical that you can identify changes or change orders quickly because they will make or break the project. Secondly, work like this should have a far greater upside than just traditional dollars. In other words, if you can make $2,000 for your time doing the work stacked up on the floor in your office and you take on work where you bear some of the risk, that same effort probably should deliver double or more if the results are as expected.

The Omnipotent Advisor: A Relationship You Can't Count on Having as Well as a Risk You Can't Afford

In chapter 2, we introduced the concept of the CPA as a process facilitator under which the MTBA is guiding the client to help him or her determine the answers, rather than the CPA individually providing the answers. Figure 7-1 (the same one we used in chapter 2) illustrates this concept, which is foundational to the MTBA Framework.

CPAs come from a "content" or technical expert background by virtue of the training and the roots of the profession. When providing advice in the traditional services arena, the CPA is the expert, providing answers to the client in some narrowly defined range of subject matter. But when the CPA is working as the MTBA, he or she *has* to default to acting as a facilitator, assisting the client's people in determining their own answers. We want to repeat this point: As an MTBA, you cannot afford to try to provide expert answers to broad strategy questions—you need to help the clients so that they can solve their own problems.

Think about it as a "substance over form" issue. In this case, we define substance (content expertise) as being some unique combination of technical skills, experience, and expertise

Figure 7-1: **The CPA as Process Facilitator**

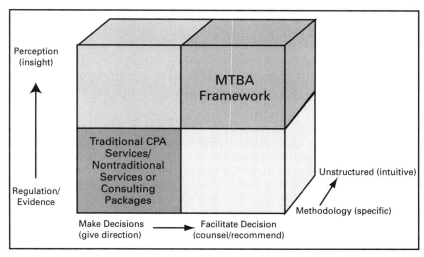

rooted in regulation or evidence delivered through detailed methodology. We define form (process) as encompassing persuasiveness, listening skills, communications ability, and selling competence, rooted in perception and insight, delivered in an unstructured or facilitated manner. Our profession's approach historically has been that if you have enough substance or are a strong enough content expert, then to heck with form. Or put another way, if you have enough knowledge, then who cares about your bedside manner or the way the service is delivered?

For a variety of reasons, with a few of your clients, you and your personnel have been able to build "substance over form" relationships. These clients regularly pick up the phone and bounce ideas off you. They sit down with you several times a year to review issues "that keep them awake at night." You, in turn, deliver the "substance" or technical content with virtually no "form" (or process) by taking on the undisputed expert role and telling your clients exactly what to do to fix their problems.

However, strategically speaking, how many *expert* confidantes can your firm truly expect to create and maintain? Certainly, a few of these relationships will evolve naturally with the more experienced members of your organization in specific circumstances. However, these are not relationships *you can count on having* with the majority of your clients. And even if you could build as many of these relationships as you desired, the risk and costs associated with this level of expertise, intimacy, and specialization are extraordinarily high. On one hand, it's expensive to train (if even possible) all of your personnel to be skilled enough to tell people what to do and be right. On the other hand, based on many situations we have encountered, every employee that comes close to achieving this unrealistic level of competency is likely to leave and take your clients with them.

Given that it is difficult (we believe it's really impossible) for any (and certainly not all) of your people to be visionary enough to be able to consistently get away with telling your clients what to do, the liability that goes hand in hand with unquestioned expertise is ridiculous. Unless you are charging about $1,000 a minute, it would be hard to feel good about this approach as a business strategy. Think about it. Which strategy do you think carries more liability exposure?

- Telling people exactly what to do
- Teaching someone how to become an idea springboard who can help clients arrive at their own solutions.

The answer is clear to us. There is no comparison. The approach of developing everyone's skills toward being a client's idea springboard (MTBA framework skills) returns a quicker payback, greater profitability, little to no liability, and will slow the growth of splinter firms. The omnipotent advisor is a high risk, high cost, low reward approach to the MTBA Framework: a relationship too difficult to establish, even more difficult to maintain, and one destined to fail in time.

If This Is So Straightforward, Then Why the Opposition?

Because being the trustworthy, loyal, friendly, courteous, kind, brave, clean, and reverent scouts that we are, we've been taught to "dance with the one who brung us." Which, generally speaking, translates to the success CPA professionals have achieved is based on "providing substantive (expert) advice." The thought that we may work with a client and *only* help them better organize their strategy, feel better about their approach, fine tune an idea, identify necessary missing skills, and so forth doesn't register as a valuable service in the minds of most CPAs. These kinds of services certainly don't fit the traditional "substantive" or "expert" advice objective that we historically have endeavored to deliver. Our professionals have made a living by providing expert solutions. However, in the business advisory role, coming up with the solutions is often not nearly as important as asking the client the kind of questions that will uncover the real problem (rather than just uncovering a symptom or two).

Our misperceptions about "what is valuable" can get us into a great deal of trouble. Reconsider the Accounting Office Management & Administration Report (AOMAR) client satisfaction survey (introduced earlier) that stated that clients are looking for new ideas, customized advice, guidance, and direction for the future and advice based on perceived opportunities, just to name a few. In response to this request, the members of our profession have screamed even louder for guides and checklists in order to provide this unique advice and guidance (putting greater onus on the CPA to become an even *more* specialized content expert).

As we facilitate CPA firm strategic planning sessions, the demand for more focused skill sets rings louder and clearer than ever. The problem is we've missed the bigger picture. Have we forgotten, or just chosen to ignore, the fact that there have been specialized guides, checklists, and methodologies available for purchase for decades? With this kind of support, why have firms across the country committed to increased specialized training, subscriptions to vertical industry information, and more, with less than stellar results? Because we are still trying to "dance with the one who brung us." We are seeking the undisputed expert role so that clients will seek us out. Think of the arrogance of this approach. We think that if we spend a couple of months (or even a year or two) developing an expertise, we will know as much, or more, as our clients do about the businesses they have been operating for generations. All the training in the world may not accomplish this. We believe that if we looked for a thousand years, we couldn't find a harder, more costly, less rewarding, riskier way of trying to implement the MTBA Framework.

That being said, let's look at some more advanced issues relating to the communication and people skills necessary to function as an MTBA who truly helps facilitate their clients' decision-making processes.

Perspective Is the Key

CPAs need to shift their perspective from delivering products to delivering services—services that not only help the clients articulate and understand their goals but also help them find ways to achieve them in a dynamic competitive environment. Along with this shift comes the need to let go of the idea that you have to show up with all of the solutions prepackaged in your briefcase. As MTBAs, you are expected to help facilitate the client's solution, not create it individually. The more quickly you believe in this concept, the more quickly you can take a lot of pressure off of yourself.

For example, when working in the advisory role, you might be helping a client decide how much to expand the company's factory floor space, or whether or not to take on the distribution of a new line of products. In this type of situation, how are you going to know with expert certainty what the right answer is to either of these two questions? You are not—you simply cannot in most cases. To attempt to do so is taking on an incredible risk as well. Let's say the client doubles factory floor space based on you telling them they should do so, and then the market for their product tanks, leaving them with huge debt service requirements they can't cover from operating cash flow. What do you suppose they're going to ask you to do about it?

On the other hand, if you work as a facilitative advisor, as an MTBA, you don't tell clients as experts what to do. So in the preceding example, when your client is thinking about expanding his factory floor space, you, as a facilitator, would not have *told* him what to do, but rather you would have been working with him to identify objectives, possible benefits, and possible downside scenarios. At the end of the process, the client is the person who will have to make the decision after considering relevant information. If that doesn't pan out for the client, he or she most likely will be calling you to let you know it's not going as initially expected and will be asking you to help them determine what to do in response to the situation that has developed. This is far different from the outcome you could expect if you had told them, as an expert, what decision to make on the factory expansion. We have lived this both ways (with the expert role teaching us these lessons quickly). As we previously stated, we've had clients take their best guess and find that their guess was wrong, at which time they called us in to try to determine what to do next.

You are there to help your clients formulate their thoughts, to help them find inconsistencies between what they say they want and what they are actually doing, and to help them prioritize what they feel they should be focusing on. The difference is the word *you*. Your opinion in this role is just one of many educated opinions. Your opinion is one that provides them with a sanity check against their own. But their opinions, their direction, their emphasis, their comfort zones are the real issues. You might give them some ideas to consider, but throughout all of your dialogue, you and the client need to consider your advice as "information of interest," not authoritative direction.

The more quickly you can change your perspective and adopt this MTBA approach, the more quickly you will be able to provide those value-added services that your clients really need. This is critical to long-term client satisfaction and retention. And remember that value lies, like beauty, in the eyes of the beholder. Your clients are the judge of what adds value to them. Although most of them certainly value having their financial statements or tax returns completed correctly and on time, they value the help they receive in addressing their general business questions even more. Being the president or general manager of an organization can be a tough, lonely job, at times, and the people who fill those slots appreciate the opportunity to bounce some ideas off of an objective friend who has their best interests in mind. Most of your clients are looking for someone to provide MTBA advisory services in this regard. With the proper perspective, you are almost ready to assume the MTBA role immediately (but hang on, we have a few more ideas to share with you first).

Different Approaches Are Necessary for the Advisory (MTBA) and Expert Advice Roles

When you are functioning as an expert who is called on to provide answers for your client, you approach the job of information gathering in a way that helps you gradually narrow down the potential causes and most likely technical solutions that apply. This is illustrated in figures 7-2 through 7-5 as explained in the following text.

In figure 7-2, the gray box represents, as a whole, the breadth of information available. As the CPA asks his or her questions, the CPA, as the expert, through expert questioning techniques, quickly and almost surgically cuts away all of the data that is not relevant to the issue at hand. This is represented by figure 7-3.

Figure 7-2: **Information Available to the Expert or Advisor**

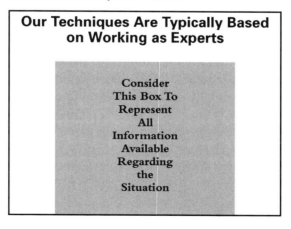

Figure 7-3: **Narrowing the Possibilities as Experts**

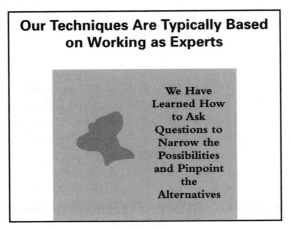

In figure 7–3, what we are pictorially trying to portray is that after a short period of time, content experts quickly cut away the distractions, leaving the information on which they need to focus and respond (the larger, lighter gray box represents cut-away data, with the darker gray area representing the remaining relevant information). For decades, this process has served CPAs well. It is very effective when you are functioning as the content, or technical, expert.

However, the surgical cutting process works against you when you are functioning as a process, or facilitative, advisor. As a facilitative advisor, you need to be expanding the information available to be sure that you identify the broader challenges, real issues, and true causes at the right level. As you can see in figures 7–4 and 7–5, in an advisory role, we need to learn to do the opposite of what we've been doing for years as technical experts.

Figure 7-4: **Information Needed for Advisory Work**

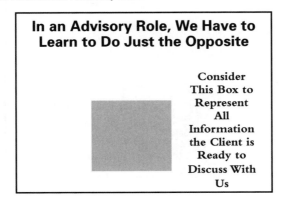

Figure 7-5: **Expanding the Information Available for Advisory Work**

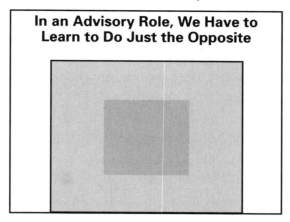

For example, consider the small gray box in figure 7-4 as representing all of the information that the client is considering talking through with their CPA.

In figure 7-5, the larger, lighter gray box represents the information we gathered while expanding the discussions with our clients beyond what they intended to share with us (about broader opportunities, challenges, and so forth) As you can see, the small gray box from figure 7-4 (planned shared information) is included within the boundaries of the larger box (information about the business as a whole, not just their financial information for example).

How do you go about expanding this information? As we've mentioned before, it's all about asking open-ended questions, recognizing that your next question will likely come from the answer to the last question, and staying at 30,000 feet initially. Once you've had your initial discussion with your client to identify the top issues they need to address, you need to spend some time with the client to help them prioritize them and quantify the impact of addressing the issues.

The Hierarchy of Sources

Previously, we touched on the need to get information from the employees once you begin to help clients solve their problems. Consider your hierarchy of sources when you work as an expert to solve a tax problem. Where do you go for help? You might use the following hierarchy or process:

- Look in the U. S. Master Tax Guide
- Read other, more complete expert sources, such as BNA, RIA, CCH, and so forth
- Look at code and regulations, and relevant case law, and private letter rulings
- Ask your tax partner
- Consult a tax attorney

The preceding list is an example of an expert approach to resolving issues or problems. A logical time to act in the expert role is when

- you are trying to apply rules, laws, standards and regulations to a situation.
- based on your interpretation of those, you are retained to provide an expert opinion.
- you are expected to find the necessary knowledge through your expertise, your organization, your research, or your network.

The point of this list is not whether these are the actual steps you take, but that as experts, it is a reflection of the hierarchy of sources we call upon to resolve problems (whether it is a subconscious process we follow or a written firm methodology).

When it comes to working as your clients' MTBA, your hierarchy of sources needs to change if you want to be effective. For example, your advisory hierarchy might look like the following:

- Talk to senior management
- Talk to middle management
- Talk to supervisory management
- Talk to the people in the field or on the factory floor
- Survey management or employees, or both
- Facilitate management team discussions
- Create brainstorming teams
- Survey or conduct focus groups with customers and with vendors
- Hire an information research firm

This approach, in the abstract, is similar to the preceding expert approach. The difference is in the answer to the question, "Who has the knowledge?" As an expert, you are supposed to have the knowledge or possess it through use of your contacts and resources. As an advisor, the client and his or her resources have the knowledge you need to turn to for help. Your job is to tap into that knowledge base and bring it together in a way that can be useful to resolve or leverage whatever issues you are trying to address. This is a significant difference that we cannot overemphasize.

Someone once wrote that in a typical, multilayer, hierarchical corporation, top management knows as little as 4 percent of the truth, whereas the people at the bottom rung of the company know 100 percent of the truth. We are not saying that these percentages are necessarily true, but we do agree that management often doesn't have all of the information they need to solve their problems as effectively as they could. An illustration of this concept was presented when senior management assumed that the workers in a small factory were unmotivated slackers due to their less than optimum output. As we pieced together the puzzle, we learned that most of the workers wanted to do a good job, but an operations manager (who was a blockhead) was creating drama and trauma that was the key cause of the poor production.

As MTBAs, we are tasked with helping round out our client's picture of reality so they can make better decisions, and this often requires us to talk with lower level employees. Just to be clear, we want to repeat that it is not our job to have the answers but to know how to find them.

Before You Move On

We have included a role play exercise to give you an opportunity to practice quantifying your clients' potential benefits from addressing their issues (exercise 7–1). Feel free to modify it to suit your organization. The purpose of this exercise is to help increase your comfort level in addressing quantification issues with your clients in a nonthreatening environment. Assume that after your initial meeting with your client (the one you used to determine the branches or the issues of concern), the client decided there were enough issues to resolve that you were invited to the office to help them determine how to improve their situation. This exercise should start by the advisor quickly summarizing the issues uncovered at the previous meeting to verify accuracy and completeness, then prioritizing them (at least the top two or three), and then drilling down on them to determine what is at stake or to gain in order to address them.

And as always, please walk through the self-assessment exercise (exercise 7–2) to outline areas you want to focus on in the future to improve your MTBA skills.

Exercise 7-1

Quantification Exercise

Put yourself in the shoes of your client. For the sake of this exercise, consider that you have a good relationship with your advisor. You call and see him or her two or three times a year, and you have gladly accepted a lunch or office appointment. Be prepared to introduce the business and some fundamental things he or she should know to your advisor before the exercise. On this form, list your current priorities or areas of concern in the business. None of these areas have to be financial. As a matter of fact, we want some of them to be nonfinancial. Finally, think about at least 3 of these areas and what those problems and lost opportunities could cost you in higher expenses, lost revenue, profits, and so forth. In other words, if you do nothing and just ignore each problem, what will likely be the financial ramifications?

☒ _____

_____

_____

What is the value of resolving this opportunity or problem? _____

☒ _____

_____

_____

What is the value of resolving this opportunity or problem? _____

☒ _____

_____

_____

What is the value of resolving this opportunity or problem? _____

☒ _____

_____

_____

What is the value of resolving this opportunity or problem? _____

☒ _____

_____

_____

What is the value of resolving this opportunity or problem? _____

Exercise 7-2

Self-Assessment Timeline Relative to Developing My MTBA Skills

Name: _____

The following are skills I plan to improve:

- _____ By when: _____
- _____ By when: _____
- _____ By when: _____
- _____ By when: _____
- _____ By when: _____
- _____ By when: _____
- _____ By when: _____
- _____ By when: _____
- _____ By when: _____
- _____ By when: _____

The following are activities I plan to attempt:

- _____ By when: _____
- _____ By when: _____
- _____ By when: _____
- _____ By when: _____
- _____ By when: _____
- _____ By when: _____
- _____ By when: _____
- _____ By when: _____
- _____ By when: _____

Delivering Value-Added Services

"Customers pay only for what is of use to them and gives them value."

~ PETER DRUCKER

The objective of this chapter is to better prepare the MTBA to *deliver value-added MTBA services*.

The implementation of this concept starts by taking a closer look at each of the words in this phrase.

Deliver bears the distinction of being more than just offering or performing services; it includes the ability to provide the right product or service, at the right price, in the right quantity, of the right quality, at the right time, in the right manner or fashion, and at the right place for a particular situation.

The words *value-added* represent a perspective. Delivering value-added services means more than obtaining results. It encompasses the balancing of the benefits achieved against the costs to obtain them.

The term *value* also denotes that a transition is in order. This transition is for advisors to move from primarily dealing with their clients' pasts to concentrating on ways of enhancing their futures. Because the future is not bound by regulation and evidence (different from traditional compliance type of work), as your client's most trusted business advisor (MTBA), your recommendations often are merely educated guesses. Because solutions are rarely clearly right or wrong, good communication skills become essential to the MTBA process.

Good communication, future-focused services, and the proper balancing of benefit versus costs (we call it the "benefit ratio") is the foundation to providing value to your client. But keep in mind that value is a judgment that only the client can bestow. Value, like beauty, lies in the eyes of the beholder.

The term *service* is a reminder that advisor work is often intangible and relationship-sensitive. A major portion of the product MTBAs provide relies on their ability to create and maintain a problem resolution environment.

 Keep In Mind

Good communication, future-focused services, and the proper balancing of benefit versus costs is the foundation to providing value to your client. But value is a judgment that only the client can bestow. Value, like beauty, lies in the eyes of the beholder.

Cash, Capacity, and Capability

Helping companies come up with implementable solutions is not an "at any cost" proposition. Therefore, we have to consider the resources of the client in determining how to deliver the services requested.

As CPAs and MTBAs, we have two basic offerings. The first is knowledge and methodology (the "how to" get something done), which is been gained through years of education, experience, and process refinement that we have learned through our dealing with business, accounting, and tax matters.

The second is manpower; it is common for CPA firms to supply the necessary management skills and labor force to complete a project. Historically, these resources have been packaged as one service. But for advisory service or non-traditional work purposes, they need to be thought of, sold, and delivered separately. Why? Because, in order to be effective and efficient in delivering non-traditional services, we need to execute the services in a manner commensurate with the client's resources. Simply stated:

Offer the services in increments the client can afford.

The larger the client, the more likely he or she can afford to retain you for advice, vision, and labor. Conversely, the smaller the client, the less likely it can pay for this bundle of services. Interestingly enough, Fortune 1000-sized businesses often provide their own advice and vision and outsource the labor. This has become a huge marketplace for large accounting firms, especially for the top 10-sized firms. Middle market sized operations will just as likely be in need of the advice and vision as the labor side of the nontraditional service, depending on the project. And finally, small organizations will want the advice, vision, and labor, but can rarely afford more than the advice and vision components of our offerings.

About this time, we often get asked, "How large is a small business?" In our opinion, the key does not lie in the words *large* or *small*, nor in the number of employees or sales dollars. Rather, it lies in the resources the business has available. Every company is made up of some combination of cash, capacity, and capability. When cash is the most limited resource within a company (for instance, if paying your firm $2,000 in a month would be a significant financial burden), then we approach our work as if the business were small.

For these clients to gain the greatest impact from their dollar, we unbundle each of our services and make a clear distinction between the costs for advice, direction, and vision, and human resources required to complete the work.

By unbundling services, the small business can opt to supply its own labor force. This person or group of people (usually part of, or all of the management team) then work under the direction of the MTBA CPA. Because the management team rarely receives additional compensation for performing extra assignments, this option allows the company to save a significant amount of money.

The idea of unbundling services is simple and hardly seems worthy of so much attention. But the problem is it is almost second nature for CPAs to package solutions that contain both expertise and manpower. Although this combination is easier to manage, control, and complete, it is a luxury many small businesses can't afford.

The tradition of the CPA performing all the work has evolved from years of practical real world experience. Why? Because CPA firms first focused on large companies regulated by the Securities and Exchange Commission. As time passed, that support has filtered down into smaller and smaller companies. Now CPAs provide services from the Fortune 100 companies to the start-up Mom-and-Pop shops. However, many CPAs attempt to use the same methodology for delivering services to businesses of all sizes. The problem is that "one approach fits all" just doesn't work.

For years, the philosophy behind being a client's MTBA has been, "If the client wanted to do it themselves, they wouldn't have hired us." This is a fairly realistic perspective for a business that has more cash than capacity or capability. However, cash usually is <u>the most limited</u> resource of the small business. With this in mind, the philosophy behind working with smaller businesses should be:

> The client has done everything they know how to do. They have hired us as advisors to help them identify what needs to be done next, direct and train them as to how to do it, and orchestrate the completion of various projects.

The bottom line is that time-consuming, tedious, repetitive tasks have to be delegated to the client when performing certain small business consultations or advisory engagements. This change in approach is difficult because old habits, like providing both the *brain* work and the *grunt* work, have to be broken. Small business owners tend to be the designated fire fighters, managers, salespeople, janitors, bookkeepers, and everything in between. Unfortunately, this day-to-day involvement keeps them focused on the now. Because many small business owners are overburdened just trying to manage daily operations, they don't have the time-luxury to spend nearly enough energy focusing on the future of their organization. Therefore, a void in the company's perspective is created. That's where advisors are needed most: to fill that void by regularly setting up time on the calendar and then helping the client with the brain work of planning, organizing, growing, and becoming more profitable.

Ultimately, the differentiator for building loyalty and creating very satisfied clients lies in the MTBA's ability to quickly and correctly identify the proper level of service (brain work vs. grunt work) for each client. Here's a process we follow that might be of help:

- *Identify project tasks.* Itemize the specific tasks required to complete the job. Sequence these tasks in the order in which they should be completed. Then identify scheduling conflicts (both yours and your client's) that might exist.
- *Identify task requirements.* Find the skill level required for each specific task. In other words, identify which areas require your expertise and identify which tasks can be delegated (preferably to your client, or if that is impractical, to a less experienced member of your firm). Next, consider the time required to complete each task.
- *Match client resources against task requirements.* Your client has some level of capability, capacity, and cash. Evaluate each area for strengths and weaknesses.

This does not have to be a formal process. With small projects, this is a very quick mind exercise that you most likely go through, at least subconsciously, right now. Obviously, the larger the project, the more likely formality should be injected in this process. The following example should clarify this three-step process:

Todd, a new client, has spent two years writing a software program in his spare time. He feels his package has a great deal of revenue potential, so he wants to market it. Unfortunately, Todd has very little money. He comes to you for suggestions on financing. Additionally, he would like to open an office but is afraid he may not have the negotiating skills required to obtain a competitive lease. Finally, he says that he may need some help automating his financial information.

Your first step, as discussed previously, is to identify the projects:

1. Financing
2. Office space/negotiating the lease
3. Setting up books

Next, break each project into tasks and itemize the requirements. Continuing with our example, let's take a look at Todd's situation.

1. *Financing.* In order to obtain a loan, specific information needs to be provided to the lender. Although this can be time-consuming, the critical skills are (*a*) determining what information should be prepared, and (*b*) massaging that information into a marketable format.

    Assembling most of the documentation does not demand a high level of expertise. With this background, the tasks might include the following:
    • Identify the required loan documentation.
    • Prepare a draft of each item required by the loan document.
    • Massage the documentation to maximize its presentation.
    • Present the loan package.

2. *Office space/negotiating the lease.* The actual negotiation of a lease generally is not time-consuming. However, the expertise required is high because the negotiator must be able to quickly recognize a fair offer when it comes to monthly charges, utilities, common area maintenance, taxes, insurance, finish-out allowances, and so on. The tasks associated with this phase might include the following:
    • Identify two or three acceptable locations.
    • List the pros and cons of each space.
    • Prioritize the locations.
    • Compare financial commitment.
    • Negotiate the lease.

3. *Setting up books.* Setting up a small company's books requires a high level of skill due to the demand for accounting expertise and computer knowledge. Both types of expertise are required because Todd plans to automate this function. The time necessary to perform this task also is high. So, in this example, the task breakdown might include the following:
    • Identify the best accounting software alternatives.
    • Investigate which package is the best fit.
    • Install the application.

- Create a chart of accounts.
- Design reports.
- Start entering financial information.

After the project is analyzed and the tasks identified, the next step is to review the client resources and match them to the requirements. Continuing with Todd's situation, we will look at the resources of money, time, and skill.

1. *Cash.* This is Todd's tightest commodity, which indicates that most of the detail work has to be done by the client in order to minimize the cash requirement.
2. *Capacity.* Because Todd quit his previous job to focus on his software company, for the most part, all of his time is available. Todd's capacity, or time available to take on more work, is his most abundant resource.
3. *Capability.* Consider the following:
   a. *Financing.* With a little guidance, Todd has the ability to put together a draft of most of the loan documentation. However, the cash flow statements and break-even analysis are going to require some extra coaching.
   b. *Office space.* Todd knows where he would like to locate and can pull together an analysis of his top candidates. However, he does not feel prepared to adequately haggle over the lease particulars.
   c. *Automated books.* Todd, as a programmer, has an abundance of computer skills that will aid him in automating his accounting. Like many programmers, he has a good understanding of accounting, but will need some occasional technical guidance.

The Balancing Act

Having reviewed Todd's resources, it is time to match them against the task requirements. Because Todd has more capacity and capability than he has cash, the approach is clear: to limit his cash outflow yet achieve his objectives, Todd must do most of the leg work!

This is one of the highest and best uses for the MTBA role because it focuses on the *brain work*: planning, task identification, and project orchestration. For instance, here's how we might approach this project.

1. *Financing:*
   a. Create a "to do" list for Todd of the required loan documentation.
   b. Instruct Todd to prepare rough drafts of the assigned documentation. You may need to coach him in advance on what these documents should look like regarding format and what key information should be presented, with an idea of the order that information may be sequenced in. You may even refer him to Horan's *One Page Business Plan* workbook and CD, for example.
   c. Once the drafts are delivered back to us, look them over for errors and suggest improvements. In this phase, the focus is to improve the overall marketability of the package to verify that the package emphasizes the strengths of the information.

For example, make sure Todd's many contacts and good standing in the local software market are highlighted. Check his projections for feasibility and thoroughness. Look over the projected income and expenses to verify that the anticipated profits are ample to repay the requested note. Help Todd with any necessary revision of the presentation of his documents—in other words, assist him in preparing a loan proposal that can sell his ideas.

   d. Finally, because Todd does not feel secure with his presentation skills, accompany him to the meeting, and aid him in selling his loan package to the bank.

2. *Office Space/Negotiating the Lease:*
   a. Ask Todd to select three places in which he would like to locate.
   b. Once these sites have been identified, have Todd create a list of the pros and cons of each space.
   c. Review his choices with him, guiding him by pointing out the relative importance of each item on his list. After getting an idea of Todd's needs and desires in office space, it's time to choose the preferred location.
   d. Schedule a few hours to meet with the landlord to negotiate a lease.

   By having Todd do all the leg work, you minimize your involvement, making your services affordable. But most important, you can offer your expertise where it is most beneficial: negotiating and finalizing Todd's new lease.

3. *Setting Up Books:*

   Because Todd is a programmer, he is familiar with software. However, he doesn't know much about accounting software for personal computers.
   a. Give Todd a list of several systems that will accommodate him. Then refer him to a local software and computer store to find more information on each. Advise him to call if any questions arise during his investigation.
   b. Advise Todd to choose the package with which he is most comfortable.
   c. Next, instruct Todd to install the software, establishing the default chart of accounts and financial statements.
   d. Tell Todd to print whatever information he creates. Meet with him to review it. Suggest additions, deletions, and changes to the information presented.
   e. Advise Todd to make the corrections that result from your meeting with him.
   f. Look over the corrected information. Finally, identify the monthly information necessary to prepare the financial statements and define procedures for accomplishing this task.

How Do You Find the Right Balance?

Obviously, the preceding example represents a simple situation. However, the general principle is always the same: find the appropriate balance between the requirements of a project and the resources of the client, whether the resources are in the form of cash, capacity, or capability.

In Todd's case, the total project is estimated to take about 60 hours. If the MTBA performs all the work, at $250 per hour, the charge would be around $15,000 (which is out of line with Todd's financial position). However, if you take on the role of planner/project manager/delegator, the MTBA's involvement is reduced to only about 20 hours, or about $5,000 (however, you might charge $6,000 or even $7,500 because the work you did always required your highest levels of expertise). This approach not only saves Todd a great deal of money but allows him to learn more about his business along the way.

It is your job to help your client find the right balance for each project. In each of your planning meetings, always be candid and set the proper level of expectation. Remind the client that the level of your involvement is under *their* control, and that the more time you spend on the project, the more it will cost. Conversely, the more work they do, the less you have to do, which in turn, saves them money. Whenever possible, provide your client with ranges of dollar estimates for the various levels of service. By doing this, you give your client the tools necessary to logically manage your efforts.

As your client's situation changes, so will your involvement. As a client grows and becomes more profitable, management skills may be more in demand than cash. Therefore, additional services (capability and capacity) may be appropriate. And that's great, as long as the services provided are in line with the budget available.

A Simple Format

We offer this simple, four-point MTBA format to help you maximize your effectiveness and minimize the advisory dollars:

1. Meet with your clients and assign them tasks or "homework."
2. From time to time, assist them when they call for additional direction.
3. At designated regular intervals, meet with your clients and review their homework.
4. Conclude each meeting with a new list of assignments.

By keeping this in mind, you will find yourself delegating more and more work. And that is the first step towards providing valued services to the small business.

Another note is in order here as well. As your client grows, you may be asked to help them on a routine basis, with or without some specific tasks to monitor. For example, with some of our clients, we meet monthly at their owners' or directors' meetings. We sit in and observe the meeting, participating in discussions as appropriate, asking questions, and raising issues for their consideration. This allows us to confirm that their action plans from previous meetings have been accomplished and to keep their eye on the ball, so to speak. We'll talk more about monthly retainers and this type of service later in this text.

What If the Client Doesn't Want to Do the Leg Work!

Let's consider for a moment that your client has little money and no inclination to provide the time or skills to keep the advisory bill within reason. What should you do? This is the easiest answer in the book: don't take the job. For the MTBA framework to be effective, the client has to be engaged and actively participating throughout the process. Too many CPAs get burned when the client doesn't have a strong commitment to the process. Knowing when to walk away is the key to both your profitability and your sanity. Given this situation, it's time to draw your unreasonable client a map as to how to get to one of your competitors' offices.

The End Result

By looking at each project and balancing each task's requirement with the resources available, the MTBA can

- deliver value–added services.
- make a significant contribution to the client's prosperity.
- maintain high billing rates.

The challenge in delivering these small business MTBA services lies in the CPA's ability to change to and from the doer role to that of project leader or coordinator, or both.

Your focus needs to be on working to improve your project management and task identification skills. The ability to quickly reduce a large project into bite-size pieces is paramount if you want to step up to the small business challenge.

Even though this strategy can be demanding and, at times, stressful, we believe that fulfilling the role of being your client's MTBA is still the most exciting and rewarding job in accounting. You're involved, you're contributing, and you're making a difference in your clients' future. But remember, anyone can provide MTBA services, but few can provide real value. And that's our constant challenge.

Estimating the Project: Pricing Approaches

Upon initial glance, this might seem to be a topic that should be covered later in this text. However, it's important that we cover it now. Why? Because we need to be comfortable with pricing in order to effectively deal with the questions that arise during the selling process. This book is organized so that each chapter builds on the skills and techniques discussed in the previous ones. But before we get started, please take out a blank sheet of paper and respond to this situation:

> You have a bookkeeping client for whom you prepare monthly financial statements. She pays you $500 a month. She recently commented that she would like to bring this function in-house. Your client is willing to use the same software you use in-house to do her monthly processing. What will you charge her to make this transition?

Now that you have written down your estimate, it's time to continue reading. We will ask you to redo this exercise at the end of this chapter to see if our approach affects the estimate you have just completed. Given this, let's move on.

One technique that maximizes your ability to get a commitment is Phasing. *Phasing* is nothing more than breaking projects into bite-sized pieces. Phasing also incorporates the idea that each phase should have a logical completion point, one at which a client gains additional insight about the probable benefits that should arise. Projects under this approach are typically estimated by phase, and although a general idea about the total cost has been identified, the more tightly controlled budget is at the phase level. The client understands that each phase creates a management decision point—an opportunity for the client to restructure the project, reassign personnel, stop the project, or continue the project as planned.

For our firm, when using the Phasing approach, our first phase is almost always the "We need to get a first-hand look at what's really going on" phase. The best description of Phase I is information gathering. Typical techniques include the following:

- Interviews with key personnel
- Observation of operations, technology, and other relevant functions.
- Surveys (often the survey gathers information from many more than the key personnel that normally would be interviewed),
- Review of documentation, including financial, organizational, procedural, and legal information
- Often times, Phase I consists of a simple organizational flowchart, which overviews the business processes.

The first phase usually includes the preparation of a general project plan with a detailed description about what should happen or be expected in the next phase. Although that sounds easy, determining what you are going to do in each phase (even if it's just the next phase) can be a mind-numbing, time-consuming process. Obviously, a great place to start is to review the approach, timetable, and outputs from other similar projects you have completed.

If your project is a totally new experience, don't get caught up in detailing the entire job; just lay out the objectives from a broad, conceptual perspective, and only create a detailed plan for the next phase. At the completion of each phase, once again, only lay out in detail the next phase. Why? Because even a project with which you are intimately familiar, there are always surprises that create problems or delays, or both. Therefore, trying to identify every step along a road for which you are unlikely to travel is usually a waste of time. In other words, when the project is an unknown, we rarely plan in detail beyond the next immediate objective because we are so unsure of what we are likely to encounter. And by the way, we make this known to our clients. The clients not only understand, but they get a better understanding of how we work while we simultaneously gain more project freedom and flexibility.

For example, let's assume one of our clients wants our firm to help them with their marketing program. As previously stated, the first phase is about getting a first-hand look at what's really going. Although we would outline generally what is entailed in a marketing plan, going much further than that doesn't make much sense until we know how their organization works, the strengths and weaknesses of their products and services, as well as what's been done in the past. It would be a waste of time to detail much of a marketing plan early on because so much of it could easily be rewritten by the results and finding of each phase, especially Phase I. With this in mind, some guidelines to follow when using the Phasing approach are as follows:

- Generate a project timetable or timeframe
- Break the project into reportable phases
- Each phase should have a logical completion, one from which the client obtains new information about the benefits that should be attainable
- Preferably, each phase should not exceed a threshold that is unreasonable for the size of business. That threshold might be $5,000 for a small business; $15,000 for a medium sized business; and $50,000 for a larger business. The number that is right for your client and the specific situation is up to you. But a guiding principle to determine that pricing threshold should be a cost that is easily manageable considering the monthly expenses of your client.
- You should plan an oral presentation of the progress and findings at the end of each phase (and build that into your pricing).
- To manage the phases and total project cost, plan to utilize the client's personnel wherever possible.
- Identify the tasks required in detail for the next phase.
- Typically, phases are estimated in 4–8 hour blocks of time (At $250 per hour, you can see how you can limit the client's cost to $1,000 to $2,000 within these blocks of time.). If this is a small project, 2-hour blocks would be common. Don't try to estimate price down to the half hour because there are too many surprises.

When it comes to pricing a phase or a project, several factors can drive price up or down. Consider each of the following (as well as combinations of them) before quoting any prices to a client regarding a potential MTBA engagement:

- *Timeframe.* When will the project start, and when does it have to be completed? The narrower the timeframe, the higher the rate. The longer the timeframe, the more flexible the rate. When a client calls you and demands your availability the day after tomorrow, and you have to make arrangements to accommodate that demand, then it makes sense that your time should be billed at premium rates. If a project calls for you to complete it in record time or under tight deadlines, once again, the price for your work should go up.

- *Client work.* Is the client contributing personnel, or is your firm supplying all the labor? Logically, the more work your employees are expected to perform, the higher the project price tag, but the more leverage you have. Therefore, your personnel hourly rate flexibility is likely to increase. The more work the client is willing to perform, the lower the project price tag, and the less flexibility you should allow your rate structure. Why? Because when you are leveraging the use of your client's personnel, your work is going to be confined primarily to high-level project planning, orchestrating, managing, coordinating, monitoring and review, which are all premium rate work activities.

- *Documentation.* What are the documentation requirements? The more documentation required (especially if numerous memos must be entered into the file due to the liability exposure of the project), the more you have to charge. Documentation typically comes down to two elements: quantity and quality. If you are responsible for maintaining both, factor in additional dollars to cover your administrative burden. Whenever possible, we try to off-load the burden of meeting documentation to the client because rarely can we bill as much time as the effort requires. This way, our involvement is limited to the review and editing of the information, an effort that takes considerably less time and converts to a bill that is palatable to the client.

- *Experience.* What is your experience performing this type of project? If the work you are being asked to do stretches your 15+ years of experience, then the project price, or your rate, should go up. If you have little experience in a particular area, or the work could easily be done by less experienced personnel, then your standard rate, or a competitive price, would be more in order.

- *Work schedule.* Who controls the work schedule? If you can come and go as you please, filling in gaps of availability in your schedule, then a competitive or lower rate might be justifiable. When the client regularly demands your appearance based on their schedule and timetable, then you certainly should be at standard rates or higher.

- *Politics.* This is one of the most common billing factors that is overlooked. Is the project one that will involve more than normal company politics? This is also a factor that is constantly underrated. Company politics burden the MTBA's work in every company. However, some companies are far worse than others. Be careful when taking on family business engagements, for example. It's easy to think you can just get in and do your job. But what you quickly find out is that you have to spend an inordinate amount of time sitting between powerful fighting factions within the organization. These fighting factions often feel that updating the other one is a waste of money. So you are caught in the middle arguing over higher than normal fees because the reality of the job is that you have to keep everyone informed in many complex projects. Obviously, the more political the project, the higher the risk and the higher the price.

An easy rule of thumb is ... the more departments (or in a family business, the more executive-level family members) that are involved in a project, the more political that project will be.

- *Retainer.* Is a replenishable retainer part of the fee arrangement? This is simply a financial consideration. Certainly, it makes sense that if you are holding a client's money and applying your charges against that money, that client is more likely to deserve some concession, be it price or otherwise.

- *Number of hours committed.* What is the magnitude of time and fees this project will consume? Generally speaking, the more hours the project involves, the better break on fees the client should expect. This is not a new concept, it's simply volume-buying. The shorter the project, the less discounting should be considered, or even premium rates might be in order.

  While the following is a theoretical statement, we make it to relay a point. When you sit and talk with a client, during the first few hours, they are getting access to an encyclopedia of knowledge gained from years of experience at the "hard-knocks institute" for next to nothing. After the discussion has rambled on for 40 or 50 hours, these same clients mostly are accessing day-to-day capabilities, which include your logic, gut instinct, business savvy, and implementation skills. The point is that your hourly fee for the first few hours should be thousands of dollars per hour, and after 10–20 hours, your rate should approximate your standard rate. When you start to accumulate hundreds of hours on a project, then a discounted rate is fair for the value provided. By this time, you are figuring out many of the issues as you go. So in theory, the more work you do for a client, the less significant the leverage they access for their fee. So it makes sense that the greater the number of days your client commits to, the more consideration should be given to discounting hourly fees. This theory also makes you think twice about how little you charge (or conversely, what a deal you're giving) those clients that pick your brain for a few hours every few months. Doubling your rate might be more in order for them.

Another analogy we use in our firm is to compare ourselves to a hotel. Whether the hotel is fully occupied or almost empty, the overhead it takes to run our operation doesn't vary that much. However, when you reserve a room early, you get access to discounted rates. When you demand a room at the last minute while a convention is in town, you'll likely get the worst room for the highest price. When you guarantee to stay a certain number of nights per year, depending on the magnitude of that commitment, deep discounts are given with greater access to quality rooms.

We have some of the same dynamics at work in our profession. Yet as we travel the country, so many firms pretend that each person has a rate appropriate for every hour of their time. This is certainly true if there is always a queue of work waiting that requires the same effort and experience. However, in most firms, this level of consistent activity only occurs during tax time or during a few large audits and, even then, changes in the expertise likely are required for different tasks within the project. This is why we have changed our pricing

Figure 8-1: **Pricing Model—Rates vs. Hours Demanded by Client Project**

structure to look toward the above factors to determine how much to deviate from standard pricing (both up and down), or which rate is appropriate for the project at hand.

Over the years, we have found that there also should be a threshold on discounting fees for volume. In our previous description, we say "that the greater the number of days your client commits to, the more consideration should be given to discounting hourly fees." In our hotel analogy, we also mention that when the hotel is at capacity, you get the highest price available for the worst room. So here is our retraction of volume-discounting in context of both of these scenarios. Instead of "discounting fees" being directly proportional to the "number of hours consumed by the client" (forming a straight line), that pricing model should look more like figure 8-1 (a stretched "U"). So fees should be at their highest with very short projects, and then as clients commit to using more time, discounts are appropriate. Those discounts can be appropriate due to likely gains in our firm's overall utilization because so much time is being extended to one project. However, at some point, as clients demand more of your time, they actually are buying time in excess of your capacity. As you sell off that remaining capacity, you create additional problems for your organization to service your other clients. Therefore, it is common to see rates being discounted as projects grow, but at some point, those same rates start increasing again because the length of this project either (1) makes conducting your normal business more difficult, or (2) increases the firm's risk because too much work is being done for one client.

As you consider this more complex rate adjustment system, consider this hardly discussed fact:

Underestimation of our value is what we do best.

The best way we know to ensure that your compensation is fair for both your firm and your client is to price each phase or project, or both, only after considering the factors listed previously first individually, then as a group. How they interact with each other plays a big role too.

For example, if we are hired to complete a project under a tight deadline with quality documentation in a highly political environment, then we likely would estimate the project at our standard hourly fees and then double that amount. If the project is very competitive and our overall fees are not as negotiable, then we take a counter approach. We look at each of the criteria and determine a way to contractually limit their impact. For example, to limit documentation exposure in a strategic planning engagement, we would demand as part of our proposal that someone from the client's office write up the notes from the planning sessions and forward them to us for review and editing. As a safeguard against a highly political environment, we would demand a refillable retainer as part of the contract. If the deadline was very tight, we would specify the exact expected outputs and implement a formal change-order process to insure the communication of the impact of project modifications. It boils down to this: Consideration and incorporation of pricing factors and phasing are keys to profitably pricing engagements.

Commissions and Contingent Fees: Where Do They Fit in?

Commissions and contingent fees are here to stay. Now part of the present, commissions and contingent fees will be more and more a part of the future. Let's consider when and how these can be used to your benefit.

First, we'd like to paraphrase a recent *Journal of Accountancy* article:

> If you are engaged to perform audits, compilations, or reviews for clients, then you can't charge your client a commission during the period of engagement unless it is by a ruling of the court. However, if you are not engaged to perform the attest function, thereby obviating the opportunity of an independence issue arising, you can charge commissions and/or contingent fees. However, disclosure is required.

Some state boards of public accountancy have added a little more bite to the disclosure mentioned in the AICPA article. For example, we interpret the Texas State Board of Public Accountancy, in section 501.13 (Payment and Commissions) under *Rules of Professional Conduct*, this way: "Any time commissions are to be paid, a written disclosure specific as to source and amount must be acknowledged by the client before any party becomes contractually bound."

Charging commissions and contingent fees for nonattest projects is an issue that has been violently opposed for years. The rules as they are today came about because the AICPA settled with the Federal Trade Commission in order to protect the attest function. This position was taken because a strong case was made that licensing restrictions regarding commissions would be restraint of trade for CPAs. Because of this, we believe that the potential of future restrictions regarding this topic are infinitesimal. Each CPA needs to consider ways to incorporate or compete with the effects of these relaxed restrictions. Obviously, your latitude in this area varies from state to state. However, by ignoring the changes occurring in this area, you may find yourself seriously disadvantaged in upcoming competitive situations.

Some ideas regarding when charging a commission or contingent fee might be advantageous include

- charging a percentage of
  - funds raised in a financing scenario.
  - the revenues of the acquisition target.
  - negotiated lease or note reduction.
  - percentage of sales or excise tax overpayment discovered.
  - increased profits for some specific period of time after a marketing MTBA engagement.

The point is the possibilities are limited only by your resourcefulness. Commissions and contingent fees boil down to a risk-versus-reward decision. If you are willing to gamble that your efforts will produce the desired outcome, then you can leverage your income by charging a results-oriented fee. This leverage occurs because people often are willing to share a greater percentage of their gain than they will pay in upfront costs that have no guarantee of positive results. But remember that many variables can enter into how well the client's people do regarding their part of any implementation. As well, have you pinned down exactly how the metric being used will be calculated? For example, consider the last point previously listed about sharing in the increased profits after a marketing engagement: how will you control what the owners run through the income statement when determining bottom line profit?

Before We Move On

Earlier, you were asked to take out a blank sheet of paper and respond to the following situation:

> You have a bookkeeping client for whom you prepare monthly financial statements. She pays you $500 a month. She recently commented that she would like to bring this function in-house. Your client is willing to use the same software you use in-house to do her monthly processing. What will you charge her to make this transition?

As we mentioned, it's now time to redo this exercise. We have included an Engagement Pricing Form on the following page to facilitate this process. This time, think about whether there should be a short investigative Phase I. In other words, is installing your general ledger system really the right solution? What about training on either the hardware or software? If you included training in your estimate, was it a fixed cost? What happens if it takes more time to train than anticipated? Did you assume that you did all the set-up (like installing Windows, the new accounting software, or any other related applications), or did you have the client install everything but your data files? Did you provide your client with a total fixed fee for the project, or did you identify the phases required and only provide an estimate for each one? Did you allow yourself a large enough margin of error in your estimate? Although there is no right answer, the ideas discussed in this chapter may have given you a few extra tools and a little more leeway the next time you are asked to price a service.

Typically, this exercise reveals either one of two things, or both. First, we normally estimate price too conservatively, missing important project steps or phases as well as underestimating the time to complete each one. Second, we tend to estimate projects in too exacting of a manner. An estimate is just that: an estimate. The original number you identified at the beginning of the "Estimating" section of this chapter should have been rounded up, for example, to the nearest $250 or $500. We often see numbers like $935 or $2,150 compared to $1,000 or $2,500. The difference comes in client perception. A number like $935, much more so than a number like $1,000, will set your client's expectation that you know exactly what his or her particular project will cost, which is a fact we rarely really know.

We have included another form as well at the end of this chapter. You guessed it: a self-assessment exercise. You know the drill. This is a personal exercise, one that is easy to skip over. But as we have stated each time, it's an important process that you should participate in so that you can better identify the changes you want to incorporate into your MTBA capabilities.

Given all of this, take time now to fill out the Engagement Pricing Form (exercise 8-1) and then compare this price estimate to the one you completed earlier. Finally, complete the Self-Assessment Form (exercise 8-2).

Exercise 8-1

Engagement/Phase Pricing Form

Client:_____

Project: _____

Current Phase Name: _____

Task	Hours	Rate	Total

Total For This Phase:

Remaining Phases: Name	Approx. Hrs.	Dollar Est.

	Total Project Estimate:

Exercise 8-2

Self-Assessment Timeline Relative to Utilizing the Techniques Discussed in This Chapter

Based on the materials covered in this chapter, please take a few moments and assess your weaknesses. Then, using the form below, make note of any skills you plan to work on as well as a timeframe to reassess your progress. In addition, if there are activities or exercises, or both you plan on attempting, jot them down and note your intended completion date. This form is provided solely as a self-improvement tool.

Name: _____

The following are skills I plan to improve:

- _____ By when: _____
- _____ By when: _____
- _____ By when: _____
- _____ By when: _____
- _____ By when: _____
- _____ By when: _____
- _____ By when: _____
- _____ By when: _____
- _____ By when: _____

The following are activities I plan to attempt:

- _____ By when: _____
- _____ By when: _____
- _____ By when: _____
- _____ By when: _____
- _____ By when: _____
- _____ By when: _____
- _____ By when: _____
- _____ By when: _____
- _____ By when: _____

9

Advanced Advisory Skills and Practices: Conducting Effective Sales Calls With Clients and Prospects

"Approach each new problem not with a view of finding what you hope will be there, but to get the truth, the realities that must be grappled with."

~ BERNARD M. BARUCH

Where We've Come From

Up to this point we have covered why the most trusted business advisor (MTBA) Framework is important to implement, tips on how to improve your communication skills, and some ideas and techniques that should help you function effectively as your clients' MTBA. We've also discussed pricing, organizing, and delivering advisory and consulting services. If you actively embrace and implement what you've read and learned in the first eight chapters, you will be on your way to being a successful, or even more successful, MTBA to your clients.

We encourage you to continue in your development and not stop at learning what we've addressed thus far. By taking the time to review this chapter's material on advanced skills and techniques, you should find yourself positioned to be even more effective.

Going Even Further

For those of you who wish to take your MTBA and advisory services to the next level, this chapter will explain how to prequalify prospects, how to frame up engagements, and how to close the deal on new engagements. While this material should quickly prove to be helpful in building your advisory work backlog, it also will help prepare you to better identify and close any type of work with your prospects or clients. As well, this text provides guidance about a process for calling on prospects or clients and then working with them to define and agree to the terms of an engagement.

To do this, we will cover a variety of calls: the Discovery Call, the Sales Call, and the Consulting Call (Advisory Call). Structurally speaking, all three types of calls have a great deal in common. All of them have an investigation phase and a closing phase. Within each of these phases, there is significant similarity in the methodology. However, each call type has a different objective; therefore, the structure varies to accommodate that difference. And by the way, please don't be put off by our references to "sales" or "sales calls." These are not dirty words. In any business or profession, all of us are involved in sales of one type or another. It is not demeaning to "sell" services that clients need. In fact, by conducting effective Discovery Calls, you can avoid wasting time with nonqualified prospects. At the Sales Call, you can avoid chasing economic rabbits down business process holes that lead to nowhere because the client has no budget for the work or the net results of a change are outweighed by the cost to make the change. Similarly, when it comes to the Sales Call, what you are doing is helping the client frame up the issue, the solution to address it, the approach to be used, and what success looks like. Don't you think this type of framework will make life simpler for you? We can most assuredly state, from our own experience, that it will indeed! Before we get into detail about each, take a moment and review the outlines of all three calls.

The Structured Discovery Call

The Discovery Call is comprised of the following phases and activities:

- Investigation Phase
  — Introduction
  — Become acquainted with the business
  — Qualify the prospect
- Closing Phase
  — Abbreviated sales pitch
  — Identification of the next step
  — Seek agreement

The Structured Sales Call

The Sales Call is comprised of the following phases and activities:

- Investigation Phase
  — The opening
  — Information gathering
- Closing Phase
  — Sales pitch
  — Our approach
  — Summary
  — The close

The Structured Consulting or Advisory Call

The Consulting or Advisory Call is comprised of the following phases and activities:

- Investigation Phase
  — Relating
  — Discovery and interviewing
- Closing Phase
  — Review of findings and identification of suggestions
  — Presentation of action plan
  — Persuading and facilitating
  — Supporting

As we stated earlier, the objectives for each call are different:

- For the Discovery Call, the objective is to qualify, qualify, and qualify.
- For the Sales Call, the objective is to close, close and close.
- For the Consulting or Advisory Call, the objective is to solve, solve and solve.

When you look at each call outline, notice the similarity. A question that could easily come to mind is, "How can the steps be so similar, yet be effective with call objectives so different?" Well, at a conceptual level, all three call types come from the same methodology, The Sales Call. But in practice, because the implementation is different, we have incorporated some unique wording in the processes to highlight their nuances. Each call type requires the MTBA or consultant to (1) uncover relevant information, and (2) do something with that information.

Uncovering Relevant Information

In a sense, to be effective in this phase of the calls, your investigative skills will be seriously challenged. For example, with the Discovery Call, before you commit a great deal of your time, you need to uncover the following:

- When is the project expected to get underway and to be completed?
- Who will be involved in making the final hiring decision?
- What is the budget for this project?
- How high is this project's priority to the organization?

The answers to these questions will *qualify* the prospect or client and help you identify the appropriate next step. If the next step is a Sales Call, then once again, your investigative skills will be taken to task. In the sales call, you are trying to determine what will motivate the prospect or client to buy your services. Therefore, your mission is to uncover the following:

- Information that identifies the client's concerns
- Whether these are concerns for which you can provide assistance or find people in your network to address
- What creates enough urgency for the client to hire your organization
- Expected benefits that your involvement will bring
- Whether those benefits are worthy of the expected price to obtain them

When you have found the answers to these questions, then your chances of closing new advisory or consulting opportunities have improved exponentially. If you don't know the answers, then most likely, you will attempt to "close on air," which has a high failure rate (we will have more on this later). As for our final call, the Consulting or Advisory Call, our focus is to dig deeper and obtain enough detailed information about the client's concerns that possible solutions can be determined. The difference is "cut-off." Consider figure 9-1, "Call Information." The shaded box represents all the information available about a particular business. The cut-off point for each call type is where the line intersects with the box. Note that in order to achieve the desired outcomes for each call type, a different level of understanding about the company should be uncovered during the process. As you can see, the Discovery Call requires the least amount of depth regarding company-specific information. On the other hand, the consulting call requires the greatest amount of company knowledge.

Figure 9-1: **Call Information**

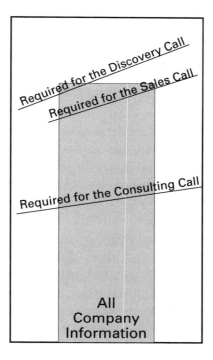

In the Discovery Call, we just need to ask a few basic questions in order to differentiate a "tire kicker" (someone more interested in pretending to buy than actually buying) from a legitimate prospect. Then, we try to understand the urgency and budget of the project so the most effective course of action can be taken to close the sale (assuming it is a sale worthy of closing). With the Discovery Call, the cut-off is very high (little company information needs to be uncovered) because the focus is on qualifying the buyer, not understanding the business.

With the Sales Call, our understanding of the company has to go deeper in order to identify the business concerns and anticipated impact of our involvement. We are trying to find ways we can help the organization that deliver savings or profit opportunities, or both, far greater than the cost of our participation. But the call type requiring the greatest understanding of the business, by far, is the Consulting or Advisory Call. With this call, we need to get a broad enough understanding of each problem so that we can determine the following:

- Causes of the problem
- Conditions that exaggerate or diminish it
- What has been tried in the past to correct it
- What are some of the probable fixes at this time
- Skill level required to implement the suggested solutions
- Potential cost and benefit of each solution

Too often, CPAs ignore the lines in the Call Information graphic. For example, during the information gathering stage of the Sales Call, rather than getting the last bit of information needed to wrap-up and close the business, CPAs often prematurely jump directly into the discovery and interviewing stage of the Consulting Call. This usually not only blows the effectiveness of the sales call, but puts the CPA in the position of giving away free advisory or consulting advice. Why do we do this? We are not sure. But our guess is that as CPAs, we not only have been trained, but our professional ethics tell us that we can't take on any work unless we have the skills to do it. Therefore, during the sales call, we actually try to gather enough information to determine the specific approach we would use to solve the problem in order to verify that we meet the skills test.

The problem with this type of behavior is that half (to sometimes all) the working time of a CPA functioning as an MTBA or as a consultant often is spent determining a logical approach to solving the problem. We are reminded of an experience that happened some time ago when a large hospital asked Bill's CPA firm to bid on a contract to provide business advice and administrative support to each new doctor setting up an office in their about-to-open hospital. This was a big project, especially for Bill's new firm, which was just created after spinning off from another one. They were primarily competing against three of the Big 6 firms. Bill's firm was included because of the exposure of his weekly newspaper column and a couple of other very visible projects he had worked on.

They put together a lengthy proposal, which they rarely did otherwise. (There is more on our criteria for preparing proposals later in the "Billing and Engagement Considerations" chapter). An exhibit in this proposal was a two-page outline of all of the steps they would take to assist each new doctor. After the hospital administrator reviewed all of the proposals, Bill's firm and one other were selected as finalists. Both firms were asked to prepare an extended proposal providing even greater detail about their planned approach. Bill's firm responded by stating that they were not going to update the proposal, but that they would be delighted to perform the request for fee. However, the competing firm provided the enhanced proposal. To our knowledge, no firm was ever hired by the hospital to help the doctors in the manner suggested in the proposal. Why? Because the hospital decided it could do much of the work internally. Dom's former CPA firm had a similar experience with some organizational change consulting for a regional building department (government agency) where the Executive Director just took his firm's approach, fleshed it out, and handled the situation internally. The point here is that what we do best—and our most unique work product—is how we approach the work (the plan). After you have given away the plan, people with far less skill than us can implement it. That's why it is so important to differentiate between information you are gathering and delivering in order to close a sale versus information needed to determine what you would do to improve the situation.

The single biggest problem CPAs have in the implementation of the various calls is that we lose sight of what we are trying to accomplish during the investigation phase of each call type. We always need to keep in mind this one critical distinction. Because you've just been introduced to how we differentiate these call types, we feel it is important to summarize again.

- In the Discovery Call, all we are trying to determine is what kind or level of attention the prospect or client needs now, from immediate personal attention to just sending information in the mail or by e-mail.
- With the Sales Call, we are asking questions in order to identify problems or concerns that carry a sense of urgency and to find expected results that will justify the fees we would charge for our involvement.
- The investigation we perform in a Consulting Call is to dig deeper into the problem areas in order to arrive at a plan of attack. The plan of attack is definitely, unquestionably, a "for fee" function. As noted earlier, by outlining in excruciating detail the blueprint for helping doctors, the hospital decided that it didn't need any of us. So although the concept of the investigation process is similar in all three call types, in reality, they are not structured to uncover the same information.

One last note: don't worry about failing the professional ethics test of not having the right skills. This book reminds you of all the skills you need, all of which you already have (even though some fine tuning may be in order). For example, you may not be able to install a network, but you are more than capable of identifying processes that are ripe for automation. Being able to identify, manage, and facilitate necessary change within your clients' organizations is the most important skill to bring to the table. Once you have identified the issues that need further investigation or need to be addressed, or both, the client (with your assistance as the General Contractor) can hire the necessary specialists. And if you possess a required specialized skill or two, that's icing on the cake.

With this explanation and distinction behind us, let's first take a closer look at the Discovery Call.

The Structured Discovery Call

Let's start out by reviewing our call outline:

- Investigation Phase
  — Introduction
  — Become acquainted with the business
  — Qualify the prospect
- Closing Phase
  — Abbreviated sales pitch
  — Identification of the next step
  — Seek agreement

Next, let's review our call objective. It is to qualify, qualify, and qualify. The Discovery Call usually is made via a phone call. Why? Because you typically are responding to a request for information, a referral from a client, a telemarketing lead, or a number of other blind inquiries. The phone call is your best approach because it allows you to determine, in a fairly short period of time,

- the interest level of the inquiry
- whether there is work to be done.
- if it's the kind of work that should be profitable;
- whether you can perform the work given the project's timetable, and so on.

These are typically "lukewarm" calls (as opposed to "cold" calls) because they are invited; however, you have little to no idea where they might lead. You might find a $50,000 fee per year opportunity or someone who is trying to gather information for a term paper in school. That's why the Discovery Call's objective is to qualify the prospect or client to see what the best course of action is. Before we look at this call type in detail, note that we will be referring to the contact person as a *prospect*. Why? Because this is the process for determining whether there is any opportunity or desire to convert this person or business from being a prospect (a potential candidate to be a client) to becoming an actual client. Without further adieu, the following contains more detail on each phase of the Discovery Call.

Discovery Call—Introduction

The introduction in the Discovery Call is very brief, usually just a sentence or two. For example, here's a scripted opening we would use with a typical phone call:

> Hello, my name is Dom Cingoranelli, and I am a CPA with the CPA/consulting firm of Cingoranelli and Reeb. I am calling in response to your request <u>for more information regarding our planning services</u>. Is now a good time for you to talk?

The underlined portion of this script has a variety of inserts depending on your organization's promotional approach. Some firms might offer a free tax review, a free hour of consulting, a free information packet (a do-it-yourself type of document or book), a free first phase of a project, or similar incentives to entice the prospect to respond. In addition, this script works equally well on almost any lukewarm telephone solicitation, such as responding to a client referral lead.

If the prospect doesn't have time to talk when you call him or her, immediately respond by asking when would be a good time and volunteering to call back then. Assuming that now is an okay time to proceed, the next step follows.

Discovery Call—Become Acquainted With the Business

It is at this point in your script that you need to identify a question or two that will facilitate a discussion of the background of the person or company you are calling upon. You are just trying to solicit a brief introduction so that you will have a general feel for the size of the business, the industry it is in, number of employees, and related, high-level information as applicable. Therefore, a comment such as, "Before we get started, could you tell me a little about your business (yourself)?" is one of our default questions. A question that could follow this one might be, "Can you tell me what caught your interest in <u>our mailing</u> (the underlined portion could also be substituted by phrases such as "our telemarketing call," "your conversation with our client," and so on) enough to request <u>more information</u> (or , "a return call," or "a tax return review," for example.)?

If the prospect says he or she was referred to your firm, you also should add, "That's great to hear. Can you share with me who referred you? We like to be able to thank everyone who refers us to someone else" Then make a note and be sure to call or send, at a minimum, a handwritten note of thanks to the referral source.

As we said earlier, only a couple of questions are required at this stage.

Discovery Call—Qualify the Prospect

Once you have a view of the business from about 30,000 feet, it's time to move on to the most important part of this call: qualification. *Qualifying* prospects is simply asking them a series of questions to find out whether they are really in the market for a specific service, who is going to make the decision, when, and why. People who don't take this step seriously find themselves wasting an inordinate amount of time and giving away a bundle of free advice. They fall prey to the infamous "tire-kicker," who we introduced earlier in this chapter. Tire-kickers love to talk to you and barrage you with questions for the sole purpose of uncovering your approach to solving their various problems. So how do you smoke these people out? You can eliminate about 95 percent of them by qualifying them using the following questions and techniques.

The first issue to address is timeframe. Ask the potential client, "What is your timeframe for getting this project underway," or "When do you want this [some service] to be completed." It's amazing what people say when you ask them direct questions. With just one or two direct questions, you'll find many tire-kickers confessing right then and there that they are just looking for information. Once a date or period is identified, you have taken a giant step in starting to determine how to best allocate your time regarding this prospect. Often, the caller states that the timeframe for starting the project is still months away, but that his or her organization is in the information-gathering stage. This is exactly the kind of data you are trying to uncover because instead of setting up a face-to-face appointment, a more appropriate strategy might be to send information about your firm and references and set up a meeting a little closer to the decision date. Why? Because you want to make your sales pitch as close to the decision-making time as possible. There's a general rule in selling which translates to whoever is the last to impress has the greatest chance of success.

If you show up and make a great impression three months too early, by the time the client narrows the field, you easily can get left out because others are etched more firmly in the client's mind. It's the old adage of "out of sight, out of mind." However, with larger engagements, the strategy is a little different due to the longer selling cycle. So although being visible close to the decision point is critical regardless of engagement size, with very large engagements, getting in early plays an important role too. For example, arriving on the scene early for a $50,000 or greater project can provide you with an incredible advantage. This occurs because you might get the chance to mold the requirements of the proposal process to best suit your organization. And as everyone knows, the closer the skill set required to do the project match those of your firm, the more likely you are of being awarded the project.

Therefore, understanding the decision timeframe is a strategic piece of information. You want to maintain your visibility throughout the process by staying in touch with the potential client, with the vast majority of your face-to-face energy expended near the time the decision is to be made.

The next critical piece of information to collect is who the decision maker is. This is a tough question to ask, and most versions of the question cause more harm than good. For this reason, we ask you to memorize these words:

Besides yourself, is there anyone else who will be involved in making the final decision?

This question assumes the person you are talking to is a decision maker.

 Keep In Mind

One of the base rules of communication is never challenge either someone's status or independence.

This is a concept we included in our communication framework based on the book *You Just Don't Understand*, by Debra Tannen, Ph.D. Without going into much detail, recall the comment we made in a previous chapter that once a threat is perceived, all communication is over. According to Dr. Tannen's book (and our experience as well), anytime you challenge someone's status or independence, you are likely to threaten that person. And if you do, you have an uphill battle to either get good information or close the business.

You see, if you ask the question, "Are you the one that's going to make the final decision?" you've created a high-risk, low reward situation. What happens when the person is the only decision maker? You'll hear a confident and potentially arrogant reply, "Yes!" So, you were lucky, you dodged a bullet. Because this person is the only decision maker, he or she rarely would take offense and often be delighted with the wording of the inquiry.

But what happens if the person you are speaking with is not the only decision maker, or worse yet, is not a decision maker at all? You have put the inquirer in the position of having to admit to you that they are unimportant and just a pawn in the information gathering process. In this situation, you have not gained an ally. You may have embarrassed someone that could help you get the job.

By asking the question the way we suggest, regardless of the inquirer's position in this process, no one has to lose face. The interesting part of this is that by including someone as a decision maker with the expectation that more people are likely to be involved as well, callers seem to readily admit their position without feeling backed into a corner.

Given all of this, why is it so important to know who is making the decision? Because the worst position you can get yourself into is selling your services through someone. We are not saying that you don't have to appease and provide support to the decision gatekeepers. But from the beginning of the sales or consulting process, you have to set your sights on being face-to-face with the people who call the shots. They often are referred to as the *economic buyers*. Otherwise, you will spend an inordinate amount of time convincing the wrong person to do business with you. You can rest assured that 9 times out of 9.1, if you can't get at least minimal visibility with the decision makers or economic buyers, you might as well be throwing money out the window because the odds of your selling efforts turning into revenue are virtually none.

The next question to ask pertains to the project's budget. This is not a sensitive question to ask, even though you may not get an answer. Something like, "How much have you budgeted for this project?" or "What did you plan on spending?" are acceptable alternatives. You need to know this information in order to assess reasonability. If the client won't divulge their budget, then suggest some broad price ranges in order to level-set their expectations. For example, make a comment like, "The past few strategic planning meetings we have facilitated, depending on the nuances each client has requested, ranged from $12,000 to $20,000." What you are trying to avoid is the client saying all the right things, is clearly ready to go, but has an unrealistic expectation of fees. If you don't qualify on price, it is easy to find yourself expending a great deal of effort only to find out that the client expects a $10,000 service delivered for a $1,000 fee. We have a philosophy at our firm that is appropriate to reiterate here:

> When a potential client expects far more than can be delivered for a price far less than is reasonable, this is the kind of prospect that needs a map detailing the directions to your fiercest competitor.

Once a prospect acknowledges a price range that is within the realm of reasonableness, the last question we ask concerns priority. Simply stated, "What's the priority of this project to your organization?" This is a more important question to ask when working with larger companies than with smaller ones. For example, when your prospect is a $10 million dollar company, you likely are interfacing with the owner or the senior management team, and we might not even ask this question. The involvement of the owner or board is clear enough that the project has a high priority. On the other hand, when the company is a $500 million dollar organization and certainly larger, you likely are dealing with middle management. And their focus is driven by the priority of the project dictated to them. Therefore, their commitment to any project can change in a heartbeat if the orders come down from above to reassign resources. For example, if we had a meeting with a Fortune 1,000 company, then this would be a very important question to ask. As well, some issues don't need the additional priority question because the situation alone signifies urgency. For example, there is no need for the priority question if a prospect said, "I am very dissatisfied with my CPA, and I just learned I am being audited and am looking for a new CPA firm to respond to the letter I received."

Basically, we are trying to determine whether this is the president's pet project, was mandated by the board, is an identified component within the strategic plan, is just one of many projects going on simultaneously, or something totally different. The higher the priority, the more urgency it has, and the more likely the client is focused on getting the project completed. The investigation being conducted by the client is often to find skill sets, not justification. The lower the priority, the more important justification may become in our efforts. In other words, the client may have little commitment to the project but is testing for feasibility. Under this circumstance, it may be up to you to create a sense of urgency and identify lost opportunity or overexpended costs in the scenario where no action is taken. Logically speaking, the lower the priority, the greater the possibility that the project will be canceled or postponed.

Going back to our telephone script, here's a summary of the kinds of questions you might ask in this stage of the call:

- *Timeframe:* "What is your time-frame for getting this project underway?" or "When do you want this [some service] to be completed?"
- *Decision-maker:* "Besides yourself, is there anyone else who will be involved in making the final decision?"
- *Budget:* "How much have you budgeted for this project?," or "What did you plan on spending?"
- *Priority:* "What's the priority of this project to your organization?"

Once you have asked, and the client has satisfactorily answered all four of these questions, you have performed the essential time-saving, tire-kicker avoiding job of qualifying. Does it always work? No, but almost always. And typically, based on the answers to these questions, a selling strategy will unfold. You may have to drop everything in order to respond, or you might create a plan to stay in touch with the client over the next few months so that when the urgency increases, you are in a position to step in and take on the business. The main thing is that by qualifying your prospects every time, you avoid the free exchange of billable time for wasted time.

Discovery Call—Sales Pitch

This is the first stage of the closing phase of the Discovery call. By this time, you have spent 5–10 minutes finding out about the business and qualifying the prospect. You already have expended the bulk of your time commitment, and you are only a few minutes from finishing this call. Before you tell the prospect what you think, the next course of action should be providing a brief introduction to your firm's capabilities.

The question to answer during this exercise is why is your firm special? This is done by reviewing the firm's credentials, describing its various services, identifying its employees' diverse levels of experience, and conveying a sense of compassion and caring for the welfare of the client. There are a million ways to approach this part of the call. But to ensure that you don't ramble at a point you need to appear the most confident, jot some notes down about points you want to make. An example of something we might say would be as follows:

> "Our firm is made up of four CPAs, one programmer/analyst and three administrators. Because of our small size, when you hire us, you work directly with the owners. You are not immediately transferred to a person with just a few years of experience. We have a mission statement at our firm that's short, but gets to the heart of why we think our clients do business with us. Our mission statement is, "Turning Vision into Reality." We work

as closely as you want us to in order to help you identify and implement *your* plan for success. We want to be more than your CPA firm; we want to be one of the reasons for your future success."

Although this may sound hokey, it's the way we feel, and it is an approach that has served us well. Interestingly enough, it's the way many small businesses want their advisor organizations to feel. So we use it to our advantage. Sculpt any narrative you are comfortable with that will allow you to quickly and succinctly share with your prospect why you are the firm of choice. However, if you have determined that this prospect is not worth pursuing, you might want to skip this stage altogether. You don't want them holding on tight as you are trying to walk away because your sales pitch about the firm was too good. Anyway, as soon as you've said your piece or skipped it because you want to send this prospect elsewhere, it's time to identify and go to the next step.

But before we go to the next step, what if you think you'd like to pursue the project, but now the prospective buyer starts raising objections about your qualifications based on the sales pitch you just made? First, never shirk from addressing questions or rebutting objections—they are simply opportunities to succeed. Unexpressed questions or objections are a death knell because you don't know they are an issue, and you never get a chance to address them head on.

Second, always be prepared with answers for some common or expected questions and objections such as, "From your introduction, it doesn't sound like you have worked with a company like ours (perhaps a company of that size, the specific industry it's in, or the way that ownership is held)." Don't get scared off by this. You now have a chance to position yourself and your firm wherever you are strongest. Have you worked with other companies in a similar industry or of a similar size? And even if you have not, the project you're interested in very often requires skill sets or processes that most likely cut across type of industry, type of ownership, and size of the company. So rather than focus your answer on what you don't have, use this opportunity to recast the question so that your answer makes it clear that you have a lot of experience solving their type of issue or problem. At this stage, a confident rebuttal to some of the standard objections will almost always be enough to allow you to pass to the next stage of the buying process if that is your desire.

Discovery Call—Identification of the Next Step

Usually, the Discovery Call ends up with one of the following outcomes, organized in order from highest to lowest qualified:

- Face-to-face appointment at their office.
- Face-to-face appointment at your office.
- Sending additional information, including your business card and a note that states you will be calling on a specific date if you haven't heard from them.
- Call-back note to your files. Although these prospects are found to be worthy of more of your time, they are not ready to meet with you yet, and there is no information appropriate to send. This is one of the main justifications for a general brochure about your firm because this is a situation where you can put something about your

organization in the prospect's hands, even though it really doesn't address any specific issues. Nowadays, your Web site or downloads from your Web site should be serving as, or allowing prospects to download, your general brochure information if you've designed it properly and kept it up to date. Therefore, an e-mail contact asking your prospect to check out something specific on your Web site should work great here.

- Sending additional information via e-mail (best if augmented by reference to your Web site or a specific download), including your business card (or v-card) and a note asking them to call if they ever need anything in the future.
- Referral to another organization more appropriate for meeting their needs.
- Referral to a competitor because you want this prospect to waste someone else's time, preferably someone who is constantly getting in your way on good business opportunities.

Based on the information you gained during the investigation phase (the introduction, becoming acquainted with the business, and qualifying the prospect), it should be clear at this time what course of action you want to suggest. But before we go on, we want to remind you of something that may seem like a stupid comment to make. We are making it anyway because so many CPA MTBAs and consultants ignore it. Remember: A waste of time is a *waste of time*, regardless of how you package or document it.

Just because you have some time to spare or you felt too pushy to ask the preceding questions, you are not doing yourself or your business a favor by staying busy meeting with people who are not interested in buying anything from you. Even if you are very sophisticated in your use of communication and persuasion techniques, don't expend significant energy on prospects without promise. You undoubtedly have plenty of clients to work closely with as their MTBA already. And if not, go home and relax, play golf, or do something fun. The point is you should not set up face-to-face calls with clearly unqualified prospects. Your return on your time invested will only look good if "busy" is the sole criterion for success.

Discovery Call—Seek Agreement

The last stage of the closing phase of the Discovery Call is seeking agreement. After you have suggested one of the preceding alternatives (or any other alternative you create), ask the prospect if they agree with your approach. This is often as simple as, "Is this okay with you?" If it is not, find out why. If it is, all that is left to do is follow through. If this is just a note to your calendar and an information drop, that's easy. However, if the next step is to meet face-to-face in a sales call situation, that can be a lot harder. So we've included our 1-2-3 approach to making that sales process work in your favor.

The Sales Process

A common misconception exists that learning how to make a sales call is an exercise reserved for salespeople. This is disturbing because **everybody sells, regardless of job titles or duties**.

From the executives to the cleaning crew, those who develop the art of persuasion (with few exceptions) lead the pack. But before we start dissecting the structure behind selling, consider a few general issues. The first is once a prospect is qualified, selling opportunities should be conducted face-to-face whenever possible. So avoid selling over the phone.

Here are a few reasons why:

- Some of the issues being discussed may be complicated. These can be difficult to communicate over the phone. With face-to-face selling, you can utilize aids like sample documents, pictures, marker boards, and flip charts to clarify the material being presented.
- When your initial meeting is by phone, it rarely is billable. Even if you are hired to perform an advisory or consulting project via a phone conversation, often a free intro-ductory meeting is still scheduled. When your initial meeting is face-to-face, not only can you save time, but depending on the content of the meeting, it may be partially billable.
- Because the client hasn't hired you yet, a great deal of marketing still needs to be done. It is difficult to establish the kind of rapport required to close a deal via the phone. Also, you have little control over your selling environment when using the telephone. Therefore, face-to-face communication gives you an edge. You not only have greater control over the environment, but you can utilize visual tools in your marketing strategy.
- It is much easier to motivate clients into making a commitment when you are sitting across from them at a table. You also have the advantage in a face-to-face meeting of being able to read their nonverbal cues and adjust your behavior for more impact.

Feature, Benefit, Result

Now the stage is set. The prospect is in your office requesting assistance (or you are in theirs), but the prospect has yet to engage anyone to perform any work. Before we start selling, there's another issue to consider. Let's make sure we remember what we are really selling. The "feature, benefit, result" technique will help you stay focused.

Most people sell features and a few sell both features and benefits. However, only the best in your organization tend to incorporate results into the sales pitch. Consider the following:

> Assume you are attempting to sell a burglar alarm system. The feature is the physical electronic components. The benefit is a warning sound, which will occur should an intruder break the electronic barrier. But the result, and what the customer is looking to buy, is greater protection for the family. *People buy perceived results.*

Let's make the example a little more applicable to this situation. A new client comes to you seeking tax assistance. The feature is the tax return. This is the physical product you sell. The benefit is that the client can meet the information filing requirements imposed by the government. The anticipated result is two-fold: first, that the IRS will be satisfied and leave your client alone, and second, that you will have found most (if not all) the money they are entitled to. For the most part, we believe the results clients are trying to buy is peace of mind when they hire CPAs to prepare their tax returns. If you don't believe this, ask yourself this question: if you could legally and enforceably write your clients a letter that released them from all future tax liability regarding a particular year, would they care whether a tax return was filed?

We believe the answer is, "No." What motivates people to action (that is, creates a sense of urgency) is an expectation of results. Therefore, we need to incorporate results-oriented thinking into our sales kit by utilizing the "feature, benefit, result" technique. This is best accomplished by taking our clients' requests and breaking them down into features, benefits, and expected results to make sure we spend more time selling the results they are looking for-which is what the clients really is looking to buy in the first place.

The Structured Sales Call

It's time to begin pulling all of these tips and techniques together. These tools are most effective when incorporated into a logically organized selling strategy. Everyone approaches this a little differently, and that's fine. However, we offer the structure of our Sales Call as an alternative for you to consider. Its components are as follows:

- Investigation Phase
  — The opening
  — Information gathering
- Closing Phase
  — Sales pitch
  — Our approach
  — Summary
  — The close

Our version of the Sales Call has two phases with six total steps. As you can see, it is very similar to the Discovery Call. Just as with the Discovery Call, most of the time and effort is spent in the investigation phase, which is the first two steps of this process. Why? Because if you don't gather the right kind of information upfront, all the sales skills in the world won't help much during the closing phase. So let's jump right into the process, with the first stage being the the opening.

The Sales Call—Opening

The first few minutes of selling are political, not technical. The objectives are simple: introductions and rapport building.

Introductions

This step of the opening stage of the Sales Call not only includes introducing yourself and your staff (if present in the meeting), but making sure you know the client's name(s) and correct spelling(s). Commit these to memory. A technique we use is to immediately use any participant's name (and use it at least two or three more times in the first 10 minutes of the meeting) in the conversation like, "Well Joe, how did you find out about our firm?"

Additionally, during this step, we need to find out about the client's background, the company, and his or her authority within the company. This information is critical in order to gauge the kind of questions to ask later.

Finally, it is crucial for you to review in advance and consider the "first impression" issues introduced in our previous chapter in order to start this step of the call as positively as possible. Note that it is premature for you to begin selling the skills of your firm at this time. The objective of the introductions step of the opening is to move through the formality of meeting each other so you can begin to build rapport.

By the way, little things can make a big difference.

- *Be careful of seating arrangements.* If you sit next to a client at a table for a meeting, it might be too awkward to make eye contact. Always think about being able to make good eye contract with all those present. As well, don't trap the client. If two or more from your firm are making the sales call, avoid one of you sitting on each side of the client. If you do, besides potentially feeling trapped, you make it much harder for the client to maintain eye contact with both of you. A number of other issues also exist regarding seating, such as being cognizant of the formality created by putting a barrier or distance between you and the client or positioning yourselves so that you easily can use a flip chart or marker board.

- *Phrase introductions carefully.* Introduce yourself as a business consultant as well as a CPA to avoid being pigeonholed as a "tax guy." If someone else uses tax terminology to introduce you, say, "Although it's true that I have substantial expertise in tax and accounting, I spend a great deal of my time advising business owners on a variety of issues, such as ... (the blank can be filled in by whatever suits you, such as loan assistance, strategy, operational planning, marketing, technology implementation, and so forth.). Then continue by stating something like, "These are areas where I have been able to really add extra value to my client relationships in the past." The point is don't set yourself up as someone who just delivers a product. You also can, and do, deliver advice. Make sure your client or prospect understands that distinction.

As we previously mentioned, don't drill down too much into your expertise yet unless you have been introduced in a way that might pigeonhole you in a place you don't want to be. Give a short comment or two now because you want to save the details of your full experience until after you know what the client is looking for. For example, if you spend five minutes upfront talking about your health care experience and the client is looking for help in manufacturing, you might have convinced the prospect that you are very talented but not in his area. So keep it short. This entire step typically only takes three or four minutes, but they are important minutes not to waste.

Rapport Building

Building rapport is the second part of the opening stage of the Sales Call. Rapport is most easily established when the client does the vast majority of the talking. To make sure this happens, ask open-ended questions, questions that require a response other than yes or no. For example, "Tell me about yourself," or "What do you do in your spare time?" The objective here is to make some personal connection with your client, which then allows him or her to become more comfortable with you. Consider these three strategic facts: (1) people do business with people they like, (2) people like people who listen, and (3) people are more comfortable with others in whom they see similarities (for example, similar interests, views, backgrounds, and so on.)

So let your potential clients talk about themselves and their interests. This quickly accelerates the rapport-building process because almost everyone would rather talk than listen. Why? Once again, because listening is hard work.

> *To talk is human, to listen is divine. In the selling environment, listening is your job.*

The rapport-building step might take as little as a few minutes or as long as half an hour. But you're in control; you're asking the questions. When you feel the time is right, change the tone and get down to business. Some say that once you have identified three common interests with your client or prospect, you have sufficiently covered the rapport building phase. But rest assured, when the client is ready, he or she will give you a sign. It might be as obvious as the client starting to discuss their situation or as subtle as sending nonverbal signals like watch-glancing, chair-squirming, or eye-wandering. There are many clues to monitor. When you encounter several messages denoting impatience or disinterest, get down to business. Otherwise, you will lose them.

Sales Call—Information Gathering

At this point, you've decided that it's time to get down to business. This can best be accomplished by asking a transitional, open-ended questions such as, "So, what prompted you to call and set up this meeting?" or "So, what's been keeping you awake at night?" or, if this is a continuation of the Discovery Call, "In our conversation last week, you mentioned ..." There are many acceptable variations. The two major ingredients are tone (casual, not negative or accusatory) and phrasing that allows the client to easily answer. Normally, CPAs will say something like, "What's your problem?" or "How can I help you?" Both of these questions often lead down a road you don't want to go.

The question, "What's your problem?" is negative because it focuses on the word *problem*. It also assumes that the client has identified the problem. In reality, the client may just have a feeling that the company is inefficient in the way it is currently invoicing and collecting from its customers. The client may have come to you to kick around a few ideas in order to determine whether or not there is a problem to discuss. There may not even be any problem, but rather an opportunity the client wants to talk with you about.

An even bigger issue regarding the question, "What's your problem?" is that it is a status-attacking question. Remember, good MTBAs or consultants don't challenge status (at least at this time)! One commonly construed underlying message of this question is, "Tell me, you lowly ignorant business subhuman, what wisdom can I, the Great One, bestow on you today?" In providing advisory or consulting services, you want to avoid the role of "the omnipotent one." Rather, you want to be thought of as a skilled person with loads of relevant experience to kick around ideas with or someone to talk about issues to determine whether action should be taken. The question, "What is your problem?" does not reflect a role of equality, but one of advisor and advisee or manager and employee.

The second question, "How can I help you," seems innocent enough. But it assumes that the client not only knows what the problem is, but that he or she is familiar enough with your firm to request a service you offer. In a way, this is a very limiting question. Why? Because most clients see their CPA in a very narrow light. That light shines based on what-ever specific services you perform for that client. For example, although your firm might be outstanding in the strategic planning arena, if the only work you do for that particular client is their audit, you are likely to be categorized as the auditor. So when you ask the question, "How can I help you?" you might as well be saying, "Do you need any audit services today?" Don't allow your client the luxury of narrowing the subject matter to their interpretation of what you can and cannot do.

We know this sounds as if we are nit-picking the process. However, we are trying to point out why CPAs so often wind up exactly where they don't want to be. Our ability to deliver needed services to our clients rarely is limited by our capabilities; it is almost always hindered by misunderstanding, miscommunications, or misinterpretation. Stated more succinctly, CPAs often are careless with words.

In the world according to GAAP, we have been technicians for too long. Successful advisory and consulting services require a good balance between political and technical skills. For example, we performed some internal control work for a manufacturing client. The real issue was that the department heads for manufacturing and accounting were at odds with each other. Our role was to implement a solution acceptable to both sides. This project was 20 percent technical and 80 percent political. There were plenty of acceptable solutions; the problem was getting agreement on one. In this case, communication skills were far more important to the success of the project than was technical expertise. As a matter of fact, the client company had several people with more technical expertise than we could supply. However, after two years of attempting the project internally and getting nowhere, they hired our firm, and the project was completed in less than a year. Communication skills often play as large a role (and many times, a larger role) in the MTBA Framework and consulting services as do technical skills.

After the Transition Question

Once the discussion is focused on the business concern, continue your role as Sherlock Holmes (renowned for uncovering the obscure) and investigate further. At this stage of the Sales Call, your job is to unveil issues, concerns, opportunities, and so forth, many of which are far from being volunteered, in order to find out how to motivate someone to buy your services. The objective of the information gathering phase of the sales call is to gain knowledge about the client's situation and identify his or her "hot buttons."

To gain the necessary knowledge, your investigation needs to

- uncover your client's concerns.
- identify what your client expects to gain, protect, or reduce by addressing these concerns.
- quantify the value of resolving each concern.
- estimate (roughly) the cost associated with fixing each problem area, which includes your fees.
- weigh the expected gain, the likelihood of achieving that gain, and the cost of implementing the needed changes against each other to ensure the end justifies the effort.
- determine whether you have (either internally or access externally to, as a General Contractor) the required resources, including both time and skill, to manage or perform, or both, the detailed work relative to this project.

The information required to satisfy issues such as these can best be gathered by utilizing questioning techniques such as those found and explained throughout earlier chapters. Also, pay special attention during this stage to taking notes and using the investigative tree notetaking technique. Be careful not to sound as if you are interrogating the client. You are attempting to gather information, rather than putting the client on the spot. And finally, do whatever it takes to avoid the desire to

- jump to conclusions.
- give premature solutions to problems you have just identified.
- tell clients what to do (instead phrase your ideas as questions).

In addition to obtaining general knowledge about the client and his or her situation, another important aspect of this stage is to identify your client's hot buttons. *Hot buttons* are issues or needs that push your client into action because there is a sense of urgency about them. Hot buttons are the key to persuasive selling, and they are rarely obvious. The problem is if you haven't discovered the hot buttons, and when necessary, quantified the value of resolving them, when it comes time to close you will be "closing on air." If you try to close on air, the client will *not* be motivated to buy.

Closing on air means that you are trying to persuade the client to commit to doing business with you when no tangible reason to do so exists. With traditional services, there are built-in client motivators like bank requirements or governmental deadlines. Therefore, our role is to convince our clients that we can do the work, not that it is necessary to do it. Consider this:

> In the tax business, we have built-in hot buttons or drivers for clients to feel a sense of urgency. For example, the clients have to file their tax returns by a certain date. As these due dates draw near, people automatically will be motivated into action in order to avoid penalties, interest, and exposure to the IRS. People also typically are motivated externally regarding audits and financial statements, especially if an outside source (like a lender) is demanding them. In these cases, the clients come to us boiling over with anxiety, focused on meeting someone else's deadline that has become theirs.

With consulting, rarely are there due dates that create this sense of urgency. Even when due dates exist, they often are generated internally (which means they are subject to change). Therefore, just as we covered for your MTBA follow-up discussion, during the investigation phase of a sales call, you not only have to pinpoint the ideas or concerns that are keeping your client awake at night, but you have to quantify the expected results of addressing them. Otherwise, the client may walk away from a meeting with you knowing that a problem exists, but thinking that it's just one of those irritants that's not worth the cost of resolving. For example:

> Let's say Mike wants your help in selecting an accounting system for his small business. He spends several hours outlining the requirements for this new system. Although Mike has done a good job, you know through experience that even if you found a system that satisfied every wish on his list, he likely would be unhappy. This dissatisfaction would occur because the price would be beyond reason, the system would require that he change the way he has always done business, or it wouldn't perform many of the "not listed" but assumed functions.

> Therefore, you feel a work flow analysis should be done in order to identify what and how paper travels through the company, the information outputs that are required, and the bottlenecks that cause the organization problems. You know this preliminary step will cost from $5,000 to $20,000 (depending on the size and complexity of the small business), and will be in addition to the research he is requesting that you do. Mike already has commented that he is concerned about money so you know he is going to resist this idea.

In order to sell the work flow study, which you know from experience will make him far happier in the long run with whatever decision he makes, you are going to have to find a hot button to push.

> During your investigation, Mike told you about several friends who spent hundreds of thousands of dollars on computer automation that proved to be marginally effective. He also commented that his greatest fear was making the same mistake. For that reason alone, he has never made a real transition into the world of technology. However, when asked why he has decided that now is the time to automate his accounting, Mike replied, "Because my inability to adequately manage my inventory, invoicing, and accounts receivable is not only putting the company in a major cash bind but causing me to lose customers because of too many out-of-stock conditions."

Well, if you ever wanted a hot button to slap you in the face, there you have it. By the way, if most CPAs actually quantified their clients' hot buttons to the degree we are going to do right now in this scenario, our closing ratios in advisory services would be excellent (typically a CPA firm's closing ratio relating to compliance services is very high, but low when it comes to client-driven additional services). So where are we?

Mike has said he is scared of spending a couple hundred thousand dollars acquiring a marginally effective system. He also has told you that by not doing something, he is losing business. The next logical question, and we can tell you this after monitoring hundreds of role play scenarios, is rarely asked. The next question should be "So how much revenue do you feel you are losing each year due to stock-outs?" He replies, "half a million dollars in sales." Then you ask, "If you had the automated accounting system you identified earlier up and running, how much of that stock-out revenue loss could be avoided?" Mike states confidently, "At least 75 percent of those stock-outs wouldn't happen with a better inventory system." Finally you ask, "What would you say your average gross margin is on the items that are typically out-of-stock?" "My average gross margin is 35 percent on almost everything we sell," is his rebuttal. So, 35% of $500,000 x 75% is lost gross profit of $130,000 per year—or more than $400,000 over a three-year period.

Even with all this great information, you also need to quantify what Mike thinks is his downside of purchasing a marginally effective system. Maybe you should ask a question like, "You stated earlier that you have had several friends who spent hundreds of thousands of dollars on marginally effective automated accounting solutions and that your greatest fear is making the same mistake. What do you feel a mistake like this will cost you?" Let's assume that he replies, "I am concerned that I will spend $75,000 to $100,000 by the time I am done installing a new system and will still have the same problems I have today."

Then the MTBA might ask, "You also mentioned that your company is in a major cash bind partly because of poor invoicing and receivable collection. Can you tell me more about this?" Mike says, "Well, my invoicing process is too slow because it is very time consuming right now based on the way we do it. As well, because we are always running around trying to salvage a sale because of our constant out-of-stock situation, we don't spend the time we should staying on top of either our invoicing or our accounts receivable. We have a line of credit against our receivables, but the bank won't loan us money against anything over 90 days, so between slow invoicing and old accounts receivable (A/R), we get caught in a real bad place sometimes." The advisor, chaining questions based on the client's responses says, "What do you mean by 'being in a bad place?'" Mike responds with, "For example, three months ago I had to walk away from $25,000 worth of discounts because I did not have the borrowing capacity because my credit line was fully extended. Something similar to this has happened at least three other times in the past 18 months." The advisor adds, "If you had the automated system you have been talking about, what percentage of those discounts could have been capitalized upon?" Without hesitation, Mike explains, "Almost all of them. Even if we didn't do a better job of collecting on the A/R, which I know we would, the amount of uninvoiced inventory always would have given us the borrowing line to take advantage of the discounts being offered."

So far, the MTBA has just quantified the risk of failure of finding the right system at $75,000–$100,000, lost discounts of $75,000–$100,000 over 18 months and lost profits of $130,000 per year in additional sales. Thus far, we are already sitting at, conservatively, over $300,000 of quantified dollars to protect over an 18-month period ($75,000 system risk, $75,000 in lost discounts, and $195,000 of lost profits over an 18-month period). You can ask a lot of question to quantify the value of doing or not doing something. And those questions vary based on whatever the client said last.

Before you end this phase of the sales call, you want to make sure you have identified all the issues Mike is concerned about. As discussed in the "Refining the Most Important Consulting Tool: Communications" chapter, when this time occurs, visit the global functions checklist. Consider this continued exchange with Mike:

MTBA:	Mike, so far you've identified cash shortages and inventory stock-outs as critical issues costing you money. Are there any other areas of the business that you are apprehensive about at this time?
Mike:	No, if I can get a system that will help me better manage my inventory, everything else will fall in line.
MTBA:	Well, if you don't mind, I would like to review several functional areas of business that our clients constantly struggle to improve.
Mike:	Go ahead.
MTBA:	First, are you getting the kind of information you feel you need on a daily basis to run this business?
Mike:	Yes, except for inventory of course.
MTBA:	How about your people? Do you feel you have motivated personnel?
Mike:	Yes. I try to treat and pay everyone fairly. Most of my people think they should earn more, and I don't blame them. I think I should earn more too. However, I am wondering if I should put my sales people on commission. Right now, because there are so many service issues the sales people have to deal with, they are all paid a salary.
MTBA:	A number of our clients have struggled with that same issue, and we have some ideas to share. However, I would like to ask a few more questions in this area first. Do you feel your company is at much risk due to the expanded laws regarding sexual harassment and discrimination based on regulations like the Americans With Disabilities Act?

Note several things in this example. First, we have begun the process of reviewing the global functions (information management was touched on, followed by personnel) to broaden our understanding about the problems our client's business is facing. While we try to get clients to volunteer this information with questions like, "What do you see as your biggest opportunity (or hurdle) in the coming six months?" for many reasons, they might not think about many areas for which we could provide valuable assistance. Therefore, we can fall back to the global functions checklist to assist in our efforts.

Also notice an important characteristic about the previous questioning. When the idea of salary versus commission was introduced, many CPAs would have focused intense attention on this topic. While we are admitting that more questions can be asked, during the sales cycle, you want to keep the conversation on a high level. Keep your questions on a quantification level. For example, asking a question like, "What do you feel like you would gain by putting your sales people on a commission system?" might be appropriate. This might lead to more justification for getting you involved. However, if you have plenty of justification already, you might set this issue aside as something that should be discussed in more detail later.

The key is to keep from succumbing to the temptation to dive in and solve problems at this stage. Once you have quantified an issue, or found out it can't be quantified easily, the investigation needs to quickly revert back to high-level questioning. And in this case, once the personnel area had been covered, another global function should be introduced. Remember figure 9-1. Selling requires that you maintain high-level investigative questioning whereas consulting or advising requires that you dive down into the details to better understand possible solutions. If you are not diligent about maintaining that high-level perspective, you will find yourself to be the most popular overworked, underpaid MTBA or consultant around.

The point is we're not trying to tell you what questions to ask. Rather, we are reminding you that you need to gather the kind of information that allows your client to better understand the magnitude of the decision he or she is about to make.

Consider the previous scenario. By quantifying the risk of making a hasty judgment regarding which new accounting system to implement, you begin to build a wall of reasoning that adds support to your involvement. For example, Mike has said that he doesn't want to do what his friends have done and virtually throw away several hundred thousand dollars. On the other hand, he feels he is walking away from over $130,000 a year in lost profits due to his mismanagement of inventory ($500,000 in lost revenue times a 75% recapture ratio if a good inventory system were implemented times a 35% gross margin), as well as $75,000 in lost discounts. By asking the right questions, Mike is allowed to convince himself (which is the most persuasive way) that it is time to take action. Although his fear of buying the wrong system is costly, his inaction is carrying an even higher price tag.

Now that there is adequate information, later when it is time to ask for the business, your fees of $10,000 to $50,000 (which might have seemed enormous in the early stages of this conversation) are being fairly compared to the anticipated results. In other words, by spending the money upfront to do adequate investigation about the needs of the business, you not only significantly reduce Mike's chances of wasting several hundred thousand dollars, but you also stop the annual profit bleed of close to $200,000 that currently is occurring.

If we don't quantify the expected results, we cannot create the proper perspective regarding our fees or a high enough level of urgency. Simply put, without this required information, you will be closing on air, which rarely converts into business opportunity.

Keep In Mind

This is not a technique to trick your clients into spending money with you or hiring you, but rather, by utilizing this process, you are in a position to help your clients see why their inaction to address a particular situation is more damaging than they realize! Yes, you win by adding additional business and profits to your organization, but your clients win by adding more money to their bottom line as well.

The Last Step to Information Gathering

Once you have asked all the questions you can think to ask, it's time to briefly summarize what you have learned. Review the issues the client has identified as problems that need to be addressed. Note the emphasis on client. Be careful not to take on the task of establishing the priorities yourself. This sets the stage for the next step of the sales call, which will be covered momentarily.

Investigative Questioning Wrap-up

The difference between selling investigative questioning and consulting or advisory investigative questioning is that with selling, all we really want to know is what's bothering the client, what's it worth to him or her to fix it, and how does that compare to what it will cost to fix it. When you start asking detailed questions about what kind of commission structure Mike has in mind, what do his competitors do, and so forth, you are attempting to determine the feasibility and implementation steps of the idea. This is consulting. It is being an MTBA. This is what you need to get paid to do.

 Keep In Mind

This could be the most difficult transition you will be asked to make in this book. However, there is nothing that will provide you more opportunity, more revenue, higher client satisfaction, and greater success with your projects than improving your investigative skills. Improving this process is not only powerful for selling, but essential to being a quality advisor or consultant.

The Closing Phase of the Sales Call

Now that we have covered the investigation phase of the sales call, it's time to move to the closing phase.

Due to the quality of the information you gathered earlier in the sales call (because you were listening, taking notes, qualifying, quantifying, and so forth), let's find out how to convert this into new business. Remember, however, that this is a dynamic process. If you are in one of the later stages of the sales process and new information is uncovered, if necessary, put your investigative hat back on and ask more questions. Based on what we've accomplished thus far, it's time to move to the first stage in the closing phase, which is the sales pitch.

The Sales Call—Sales Pitch

The intent of this stage is to discuss who you and your firm are and what you and your firm do.

Many cover this information in the rapport-building stage. However, we believe that the beginning segment of a sales situation should be conversationally dominated by the client; let them "empty their buckets." In other words, until the clients have had ample time to express their feelings and concerns, we know from experience that it will be hard to get their full attention. Once their buckets are empty, the stage is set. Also, waiting until you discover the issues that need to be addressed allows you to tailor your sales pitch to present the services that fit the situation—this is known as *adaptive positioning*, where you adapt your pitch to best address the client's needs. It's time to begin the firm's floor show. This includes the following:

- Discussing partner and employee experience and credentials
- Outlining the various services your firm performs
- Distributing firm brochures, newsletters, and other sales information
- Introducing references and so on

As we stated in this same stage of the Discovery Call, the question to answer during this exercise is, "Why is your firm special?" This is done by reviewing the firm's credentials, describing its various services, identifying its partners' and employees' diverse levels of experience, and conveying a sense of compassion and caring for the welfare of the client. This is not accomplished by running down a competitor but by making sure the client sees the value-add your organization brings.

As previously noted, during this step of the closing phase is a great time to tell stories that demonstrate how you have helped others in similar circumstances, that your firm has numerous clients in their specific industry, and so forth. This is also the time to assure the client that, together, you will form the kind of team that can identify and uncover solutions that will be beneficial to the organization. Unlike the Discovery Call, the sales pitch in the sales call is much more detailed. Although this stage would only be a paragraph of words in the Discovery Call, in the Sale Call, you want to make sure your client understands why your organization's skills match the requirements he or she has previously outlined. This stage is likely to take anywhere from 5–15 minutes in the Sales Call, depending on the complexity and likely price tag of the work to be performed.

The Sales Call—Approach

By following the structured sales call process, here's about where you should be at this time:

- Everybody knows everybody.
- Everybody likes everybody.
- The client's bucket has been scraped clean.
- The client is in awe of your firm's capabilities.

The next step is to discuss how you would approach solving the client's problems. Most often, we start this section by discussing the "cash, capacity, and capability" technique. It always seems to comfort clients when they understand that

- we offer various degrees of involvement.
- they control our degree of involvement.

After everyone is comfortable with this concept, we lay out a game plan that could resolve their dilemma. At this point (because our earlier investigative process was focused on identifying hot buttons and quantifying them), rarely can we specify the exact details of our approach, but we can speak in general terms. Remember, this is a sales call, not the actual advisory or consulting call. This is not the time to lay out the intimate details of the plan, even if you have a good idea what they are. We can't say this enough: don't give away the plan. That's what advisors and consultants are paid to do. In this stage of the closing phase, all you are trying to do is convince the client that you know what you are doing.

For this reason, phasing becomes an essential technique. It is logical that we need to do more investigation before we can give the client a more definitive outline of our game plan. Based on the information we have gathered about the company, we can estimate the cost of phase 1 (as we discussed earlier, the first phase usually doesn't exceed something between $2,000 and $5,000 for most small business engagements).

If we have performed a similar project for a similar sized company with similar circumstances, we would provide the client with an overall estimate for the project at this time. If we haven't, then we might relay a wide range, quoting a past project or two as a point of reference until we know more. Or more commonly, we tell the client that we can only provide a reasonable estimate after having a better understanding of the business, its people, and the obstacles. We know what many of you are thinking, this strategy would never work with your clients because they demand to know the cost before they will hire you. Although it's true that clients do demand a cost estimate, they don't require one. We've been selling services this way for three decades with minimal resistance. The key is to make sure that you are not trying to close on air.

During the investigation phase of the sales call, you should identify enough of the client's "at-risk" money that your client feels like it's worth spending several thousand dollars in order to get a better understanding of the problem. We remind our clients that if they decide not to proceed with our involvement after we have completed phase 1, then they can use the information we gather to proceed on their own or with another firm. This lets them know that we are confident in our work and that the effort has value even if the project is not feasible at this time.

Using our phasing technique, the client can commit to the overall project in general but only has to specifically commit to one stage within the project. Even though it is incredibly rare when we don't perform all the various stages of a project, the client commits to them one at a time. This creates a type of safety net for the client and for us. If the client doesn't like the way the project is progressing, then at the end of every stage, there is a logical place for us to be dismissed and for someone else to take over. For example, let's say that a very small client was interested in obtaining financing. Our first step would be to analyze their situation. Let's assume that in this scenario, based on the information we gained during the investigation phase, we estimate that it will take three hours to take a cursory look. If the client's actual situation was similar to what we expected, our second stage might be to help identify the funds required and how they are expected to be spent. This could take another couple of hours. Specifying the information that needs to be prepared for the loan proposal is a likely third step requiring two more hours. At this time, we would jointly decide who is going to prepare what.

The point of this is that we lay out a simple approach in multiple stages. In doing so, we make it clear that our estimates are merely rough guesses, except for the stage we are about to perform, and that we charge by the hour or the day (or whatever pricing strategy you employ). Therefore, unexpected problems, lack of information, unusual complexity, and other unforeseen circumstances will affect the time requirement for future stages. As well, any unmet commitments by the client during the current stage will create a change-order, which will likely affect the price of the phase we are currently working.

A downside to our multiple phase approach is that occasionally a client gets the wrong impression about the overall cost of a project because of too much focus on early phases. So we work hard to ensure that we don't have any misunderstandings in this area. We attempt to

1. establish the appropriate expectations about the anticipated results.
2. make it clear that the price quoted is for a certain phase only.
3. mention, in general, likely future phases.
4. if appropriate, inform the client that our fees are for the services we perform and not for achieving specific results.

Given the preceding list and considering this example of a very small business, we might conclude this way. Assuming that the client does most of the detailed preparation of the loan package, by the time we lay out the required documents, look over and critique the loan package, and attend several meetings with bankers, a loan package like this typically might cost around $4,000 to $5,000. If we did this work fairly regularly and were comfortable with the typical stages of this type of project, not only would we provide a fixed price for the first phase, we would probably provide a likely overall ballpark price for the project.

So we lay out our approach in multiple stages, give a specific price for the next phase of the project, provide some general estimates for future phases, and allow ourselves plenty of flexibility. The clients usually are satisfied because they only have to chew on this project one bite at a time. And we have offered ourselves a very important protection. If we were wrong about the work effort required and the client has not changed the scope, we have limited our risk to only one phase, not the entire project. Because we have a fresh slate to price the next phase, although we may not fully recover from profit shortfalls in the last phase, we can make sure we are proposing profitable phases for the rest of the project.

The Sales Call—Summary

By this time, you and the client have covered a great deal of information. This step is to bring it all together in preparation for the close. What you are doing in this stage is summarizing the issues, quantifying the reasons for taking action, and reviewing the game plan that has been identified.

Here's where you can pull all of this work together and make the client beg for your involvement. For example, reconsidering Mike's computer dilemma, the summary might sound something like this:

> Mike, you mentioned earlier that you really wanted to avoid making the costly mistake of purchasing an ineffective computer system. You even said you felt like you could easily throw away several hundred thousand dollars by making a poor decision like some of your friends have. You also told us that you feel you are walking away from at least $130,000 in lost profits and $75,000 is lost discounts each year because of your current inventory control capabilities. Over a three-year period, that could easily represent additional profits in excess of $600,000 that you are walking away from if you do nothing.
>
> Just a few minutes ago, we talked about our firm and how we have developed a great deal of expertise in this area. You even commented that you hold one of the companies we've assisted in high regard concerning their effective use of automation.
>
> With this in mind, let me summarize what we see as the financial side of this situation. The last two projects like this we performed for clients similar to your organization ran in the $40,000 to $75,000 range for consulting services. And as we discussed earlier, we will be betterable to pin this number down after we complete phase I of our work. Phase I, which is our preliminary investigation as well as an outlined go-forward plan, can be performed for a fixed price of $15,000.

As you may have noticed, not only did the summary recapture the reasons uncovered in the investigation phase about why action is necessary, but the firm's capabilities and experience were directed towards solving the problem as well. This client should be chomping at the bit to say, "I'm ready. Please, please! When can you get started?" This is why the close follows the summary. The close, in this situation, would be a "no-brainer."

This closing sentence has several complexities to it. For that reason, it's time to take a look at the many variations of how the close works.

The Sales Call—Close

It's time to examine the final stage of the Sales Call. By this time, you have successfully

- gained your client's trust by building rapport.
- asked a transitional, open-ended question.
- investigated the client's problems by listening and questioning.
- fine-tuned the flow of the meeting by using all of your available communication skills—both verbal and nonverbal.
- identified your client's hot buttons.
- quantified the reasons for the client to take action.
- given your sales pitch.

- summarized the key points.
- outlined the approach you will follow to resolve the various concerns.

Therefore, the close is imminent. The close is a critical part of the Sales Call because that's when you ask for the business. Given our preceding scenario, the close might be as simple as a statement like this:

> Mike, we know we can help. We are asking you to invest $15,000 now so that we can develop a go-forward plan and pin down the likely total cost of implementation against a solution that, in your words, could augment your profits by $200,000 a year while simultaneously minimizing the risk of your making a bad decision regarding the automated solution you choose. We have availability to get started either in about 10 days, or after the first week of next month. When would be better for you?

Until now, you could have made a great deal of mistakes that would have little impact if you finish with a strong close. On the other hand, you could have been flawless up to this point and blow it all here. Based on the facts of our scenario, as we previously mentioned, the client probably wouldn't have even let you get to the closing statement because he or she would have just asked, "When can we get started?" But let's assume the client is still a little resistant and pushes back after your closing statement. This is the point at which most people fall on their own sword. Unfortunately, most CPAs consider objections or pushback from the client as a loss rather than seeing it as the client trying to go where we want them to go, but still needing a little more convincing or assurance.

A technique that dramatically can minimize the frequency of one falling on the proverbial sword is called the trial close. *Trial closes* allow you to identify, further define, or eliminate obstacles hampering the selling process. In other words, if everything seems to point to a logical "yes" response, why are you still hearing "no?" For instance, let's say the preceding client says

> I am not comfortable at this time with the idea that your consulting fees could be any amount. Although the price range you suggested is within reason, doubling or tripling that amount changes the decision about whether we move forward with you or someone else.

You might respond with a trial close such as

> Let's assume that after our $15,000 upfront preliminary investigation phase and report, although we might not be able to pin down the exact price of our implementation involvement, we would be able to give you a "not-to-exceed" price as a protection for you. Would you be comfortable working with us then?

This trial close conditionally asks for the business. In this case, it takes away the possibility of a totally uncontrolled engagement cost on the client's side. If the client has no objections, he or she is allowed to accept the proposition on the condition that the next proposed phase (after the initial phase) would include a ceiling on your consulting fees. By asking for the business in a trial close format, this allows you to bring unresolved issues to the surface. For example, the client might respond with

> Well, your identification of a "ceiling" price would certainly make me more comfortable knowing that I have some protection on this project getting away from us. However, the

stories I hear about technology implementations are that before you know it, you find out that you have spent the entire budget and are not even close to being ready to turn the system on. Even if you have a ceiling on your fees, that doesn't mean I will end up with anything like the system I am expecting. That is not the kind of surprise I am comfortable with and, quite frankly, it is my greatest concern.

The client's response shows that although the price ceiling is helpful, the even greater concern is about being surprised with an inadequate automated solution and a totally blown budget. Therefore, the trial close has minimized one hurdle and identified an even bigger one. So another trial close might be in order to see if you have heard all of the objections or if there are more to follow. Consider this response:

We understand. That is one reason we would like for you to talk to a couple of our references because we believe your comfort with us regarding this possible occurrence will improve dramatically. However, what if we also set up weekly meetings between you and me to review, at a high level, where we are budget-wise on the project, go over what we have done that week, and compare this to the timeline and budget expectations for the overall project. This is an approach we have taken with many of our clients, and it keeps you in the loop and minimizes the possibility of surprises. Assuming you get the positive responses you are looking for from our references and we utilize the weekly reporting format I just mentioned, would this make you comfortable enough to get started?

The point is by properly utilizing the trial close technique, you can identify the hurdles that stand between you and your final objective: approval. This process also is incredibly worthwhile because you can obtain commitment before wasting enormous amounts of time doing work (proposals, investigations, and research, that will not make any difference in the client's final response.

Once you have jumped the various hurdles (satisfied your client's objections), it's time to ask for the business. There are several guidelines to follow when attempting to do this:

- *Don't let your potential clients leave without asking for their business.* People normally avoid making decisions. By forcing the issue face-to-face, you increase the odds of obtaining a positive response. It's much easier for them to refuse you later, over the phone, or by letter than right then in person. This fact clearly has influenced a whole category of product sales that fall under the consumer credit contract provisions. For example, products such as swimming pools, sunrooms, magazines sold door-to-door, and hundreds of other products fall into this category and require several days to pass (often three) before the contract is valid (providing ample time for the customer to back out). Why? Because it is hard to turn people down face-to-face.
- *Before you ask for the business, discuss your rates and how you will bill for the project.* Try to minimize the number of possible put-offs, or buying objections, before you ask for the business. Don't let rates bog you down; cover them upfront in a matter-of-fact style. When your potential clients are forced to ask you for this information, or when you are shy about revealing your fees, the cost of doing business is given more of a spotlight then it deserves.

- *If you require a retainer, discuss it with confidence.* Be confident when asking for a retainer. Nothing is worse than someone requesting a retainer and then stumbling all over themselves trying to explain why. If the client wants to know why, he or she will ask. After you mention the retainer, expect your client to be silent. This is not a bad sign, it's normal. Everyone seems to require a few moments of silence before deciding to spend money. These quiet seconds often are used by the client to decide some financial specifics like is there enough money in the checking account, what bills are due this week, and so forth. Regardless of why, the point is do not overreact to the silence.

- *Ask for the project in a way that suggests an affirmative answer.* As we previously stated, most people avoid confrontation. In other words, they would rather say "yes" than "no." Phrase your closing question in a manner that takes advantage of human nature. For example, consider the last sentence in our previous first closing attempt:

  "We have availability to get started either in about 10 days, or after the first week of next month. When would be better for you?"

  By phrasing your question in a positive fashion, there is an implied "yes" to doing business together. So in order for your client to turn you down, they almost would have to argue with you. In contrast, a statement like, "Why don't we give you a couple of days to think this over" offers an easy out for the client to postpone making a decision, and one likely taken even if the client was ready to decide.

- *When it's time to ask for the business,* ASK and SHUT UP. At this point in the marketing game, after you have asked for the business, the old saying goes: whoever talks first ... loses. In other words, learn how to live with the silence that follows tough questions. If you say anything, you divert attention away from the question, giving the client an opportunity to change the subject, postpone the decision, or many other less desirable alternatives. If your client has a real objection, this silence will give him or her time to formulate a response. Remember that an objection is not fatal; each time you satisfy one, you get another step closer to getting the commitment you are looking for.

- *If the client does postpone the decision, find out what must be done to finalize the deal.* If your client must postpone the decision for good reason, such as needing approval from a higher company official or wanting time to check your references, be sure to agree on the next course of action before your meeting is adjourned. This might entail creating a "to do" list, scheduling another meeting, or identifying who should contact whom and when. If the responsibility of contact falls on your client's shoulders, always give yourself another in, such as, "If I don't hear from you by Friday, can I call you on Monday?"

By following the structure of the Sales Call and by paying attention to what may seem to be the minutiae of detail surrounding each step within it, your ability to close tough business situations will improve dramatically. The good news is once you get comfortable with the process, it will become natural very quickly. After you close the business, it's now time for you to move on to the Consulting or Advisory Call.

Service Delivery

The Structured Consulting or Advisory Call

We've been referring to this as the Consulting or Advisory call throughout this text. In order to streamline the material and enhance your reading, we're simply going to call it the Consulting Call from this point forward. As stated in the beginning of this chapter, the Discovery Call, the Sales Call, and the Consulting Call have a great deal of similarities. Because we have gone into the Discovery and Sales Calls in detail, we want to mainly point out the nuances of the Consulting Call. The place to start, as we have done with each call type, is to review the structure:

- Investigation Phase
  — Relating
  — Discovery and interviewing
- Closing Phase
  — Review of findings and identification of suggestions
  — Presentation of action plan
  — Persuading and facilitating
  — Supporting

Consulting Call—Relating

The first stage in the investigation phase is relating with the client. How is this different from the opening (the combination of the introduction and rapport-building) in the Sales Call? Simple. By this time, you already have sold the client your services, and hopefully, have built some rapport with the owners or management team. Therefore, although we always have to be concerned about maintaining good impressions (or making a good first impression every day), our dialogue at the beginning of the meeting should shift from making a connection to building on the connection we have already established. That's why we refer to this step as relating, which is defined by Webster's as "to establish a meaningful relationship with a person or thing."

There is nothing we need to say about this area; this is nothing new. One of the reasons our profession has thrived over the years is because our professionals know how to build strong client relationships. The foundation of this relationship often rests on our ethics, including trust, honesty, and integrity. It certainly doesn't hurt, however, if you also make a concerted effort to accelerate the relationship-building process by talking about shared hobbies, enjoying some after work activity together, or showing interest in subjects that you know are of interest to the client.

Consulting Call—Discovery and Interviewing

The second step in the investigation phase is discovery and interviewing. Discovery is virtually the same as information gathering, except rather than looking to quantify why something should change, you are now looking for ways to facilitate the necessary changes. Interviewing is self-explanatory. Although this could be said to be a tool of the discovery process, because so much time is spent utilizing this technique, we included it to differentiate the kind of analytical investigation a consultant performs on his or her own versus that information gathered through formal interviews with key personnel. We covered questioning and listening (which is what interviewing involves) in more detail earlier in this text.

All of the tips and techniques discussed throughout the book so far regarding communication skills, questioning techniques, avoiding premature speculation, paraphrasing your ideas as questions, not feeling like your job is to have all the answers, and more absolutely apply here. Remember when we were covering the Sales Call process, that we discussed making sure that both you and your clients understand the value of hiring you (quantifying the reason for fixing the problem). Well, in the Consulting Call, you are attempting to solve, solve, and solve. Once again, this does not mean that it is your job to have the answers. It means that it is your job, with heavy involvement from the client, to arrive at alternatives and help evaluate them. For example, in a recent workshop, a real client participated in the role play scenarios. Here's an excerpt from that dialogue that supports our position.

> **Consultant:** Tell me a little bit about your business.
>
> **Client:** I am the president of a restaurant chain. We have seven successful company-owned locations and have franchised four more.
>
> *Later in the conversation*
>
> **Consultant:** Why the mix between wholly owned restaurants and franchised ones?
>
> **Client:** Years ago, all of our locations were wholly owned. But as you know, the cost of expansion is high. There is not only the cash flow requirement to fund new locations, but you need to know the area in order to select good locations, you need to find management that you can count on and trust, and a number of other issues. The bottom line is that we saw franchising as being an excellent alternative in that it looked to be very lucrative, provided us with more buying power (which would be good for both the franchisees and our own locations) and allowed us to grow much more rapidly with significantly less risk.
>
> **Consultant:** How is the franchising going?
>
> **Client:** Not nearly as well as we had hoped!
>
> **Consultant:** Why?
>
> **Client:** I don't know. We've sold four locations, and they seem quite happy. But we need to do more to support them on an ongoing basis, especially if we want them to remain happy.
>
> **Consultant:** Like what?
>
> **Client:** More products, better marketing, lower costs ... you know ... anything to help them attract more customers and make more money. Because we take a cut of the gross revenue, it's in both of our best interests for us to help them grow.
>
> **Consultant:** What's stopping you from making all of that happen?
>
> **Client:** Time! I just don't have enough time to get all the things I should be doing done.

Consultant: Is there someone you can delegate more work to?

Client: No. Everyone here is already so busy. Besides, the kind of person I need to help me would cost us about $80,000 per year. I am just not ready to spend that kind of money.

Consultant: I'm just curious. If you had this $80,000 per year person working for you, how much OF YOUR TIME do you think you could realistically free up?

Client: Probably about half, easily more than a third.

Consultant: If you spent that freed-up time selling new franchises, conservatively, how many could you sell in a year?

Client: Maybe five, but conservatively, three or four.

Consultant: How much revenue in franchise fees would you expect from each of those newly established franchises in a 12-month period?

Client: In the first 12 months, probably around $50,000 each, but that is conservative, and it usually climbs to $75,000 or more by the second year.

Consultant: Are there any other benefits that you would enjoy by having, let's say, three new franchised locations?

Client: Definitely. Like I said earlier, with each location, we gain greater buying power (which makes every location more money, including company owned restaurants) and spread the cost of promotional and advertising pieces because there are more operations sharing the cost burden.

Consultant: What do you think that would be worth to you?

Client: I don't know, but it would be in the thousands of dollars.

Consultant: So, you feel that you could conservatively add three new franchised restaurants per year netting you an average of $50,000 each, and that you would gain thousands of dollars in savings per year through greater buying power if you had more time you could devote to this area?

Client: (*Long pause*). It seems kind of silly that I have hesitated hiring someone to help me, doesn't it? Your question doesn't even consider the compounding nature of adding three franchises a year because by the end of the second year, I would have added the equivalent of six $50,000 a year income streams. I have to admit, putting off $300,000–$500,000 in revenues or savings just to save $80,000 in payroll cost doesn't make much sense.

This is a perfect example of how advisory or consulting services heavily utilize communication and questioning skills, why you should avoid premature speculation, and how it is so much more powerful when ideas are paraphrased as questions. It also points out how the process requires patience to refrain from too quickly providing clients with answers. This is not to say that the advisor or consultant doesn't have to have any knowledge at all. But when you believe that your clients and their employees have the necessary answers, the Discovery and interview step of the Consulting Call become kind of a fun game. You know there is buried treasure in your client's company and that a map exists, even though no one person has the entire map. Can you successfully piece that map together by combining your expertise with theirs?

It wouldn't surprise us if some of you were thinking, "Being an MTBA or doing consulting can't be this easy. These guys aren't telling us the entire truth. My clients would never pay for this kind of service. And even if they did, they would be mad at me for billing for this!" Well, we certainly can't speak for the world. But we can repeat what thousands of CPAs have said after they have tried this: "I wish I would have starting doing this a long time ago. It's easy, it's profitable, and the client is really happy with the outcome." Anytime actual clients of the CPAs are involved in our workshops, we ask them if the information discussed in the role plays were valuable to them. Each time, to the amazement of the participants, the answer is emphatically, "Yes!"

While doing your MTBA work or consulting, many of the answers or potential solutions will fall out just as they did in the previous questioning dialogue. However, many will not. And that's perfectly fine. This is to be expected. But during the Consulting Call, you need to resolve each branch identified on the investigative tree. Resolution can be as simple as uncovering that nothing of real importance was related to that particular branch, or that the cost of a solution far outweighs the gain of fixing it. But for those branches that need to addressed, you need to develop a go-forward action plan. This is where you apply techniques such as "to do lists;" planning; "cash, capacity, and capability;" phasing; acting in the role of the General Contractor; and others to satisfy the needs of your clients in a way that matches the resources of your clients.

Consulting Call—Review of Findings and Identification of Suggestions

This is the first step in the closing phase of the Consulting Call. Review of findings and identification of suggestions is the analytical part of your work. After you have gathered the information you need, take it back to the office or to your cubical in the client's office and reflect on what you have found. Reflection is an important tool for CPAs. But as we discussed earlier, our desire to provide instant answers gets in the way of utilizing this as often as we should. Usually, after allowing yourself even minimal time to think through the events that transpired and the information you gathered, you arrive at some startling revelations. Many times reflection allows you to envision ideas far better than those you originally pictured. Or even more important, after some thought you realize that you are operating without some critical information. This realization would force you to take a quick step back into the information gathering process to collect more information, which is common. At this stage, you need to keep bouncing back and forth between gathering information and analyzing it until you feel like you really understand what is going on.

CPAs are uniquely qualified for work like this. We, as a profession, have excellent skills when it comes to looking at business systems, processes, procedures, and workflows, and deriving more efficient and effective ways to meet or exceed an organization's objectives. Our only drawback here is that we often expect these revelations to come instantaneously. So make sure that you allocate time to this creative process. This not only includes quality thinking time (several hours of uninterrupted thought), but a few days to let your brain subconsciously do some work on its own. Obviously, the more complex the project, the more think time you have to allocate to it. The time-saving, money-generating, cost-reducing ideas that seem to almost magically appear when you give yourself enough flexibility are amazing.

Consulting Call—Action Plan Presentation

This is the reporting step of the Consulting Call. Large firms do this well. Formal reporting is part of their methodology for managing projects. For smaller projects, which are often done by smaller firms, we change the rules slightly. Although the reporting element is still essential, we suggest changing the delivery from written to oral reporting or oral reporting with a brief, bulleted list of points that you cover. Chapter 11 addresses many of the techniques required to manage meetings and make high quality presentations. At this point, we just want to drill in why reporting is so important.

In almost any project, many aspects will work as planned, a few better than planned, and a few (and it sometimes seems like all the important ones) worse than planned. This is just a day in the life of an MTBA or consultant. We've seen from our own experience, as well as our CPA firm clients, that too often we are faced with enormous challenges and constantly are asked to scale the highest peaks. Upon arrival at the summit (overcoming the continual barrage of hurdles), in total exhaustion we might add, you inevitably will be greeted by the dreaded phrase, "What did you get done today (this week, this month)? It seems we haven't made any progress at all." Often in these cases, an unexpected problem arises that you and your team work furiously for hours, days, or weeks to resolve. Many times these problems are caused by the client, their personnel, or are just unexpected and unique to that particular situation. Instead of being greeted with accolades and gifts for your creativity and genius, you are slashed by the penetrating suggestion that you have underperformed. There are few moments harder to take than these. Why do they happen? How do you avoid them? Client reporting is the answer.

The point here is that the action plan presentation is your minimum presentation requirement. When you use phasing, this step comes up quite often. But if you have a project with a phase that lasts weeks or more, then you have to incorporate mini-updates along the way. Our rule: martyrs don't live long and prosper in the field of consulting.

Translated, this means that when you encounter a significant problem (one that requires more time than planned), let your client know immediately. If the answer is easy, the client will quickly steer you in the right direction, and you won't waste any of your time or theirs. And if it is not, then you not only want to make them aware of what you are up against, but you also want to assure them that their problem is in good hands. Why would you put forth this much effort? Because we believe that when we are losing sleep attempting to solve a problem, so should the client. Although they have the luxury of leaving the project in your hands, they typically will also try to gain an understanding of how a problem might poorly position them.

What makes this all worthwhile is when you finally identify an implementable solution and share it with the client, they are as excited about your accomplishment as you are. This is a hard lesson to learn, and one we didn't take to heart easily. We spent the first few years of our consulting lives accomplishing incredible feats with less than overwhelmed clients. When we shortened our phases and added this reporting step to the process (and occasionally threw in extra reporting steps along the way), we found a much greater appreciation for our work, higher client satisfaction, and less friction over fees.

In the Consulting Call, the action plan presentation step is an excellent way to let your client know where you are and to open a dialogue about where to go. This is not something that should take days to create. Obviously, the more complex the project, the more formal the oral report. For example, instead of using a typed meeting agenda like you would for most meetings, you might use presentation tools such as PowerPoint™ or any other software package that would help you deliver complex materials succinctly and easily. Don't be shy about keeping your client informed. It's funny, CPAs tend to think this is a nonessential, costly step compared to the other work performed. However, the less your client knows about what you are doing day-to-day and what you are accomplishing, the less satisfied they are likely to be with your work. Just remember that conjecture in the absence of good information creates an information vacuum that normally is filled with misinformation that assumes the worst. Communicate actively and often. This is just another case in point where the politics of doing the work easily can be more important than the actual work itself.

Consulting Call—Persuading and Facilitating

A great plan or a superior idea is meaningless if there is no consensus to take action. As an advisor, being able to take on the role of change agent is critical to ensuring forward momentum. Too often, we get bogged down in our analysis and our quest for the right answer. After hours, days, and even weeks of deliberation, it is common for our professionals to enter a room of their peers with their statistically valid or most successful approach to choosing an action plan. We weigh the pros and cons of each alternative, assess the risks, and then hold steadfast to the idea that one solution is better than another. Unfortunately, although our analysis is quite likely correct, it often contains a fatal flaw. We don't consider the "people factor," which easily can undermine even the best of ideas.

We are not suggesting that CPAs change their deliberate, conscientious approach to problem solving. However, once your analysis is done, when you sit down with your client's management team, peel your pride of ownership from around your suggested alternatives and open your mind to another set of decision-making parameters. The new parameters are simple and straightforward:

- Does the client (or the management team) believe in the alternative?
- Does the client (or the management team) understand the nuances of implementing the alternative?
- Will the management team know, at a gut level, how to respond when the alternative goes awry?
- Will the alternative receive a great deal of resentment or undermining from the rank and file?
- Is the alternative one that fits the style, culture, and capabilities of the company's personnel?

Depending on the answers to these questions, the best solution easily could move from last on your list to the number one position. The "people factor" is what makes advisory and consulting work so difficult. As an MTBA, you are not trying to find the perfect solution for you but one that achieves the greatest results for your client given the environment and personnel who will implement it. And as an advisor, you will not always be there to implement it. You have to strive to install systems and procedures that will endure when you are not around.

It is here, at this step, when you have to determine if it is best to motivate, educate, and persuade those around you about why one option is better than another, or for you to do everything in your power to make an inferior idea work because of the commitment and support the client has for that idea. The persuading and facilitating step does not, by any stretch of the imagination, mean that it is your job to get people to do what *you* want. Rather, it is your job to help your client achieve success by taking action, with the appropriate personnel working as a cohesive team on whatever solution is most likely to work given the situation. As we just stated, this sometimes means that the theoretically best ideas get scrapped, and you have to scramble to shore up all the holes that exist in whatever alternative is chosen.

Before we leave this step of the Consulting Call, we would like to remind you of what we consider to be an important perspective. The day you believe your answers are always the best ones is the day you need to stop doing this kind of work. People are unpredictable, projects are always unveiling unforeseeable difficulties, the work environment is changing constantly, and the marketplace is shifting perpetually. Given this, is it even conceivable that any one person has the vision to predict the result of an action taken amidst this evolving chaos? Keep in mind that taking on the role of change agent is difficult. It not only requires the skills we cover in this text, but also a great deal of business experience combined with uncommon patience and humility.

Consulting Call—Supporting

This is the last step of the Consulting Call. Performing this step well separates a great MTBA from a marginal one. After an action plan is identified, agreed upon, and tasks are assigned, political issues, conflicts, new priorities, and other unforeseen challenges can throw your client off track quickly. For example:

> Let's say your client is ready to implement an expanded marketing plan. A week or two (of a three-month concentrated front-end effort) after the project starts, which was deemed the number one priority by management, a new priority called "our biggest client is unhappy with our product and is threatening to change suppliers" instantly rises to the top of the list.

This kind of scenario is so commonplace it can't be considered an anomaly. Yet, a tremendous amount of work is at stake if the client doesn't immediately pick up where they left off as soon as the crisis is averted. If the unhappy client leaves, then implementing the expanded marketing plan in this case becomes even more important. *Supporting* is the step that keeps you involved and in contact with the client. Supporting occurs because of the following:

- Occasional (planned in advance by you using a contact management system) phone calls
- Pre-arranged update meetings (these could be daily, weekly, monthly, or quarterly depending on the project, its critical nature to the client, and the magnitude of its impact on the organization)
- Working on-site while performing other services so you can watch for the anticipated changes
- Strategic, tactical, and budgetary planning meetings and more

Just because your portion of the project is over doesn't mean that you should walk away. When you take on advisory or consulting work, you should include in your proposal your ongoing involvement as a critical success factor to the client's success in that endeavor. We do. Now we're not talking about this function consuming a great deal of time, or billing much money for that matter, compared to the actual implementation work. We are simply referring to the act of providing a watchful eye over the progress of your client in some systematic way. By doing this, when projects get derailed, you can step in easily and quickly to help get them on track again.

The Number One Failing

All three of the call types discussed in this chapter have some overlap, a great deal of similarity, require the same skill sets, and work in conjunction with each other. For example, before you meet with a referred prospect, you would conduct a Discovery Call. Once the prospect has been qualified and there seems to be mutual benefit to doing business together, a Sales Call is the logical next step. At such time that the prospect accepts your offer to deliver services and become a client, a Consulting Call is in order. Each call type picks up where the previous one left off. As we stated in the beginning of this chapter, the key is cutoff. Often, a natural delineation exists between one call type and another.

Sometimes, however, the delineation between these call types is vague. Sometimes, they occur one after the other, or even simultaneously, in the same setting. In these cases, you have to create the necessary distinctions. For example, if you find yourself making a Sales Call before a Discovery Call was made, then the two call types blend together. Because you are in a selling environment, you should follow the process of the Sales Call. However, once the opening phase (which includes the introductions and rapport building) is complete, the Discovery Call objective of qualification becomes the focus of the information gathering phase. If the prospect doesn't meet the basic tests of qualification, you quickly cut your losses, stop selling, and find a courteous way out. If they are qualified, then you just continue with the sales process and ask more questions. At this point, the call objective would shift from one of qualification to quantification.

If the Sales Call goes well and the client says, "Let's get started right now," then do so. You have to make the clear distinction at this point that you are "on the clock" and beginning the project. You should always make a clear distinction between the Sales Call and the Consulting Call. Why? Because one is for *free* and the other is for *fee*! Once again, the problem we have within our profession is that we continually merge the Sales Call with the Consulting Call. If we can't make the necessary distinctions between them, there is no way our client will be able to. With the Consulting Call, the objective is to solve. This is significantly different than the Sales Call's objective of quantification.

The number one failing we see in our work with CPA firms is that all three of these call types are performed simultaneously with no distinction between them. This typically results in a great deal of wasted time, prospects that just won't make the final commitment to specific consulting services, or consulting expertise being given away. By understanding the differences between each of these, their nuances, and their cut-off, you will not only find yourself generating more advisory and consulting work and revenue, you also will find yourself in a better position to satisfy your client. Why? Because your skill in performing these calls will help them better understand the priorities of their organization, the value of taking action, and the plan to facilitate the necessary changes.

Before We Move On

We have a variety of exercises for you pertaining to this chapter. This is partially the case just because there is so much material here. However, we included these exercises because it is important for you to experience these concepts firsthand. Many of these concepts, although they might seem familiar, will not reveal their full impact until you participate in a role play or two.

The Discovery Call Role Play

The first exercise (exercise 9-1) is a Discovery Call role play. The "Role Play Scenario Sheet" assumes that the CPA firm regularly sends out advertising direct mail pieces that include a return postcard. Potential clients can check any of the following:

- Yes, I want more information about the various services you offer.
- Yes, please call me. I would like to talk about ways your firm can help me.
- Yes, I would like to take advantage of your 30-minute free consulting offer.
- Yes, I would like to take advantage of your free tax return review.

This sheet identifies a few scenarios for the "potential client" in this role play. Here's the way this role play works:

1. The advisor makes the discovery call in front of the entire group.
2. If a phone system is handy, then have the prospect go into another room so that the MTBA can call using a speaker phone so that everyone can listen in on the interaction (this is the best alternative because it most closely emulates the real situation). If the

technology is not easy to put in place, put the MTBA and the prospect in chairs that are positioned back-to-back in the front of the room.

3. Those observing are to use the "Discovery Call Observer's Note Sheet" and record constructive advice to be passed on to the MTBA at the end of the call.

4. The group facilitator looks at the role play scenarios list and chooses one for the prospect or potential client to play (or the facilitator can make up his or her own scenario). The scenario is communicated secretly to the prospect by the facilitator with the prospect taking on that role for the role play phone call.

5. The MTBA is to utilize the "Discovery Call Prompter Form" (the next form) to help him or her prepare for the call. Feel free to review the "Discovery Call" section of this chapter as a refresher before the call. As you remember, we recommend using scripts in this type of call not only to build confidence, but because the calls are meant to be short and to the point.

The objective of this exercise is to qualify the potential client. This means that although you might have to live up to an advertising obligation, you want to either minimize how much time you waste or maximize how much opportunity you might uncover. Part of this exercise is for the consultant to correctly identify the potential client's situation. For example, if the potential client is merely a student looking for information with no business opportunity, the advisor should be able to correctly state that at the end of this exercise. The advisor also should correctly determine whether this potential client should be

- referred to some other company so as to not waste any additional time.
- sent information or referred to your Web site to download applicable material—politely responding but minimizing your involvement or effort.
- sent information and noted in a tickler file to call back because there might be opportunity in the future, although there is none imminent.
- set up with another phone call to review the sought-after information or fulfill an advertising commitment (like a free tax return review) so that you can perform the obligation and minimize the time commitment.
- set up with an appointment at the office in order to serve the client but not waste commute time in order to serve good clients with limited opportunities.
- set up with an appointment at the client's office to maximize opportunity identification.

Noting option 4 previously listed, if a free tax return review is the requested service, having the client e-mail, mail in, or fax the return and then following up that receipt with a phone call is a good way to minimize the time commitment if it was determined that the prospect's only desire was to get free advice.

Have everyone in the room cycle through this exercise. After the first exercise, the MTBA and the prospect should change roles and repeat the exercise (with the new prospect taking on a different role chosen from the scenarios list). Once they are done, the next pair of participants is called to the front of the room to go through this exercise again until everyone has experienced it.

Paper Closing Exercise

The next activity (exercise 9-2) is a two-page paper closing exercise appropriately called "Closing Exercise." A situation is described, and you are asked to identify your client's hot buttons, write out a trial close, and with additional information, propose a closing statement. This exercise is meant to make you think through the Sales Call process and have you lay out a logical close.

Sales Call (Information Gathering or Branch) Exercise

The third exercise (exercise 9-3) is the "Sales Call (Information Gathering) Exercise." We often refer to it as the "Branch Exercise" because we are trying to uncover all of the main branches (from the upside down investigative tree) of interest to the client (in other words, find out what is keeping them awake at night). This is an exercise many firms redo often. Why? Because it is focused on identifying advisory opportunities and then quantifying reasons justifying the MTBA's involvement. Skill development in this area can quickly increase revenues. The first step is for each person to work through and fill out the "Client's Priority List." Put yourself in the shoes of a client you know well and follow the instructions from there. If you have the luxury, just like with the Discovery Call, have pairs come to the front of the room and experience the exercise with everyone watching because it is more powerful learning technique when it is done this way. But because this exercise takes a little longer than the Discovery Call exercise, and because time may be short, you can always divide up into groups of three and run the exercise in small groups; one participant is the consultant, another the client, and the third is an observer. Logically, the observer should take notes on the Sales Call's "Observer's Note Sheet."

Objective: You have 8–10 minutes to identify the issues that are "Keeping the Client Awake at Night" and then prioritize them.

Steps to follow:

- Find the "Sales Call/Branch Exercise Client Worksheet" in the forms at the end of this chapter. Each person should think of a client you know well and think about the various issues they are trying to resolve (not just financial issues but *all* issues). Record those issues on the worksheet. Do not fill in the "$ Value to the Client..." column yet.
- Prioritize each issue, numbering them 1–5, with 1 being the most important.
- If you are not going to do this exercise in the front of the room, then have the facilitator break you into groups of 3.
- Please identify who will take on each of these roles in your group for the first round (after the first round, each person will rotate roles until everyone has played every role):
  — The Listener (advisor)
  — The Talker (client)
  — The Observer

- Before the role play begins
  — Listener (advisor), hand your client sheet to the Observer.
  — Talker (client), briefly describe for the benefit of both the Listener and Observer some basic background information (what business he or she is in, revenues, number of employees, industry, what the CPA firm already does for them).
  — Observer, please find the "Sales Call (Branch) Exercise Observer's Note Sheet" and respond to the questions listed, and note any other observations that you think should be shared with your group
- The set up for this role play is The Talker (client) called his or her CPA for assistance, and the CPA suggested that the person best suited to help resolve the client's problems was his or her partner (The Listener/advisor). So, the client called last week and asked the advisor (Listener) to lunch. Our role play picks up as the Advisor and Client meet for the first time at a restaurant for lunch.

Once the time expires, the Advisor (Listener) is asked to identify the issues uncovered and prioritize them. The Observer should compare that list to those found on the "Client Worksheet." Finally, the Observer shares his or her observations about the exercise. Let the role play begin.

Self-Assessment

Finally, there is the "Self-Assessment" exercise (exercise 9-4). Each chapter is building on skills found in the previous ones. However, the exercises in this chapter force you to pull them all together. After you have gone through the forms and role plays, you will find that you are comfortable in some areas and extremely uncomfortable in others. Analyze this discomfort to determine what developmental areas you should be focusing on.

Let's get started with the Discovery Call role play exercise.

Exercise 9-1

Discovery Call Role Play

Scenario Sheet

The Structured Discovery Call: Objective—Qualify

Investigation Phase
- Introduction
- Become acquainted with the business
- Qualify the prospect

Closing Phase
- Abbreviated sales pitch
- Identification of the next step
- Seek agreement

Role Play Scenarios:

1. Wants additional general information because he or she is a pack rat. Checks all information request boxes because of curiosity. Has no intention of spending $$.

2. Wants to talk to someone about providing a higher level of tax advice because he or she just found out about being audited by the IRS. He or she is unhappy with the current CPA and spends about $1,500 a year on tax return fees alone.

3. Wants additional information specific to planning. Has a company of $50 million in revenue that is ripe for a planning engagement.

4. Is a student wanting information for a project.

5. Works for a company now, thinking about starting a business, and would not blink an eye at spending $10,000 for some start-up advice.

6. Is sheepishly inquiring about tax advice because he or she hasn't filled a return in over 10 years. Although he or she doesn't make a lot of money running his or her own cash business, he or she wants to do the right thing and get caught up but is hesitant to acknowledge ignoring 10 years of filing. He or she fully expects to pay $10,000 or more for help.

7. Wants additional information. Is calling trying to find some help moving his or her business from QuickBooks to Peachtree accounting. Although, this $25 million dollar company easily can afford, and should be looking at, a full blown accounting system. However, the owner doesn't know this, but at the same time, has no problem spending whatever it takes so that the information needed is available.

8. Doesn't remember sending anything in or talking to anyone and is too busy to talk.

9. Wants a free hour of consulting, feels a need for help, and is the soon-to-be incoming President (son or daughter taking over) of a $500 million dollar business.
10. Wants free tax review and currently does a 1040EZ.
11. Doesn't remember sending anything in or talking to anyone, but is struggling with several business issues at the current time and is willing to talk. The business is about an $8 million dollar professional firm.
12. Interested, not ready now, but wants you to call back in 6 months.
13. Works for a company now, thinking about starting a business, and spending $500 for assistance would be an enormous commitment to make.
14. Wants free tax review, is having some problems with an IRS audit, and spends about $2,500 a year on a tax return.

Discovery Call Observer's Notes Sheet

*Consultant:*_____

*Client:*_____

Write down your observations regarding the Advisor's or Consultant's questioning style, use of open-ended questions, or lack thereof. Did the conversation comfortably lead to qualifying the business? Did the client drop clues that the MTBA never picked up or clues the MTBA picked up but never followed? Did the advisor or consultant make a commitment that was unwarranted given the call situation? Please note any thoughts you have that might help the MTBA in future Discovery Call situations.

Notes for the MTBA: _____

_____

_____

_____

_____

_____

_____

_____

_____

_____

_____

_____

_____

_____

_____

_____

_____

_____

_____

_____

_____

Discovery Call Prompter

Write down your scripted open.

_____

_____

_____

_____

_____

_____

_____

_____

_____

_____

Write down an open-ended question or two.

_____

_____

_____

_____

_____

_____

Were these four areas addressed during the discovery call?

Timeframe

The first issue to address is *timeframe*. Ask the potential client a question like, "What is your timeframe for getting this project underway," or "When do you want this [some service] to be completed?"

_____

_____

_____

Decision-Maker

The next critical piece of information to collect is who is the decision-maker. This is a tough question to ask, and most versions of the question cause more harm than good. For this reason, we ask you to memorize these words: "Besides yourself, is there anyone else who will be involved in making the final decision?"

_____

_____

_____

Budget

The next question to ask pertains to the project's budget. This is not a sensitive question to ask, even though you may not get an answer. Something like, "How much have you budgeted for this project?" or "What did you plan on spending?" are acceptable alternatives.

_____

_____

_____

Priority

Once the potential client acknowledges a price range that is within the realm of reasonableness, the last question we ask concerns priority. Simply stated, "What's the priority of this project to your organization?" If the issue has clear priority, this does not need to be asked, but the advisor needs to defend why the question was purposely overlooked.

_____

_____

_____

Notes:

_____

_____

_____

_____

_____

_____

Exercise 9-2

Closing Exercise

Situation:

You have just completed an information gathering meeting with your new client. She operates a computer network consulting firm and wants to expand her practice. She currently has five programmer/analyst employees working for her. She wants you to help her establish a marketing plan. She has told you that she thinks she has lost over $500,000 worth of projects due to the fact that she has been very haphazard regarding how she markets her business. This loss in project revenue is based partially on inside information about her competitors. Although it appears she spends about as much in marketing as her competitors, she consistently does not receive nearly as many inquiries regarding her services.

Your new client also is interested in improving her billing process. She feels it is slow and inefficient, and because of that she knows of over $75,000 in lost billings from last year that are uncollectable because those projects are complete and considered paid-in-full.

Finally, the owner seems to have excellent skills in attracting and closing new projects. However, she is not so good (by her own admission) regarding day-to-day firm administration. She would like to brainstorm with you about ideas on how to improve firm administration because if things stay the same, she feels her lead programmer/analyst will get so frustrated he will quit.

Step One: List your new client's hot buttons.

1. _____

2. _____

3. _____

Step Two: Without committing to a price or a cost estimate, write down an example of a trial close.

_____

_____

_____

_____

_____

_____

_____

_____

_____

_____

Step Three: Write down an example of a closing statement based on the following additional facts.

Assume that you are comfortable with the skills required to perform this engagement, that your price estimate to help your new client create a marketing plan is $25,000, that for an additional $10,000 you could review her billing system and procedures and be in a position to make recommendations, and that the three-hour brainstorming meeting regarding firm administration would run about $1,200. Assuming that all three projects have the same priority and she wants to hire someone to help her with all three immediately, what is your closing response?

_____

_____

_____

_____

_____

_____

_____

_____

_____

_____

Exercise 9-3

Sales Call (Information Gathering or Branch) Exercise

Rules of the Game

The objective is for the advisor to find out what the client's top priorities are and to refrain from diving into the details until we fully understand what is "keeping the client awake at night."

The rotation of the game is: the new player becomes the advisor, and the last round's advisor becomes the current round's client.

This exercise can become as complex as the facilitator desires. The first focus is to get the advisor more aware of the various branches the client identifies. So as the exercise facilitator, please break in and comment anytime the advisor doesn't recognize that the client has created a branch in the investigative tree. In other words, if the client was to say, "I called you because I thought it was time we started wrapping up last year' tax return, and because I wanted to talk to you about planning for my retirement." In this case, two important topics are on the table for discussion: the client's tax return and retirement planning. Every time a topic that needs consultative investigation is introduced by the client, the advisor is to yell, "Branch." If the advisor does not say, "Branch," the facilitator should break in and comment.

Other more advanced areas might be to listen for the advisor asking multiple questions at a time without recognizing it. It is okay that this happens, but the advisor should catch himself or herself and go back and ask each question individually. If that does not occur, the facilitator should break in.

If an advisor keeps trapping himself or herself by asking closed questions, this is another area for facilitator involvement.

Sales Call/Branch Exercise Client Worksheet

Put yourself in the shoes of one of your good business clients. For the sake of this exercise, consider that you have a good relationship with your advisor, you call and see him or her two or three times a year, and that you have gladly accepted a lunch or office appointment. Be prepared to introduce the business to your advisor before the exercise and some fundamental things he or she should know. Finally, on this form, list your current priorities or areas that are of concern for you in the business. In other words, list what is keeping you awake at night. None of these areas have to be financial. After you have listed at least three areas of concern, indicate their priority to each other in the "priority" column. **DO NOT** fill in the "$ Value to the Client" column yet.

Description of Issue	Priority	$ Value to the Client of Resolving This Issue

Sales Call/Branch Exercise Observer's Note Sheet

Make notes regarding the progress of this exercise. As potentially sensitive situations occur, jot down how well or poorly the CPA handled them. Some issues to consider are as follows:

Did the CPA listen carefully to the conversation, or did he or she talk too much?

_____

_____

How well did the CPA make eye contact with all the players, use gestures, have a confident tone of voice, act interested, and so forth? Write your thoughts regarding nonverbal messages?

_____

_____

Did the CPA seem to pick up on subtleties of the client's comments or concerns, or both?

_____

_____

Did the CPA interrupt the client or start talking before the client completed his thoughts?

_____

_____

Did the CPA miss consulting opportunities (branches)?

_____

_____

In what area(s) did the CPA seem most comfortable?

_____

_____

Other comments regarding this exercise.

_____

_____

_____

Exercise 9-4

Self-Assessment Timeline Relative to Improving My Call Skills

Based on the materials covered in this chapter, please take a few moments and assess your weaknesses. Then, using the form that follows, make note of any skills you plan to work on as well as a timeframe to reassess your progress. In addition, if there are activities or exercises, or both, you plan on attempting, jot them down and note your intended completion date. This form is provided solely as a self-improvement tool.

Name: _____

The following are skills I plan to improve:

- _____ By when: _____
- _____ By when: _____
- _____ By when: _____
- _____ By when: _____
- _____ By when: _____
- _____ By when: _____
- _____ By when: _____
- _____ By when: _____

The following are activities I plan to attempt:

- _____ By when: _____
- _____ By when: _____
- _____ By when: _____
- _____ By when: _____
- _____ By when: _____
- _____ By when: _____
- _____ By when: _____
- _____ By when: _____

Section 3

Administrative and Organizational Issues

Billing and Engagement Considerations

"If you really do put a small value upon yourself, rest assured that the world will not raise your price."

~ ANONYMOUS

The material in this chapter covers an area where personal preferences, organizational structure, and risk management all play a role. For example, even though advisory or consulting service collectability should improve by utilizing multiple billing cycles in a month, this administrative hassle may be deemed disproportionate to the gain (especially if collections haven't been a problem in the past). With this in mind, we would like to share with you our approach regarding a few billing and engagement issues.

Tracking Your Time for Billing Purposes

There are perhaps three broad approaches to billing for advisory assistance:

1. Time and charges
2. Project billing
3. Value billing

We will cover the pros and cons of each of these approaches in this chapter.

Time and Charges Approach

This approach is what most CPAs have been doing forever—keeping track of time and related costs and billing the client periodically to clear out the work-in-progress that accumulates from tracking the time and charges. Accounting for hours and minutes has to be the most tedious and boring task associated with our profession. It is so hard to keep track of miscellaneous phone calls and other interruptions. But, over time, these minutes add up. This is especially true for most trusted business advisor (MTBA) type of work because you easily can find yourself delivering 6 hours worth of advisory services in 15-minute increments (that is, through telephone calls), an amount of time you can't afford to give away with numerous clients month after month. So making an effort to record all of your time is essential if you want your advisory services to be profitable. However, because of the management policies of many organizations, although recording all of your time is administratively feasible, it may not be politically practical. Let us explain.

The problem of recording time often is tied to that of billing it. Not all time is worthy of being billed, at least not at full rates. (And the converse is true, but we'll cover this in a few moments). In a fair number of firms, certain time is *not* recorded because the worker does not want the time billed. More importantly, the worker doesn't want to argue with the billing partner about why the time wasn't valuable or why their realization percentage went down. In other cases, partners might not log the time because they have already made the determination that the time wasn't going to be billed. So their theory is, "why create meaningless entries and paperwork?"

For those of you using the time and charges approach, this dilemma can be solved by deciding to record all time, understanding that all time won't carry the same value or charge rate (maybe more, maybe less, if one at all), and then itemizing everything on the advisory bills. This includes billable and what we call "no-charge time." By doing this, you will find that clients will

- not call as often asking for an explanation of fees.
- pay on a more timely basis.

Historically, the CPA profession has created bills that have a one- or two-line description along with a fee. When providing advisory and consulting services using the time and charges approach, this can be deadly. Not only does this type of bill jeopardize getting paid, but it potentially impairs being hired for future work. Why? Because traditional work, as discussed earlier, is not completely understood by your clients. Therefore, it is hard for them to judge if the actual time spent was necessary. Consulting is different, at least in some cases. Because the client is usually very comfortable with the objectives and implementation plan of most management projects, the manner in which your implementation time was spent is more likely to be scrutinized. By providing an itemized bill, you allow your client an easy way to review your efforts and progress. For example, an itemized bill using the time and charges method might look something like this:

For professional services rendered in connection with:

Lease of an office building: 4/21/09

Telephone conference call regarding lease of an office building between Lynda, Sam, and Prominent Point leasing agent Jim.	1 hour	$ 350.00
Discussion with Lynda and Sam about conference call, pros and cons of leasing the building, various other issues regarding the same matter.	1.2 hours	420.00
Meeting with Sam concerning: 4/25/09		
Americans With Disabilities Act requirements	3.5 hours	1,225.00
Telephone conversations with: 4/22–4/30/09		
Leasing agent regarding maintenance fee cap	.3 hours	105.00
Leasing agent regarding increasing the build-out allowance	.2 hours	70.00
Lynda regarding lease versus buy decision	.4 hours	140.00
Numerous quick conversations with Sam regarding various computer accounting system issues	1.0 hours	350.00
Total Bill		$2,660.00

If we incurred out-of-pocket costs, we'd add them in with line item explanations, and we'd attach copies of substantiation for the out-of-pocket costs, such as receipts and invoices. Do we mark them up? We know of some firms who do, but we choose to bill them at our cost. We don't think it matters as long as the client knows what you are doing.

Now if you have a license to some intellectual property, such as an assessment, and your wholesale cost is $45, but the assessment retails in the market for $150, we suggest that you bill the assessment at the retail price. If there's some price sensitivity, you can always decide to make special concessions on a one-off basis. And speaking of price sensitivity, let's address that further in the context of the preceding sample invoice.

When there is price sensitivity, an itemized bill gives the client an opportunity to satisfy his or her concerns by reviewing the detailed time. This often triggers a reminder of the variety of events that happened to make up that time, where one phase of the project was more complicated than expected or that additional work was requested.

Detailed billing helps in even the worst case scenario, one in which the client challenges the value of some specific portion of your work. It's advantageous because at this point, instead of arguing about the overall fee, you are now only discussing a few line items on the bill. This helps resolve issues expeditiously and, if concessions are made, they are based on smaller numbers. For example, consider the preceding bill in the following scenario:

> Let's say that Lynda was slightly upset at the $140 charge regarding the lease/buy decision conversation. She maintains that because no new information came out of that discussion, she shouldn't have to pay for it. We would then very politely remind her that we are paid by the hour, not by specific results, and that she initiated that conversation. Immediately after we explain our position, we would likely comment, "Would you like for me to remove that line item from the bill?"

Based on our experience, Lynda would likely reply, "No, I don't think removing it entirely is fair." We would then reply, "We are happy to reduce this ... just let us know what you have in mind." In a situation like this, the client rarely asks for much; and often, especially when a line item is so small, after the client suggests a discount, we reduce it to zero anyway. We follow our discount offer with, "it is important to us that you are happy with our services and that we can have this kind of open communication."

Look at what happened here. Although this is a sample conversation, many just like it have occurred in firms that use the approach we've just outlined. Several critical points should be reviewed. First, the argument was over $140, not the entire bill. Had the bill been summarized instead of itemized, we could have offered Lynda a 10 percent discount (which would have been $266) and had less affect than deleting an entire $140 line item. Keep in mind that the public is so numb from retail marketing that it takes discounts around 30 percent or more to get people excited. So putting yourself in a position to have to discount an entire bill is a bad situation. Under our scenario, you have the luxury of discounting a specific line item by 100 percent with minimal negative impact.

One last thought on recording detailed time entries: either you can spend some time with your partners and staff outlining the kind of narrative they are expected to write down regarding a time entry, or each billing partner can spend many wasted hours rewriting those entries at billing time. Note this: it is our experience that partners often procrastinate when it comes to reviewing and completing bills in the first place. Adding the extra laborious step of having to wordsmith each line item on an advisory bill will only make matters worse. Therefore, it seems the logical choice is to spend time upfront identifying the kind of work explanations you are looking for and then performing the necessary training to ensure that the partner review effort required at billing time is minimal. This has become somewhat easier with technological advancements because some timekeeping systems now allow you to build a list of billing legend codes that can be used by "checking a box," rather than requiring each legend to be customized when you are generating invoices.

Now that we've reviewed the issue of recording time under this method, let's consider some more nuances of billing under the time and charges approach. Our first topic of discussion is the time we code as "no-charge" or "gratis" time. Most billing partners attempt to charge it if at all possible. The perception is that if the time isn't billed, it didn't serve any purpose. We don't believe that is always the case. Our experience has been that gratis time is not only valuable, but at times, a necessary part of building the MTBA relationship. When a bill is created, we specifically itemize any nonchargeable time or show discounts to offset the time we believe falls into this category. This demonstration of unbilled contribution to the project easily can enhance client loyalty, allows us to operate in a martyrdom-free environment, and indicates our commitment to the success of the project. We often refer to the related write-down under this approach as our "investment in the relationship."

The idea of creating a martyrdom-free environment is critical because

- what your clients don't know can and will work against you.
- if you expect to benefit from giving your clients something, they have to know you've given it to them.

Any long-term arrangement with a client requires some give and take on both sides. This usually results in some discounted or free time somewhere along the way. Free time can have significant value as long as the client is aware of it. The bill is an excellent forum to demonstrate this supportive commitment and attitude.

Although we understand the intent to not bill certain time because you provide a service, two good things happen when you record that time anyway. First, in some cases, you find you have spent much more time than you ever expected doing free work so you decide to bill some of it (that is good for your profitability). Second, should you stay with your plan to provide that time for free, because you have recorded it, that time is easy to put on the bill and show it as gratis time or "discounted to zero" work. In this case, you win because by showing it on the bill and sharing that information with your client, you remind your client that they are getting more out of your relationship than what they are paying for.

Discounting certain work to zero or applying a credit against your time can work in your favor. The message is: *time is money, but not all time is worth the same amount of money. Some time is simply your investment in maintaining a quality and long-lasting relationship.* In other words, you are communicating two messages (1) a quality control measure, and (2) a message that you think this relationship is worth investing in. When you perform premium rate work, you expect to bill and receive premium rates. But because all work isn't always of the same value, occasionally, when a clear inequity occurs, it makes sense to adjust your bill. This can be perceived as an attempt on your part to balance the relationship between rates and value. And this kind of perception is one of the keys to client satisfaction.

Just to be clear, we are not advocating that you go out and consciously sell work at less than standard rates. We also are not advocating giving away time when you are working on a project. We are simply acknowledging the fact that everyone gives away some time to their clients throughout the year, and we feel like sharing this information creates a great deal of positive benefits and goodwill.

Project Billing Approach

Under the project approach, rather than billing for every 1/10th of an hour you spend, your agreement with your client is that assuming certain conditions exist, your fee for a specifically defined phase of a project will be fixed at the agreed-to amount. Think about going to the dentist. To clean your teeth is one price, to get x-rays is another, to get a tooth filled is a third price. The point is your dentist does not start the clock when he or she first starts poking you and then at the end decide what to charge you based on how long it took. This is a simple example of a project billing approach—each phase, each product, and each added service has a specific price depending on what is included in each configuration.

However, project billing can be difficult to use when you are trying to "guesstimate" the amount of time it could take to complete a complex project delivered over an extended implementation schedule. The reason is because there are a seemingly infinite number of variables beyond your control. The more complex the project and the longer it takes to complete it, the greater the number of these distractions and obstacles you are likely to encounter. Two common techniques can be used to mitigate this chaos and position project pricing as the option of choice.

The first is phasing. If you are agreeing with a client to do a fairly simple, well-defined phase of work under the unbundling approach we've covered earlier in this text, you easily can price and perform a short phase profitably under a project billing approach.

The second is leveraging consulting packages, which we introduced earlier. Because a consulting package starts with a great deal of experience and is wrapped with an outlined methodology, specific steps in a process, identified deliverables, and clearly articulated "out of scope" common variations, you can provide a project price profitable to even these complex longer-term assignments. The key, however, is in monitoring those "out of scope" variables and making sure that when they arise, they are addressed quickly.

The advantage of this approach, when you can use it, is that your client doesn't need to worry about being nickel-and-dimed to death every time they pick up the phone to talk to you. If you've priced the project properly, neither should you.

What is an example of this type of billing? Let's say that you assist clients with strategic planning, and you use an approach that normally consists of

- review of past company performance including certain key operating statistics.
- conducting a preretreat online survey of up to 20 managers and selected staff at the company.
- a facilitated planning meeting of one and one-half to two days.
- sharing high-level notes of the discussions taken from the meeting that outline the stated goals and actions plans identified to achieve them.

Assuming the survey for the company is similar to the commonly-used template you have, your project price might be developed as follows:

Online survey charge, with survey limited to 15 questions, including one open-ended question	$2,500
Two days of facilitation, including review of company performance, creation of the retreat agenda and delivery of the high-level notes of the meeting	<u>$7,000</u>
Total fees for project	$9,500

In your communication with your client, you would address the objectives of the retreat, the deliverables, the scope of the work, and the project fee of $9,500. There's no need to break the fee down further because it is based on specific duties or deliverables, not hourly charges. Don't forget that just as we did with the time and charges approach, we normally add out-of-pocket costs at actual cost to our fees when we bill the client, and we attach copies of substantiating documentation (receipts and other source documents) to the invoice when we bill them.

A key issue under this billing approach is change orders. Change orders for increased work would need to be discussed with the client at the time the scope change occurs. For example, let's say that you jump into the survey design, and by the time it's ready to launch, the client wants you to ask 25 questions, including several open-ended questions instead of just one (open-ended questions take a great deal more time to summarize). Or what if the client wanted to augment the preretreat discovery to include one-on-one telephone interviews of certain personnel? Both of these requests are reasons to introduce change orders to the initially quoted fee of $9,500 because the scope of work required has escalated from that originally anticipated.

A common question we get regarding project work is, "Do we still need to keep our time on this project since the fee has already been set?" Our answer is yes, but for the same reasons a contractor keeps job cost records on a fixed-price job. The time records help us better understand, for future, similar projects, how to bid or price them profitably. Being able to analyze the time after a project is completed gives you a sanity check about whether you need to change your pricing model. It also helps you review whether any of your people might need additional supervision or guidance in order to be able to do the work within the expected time requirement. Because change orders should be common in the project pricing (or fixed price) approach, time records help you uncover work that should have been flagged as a change order. Or when change orders are identified and approved, because everyone is used to turning in their time anyway, billing for those changes is made easy.

Value Billing Approach

The value billing approach has been touted by some in our profession as the billing option of choice for years. Does it work? It can, but in our experience, it is not as widely used as other methods. In fact, often when professionals claim they are using a value billing approach, we find that they actually are using what we previously covered as the project billing approach. They are, for the most part, figuring out what their average standard rates will amount to doing a specific phase or project and then quoting a fixed price for their work. A good example would be an automobile mechanic charging 3.5 hours of work and, therefore, a flat fee (plus the cost of parts) to change a water pump. The mechanic looked at a flat rate book, which estimated that this work normally requires 3.5 hours for that specific make of car for an average skilled worker. Whether it took the mechanic 3.5 hours or 1.5 hours, the charge is still the same. The commentary we often hear is the price was based on the value of the work. Because those rating books are often based on the time it would take a marginally skilled mechanic, a nice fudge factor is already built in to cover unforeseen problems when they arise. In other words, the mechanic fully expects to be able to outperform the projected estimates.

To us, true value billing requires you to bill the client based on the value generated from the work. Admittedly, in some types of work and projects, determining what that value is can be very difficult. In this text, we've covered some ways to quantify the value to be gained, or at least protected, and you can certainly use that technique to pursue value billing if you wish. However, attempting to value bill on some complex implementation projects could be difficult for you due to the myriad of variables you could encounter that are outside of your control. In many cases, by the time you built an engagement agreement that covered the contingency factors, you might run the client off or have such a complex agreement that it could make life more complicated than it really is worth to you.

In some instances, value billing can be a boon to everyone involved. Let's talk about an MTBA situation Dom encountered when he was practicing as a traditional CPA. He was at a client's office meeting with the general manager and their attorney to finalize negotiations on the purchase of a piece of land. The three of them had a conference call with the seller's agent. At the end of the discussion, as the deal was just about finalized, Dom asked the seller's agent if there was room to discount the price. The parcel had been offered at $535,000. The agent suggested they would consider an offer to that effect, after which ensued a short but spirited discussion resulting in a $15,000 discount off the price the general manager and attorney had assumed was fixed. The conversation took about 20 minutes. The overall total time involved in the client meeting was not quite an hour. At normal billing rates, Dom would have billed the client a couple hundred dollars at that time. However, he called and talked with the general manager before sending the bill to discuss what might be fair. In the eyes of the client, $1,000 was a very reasonable fee for the value he provided in negotiating this better deal for his client.

The problem in this scenario is common, which is why value billing has not become routine in our profession. It is only after we do the work that a clear value reveals itself. Usually, an after-the-fact call does not yield the optimum response. Consider Dom's preceding scenario. If he had gone to the client before this phone call and said, "Look, I will come to the meeting for free, but if I end up saving you some money, I want a third of what I save you," the client probably would have agreed (thinking most likely nothing would be saved so he will get some free advice, but worst case, he is still two-thirds ahead). But he wouldn't have made that offer unless he knew in advance there was a high likelihood of this kind of windfall unveiling itself. Otherwise, it makes more sense to just show up and be happy with the hourly bill.

Here is another example. We were called by the president of a privately-owned, but large company to help with some organizational planning. The company had been struggling with fiefdoms and finding ways to organize their diverse groups for optimum impact. A lot of the problems centered on one vice president (VP). This VP was nearly uncontrollable (and was someone the majority shareholder never seemed willing to put in the line of fire). Our client had a Big 4 consulting department come in and provide some advice, but for all the time and money that management spent with them, the outcome was marginal. Using the techniques we discussed in chapter 9 of this text, we agreed to conduct advance surveys of the management team, followed by interviews of each of them, together with three meetings spread over 6 months. The meetings ran from one day to one and one-half days in length. We facilitated difficult discussions for them and helped the key shareholder put the troublesome VP on notice that he was not the heir-apparent and would, in fact, need to make a few changes if he wanted to continue being just plain apparent at the company, if you know what we mean. The price, negotiated in advance? About $80,000, plus costs, which was definitely a value bill on our part.

Finally, certain services lend themselves to value billing, like taking a piece of the sales price when you help your client sell his or her business or taking a percentage of the research and development tax credits your firm found, articulated and presented to the IRS, which are approved. As we have previously described, there are times when value billing has its place in a CPA practice, especially in the advisory or consulting service areas. But in each of these examples, they work best when we have so much experience delivering a specific service that our history allows us to predict a greater-than-average payoff most of the time.

In conclusion, we are not saying that everyone should run out and try to change to value billing as their standard method. Rather, we are saying that it is a viable method, one that should be considered more often than it is, and one that can be very lucrative when the right situation presents itself. But then again, we can make the same exact statement about the project pricing and time and charges approaches as well.

Frequency of Billing

The frequency of billing in most CPA firms is monthly. This cycle is not only in line with cash-flow requirements, but it's easier to manage (and requires less overhead) than weekly or biweekly billing.

With advisory and consulting projects, whether it is a retainer refreshment, a portion of a fixed project fee, or regular billing, being paid is an indication of management's satisfaction with your performance. Because the perception of your value as an advisor is usually more emotional than when you perform traditional work, you need to keep a close watch on the current feelings.

Frequent billings are suggested. Billing something upfront to kick off the project also has merit. In fact, when you are working on a project billing basis or value billing basis, you can give the client multiple payment options to help them manage their cash flow:

- Some portion (from 33 percent to 50 percent) to start the work, and the balance due within 30 days of completion
- The whole fee, in advance, minus a discount, maybe 5 percent to 10 percent, for early payment

Don't be surprised if they pay the discounted amount of the full bill in advance if it's a short duration project. We'll cover advance payments more under the following section, "Retainers."

Our timeline is simple. Bill your advisory time often enough so that no individual bill exceeds the client's cash flow comfort zone. For example, if a client feels $2,500 is a big project, bill them before you accumulate that level of outstanding charges. Regarding large projects, because we worked in small CPA firms, we tended to bill at intervals when the receivable became more than we wanted to carry. So if after 10 days we had accumulated $10,000 or more of work-in-process, for example, we would bill it. As a general rule, we tend to bill as soon as a project is complete, at the completion of each phase, at the end of the month, or when large balances are accumulated, whichever happens sooner. We also will send out invoices more frequently than monthly on complex or politically sensitive projects (internal politics), if we want to more closely monitor the level of satisfaction regarding the work we are doing (people pay quickly for work they are happy with and slow the process down when they are starting to get frustrated). Therefore, bill in increments the client can afford. This way, you can minimize their pain and yours.

Billing your clients frequently also reminds them that you are hard at work on their behalf. If a number of days or weeks pass before you present your client with an invoice, they may get the impression that nothing is being done.

Finally, if the project is volatile, it may be imperative to bill weekly or—in some extreme cases, where large resources are committed—every day or every other day. An example of a volatile situation would be performing a consulting engagement for a bank with imminent takeover by the FDIC (Federal Deposit Insurance Corporation). In such a situation, the agreement between the CPA firm and the client bank should be that an invoice will be prepared before day's end for that day's work, submitted to the bank for payment, with the payment electronically transmitted to your account before closing.

Survey Information You Might Find Interesting in This Context

Now that we've talked about phasing, estimating, tracking your time, billing approaches, and frequency of billing, let's take a few moments to cover some independent research on the pricing area. The best way we know to address this is by presenting you with some highlights from a 2008 report, "Fees, Utilization and Key Metrics in Consulting 2008," prepared and published by Kennedy Information, Inc., located in Peterborough, New Hampshire. The following indented paragraphs are direct quotes from this study:

- "The average consulting firm's hourly fees climbed by 2.7% in 2006 to 3.4% in 2007 and are expected to grow by 4.4% in 2008. Consultants are also billing more hours. Utilization rates set new highs across much of the profession, growing highest among the lower staffing levels."
- "Broadly across the profession, the average firm will see its operating margins (operating income on an EBITDA basis, divided by net revenues) increase from about 17% in 2007 to just over 20% in 2008."
- "Realized rates, the hourly fees consultants actually collect, are projected to grow faster at every position in 2008 than they did in 2007. The growth in realized rates for those below the director/manager level are expected to approach almost 5% by the end of 2008."

Paraphrased, partners are doing well to achieve a utilization percentage rate in the mid to high 50s, whereas the profession has seen an unprecedented climb in utilization percentages as high as the low 80s in the other levels.

The overall view is that consulting is doing well and is predicted to continue to do so. As this book goes to press, in our stumbling economy, we are seeing rates and profitability flatten, but there is still healthy demand. The following is a table of realized rates from 2005–2008 (projected) by staff level:

Realized 2005–2008 (Projected)

	2005	2006	2007	2008 (Projected)
Partner/Vice President	$294	$303	$319	$331
Director Manager	$256	$263	$279	$291
Senior/Experienced Consultant	$220	$226	$238	$249
Consultant/Recent MBA	$166	$169	$177	$185
Entry Level/Analyst	$128	$132	$138	$145

As with any competitive environment when an economy shifts, the lack of an overabundance of work causes organizations to get creative to maintain work backlogs. In the current market, we are seeing firms trying to expand their relationships and share-of-wallet within the companies they serve. Here is how KRI commented on this topic:

Due to a number of market influences, the traditional consulting 'turfs' of the five service lines are converging (Strategy, Operations Management [OM], Business Advisory Services [BAS], Human Resources [HR] and Information Technology [IT]). Strategy consulting is being pushed into projects that historically would have been handled by operations management and business advisory services firms. And at the other end of the spectrum, IT firms are increasingly trying to go upstream into traditional management consulting projects.

The convergence is occurring in part because of the gap between hourly fees among IT and management consultants. IT consultants tend to charge the lowest hourly rate compared to the other service lines. So as more IT firms compete against BAS and OM consultants, there's a natural drag on the prevailing market rates.

Meanwhile, the downward expansion of strategy practices is adding new competitive pressures. The silver lining is that strategy consultants tend to bring higher fees downstream. *Strategy consultants historically have charged the highest hourly fees of any service line,* meaning an influx of strategy consultants into OM and BAS markets should help raise market rates. However, because there are more IT consultants than there are consultants in the rest of the service lines combined, the drag by IT consultants has a much larger net effect on realized rates than does the upward lift provided by the down-river migration of strategy consultants.

This brings us to the rates by service line. The following is a table from the KRI data showing "Projected 2008 Realized Rates by Staff Level for the Largest Consulting Practices by Service Line:"

	Partner/ Vice President	Manager/ Project Leader	Senior/ Experienced Consultant	Consultant/ Recent MBA	Entry Level/ Analyst
Strategy	$536	$458	$399	$242	$170
Operations Management	$471	$435	$388	$219	$154
Business Advisory Services	$452	$405	$369	$215	$149
Information Technology	$399	$358	$315	$174	$122
Human Resources	$429	$383	$350	$202	$136

As you can see, specialized consulting and advisory rates are very healthy compared to the rates we tend to find for traditional CPA services. Even the average rates for all consulting that we reviewed earlier in this section reflects realized rates that most firms around the country, except those in large metropolitan areas, would be happy to achieve. Recognize that the 2008 projected rates shown in both tables were averages, not highs (as you can find, for example, strategy consultants charging in excess of $1,000 per hour). Of even more importance, notice the low end, where $122 was the least expensive rate projected for an entry level person across all lines of specialty service. Historically, you could partially justify the gap between entry level rates for consulting versus traditional accounting simply because of utilization expectation. However, with consulting seeing utilization percentages in the low 80s for lower level workers, that explanation is not nearly as compelling. We believe these higher rates are more representative of the value clients place on accomplishing their own initiatives versus those required of them by outside parties (banks, IRS, government agencies, and others).

Specifically mentioned in this report as to projects that tend to attract lower than average versus higher than average pricing pressure:

Lower than average pricing pressure (less price sensitive):

- Client-specific process improvement projects
- Litigation support, M&A due diligence
- Vertical expertise-driven Enterprise Resource Planning and Systems Integration

- Specialized engagements (executive compensation, etc.) where consultants have unique skills

<u>Higher than average pricing pressure (more downward fee pressure):</u>

- Anything that can be done offshore, especially coding work
- Sarbanes-Oxley compliance
- Many security solutions (physical, technological, and risk) have become commoditized
- Routine actuarial services, government projects, and distressed industries"

KRI also reported on the types of billing approaches it found in the consulting arena. As you can see, fixed price (or project, as we call it) and time and materials (or time and charges, as we call it) were clearly the most common methods, with value billing playing a minor role in the management consulting side only. The following is a graphic summarizing the "Billing Method Usage by Firm Type in 2007."

	Management Consulting	IT Consulting
Relatively Evenly Spread	14.6%	11.4%
Majority Fixed Price	42.7%	22.9%
Majority Value Based	6.3%	0.0%
Majority T&M	36.5%	65.7%

Given all of this, it should be no surprise that the executive summary of this report wrapped up with the following simple reminder (KRI noted everything but the subsequent comments in italics):

How the coming market changes will affect firms' bottom lines will be determined largely by how well firms manage the interplay of basic levers of profitability:

- How much firms pay their consultants *(don't get sloppy paying too much for your people)*
- How much firms charge clients for their services *(realized versus book rates and project versus time and materials versus value billing)*
- The ratio of senior talent to junior talent *(increasing your work leverage is key)*
- How many hours their consultants are billable *(each person needs to be responsible for a certain amount of billings, rather than just focusing on the individual metrics of billable hours, realization, and utilization, which are manipulated too easily)*

We found a great deal of the information in the Kennedy study to be interesting and helpful to our planning. As you would guess, the research contains much more detail than was previously discussed, as well as more information. For your own copy of this study, contact Brad Smith, Kennedy Research Incorporated, at 603-585-3101 or by e-mail at bsmith@kennedyinfo.com.

Gaining an Edge on Being Paid for Your Involvement

The following are three key words to remember regarding the billing and collectability of advisory consulting fees:

Retainer, Retainer, and Retainer.

Traditional CPA work has been paper-oriented. For example, during tax season, we produce tax returns. When we perform audits, we deliver an opinion. For bookkeeping engagements, we compile financial statements. The point is that even though accounting is a service, the end result to the client is commonly a tangible product.

Advisory and consulting services are just the opposite. The result often is intangible, such as the resolution of a dispute between labor and management or a new marketing approach. Therefore, many circumstances exist where adopting a retainer billing philosophy is critical to the success of the consultant. For example, after a consulting project has been completed, a client may begin to question whether the end result warranted the rates or amount charged. It is easy, especially in hindsight, to rationalize why a fee is out of line. Once a problem has been solved, management's motivation to pay for its resolution often falls in priority over time. As time passes, the perceived value of the consulting service diminishes or is taken for granted. These statements are partially true given the "beast" itself (that is, advisory and consulting service). As an MTBA, a major part of your job is to facilitate necessary change. This means that we help management help themselves. Therefore, good MTBAs and consultants work themselves out of jobs. Because MTBAs keep the spotlight and "high" reliance on others, they often put themselves into positions of being taken for granted or viewed after the fact as unnecessary. For example:

> Not very long ago, we conducted a planning meeting for an association that had been floundering in its strategic direction. After facilitating multiple sessions and working individually with several small teams, a plan of attack for the group was mapped out. On one of the last days of planning, a member of one of the teams commented, "We should have broken into small teams a long time ago. We are so effective when we work like this." The comment seemed to overlook the fact that our process and facilitation played a significant role as to why their small groups could gain the ground they did. The perception, by a number of the participants, was that the board seemed to just magically get their act together and reach consensus. The reality was that had we not been there to facilitate the necessary exchange of information, keep them on track, and have them follow a logical decision making process, they would have floundered for many more months (maybe even years). By keeping the spotlight off of us and our role, with our process focused around maximizing the talents of the management team (in this case, the association's board), it's easy for some to minimize the value of our involvement. This is particularly true anytime you are providing facilitative services. The better the facilitation is, the more empowered the group is, and the more likely you will be dealing with this issue from time to time.

This is why we made the comment that with respect to advisory and consulting services: some of the collectability issues are inherent in the beast itself. The advisory and consulting arena is no place for the thin-skinned or the ego maniac. The product we deliver is intangible, which is, therefore, constantly being challenged, interpreted, and misinterpreted. In addition, because of the high reliance and involvement of others, the success of our work is heavily dependent upon factors over which we have no control (such as the client's implementation of the action plan). Therefore, whenever possible, we want our fees to be based on performing the job, not the results thereof. Retainers, or advance payments, are tools that help facilitate the right perspective. Also, think of it as an insurance policy that protects the value of your time. Note: we don't object to being held to results. However, in "results expected" cases, we would use the value billing approach, add a premium to the project fee, or add a premium to our rates to cover additional work that might be necessary to secure the desired outcome. Given all of this, a number of reasons exist as to why retainers and advisory services so often go hand-in-hand.

The Value of Advisory Fees Is More Subjective

Clients have a preconceived perception of a product's value, such as a tax return. This judgment about what constitutes a *fair price* usually is based on two things:

1. *Comparison to a similar product.* Typically, accounting jobs are repetitive: tax returns are produced year after year, financial statements are generated monthly or quarterly. This repetition and past experience establishes an expectation about a product's value.
2. *Experience and quality of work.* Most people assume that all CPAs have the same knowledge and, therefore, that all similarly produced products, such as audits, are identical. This assumption, which doesn't distinguish between various degrees of experience and work quality, creates a commodity marketplace. Therefore, the preparation of a tax return, financial statement, or audit is subject to being *shopped*. This theoretical comparability establishes an acceptable fee range.

Ideas, on the other hand, are not subject to this same kind of price rigidity. Each advisory or consulting project is unique, so comparison to the past is not as relevant. Even in a competitive bidding situation, it's often difficult to compare one proposal to another because issues such as experience and communication ability are key ingredients. In advisory projects, the professional's skill—not time and effort—determines the value of the service. The bad news is that *value is often intangible and highly susceptible to interpretation.* Therefore, your client's perception of your work is of greater importance than the actual work itself. This makes MTBA services more political in nature than traditional CPA work; and if the internal politics aren't handled properly, the project is destined for difficulty if not failure.

The good news is that this political environment and uncertainty allows for greater leverage in pricing, especially when the results are better than anticipated. But if the outcome of your effort is even remotely tainted, then your fees are at risk. As an example, if you were hired to obtain financing, and the approved loan amount is considerably less than expected, then the perceived value of your work diminishes even if the situation was beyond your control. Collecting a retainer before the work is performed protects you from clients who tend to place a subjective value on your time.

Sometimes When Senior Management Asks You What the Problem Is, You Have to Tell Them That They Are the Problem

More than once, after performing our diagnostic work, talking to a variety of people and digging into root causes of situations presented to us, we have found that the guy or gal who brought us in is the primary, or at least a significant, cause of the problems their company is experiencing. Although we try to evaluate people and their ability to change when we're at the front end of projects, we still find one or two who talk a good line but are really not interested in changing themselves. This is because they believe everyone else needs to change instead of them. It's at times like these that it is good to have a significant portion of the project fee in our bank account already. Once in a while, the problem-causing executive decides that the project is not so important or that they will look for some sycophants to stroke their ego instead of confronting problems, causes, and effects.

Project Deadlines Are Internally Generated

There is another issue regarding retainers. With tax returns, audits, and financial statements, compliance deadlines help focus the attention of management to a project. These deadlines are often externally dictated, for example, by stockholders, banks, and vendors.

In the advisory arena, deadlines are most often internally generated. In other words, management decides on a daily basis what issues are "hot." These priorities can shift easily if an externally imposed deadline appears. Internal deadlines are subject to change for many other reasons, like the crumbling economy we have been living in as this goes to press at one extreme or a new marketing opportunity at the other. Many pressures can force management to reallocate their available resources. Internally motivated projects are the first to be reviewed, shuffled around, or canceled. Therefore, because advisory projects are often internally motivated, holding a retainer protects your fees should a resource reallocation occur. Also, collecting a retainer ensures that your project at least starts out as a priority item. Why? Because clients don't pay in advance for low-priority work.

Client Commitment Is Imperative

Client commitment is the most important component in the success of a project. This is because almost all MTBA work requires a great deal of client participation. Because problems are rarely solved with simple solutions, the people (within your firm, your client's company, or a combination of both) who implement the ideas determine a project's success or failure. The payment of a retainer demonstrates commitment from the client. Why? Once again, no one pays in advance for unimportant services.

There's one other factor to consider too. Ideas that are paid for tend to be more effective. This is because everyone likes to make good decisions. If your advice is bad, yet it was paid for in advance, then whoever hired you looks bad. So every time management refills your retainer, they increase their stake in the game. This, as a general rule, intensifies management's commitment to the project as well as their support of your efforts.

Retainers Aren't a Panacea

Retainers have their downside too. Years ago, our firm started charging everyone a retainer for consulting work. As you will see in a minute, it's not hard to ask for a retainer. As a matter of fact, once you incorporate a few "retainer-asking" tips into your toolkit, it's almost too easy to get paid a retainer. At one time, we found that we had been paid up-front for about four months of work. Although this sounds like a cash flow jackpot, it created some other problems. We backed off a bit on collecting retainers shortly after that. Or better put, we changed our retainer process. It is now less of a retainer and more of an agreed-to billing frequency and amount. For example, we might charge $50,000 for a specific number of days or hours of work. We then spread that total amount out over the number of months both parties plan on focusing on that project, whether that be 3 intense months or a much more drawn out schedule over 10 months. We bill the same amount each month and send a time update that allows the client to see how much time is left on the total time package. Clearly, this is still a retainer system, but more of a hybrid because it is really scheduled payments against a total agreement for a specific amount of time.

Basically, we ask for retainers or use our hybrid billing approach to

- verify management's commitment, both for starting the project and to secure continued support in order to complete it successfully.
- ensure that our fees are protected should the project lose its high priority.

For small projects, we rarely charge retainers. We just do the work and bill it afterwards. For larger projects, we almost always work off of a retainer or our hybrid approach. It's funny though, we hold a harder line on retainers for the organizations most people would least likely expect us to. The biggest example is we are exponentially more likely to charge a retainer to a large organization, one that would have no problem paying us, even if we are working on a small project. Why? Because it's very easy to get caught in the middle with a large company. In other words, you have support from one top manager, but not the support of another. Each might verbally have told consultants to start work, and when they find out what the other has done, a war breaks out. When this happens, even if we still get the job, either a significant amount of time winds up being lost (nonbillable) or work done before everyone has approved it is often expected to be heavily discounted. Although a mere phone call is more than enough to get started with even large projects for smaller organizations, we use a retainer with large companies to make sure the right people in the organizational chain of command have committed to the project before we expend a great deal of effort. One rule that has never failed us is

If we can get a check in our hands before the work starts, we have the top level visibility and project commitment we need.

At the other extreme, which is far more obvious, we tend to charge retainers to start-up companies and anytime a project seems outside a company's "natural" capacity to pay. With start-ups, retainers are normal. This group is commonly willing to sign up for a multitude of services. Unfortunately, they are rarely able to pay for all of them. Therefore, charging a retainer does both you and the client a service; it matches high priority work with capacity to pay. With the "natural capacity to pay" situation, we look for signals. For example, if we have a client that screams every time they receive a $2,500 or higher bill for services from anyone, whether it be from our firm, the lawyer, or other advisors, then being asked to perform a $10,000 project is suspect. Or if we were to be asked by a retailer grossing $500,000 a year to install a $70,000 computerized accounting solution—that is another example of a suspect transaction. Other than the reasons previously stated, we tend to just bill as we go (but keep in mind that we might bill much more often than on a monthly basis).

Asking for a Retainer

After accepting the idea that collecting a retainer is an important billing philosophy for MTBA work, your next step is to review the best way to ask for one. This is where a great many CPAs fail miserably. Here's a typical example of a CPA asking for a retainer for the first time:

> **CPA:** Mr. Client, we would love to get started on your project. We usually require a retainer in advance. In a case like yours, oh say ... maybe $2,500?
>
> **Client:** *(Doesn't say a word, just looks puzzled or stares.)*
>
> **CPA:** Is that alright? ... ah ... if it isn't ... well, maybe we could make an exception and lower it a bit?
>
> **Client:** *(More silence as the client ponders the words "usually," "maybe," "is that alright?" and "exception.")*
>
> **CPA:** How about $1,500 ... could you afford $750?

By this time, the client has assessed several things. First, the collection of a retainer isn't a requirement because the CPA indicated that there are exceptions. Second, the client wonders why he or she is being singled out for this retainer policy, which often makes them even more aggressive regarding the issue. Their belief that they are being singled out comes from the CPA's obvious discomfort with the idea. Third, even if the client believes that a retainer is in order, it is clear that the amount is negotiable. Fourth, the CPA's stumbling has relayed the message that the client can modify the rules.

To Avoid This Kind of Confusion, Ask for Your Retainer in a Very Positive Way

See if this next example doesn't sound better:

> CPA: Mr. Client, we would love to get started on your project. We require a retainer in advance, and on a project of this size, we could start work with $2,500.

The statement is short, sweet, doesn't leave you with the idea that this issue is negotiable, and says "we're ready to start as soon as you write the necessary check." By the way, the real mistake made in the previous example wasn't with the CPA's first statement—it was the fact that he or she made a second one before the client said anything.

Ask for Your Retainer With Confidence

Don't hesitate in mid-sentence. Avoid "uhs, " "let's sees," and "maybes." If delivered in a steady tone of voice (and assuming that you weren't sweating profusely), the previous example would illustrate to the client your confidence in the idea, and that it is important and necessary to collect a retainer.

After asking, don't say another word until the client responds. We know that this can be unnerving, but like anything else, the more practice you have with it, the easier it will be to sit silently and confidently while waiting for the client's response. As we mentioned in the last chapter regarding closing a sale, he who speaks first loses.

Ask for Alternatives If Necessary

If you are told that paying the retainer upfront is a problem for a client but you still want the business, ask them for an alternative:

> CPA: I understand your situation, what do you suggest as an alternative?

This way, the client is committing first, which allows you to give a counter-proposal if necessary.

> Client: I set aside an amount of $1,000. I can write you a check for that amount today. Any additional amount would require a meeting with the rest of the management team, and that would delay the project for at least a week.
>
> CPA: I could work with a check for $1,000 today if we can bill you each Monday and expect to be paid by each Friday. Would that work for you?

Some might feel this scenario really is no different than the first one, but it is. In this case, the client understands that an exception is being made to accommodate his or her situation. In the first case, the retainer looks more like a wish than a requirement. Note: the bigger the project, the more important it is for you to follow-up verbal agreements like this one with a letter of understanding. We rarely go to this level of formality except for projects under $15,000 dollars (which represents about half of our work).

How Much Retainer Should You Ask for?

This one is simple in theory, but difficult to pin down. The amount of retainer to request is really a risk and commitment issue. In other words, how much risk are you willing to take that you'll be paid, and what kind of client commitment are you looking for in the project?

As we previously mentioned, we moved to our hybrid approach to make this easier for us. We sell a total contract of time over a period of months at a fixed charge per month. If we get too far ahead of the time (billings far exceed time expended), we skip a month and catch up. If we get too far behind (billings far less than time expended), we simply inform the client and stay on our current billing cycle. However, a key here is that we need to constantly monitor where we are and discuss out of balance situations with our clients as soon as we see them, not wait until they become problematic.

For short-term projects (a month or two in duration) that are in excess of $15,000 (that is our threshold—we are not recommending that it be yours), our firm usually requests one-third to one-half of the expected fee upfront with the remainder due upon completion. If we work out a weekly billing arrangement (which we often do for small businesses), then smaller retainer amounts are required.

These rules aren't set in stone. They merely are a guide to consider. If your client is financially strong and you are convinced that management has a high level of commitment to the project, then waive the retainer requirement conditioned on the fact that you can bill frequently and that they pay in a timely manner. This minimizes financial risk and constantly verifies management's attitude toward the project.

Summary Regarding Retainers

Most of us would rather not work at all (that is, play golf or go fishing) than work and not get paid. Therefore, ask for retainers for advisory and consulting projects in order to minimize your financial exposure. This strategy also maximizes the likelihood of a successful project because when management advances the retainer, they are demonstrating commitment to the project.

Before we leave this subject, there is one important rule to remember when a retainer is collected: work within the limits of the retainer. Our experience is that firms charge retainers and then overwork them. For example, consider that the client pays a $2,500 retainer to get started. At the end of the month, that same client gets a bill for $3,000 of additional work. Now if the client paid another $2,500, they wouldn't even be paying for the work the advisor has already done, not to mention refilling the retainer to the $2,500 agreed-to level. Most CPAs take a retainer but really just treat it as a down payment. After the retainer is paid, CPAs just do the work and bill it every month. This is not the way the retainer system works, although it is common practice.

Working beyond your retainer usually creates problems for your client and, therefore, for you. Although you may have told the client that the total work is going to amount to $25,000 and you're working in retainer increments of $2,500 each, they still don't want to be shocked that you have way overspent the retainer they gave you. In a sense, the retainer is not only your safety net but also your client's because at the point when the retainer needs to be refilled, they can decide whether they want to continue or discontinue the work. When you work off of retainers, you have an obligation to keep your client informed and, at a minimum, communicate with them when their retainer amount has been used up. In more extreme cases, clients may feel like they've only authorized you to do work up to, but not beyond, the amount of the retainer, so their reaction to the situation we previously described also could be very strong and negative.

At the point that a retainer has to be refilled, we believe you owe your client an update. Although this update does not have to be a formal presentation, it is our belief that you have a responsibility to let the client know what you have done, where you are now, and generally what's left to be done. By doing this, you don't overspend your clients' retainers, you keep them informed about how their money is being utilized, and they tend to be much happier with your work. And the good news is if there is a problem, you find out about it thousands of dollars of potentially uncollectable work sooner. Remember to make life easy for your clients and for you, and you will enjoy your work a great deal more while building a very profitable practice.

 Keep In Mind

Work within the limits of the retainer. Working beyond your retainer usually creates problems for your client and, therefore, for you.

Proposals

We have alluded numerous times in this text to the fact that we are not particularly fond of the proposal process. We even stated that our firm does not participate in most requests for proposals (RFP). This is an odd position when you consider that proposals are the standard way of conducting business for large projects. Practically speaking, our firm doesn't do a lot of large projects (we think of large projects starting at the several hundred thousand dollar mark and going into the millions). One of the main reasons we are not enamored with the RFP process is because it takes a great deal of unbillable time to create proposals that are likely to win. In addition, often times you are asked to provide some upfront evaluation or diagnostic services as part of the proposal process. Finally, once someone has issued an RFP, it often means that they have determined, at least approximately, what the problem is, and they are now at the point of finding out what the lowest cost will be to solve it. Because of these issues, we are reluctant to get involved in very many of these efforts.

Nevertheless, proposals definitely have their place, and depending on the magnitude of the project, a certain amount of free work is not only expected but acceptable. To put this in perspective, remember the AICPA's Management Consulting Service's definition of consulting, where *consulting* comprises the following:

- Diagnosing
- Strategizing
- Constructing
- Implementing
- Operating

When you are creating a proposal for a million dollar or more project, then the diagnosing step is often thrown in for a nominal fee or given away. Many times, firms will provide specialized research, all kinds of analysis, and even hire specialized consultants to help them win the project. For example, it is not uncommon in response to an RFP to bring in consultants with the sole purpose of working with the project team to create resumes that best respond to bid specifications. Our point here is that for large projects, proposal creation is big business in and of itself. There are even people who specialize in designing proposal deliverables or packages so they look professional and give the proposer an edge. The reason the diagnosing and sometimes part of the strategizing stages of consulting are given away in these sized projects is because the real money is made by leveraging large numbers of people for extended periods of time at good rates. Therefore, the real plum is in performing the construction or implementation stages. However, for the kind of projects our firm typically does, from several thousand dollars to a couple hundred thousand dollars (with a normal big job being around $100,000 or more), if we gave away the diagnosing phase, we would lose a significant portion of our revenue. Why? Because often, our clients or other specialists will perform much of the constructing or implementing work.

It makes sense that if you want to play in the skilled labor force delivery arena (which often means you have to be able to amass large numbers of full time people in minimal time),preparing quality customized proposals is essential. It also makes sense to give away expertise to demonstrate that you are the best firm for the project. However, this is not an environment for which our firm is well-suited. There are occasions where we make exceptions, such as the hospital example provided in the last chapter. But at such time that the request for free advice becomes disproportionate to the overall project size, or when you feel the proposal process is being used as a way to access free expertise, it is time to walk away.

Think of it another way. Many organizations pay partners 5 percent to 15 percent to bring in new projects. So we use 10 percent as a guideline. When the cost of proposal preparation (both time and expense) exceeds about 10 percent of the expected revenue, it normally exceeds our comfort zone of what we would consider a reasonable marketing investment.

There is an even more important factor that drives whether we are willing to create a proposal. It can best be explained by the answer to this question, "What are the odds that we will win the RFP?" Some of the criteria are as follows:

- If we helped the potential client develop the proposal specifications, then we are certainly comfortable investing the necessary time and energy to prepare a proposal.
- If the proposal request is from a client with whom we have a good relationship, we will prepare a proposal.
- If we have a supportive ally who is one of, or is close to, the decision-makers and will use his or her influence to sway the final selection, we will participate in the proposal process.

The last reason in the preceding list was why we participated in the hospital proposal. Anyway, we could go on and on with specific situations, but the underlying key here is that we are looking for better-than-average odds of our proposal being selected.

One of the downsides of having a small firm with a good reputation is that organizations will ask you to be involved just so they can include your name in the list of candidates. The problem is that in many of these situations, management already has an inside favorite. They just want to protect themselves a bit before going public with their decision. These are the situations we try to avoid. But we want to make one thing clear before we move on. We are not against preparing proposals; we are just against spending valuable time doing "make-work." If we feel we have a real chance of winning the proposal, most likely, we'll participate. Even with these high criteria, we still lose a few. The good news is we haven't had to waste the time and money to establish a proposal department just to respond to requests that we have virtually no chance of winning.

Typical Proposal Structure

We've spent quite a bit of time and print explaining why we are not big fans of the RFP process, but as we've said, we do occasionally prepare proposals. We believe that if you are going to submit a proposal, you need to create a document that sets you apart from the competition and compels the prospect to want to know more and to ultimately engage you instead of someone else. Following is an approach we use for our proposals. Feel free to adapt it to your circumstances.

1. *Transmittal letter.* This is a *selling* tool. It needs to be short and sweet and no longer than a page or two. Preferably, it should be closer to a page in length and enthusiastically ask for the business, referring to the attached proposal. This is where you quickly can cover the most important features, benefits, and results about why the client should hire your firm to do the work.
2. *Cover or fly sheet.* The sheet simply contains the title of the proposal and "submitted by," with the date. If possible, we insert the client's logo on this page, together with ours. On shorter, smaller proposals, we often omit the cover page.
3. *Table of contents.* This is self-explanatory. We omit this on smaller, shorter proposals.
4. *Executive summary.* On very large, long, and complicated proposals, we may include a one- or two-page executive summary to allow high level decision-makers to get to the gist of the proposal very quickly.

5. *Understanding of the situation.* In a paragraph or two, this lead section of the proposal, often referred to as the *situational analysis*, outlines the current situation regarding why the client wants help. Note that it is not called a "problem statement." Clients have egos too, and besides, the situation may be an opportunity to pursue and not a problem by definition. We try to reiterate some of the terms and phrases the client used in his or her initial discussions with us in the section. Done properly, this shows the client that you really understand what they're going through and, therefore, the rest of the proposal is relevant. Spend some time getting this fine-tuned—it will pay off for you.

6. *Objectives of the project.* Tell the client what you heard them say they want to accomplish in this section. We often have a general, or overall, objective with bulleted, more specific or detailed points listed underneath it. Focus on outcome here, not on inputs or your approach.

7. *Expected benefits.* Although this section refers to "benefits," it really is a brief listing of the "results" from your features, benefits, and results analysis. It lays out the compelling reasons why the client should pursue this work with you.

8. *Measures of success.* This section allows you to brainstorm a few measures of success that the client easily can refer to with you to be sure that the project is proceeding on track and heading where everyone intended it to go. It answers the question, "How will we know it is working?"

9. *Approach and scope.* This is the section where you provide an overview or high level summary of the approach and the scope of the work you plan to perform. There are three important issues to point out here: (*a*) the approach in this proposal is necessarily high level but descriptive enough for the client to understand the general approach you are taking; (*b*) we normally provide at least two alternative approaches, sometimes three, to achieving the client's goals. The first approach meets their objectives; the second and third, if applicable, represent upgrades that meet the objectives, plus add even more value to the project; and (*c*) use this section to make clear what your work entails and what it does not—that's the "scope of work" part of this. It can help avoid misunderstandings with the client later.

   The notion of using multiple options is good because it
   • helps differentiate you from your competitors.
   • provides opportunities to suggest value-added services.
   • gives the client a choice between "yes" to alternative one, or "yes" to alternative two, rather than "yes" or "no" to your proposal.

10. *Workplan.* We don't provide this very often. On shorter, smaller engagements, this normally is omitted because a rough idea of the workplan will be derived easily by looking at the preceding approach outlines. Even on the few jobs where this is necessary, we only do a high level summary without any real specific tasks. (You probably will recall our earlier exhortation to avoid giving away the plan, which is part of the intellectual capital you bring to bear on the situation).

11. *Responsibilities of Parties.* We often include this to show management's responsibilities for making this work, including for example, the need to have the right people at the appropriate meetings, and the ability to make them and information we need available to us. We also list the key things we are responsible for here as well.

12. *Schedule or Timing.* This usually is pretty short, but it indicates when we think we could get started and, assuming availability of key people and compatibility of schedules, what sort of elapsed time period we expect for the project to be completed. We make sure the client understands that the duration and timing is contingent on the client's timely and appropriate participation.

13. *Staffing.* Normally, this is a very brief section that indicates who the partner in charge is, who will be overseeing the work, and who might be doing it, if that is important to the client. This is more critical in those jobs where you are using people's resumes to sell the work, and the client needs assurance that the "expert" will be involved. You can use a short paragraph or two here to highlight relevant aspects of key people's backgrounds or refer the reader to resumes that are attached to the back of the proposal, or both, if appropriate.

14. *Fees.* If your work is proposed on a time and charges approach, then you would explain the basis for charging fees and costs. Other approaches (project or value billing) normally only require fees for a phase, percentages of the value, or when appropriate, lump sum estimates. We cover the treatment of out-of-pocket costs, as well as the frequency of invoicing, payment terms, and finance charges. As we've mentioned quite thoroughly in this text, we may be working from a retainer, and that also would be spelled out here.

Finally, because we are providing multiple alternatives for the client to consider, the fee proposal would show the phase breakdown or total fee, or both, for each alternative. In addition, as mentioned previously, we often give the client a couple of payment options to help them manage their cash flow, with some portion to start the work and the balance due within 30 days of completion, or the entire fee in advance minus a small discount for early payment. An advantage of using multiple, proposed alternative approaches is that you've provided a variety of options to meet the client's needs and can use that as an argument against haggling. If one option is too expensive, then shift the consideration to one of the other options rather than allowing the conversation to default to you taking less.

We also have used a work discontinuation clause in this section from time to time, where we make it clear that if the client does not refresh the retainer or keep up on out-of-pocket payments or any other amounts billed to them, we will discontinue work until the account is brought current.

Attachments

Attachments to the proposal may include items such as the following:

- Sample agendas or reports for the type of work being proposed
- Resumes and qualifications
- References

With the exception of perhaps references from appropriate past projects or clients or adaptively positioned resumes, when resumes are requested, we normally suggest that you keep your proposal short and focused on your approach and why they should use you. If you include more than what is necessary to make the decision to hire you, you run a very real risk of either

- providing extraneous information that actually could be used to disqualify you or at least move someone else ahead of you, or
- weighting the proposal down with so much data that it motivates the client to skim over "your best stuff" because you have made the review too laborious.

Generally, we believe if you are not asked for it, do not include it unless you are convinced the added information will make your case stronger (not simply heavier).

We've included a sample of a proposal for a smaller project in exhibit 10-1 at the end of this chapter for your reference. Note that this sample does dual work as a proposal and engagement letter, obviating the need for another round of paperwork once the client talks with you about it and makes a decision. If you were just presenting a proposal, you might leave off the nitty-gritty details of service charges, work stoppages, and so on, and you would not have a signature block for the client to sign. However, if you separate the two, then you would have the added step of asking them to either

- send you a letter of award or notice to proceed incorporating the proposal terms, or
- request an engagement letter addressing the alternative they chose, with any modifications negotiated between you and them.

Engagement Letters

To borrow a term from another guy named Bill, "To 'engagement letter' or not to 'engagement letter,' that is the question." What it really comes down to is a risk management question that we cannot address for you. Every firm decides where the line should be drawn regarding this issue, and it is drawn everywhere from no engagement letters for any clients to engagement letters for every client. We've used the following guidelines for consulting or advisory projects. First, let's look at oral engagement understandings.

Our guidelines regarding when oral engagement understandings are appropriate with the client include when the

- consulting situation is narrow in focus with few stages.
- engagement primarily consists of meetings and discussions with the client.
- engagement costs are not significant to the client company.
- opportunity for misunderstanding the nature and scope of work is minimal.
- consulting delivered is primarily demonstrating knowledge possessed prior to the engagement.
- consultant and the client are very familiar and have a good existing relationship.

Conversely, engagement letters are appropriate and important when the

- consulting situation is complex.
- likelihood of misunderstandings is highly possible.
- project requires a variety of stages.
- project will take place over a long period of time, for example, months or years (people forget as time passes).
- future stages of work can vary significantly based on the findings of each stage.
- level of knowledge required to perform the work is beyond that currently possessed by the people working on the job (in other words, we would have to do additional analysis, research, for example, versus just showing up and sharing our thoughts).
- prospect or client has little to no existing relationship with the firm.
- firm's professional liability carrier requires formal understandings (or at least strongly encourages this formality for fees in excess of some designated amount).

These are not the only issues to consider. We also view the size of the client organization before making a final decision regarding whether engagement letters should be prepared. For example, the larger the organization, the more formal the agreement because

- it's consistent with the corporate culture; the way they do business.
- upper management wants the engagement letter to minimize the potential for misunderstandings between contractor and purchaser of services.
- the client company wants to avoid being trapped into paying for worthless services and products (they see formalized engagement letters and contracts as protecting their rights).
- persons responsible for hiring the consultant wants protection from rebuke from upper management.
- the larger company demands greater formality in order to better protect its assets.

On the other hand, the smaller the company, the more threatening an engagement letter can be because

- the client company wants to avoid being trapped into paying for worthless services and products (they see formalized engagement letters and contracts as limiting their options).
- engagement letters are not consistent with the way they normally do business.

• smaller businesses focus on building personal relationships with customers and vendors. To many small organizations, these relationships should not start off focused on legal babble. Note how many prenuptial agreements never get signed.

As we stated earlier, engagement letters often fall into the risk management zone. What is at risk versus what is to gain? The majority of the time, we do not ask for or prepare engagement letters. Why? Because much of our work is for smaller businesses (which dislike the formality of legal stylized paperwork) and is performed primarily with knowledge currently possessed by the consultant. Larger projects, often of $20,000 or greater in size, usually are accompanied by letters of understanding or contracts. For example, if we were to facilitate a strategic planning session that carried a price tag of $15,000 to $25,000, we might send out a letter or e-mail confirming the price and outlining our approach. In these situations, there would be no requirement for the client to sign or return our letter. However, when in working in our CPA firms, we performed technology consulting, whether it was finding the best software, determining what areas of the organization should be automated, software support, and so forth, we would have the client sign an engagement letter or contract. Why? Because technology is an area where misunderstandings are not only predictable but expected. Similarly, in our present consulting work, when we are called in to assist with intergroup conflict resolution on large construction projects for example, we get both parties to sign off on a proposal or engagement letter. They're already in a conflict, with all the attendant emotions running through it, so we don't take any chances here.

By considering the elements previously identified, we feel the decision regarding when to use engagement letters becomes fairly straight-forward. When in doubt or if the situation is borderline, don't take unnecessary chances. Prepare an engagement letter, and don't give it a second thought.

There is one last point we want you to keep in mind about this topic. Don't focus on the engagement letter at the expense of the engagement itself. An engagement letter should be used to clarify responsibilities and create a layer of protection between your firm and litigation. It is not a selling tool and, if interjected too early in a discussion, may kill the deal. Proposals typically are for selling, and engagement letters are for clarification and definition. That doesn't mean you shouldn't use engagement letters. We are just suggesting that you consider weighing the risks you are taking, the client situation, and the work you are performing so you can make a decision that is comfortable for you and your organization. As we said earlier, if the project is borderline, feel the fear and send out the engagement letter anyway. If a borderline deal is killed by the use of an engagement letter, the odds are high that you should have never considered doing the work in the first place.

Exhibit 10-1

Sample Proposal

HHC CONSTRUCTION, INC.—DOT SKYKOMISH HIGHWAY PROJECT
PROPOSAL FOR PARTNERING ASSISTANCE
FEBRUARY 11, 2010

UNDERSTANDING OF THE SITUATION

HHC Construction, Inc. (HHC) is an established, heavy construction business with its home office in Boise and a strong reputation within the heavy highway construction industry. It is the general contractor on a $9 million project involving roundabouts, curb and gutter, road improvements, and bridge work in Skykomish for the Department of Transportation (DOT). The construction project has been under way for about one and one-half years and is scheduled for completion during the summer of 2010. Approximately 30 percent of the work remains to be completed on the project at this time. That work is expected to resume this spring.

During the last construction season, teamwork on the project suffered as a result of interpersonal relationship issues, which led to deterioration in communication and coordination among the parties to the contract including HHC, DOT, and its consultants. Since that time, DOT has assigned a new Project Engineer to the project, and both HHC and DOT recognize the need for effective teamwork on the project management team to finish the project successfully this season. Consequently, the parties have requested a proposal from Succession Institute, LLC for partnering assistance.

OBJECTIVES

The overall objective of the consulting assistance requested is to restore effective team functioning to allow all parties to the contract to be successful on the project. Specific objectives include

- Developing processes to improve communication and coordination on the job
- Adopting processes to resolve potential conflicts quickly and in a constructive manner

MEASURES OF SUCCESS

We'll know we've made progress when

- an overall sense of the opinions of the project management team emerges.
- senior management of both HHC and DOT understand the nature of the key issues facing the project.
- alternative approaches have been examined for dealing with the key issues.
- the project management team has agreed to the next steps to take in dealing with these issues.

VALUE

The worth to you of achieving these objectives includes

- greater speed and efficiency in making the right project decisions.
- focus on the most productive mechanisms for managing potential disagreements in the future.
- meeting the "triple constraint" of managing this project—building it correctly, on time, and on budget to the extent possible.
- opportunity for mutual success on the project leading to reasonable economic outcomes as applicable for the parties to the contract.

METHODOLOGY AND OPINIONS

There is never one "perfect" approach to complex organizational issues, so we're providing some alternative routes for your review and selection.

Option 1: Interviews with facilitated, offsite meeting

In this option, we would create a process for interviewing key members of the project management team from HHC, DOT and its consultants, and key HHC subcontractors to gather diagnostic information. We would summarize the interview findings, and we would summarize our reaction to the findings and the issues facing the project management team. We then would review that information separately with, Jim Adams, the president of HHC and Joe Dokes of HHC, and with Jane Smith and Bob Jones of DOT. During those discussions, we would discuss how we think the agenda should be structured for the offsite meeting. We also would provide a summary of findings for these leaders to present to their respective project team members prior to the facilitated session.

Under this option we would facilitate a partnering session of up to one and one-half days in duration. That session would involve current project team members from HHC, DOT, and its consultants. Depending on the findings from the diagnostic interviews and the preferences of HHC and DOT, it also might include key representatives from major subcontractors and suppliers. As a result of this session, the project management team should leave with shared agreement regarding how it will deal with communication, coordination, and conflict resolution on the job for the duration of the job.

Option 2: Backstage intervention

In this option we would provide all of option 1, but would additionally

- prepare presession work prior to the interviews to stimulate participants to think about key needs and perhaps gain more of a "running start" when we're conducting the interviews. This presession work would take the form of short surveys to be completed in advance of the interviews by each person whom we would interview.
- prior to the interviews, summarize the survey responses and provide feedback separately to Jim Adams and Joe Dokes of HHC, and to Jane Smith and Bob Jones of DOT.

Option 3: Follow-up assistance

This option includes all of option 1 and option 2. In addition, it would include telephone and e-mail follow-up with Jim, Joe, Jane, and Bob for the duration of the project.

TIMING

We are prepared to begin rather quickly due to the issues you are facing. For instance, we could distribute the surveys during the week of February 13 if you choose option 2. Under any of the options, we would schedule our interviews for sometime between February 23 and February 28, subject to mutually agreeable dates, and we believe the entire process, including the facilitated offsite session, can be completed by mid-March, subject to the availability of all relevant parties and our schedules.

JOINT ACCOUNTABILITIES

You will provide us with the following:

- Documentation required.
- Access to participants as needed.
- Facilities for the interviews and for the offsite meeting we will conduct to review the interview findings.
- Scheduling and logistical support, including arranging interview schedules to allow DOT personnel and consultants to be interviewed in one day and allowing for the interviews of HHC personnel and key subcontractors in one day (preferably these two days of interviews would be conducted back-to-back.). This also would include arranging for the offsite facilities and, to the extent required, overnight accommodations in connection with the offsite meeting.

The nature of partnering is such that it may require some parties to alter their behaviors. Some individuals can alter their behavior more easily than others can. It is senior management's responsibility to see that their organizations, and individuals within their organizations, are aligned with the agreements reached on an ongoing basis.

We will provide the following:

- Work product as described
- Interviews, summary, and facilitation as described
- Timely and accurate reporting post-interviews
- Process and agendas for your review and critique

We both agree to immediately inform the other of any developments which might materially affect the success of this project.

TERMS AND CONDITIONS

We charge a set fee so that there is no "meter running," and you don't have to make an investment decision each time you may need our assistance during the project.

The fee for option 1 is $18,000.
The fee for option 2 is $20,000.
The fee for option 3 is $23,000.

A 50 percent deposit is required at commencement, with the balance due 45 days thereafter. Expenses are billed monthly as actually incurred and include hotel, meals, tips, telephone, fax, courier, duplication, clerical processing of materials, supplies, administrative expenses, and related items.

This contract is noncancelable for any reason, although you may postpone and reschedule it at any time with no penalty, subject only to mutually convenient timeframes.

Note: If you desire our assistance in actual implementation, we'll be happy to submit an additional proposal at that time. Similarly, if you require assistance in arranging for the meeting site for the offsite session, we can provide you with a quote for those services as well.

ACCEPTANCE

Your signature below indicates acceptance of the terms and conditions described herein. Please indicate the option you prefer. Alternatively, your deposit also will constitute your acceptance of these terms in lieu of a signed proposal.

You accept: _____ Option 1 _____ Option 2 or _____ Option 3

Succession Institute, LLC:

Dom Cingoranelli CMC
Executive V-P, Consulting Services
Date: February 11, 2010

HHC Construction, Inc.:

Name:_____

Title:_____

Date:_____

For State of Bliss Dept. of Transportation

Name:_____

Title:_____

Date:_____

Section 4

Identifying and Marketing Your Services

Two Approaches to Providing Advisory and Consulting Services[*]

"The aim of marketing is to know and understand the customer so well the product or service fits him and sells itself."

~ PETER F. DRUCKER

---

[*] This chapter is co-authored by Michaelle Cameron, Ph.D., Marketing Professor for Saint Edwards University in Austin, Texas

Winters and Associates, a successful CPA firm, decided to offer some new, specialized consulting services. As a logical place to start, these services were marketed to their existing client base. Immediately, there were several hot prospects. Within a couple of months, the consulting projects fully utilized what normally would have been off-season idle time by the CPA firm's management and staff. Yet, additional requests were being made. Rather than miss these lucrative opportunities, the CPA firm hired personnel for the sole purpose of consulting.

Six months later, operating with a beefed-up consulting department, the pent-up demand of the existing client base had been consumed. The consulting requests were starting to come in at a more normal pace. Over the next 12 months, the nonbillable time of the consulting staff was growing and getting out-of-hand.

Knowing that the firm's financial resources were draining fast, the firm's management put together a comprehensive marketing campaign to expand the firm's consulting visibility to potential new clients. This resulted in an even more restricted cash flow because even though there was significant interest due to the expanded marketing effort, new business was slow to materialize. The firm quickly discovered that selling consulting services to new clients was a much harder and slower sell than signing up existing clients. Because Winters and Associates was not financially strong enough to support the ever-increasing idle time of their expanded consulting department, at least for the length of time they thought it would take for demand to catch up with supply, they decided to go back to their "bread and butter" services and leave consulting to other CPA firms. Because of this decision, one of the partners that enjoyed the consulting and advisory work took several of the firm's key employees and a good number of the clients and started a competing firm. The result was disastrous. It took years for Winters and Associates to recover from their consulting service start-up adventure.

This scenario should ring a familiar bell. If you didn't personally go through it, you most likely know someone who did. History reflects that CPA firms have had difficulty implementing consulting and advisory services, and we blame most of the problems on three factors:

- Confusion between consulting/advisory services and consulting packages
- The delivery of consulting through a one-approach-fits-all strategy
- Consulting service/consulting package offerings inconsistent with firm objectives

The first item was covered in the first section of this book. The second factor, delivery of consulting through a one-approach-fits-all strategy was discussed in chapter 8 "Delivering Value-Added Services." The third factor, consulting service and consulting package (niche service) offerings inconsistent with firm objectives, is the focus of this chapter.

Understand to Whom the Service Is Targeted

Before you offer any new service, you need to understand who the service is targeted to serve and why it is important for you to serve that market. This is where the concepts of the Fortress and Empire strategies come into play. Let's take a closer look at the meanings we've assigned to these terms.

> Throughout history, fortresses were built in order to protect communities from outside forces. Barriers were created, such as walls and moats, to fend off would-be attackers. All the needs of the community were supplied from within the confines of the *fortress*.

Empires were built by conquering new territories and expanding well beyond original boundaries. The community's needs were supplied through a combination of resources available within the empire's own fortress and in the new wealth found amidst the annexed provinces.

With these brief definitions in mind, here's how these terms form the foundation of our service offerings analysis.

The Fortress strategy, which has both a client retention and service extension objective, has a short-term horizon and is directed at offering advisory services and consulting packages to a community of existing clients. The goal is:

To enhance loyalty and revenues while simultaneously denying opportunities to competitors by building a wall of essential business services around your client base.

Figure 11-1 **Specialization Areas for the Wall of Services**

With the Fortress, consideration should be given to the short-term needs of the CPA firm's client base, the profitability of delivering a particular service, the CPA firm's in-house talent, and the CPA firm's long-term objectives, in this order.

This approach is a *client base protection strategy* that simultaneously generates additional revenues. By continually offering client-desired advising and consulting, you eliminate the need for them to look to your competitors for help. So in order to keep your competition at a distance, you build a wall of services that addresses all reasonable consulting opportunities (see figure 11-1).

For example, let's say one of your major clients requires financing support. The Fortress strategy suggests that you find a way to satisfy this need. Otherwise, your client's cry for help could be heard by competitors. Should one of them respond, especially if the one responding is also a CPA firm, all the other services you provide to that particular client are at risk. By remaining visible and maintaining at least some level of involvement with the client, you minimize the chance of losing account control. Your firm also presents the positive image of being a one-stop-shop, a firm that can cater to all the needs of its community either through its own service offerings or through its professional network (taking on the role of General Contractor covered earlier).

A real plus for the Fortress strategy is that it typically returns a high profit in minimal time. Why? Because revenues can be generated quickly (inasmuch as you know the clients are ready to buy because they are requesting the services), and the cost of marketing is low (because they are existing clients; the selling cycle is short and reaching out to touch them is inexpensive). So what services should a Fortress offer? We think asking your clients what they need on a regular basis is probably the safest and most accurate way to make this determination. But if you want some anecdotal evidence for additional ideas about services we have seen firms offer that have sparked interest, consider offerings such as the following:

- Wealth management
- Business valuation
- Economic analysis
- Forensic accounting
- Succession planning

- Personal financial planning
- SEC company auditing
- Technology consulting
- Internal auditing support
- Cost reduction and cost efficiency analysis
- Special projects in the assurance area
- Fraud detection
- Alternative dispute resolution
- Business turnaround
- Developing key performance Metrics
- Building performance compensation plans
- Helping organizations transition retiring owners
- Infrastructure benchmarking
- Applying services such as those in this list to industry niches such as the following:
  — Construction
  — Health care
  — Manufacturing
  — Distribution
  — Professional services
  — Retail

The second alternative to service strategies, the Empire strategy, which for most firms has a new client acquisition objective, requires a long-term horizon and is time and resource intensive. We call it the Empire strategy because its intent is

To select a few niche consulting packages and use them to annex new clients while also supplying them to the community within the fortress.

This approach, referred to in our second chapter as the "Swiss cheese approach," is the one most commonly employed by large firms. The tools used are consulting packages, specialization, or nontraditional services. This also might be called a "niche service approach." But there's more to this methodology than just offering a few niche services. That's why we gave it the more expansive title of E*mpire*. Anyway, to continue, within the Empire strategy, firms market highly specialized consulting packages to attract new clients while simultaneously supplying these services to their current client base. As we mentioned earlier, the great news for large firms is that based on their critical mass of clients alone, it is easy for demand to outstretch supply. Large firms often don't have to consider new client acquisition as a means of justifying the expense and effort required to deliver these various nontraditional services. On those occasions when the supply for a unique service is constantly undercommitted, they just reallocate those resources to the delivery of some other consulting package.

However, for the rest of us, the Empire approach doesn't work quite so easily. These unique, packaged services, because of the small size of our client base relative to the top 20

Figure 11-2 **Example of Empire Strategy Offerings**

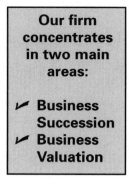

> **Our firm concentrates in two main areas:**
>
> ✔ **Business Succession**
> ✔ **Business Valuation**

CPA firms, almost always will be underutilized when the current client base is the main target. So although you may be able, in the short term, to increase revenues delivering these services to your current client base, the Empire is much more powerful when used for client acquisition. Think of it this way: with the Empire approach, you are making a few highly specialized consulting packages visible in order to create a distinction between you and your competitors. Because you have unique skills and experience in these consulting package areas, the Empire highlights these strengths to attract new clients (see figure 11-2).

As you can see from reading just these few paragraphs, randomly picking consulting packages in order to make a few extra bucks might prove counter-productive to the long-term positioning and success of the firm. The first step is to determine whether the Fortress or Empire strategy is right for your organization. Then, based on that decision, many issues from the gamut of service offerings from fulfilling your most trusted business advisor (MTBA) role, to offering new consulting packages, should become much clearer by the time you get through the worksheets at the end of this chapter.

Before elaborating more on the specifics of these two approaches, recall that we discussed in the first section of this book the General Contractor model, under which a CPA firm may subcontract out work, staying in charge of the client's project and overseeing the subcontracted service providers. The client is looking to you to keep the project and the people on track. This is clearly a more involved and rigorous approach to meeting the client's needs than simply referring the client to other parties for assistance without any expectation of further involvement.

Knowing when to use the General Contractor model and manage the project using subcontractors versus when to deliver those services with your own personnel versus when to refer, plays a major role in the successful deployment of either the Fortress or the Empire models. Let's now examine the nuts and bolts of each approach.

Building Your Fortress' Wall of Services

First, identify the wanted services. *Wanted services* are just like they sound—those services your clients want to obtain. The simplest way to do this is to listen. Clients tell you what they want in many ways—by the questions they ask, by sharing interesting comments from friends such as, "Joe tells me his CPA is ...," or by referring to issues on their business wish list, for example. More directly, you can have each member of your staff inquire about the client's near-term operational priorities at the end of meetings and phone conversations (this technique is not only simple and free, but effective, and it extends the MTBA role to everyone in the firm in one way or another. This alone will help you position your firm as a force to be reckoned with in the marketplace). More formal alternatives involve sending out surveys and questionnaires or conducting focus groups, both of which solicit this kind of information.

After gathering the information you need (and by the way, this is an ongoing process), prioritize these wanted services into a sequence of highest to lowest demand based on your clients' responses. Next, consider your competition and increase the priority of those services most likely to receive CPA competitive interference. This process helps you to

> *Distinguish the services of greatest interest to both your competition and your client base.*

After you have thought through the services that are in high demand, it's time to identify your skills inventory. You accomplish this by reviewing the background and experience of your managers and staff. A good way to begin this phase is to have each member of the firm analyze and list his or her own talents and strengths. Emphasize that this is no time to be modest or shy about abilities (for example, your data entry person may be a closet Web site designer, more than capable of expanding some of your technology service offerings). Once you have consolidated this information, you are likely to have a broader insight into the skills possessed by your in-house talent.

Another resource that you need to consider in addition to your in-house talent is that provided through subcontracting. Many firms across the country are regularly utilizing subcontractors, (outside consultants or other professionals in your network), to help deliver client-demanded services. This is a critical support system for Fortress firms because it is highly unlikely that their internal talent alone can satisfy the varied desires of their client base. Therefore, finding reputable firms that are capable of supplying quality contract services is essential. In a way, we are suggesting a kind of strategic alliance with those who can augment your in-house talent. As our professional life becomes more complicated with ongoing expansion of standards and regulations, at least some of your strategic alliances very likely will be with other CPA firms under arrangements that allow you to complement one another's skills without competing for clients who use both firms. By making such alliances, you will be able to

Figure 11-3 **Determining Fortress Services**

- build additional loyalty by becoming more responsive to client needs.
- provide a training ground for your personnel as they learn from these specialized outsiders.
- generate additional revenues. Even though there may be little to no room to mark-up the contractor's work (which we don't recommend anyway), you make your money by
  — involving one or more of your workers with the strategic-alliance partner performing the service, and
  — being the overall project manager and client relationship partner, making sure the project stays on plan.
- strengthen your fortress' wall of services and make it more resistant to competition.

Finally, determine which services your firm should offer (offerable services) by balancing wanted services with available in-house and subcontract skills (see figure 11-3). The result of this process is the identification of services that

- protect your client base
- are easy to provide.
- are profitable to deliver.

The preceding steps work well in helping you determine which services you should offer to your Fortress community. Besides those services you formally offer, you have to be ready to deliver client-tailored services as well. For example:

> Let's assume that one of your clients is about to begin the painful process of converting inventory and receivables from their present system involving a lot of manual processes and an unsophisticated bookkeeping software package to a more integrated accounting and management information system. Let's also assume that this is not one of the consulting services or packages that has come out of the service analysis you have just performed. However, your client has come to you for assistance or has commented that they need assistance.

The first question is, "Do you have access (internally or through your relationships with likely subcontractors) to the skills required to perform this project?" If the answer is no, then the AICPA's one consulting standard (Statement on Standards for Consulting Services No. 1, *Consulting Services: Definitions and Standards* [AICPA, *Professional Standards*, vol. 2, CS sec. 100]), precludes you from taking on the work due to the professional competence issue. For the sake of this discussion, let's assume the required skills are available.

The next question would be, "Is it likely that a competitor (who offers basically the same services you do) will take care of your client if you don't?" If the answer is no, then the decision regarding whether to pursue this job should be based predominantly on its profit potential. Should competitive pressure exist, the client's relative significance to your firm becomes of paramount importance. If the answer is not substantial, then once again, the project's overall economic impact determines your level of involvement. But if the client is an important player in your firm's revenue stream, then being involved in this project as the service provider, as the general contractor, or as their general advisor throughout the project is warranted to reduce the threat of poaching. All of these roles should be profitable, so don't think you have to give these services away just to keep the client. Clients that don't want to pay a fair price for advice and support are clients you want to send to your fiercest competitor so they can suck the life out of your competitor's firm.

Building the Wall Profitably

Building the Fortress' wall of services is likely to require a variety of talents and unique expertise. Few firms have the diversity of in-house talent to pull this off. So with each new opportunity, availability of talent becomes a central issue. Questions such as the following arise:

- Do we have the in-house talent required for this project?
- If we have the talent, is it currently available?
- If the in-house talent doesn't exist, is it worth developing?
- If the talent is worth developing, should we train existing personnel by contracting with someone already possessing this specialized knowledge or work out a special on-the-job training arrangement with the client?
- Should we take on the role of General Contractor and use subcontractors to do this work?
- Should we simply refer someone in our professional network to help the client because client demand is likely to be sparse?

This series of questions brings up an important point to emphasize regarding the Fortress strategy: minimize overhead! Looking back at our computer implementation example and assuming a competitive threat, if the talent is not readily available in-house, then acting as the general advisor to the project, taking on the role of general contractor, or simply referring from your network are all preferable to developing talent in-house. Why?

Because hiring or internally developing unique technical skills is a very low priority in the fortress strategy.

The reason why is simple. The needs of your clients constantly are shifting. Responding to these shifting needs is what the Fortress is all about. In other words, some of today's very specialized, demanded services are likely to be less important several months or a year from now. For example, consider the rise in interest in forensic accounting today, the cost control analysis during our recession, or succession planning in the future as our baby boomers start retiring in force. Because consulting services and packages can be sensitive to timing, adding overhead in order to meet today's client needs could be the catalyst for disaster tomorrow if that service is not part of your long-term strategy. However, we want to make an important distinction here between consulting packages and acting as your clients' MTBA. Although you have to be careful about committing overhead to support a low volume or very unique consulting or nontraditional service, investing in everyone to develop their advisory skills is a no-brainer. Being an MTBA is, to us, an essential skill every partner and senior manager should be demonstrating every day.

The importance of low overhead cannot be overemphasized. Because you have a narrow primary marketplace (your clients), and because consulting and nontraditional work, by nature, is nonrepetitive (you don't build a good client/consultant relationship if you have to solve the same problems over and over), the demand for unique consulting services is unpredictable at best. This environment often creates a string of feast or famine situations. That's why the success of this approach depends so heavily on a firm's ability to maintain lean and mean overhead. Here's another way to think of it: picture your consulting offerings as an accordion. Imagine it expanding and contracting based on current opportunities, client demands, and competitive pressures. The expansion should, for the most part, be supplemented through subcontract arrangements. This allows the contraction to occur for you, the General Contractor, without threatening the viability of your firm.

In the Real World

The Fortress is not only a viable alternative, it is also the option best suited for most CPA firms. Why? Because few firms have a large enough client base to support day-in-day-out specific consulting packages, or even more grandiose, a fully staffed consulting department.

For those of you who feel the Fortress is more theoretical than practical, we offer these examples:

Not so long ago, the American automotive industry focused on large cars. Because large luxury cars were the most profitable, building small cars was almost perceived as an inconvenience. The inexpensive small car (or on another spectrum, hybrids), are more current examples in today's climate.

Automakers (the Japanese early, on and more recently, Korean automakers) find an unattended niche that is being underserved and find market share filling it. But once they do, they don't stop there, they just continue to expand on their brand reputation and start eating away at all of the other market segments—from the small car, to the luxury car, to trucks, to SUVs, and hybrids. This expansion has significantly affected the profitability and the viability of the now-former dynasty of the big three American automobile manufacturers.

Here was a situation where the American automotive industry decided to ignore the demands of its community. However, if the Fortress strategy had been followed, so many companies would have been denied their easy invasion of the marketplace. The result: American automobile manufacturers might have been able to maintain a much greater market share than they enjoy today, or at a minimum, wouldn't be in the trouble they are today.

Coming back to CPA firms, what we are saying is those firms building their brand around acting as their clients' MTBA as well as those launching new consulting and nontraditional services may soon be found encroaching on your client base. All it takes is for one of these firms to be engaged for a specialized project or two, and within a couple of years, you might find yourself bidding just to keep some of your annuity traditional service work. The Fortress approach dictates that if one of these specialized services is required, you are better off using the General Contractor model to subcontract the services out to potential competitors (or referring them to a noncompetitor) than letting them run loose among your clients. This way, at a minimum, you maintain control of the account.

The handwriting is on the wall:

Protect Your Client Base!

Sustaining a wall of services around your clients is the best way to build a Fortress that can stand up to the competition.

Building the Empire

What do you do if you don't have a client base to protect? Or what if your current client base isn't big enough to support your desired lifestyle? Maybe the current work you perform isn't challenging enough. Are you looking for a growth vehicle that would allow you to promote and retain your quality personnel? These kinds of questions lead us to our next approach, the Empire, which is committed to client base growth.

As a starting point, the Empire strategy is almost a superset of the Fortress strategy (as illustrated in figure 11-4). When you think about it, there is some logic to this. Securing your homeland should be an integral part of an expansion program. And as you know from our previous discussion about the Fortress strategy, securing your homeland is accomplished by taking care of the needs within your current clients.

The Empire strategy focuses on the CPA firm's strategic plan, not the current needs of the client base. However, the Empire strategy does attempt to take advantage of all business opportunities within the current client base as long as they are consistent with the long-range plan. An example of an Empire firm's five-year vision statement might be

> To build a nontraditional service department that has the skills and reputation to expand and dominate new markets by providing superior services in arbitration, divorce litigation support, and valuation.

Considering the preceding vision statement, if a current client needed support in the resolution of a partnership dispute, and because arbitration is part of the long-range plan, this project would be solicited aggressively. However, if obtaining financing was the demanded service, it most likely would be referred to some other firm. Note: Empire firms should try to refer nonstrategic services to firms that complement their areas of expertise so that their referrals can be reciprocated. Or, move one more step forward in formality and form strategic alliances with those firms who deliver complementary services and expertise.

So why would an Empire firm give up a service opportunity just because it wasn't part of their strategic plan? The reason is focus. With the Empire approach, you endeavor to use specialized services (often MTBA, consulting, or nontraditional services) to attract new clients. As exemplified by those identified in the preceding vision statement, because many specialized services (*arbitration, divorce litigation support, and valuation*) typically are nonrepetitive in nature, the idea is to continuously add clients in order to maintain a steady supply of service delivery opportunities. From day one, the Empire's spotlight has to be on penetrating new territories. In order to encourage new clients to hire your firm, you must offer super-quality services to the masses. In order to provide super-quality services, you have to possess unique experience and expertise in a specific field or area. To attain this level of specialization, your firm must choose a few select services. Then, you need to continually fine tune and develop the delivery of these select services.

As your list of services becomes narrower and specialized, the geographical area of your target marketplace most likely will have to expand. As you know, the authors of this text constantly utilize the empire strategy. We offer a unique set of services to two market segments: CPA firms and the heavy construction (highway and heavy civil projects) industry. We work with organizations throughout the United States and Canada because the more unique the niche, the larger the territory you have to market to in order to define a market segment that can support your firm.

Figure 11-4 **Empire: A Superset of Fortress**

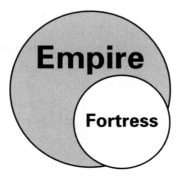

Creating super-quality service distinction and visibility is costly, both in time and money. Therefore, deciding to implement an Empire strategy is not a decision to take lightly. For it to be the right choice, you have to view whatever specialty services you chose to be the cornerstone of your future practice. As has been apparent throughout this book, we believe that the general practice advisory function—using the MTBA Framework—should be a big piece of that future cornerstone for the vast majority of small to middle-market CPA firms. However, many organizations will find themselves developing highly specialized, nontraditional services or consulting packages and leaving the general advisory MTBA work to the CPA firms that maintain account control. For example, let's say you want to develop a firm that is the best boutique forensic accounting firm in the Northeast. In this case, you will end up providing a few specialized nontraditional services within your Empire firm and leave the account control in the hands of the traditional CPA firm. What you are doing here is shifting from being a firm that is hired predominantly by clients to a firm that is predominantly brought in by other professional service firms. So in this case, your empire firm needs to be built so that it is a comfortable choice for all of the fortress firms bringing you in. This might include creating formal strategic alliances, client protection agreements (nonpoaching agreements), and other approaches geared at making you the provider of choice to secure the fortress walls of those professional service firms bringing you in. At some point in your success, you will have enough clients that you can start working with them as your own fortress (potentially expanding your forensic accounting services offerings). But don't forget, because you are so highly specialized, you always need to keep those firms that manage the broader client relationships up to speed with what you are doing.

Determining the Most Appropriate Services: The Notion of Synergy

For the past 20 years, CPA firms have continued to expand their scope of services. In the beginning, the services were more of a migration of an existing service, or even a redefinition of a scope of a service rather than a truly new service. For example, many CPA firms offered informal tax, estate, or wealth management planning as part of the tax return preparation process. However, many CPAs either gave some of these services away or charged minimally for them. Therefore, it became increasingly more important for firms to formalize these services so clients would understand that

- these unique services were not a normal part of the tax return process.
- their CPA firm had unique expertise to share, which allowed the firm to differentiate themselves from other CPA firms.
- if they were interested in receiving any of these augmented services, their fees would rise.

As you know, firms found little resistance to expanding their services. This makes sense because in the beginning, these new services, by the nature of their migration, were very synergistic with each other. For example, tax return preparation naturally can lead to tax planning, which naturally can lead to discussions about estate planning.

As the firms evolved and the redefinition or formalization of their traditional services were completed, firms continued to mine this success strategy by adding new services. Conversations among partners shifted to "what niche service or specialty area should we develop next?" In some cases, firms added new services that were synergistic to their existing services. For example, if a firm had a number of wealthy individuals for clients, it certainly would make sense for them to offer wealth management services. Or a firm that had a specialty niche, like construction, might add an estimating or bonding support service. All it takes for a service to be synergistic is for the new service to be a natural extension of the needs of the clients currently served.

CPA firms all over the country were adding new services at a phenomenal pace with little resistance and mostly encountering success. But as with everything in life, we found that the service expansion strategy had its limits. One of those limitations arises when we offer a nonsynergistic service. Why? Because we have to develop a new marketplace for nonsynergistic services if we want them to be profitable long-term. And most CPA firms did not understand this. Therefore, they lost a great deal of money during this educational process. Our story regarding technology consulting at the opening of this chapter was a common example. Technology services are synergistic if most of a firm's clients are businesses, and you already offer a variety of operational support services. However, they are not synergistic if most of your clients are individuals, businesses too small to be able to afford this level of expertise, or so large that they have this expertise internally. For the sake of definition, we call any service that is not synergistic with the needs of your existing clients an *island* service. This simply means that it stands alone. For an island service to make sense for a firm, it

- needs to be part of their long-term service strategy (it may be an island service now, but given the clients the firm is trying to attract, the current island service is just the beginning of a set of synergistic services).
- should be a differentiator service (in other words, you might not plan to make much money on the service itself, but you use it to open new doors and attract clients away from competing firms because it is a service that is seen as valuable).
- needs to be profitable.

For a long time, many firms had the idea that you could choose a new service out of a hat and it had as good a chance of succeeding as any other. However, over the past 10 years, one firm after another has found out that adding new services can be very expensive. This cost has come in the form of financial losses, separation of partners that developed island specialty niches, and lost focus of the firm. Before a firm launches a new service, it needs to answer some key synergistic questions. Some of those questions include the following:

- Why are we launching this service? (Is it because our clients are demanding it, or is it because we have a partner interested in providing it?)
- What will likely happen if the service succeeds or fails? (What is the business plan for this service? Are we building this to support one person, or do we intend to grow this group to multiple people so that it has a chance of continuing beyond the original

champion? If the service succeeds, have you protected the firm so that you haven't just incubated a spin-off organization for one of your partners to steal if no one else is interested in supporting this service?)

- Is this service one that logically fits with the other services we offer?
- Is this service one that logically serves the current clients we have? (If not, then do we have a strategic purpose to attract a new set of clients? And if we have a strategy to attract a new set of clients, what other services do we plan to sell them so that we are not supporting a client base with one service offering?)
- What are the expectations we have for this service? (When will it break even, how long are we willing to support it, how do we define success so we know when we have achieved it?)
- Who is going to champion this service (and does that champion have any clout with the existing partner group because there is no point in launching a new service with a champion who is not a partner or a champion the partner group does not see as a future partner)?

Some key points to consider are as follows:

- All services are not alike.
- Just because a service is synergistic for one firm doesn't mean it is for yours.
- Island services that are not initiated strategically will be very costly to the firm.

Once you have decided what services to offer and promote, the next question to address is "who is going to buy them?"

With the Empire approach, as we have said before, services offered are based primarily on the CPA firm's long-range plan. So, performing some business planning internally at your firm is the right place to start.

 Keep In Mind

By having one of your firm's MTBAS or CPA consultants facilitate the internal planning sessions, you will provide an excellent forum for training and confidence-building. If you would rather bring in an outside facilitator, assign one of your CPA consultants to work very closely with the facilitator in order to glean as much information as possible from the experience.

The CPA firm's skills also are a major ingredient to the future services of an Empire-focused firm. These can be divided into two categories: current skills and planned skills.

Current skills should be fairly self-explanatory—those skills currently in-house or available through other sources. *Planned skills* are those to be obtained through training or future hiring. Both are viable alternatives. In order to choose the best option for your organization, you need to consider the technical expertise needed as it compares to the aptitudes and interests of the current staff, managers, and partners. This is the classic "make or buy" decision.

What will it cost to ramp up the new service assuming you have someone in-house with the aptitudes and interests who can take it on versus what would it cost to hire in someone to be the practice leader for this service? This is the "make or buy" decision you need to make. And make no mistake about it, ultimately, someone at the owners' level needs to be tasked with responsibility for rollout and growth of the new offering.

As an interim solution to this development process, an idea worth considering is to establish a good, strong professional network to lean on to provide the initial support for new service offerings or create working relationships with a subcontractor or two in the niche specialty area of interest. This allows you to first test the water regarding whether the momentum and interest for a new service is truly strong enough before you commit your firm's limited resources. For example, if you think asset management would be a highly valued service your clients would want, then first align with an investment house, and when they are managing enough of your client's money to make it worth your while to bring that service in-house, then make the transition. So that means that when you initially sell the idea for your client to utilize someone from your network, don't oversell them so much that you inadvertently close the door for your next move. The only thing you want to constantly sell hard is the idea of your involvement in the process: your oversight and your interest in their future. That way as you change the various pieces of the puzzle, you and your firm are the constants throughout each transition. Using your professional network or hand-picked subcontractors not only allows you to offer super-quality services from the onset, but your network also can double as trainers for your staff should the time come to bring the service in-house.

Offered services are the end product of blending a CPA firm's long-range vision and strategy (or plan) and its skills. Another way to put this is offered services are merely those services identified within the long-range plan that can be presently supported. As additional skills are developed, offered services should be expanded to encompass these changes. (See figure 11-5.)

Before any offered services actually are delivered, the central focus turns to the project. Remember, with the empire, you are attempting to deliver a few super-quality services, which often means you have to expand your marketplace (or the geography you cover) to

Figure 11-5 **Determining Empire Services**

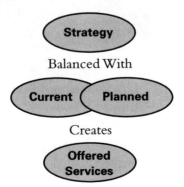

create an audience size large enough to support that unique offering. It is the intent of the empire approach to skim off, or cherry pick, those projects with the highest profit potential.

This expansion philosophy takes a great deal of time and money to implement, especially compared to the Fortress. In order to be successful, from the onset you need to simultaneously sell to both your clients and prospects. Why? Because today's prospects will be slow to react to whatever marketing effort you put in place. Experience dictates that it takes about a year to 18 months before a new target audience builds enough trust and confidence in you to solicit help. This means your current client base plays a critical role in allowing you to bridge this span of time. Especially in the beginning of this transition, every consulting opportunity within the current client base that is consistent with the long-range plan must be pursued aggressively. Some projects inconsistent with the long-range plan also may be undertaken during this initial timeframe if excess consulting capacity exists (as long as you don't lose sight of your final objective).

Because your current client base is limited in size, at some point you will have capitalized on all of the lucrative projects matching your current and planned skill set. The trick is to create an effective marketing campaign that produces new clients and service opportunities before you have depleted the excess service demand from your existing clients. This is the risk associated with the Empire. If you don't create the necessary stream of new clients fast enough, your firm will have to be financially prepared to carry your newly launched nontraditional service and consulting department during this transition. The hope is that eventually a transition actually will occur, and there will be adequate demand for your select group of super-quality services. For many firms, this transition never occurs, mostly due to haphazard marketing efforts, minimal financial commitment from the beginning, and lack of accountability for performance. A common trap occurs when a firm launches a new service and immediately starts enjoying the pent up demand within their client base. This immediate success lulls management to sleep, and they don't get a jump on implementing a well thought out marketing campaign to the Empire marketplace, which needs about a year to 18 months to incubate and start working.

This is one of the main reasons why the Empire is riskier than the Fortress. The Empire assumes that you are building a long-term niche specialty firm. This equates to a higher cost structure consisting of overhead and marketing. Higher overhead will come in the form of subcontractors, developing people, training, and marketing costs. In the beginning, when demand for your new niche services often outstretch supply (because you are cherry-picking projects from your current client base), the expenses associated with your Empire start-up are likely to be reasonable. And on the other end of the spectrum, once your marketing campaign gets into full swing and you begin to sign up new, lucrative opportunities, then your overhead should be very manageable. At this stage, you not only have the opportunity to enjoy the profit for supplying the new niche service, but because that service is attracting new clients to the firm, it opens the door for your firm to provide other, more traditional services as well. However, the interim is the danger zone, when overhead costs are high to support the new service, current client demand has been supplied, and there is no real momentum attracting new clients or prospects. This is the point when many firms discontinue a service or minimize the commitment to resources, and the new niche service starts to die a slow death before it starts providing its true benefit. But to also be fair, many niche services launched by CPA firms are not synergistic, not part of the firm's strategic plan, but rather they represent a specific partner's personal interest. Often these services are not unique or valuable enough to attract new clients or stand on their own. These services should have never been offered in the first place, and they need to die a quick death as soon as it is clear where they are heading. Some of the signals to look for include the following:

- Slow growth and the lack of traction within the current client base.
- Partners who have no interest in providing leads or supporting the new service.
- The champion of the service really only focuses on his or her personal gain rather than what is best for the firm overall.
- The champion, for any number of reasons, never leverages the work through anyone else in the firm.

The best way to minimize this risk is by understanding that marketing is forever in the Empire. Marketing must be consistent and continuous. The sooner you start marketing to these vast unconquered territories, the sooner you will reap the rewards. Too often people become overconfident due to the responsiveness of their current clients. By the time the firm gets around to launching the expansion marketing campaign, too much time has been wasted, and it is often too late. The transition period discussed becomes too much of a financial burden. The result: the Empire crumbles.

The point is the Empire is for aggressive, marketing-minded, growth-oriented CPA firms. Firms adopting this approach will, no doubt, face a few Fortress-minded CPA firms. Don't be concerned because these firms have to be part of the Empire's marketing strategy. The Empire firms should position themselves as subcontractors to Fortress firms. These two methodologies really work hand-in-hand, especially when Empire firms support the idea that the Fortress firms maintain control of the account. The Empire firms manage their unique services; the Fortress firms manage the client relationships. Therefore, as an Empire-builder, you should expect to sign agreements that prevent your firm from invading other services, which are provided within the Fortress of the contracting firm.

Many lucrative client-requested projects are being ignored today by almost every CPA firm. Delivering a few super-quality services using an Empire approach can not only be profitable, but the work is fun and challenging as well. And if our prediction is correct, over time and in the future, many successful, prosperous firms will be highly specialized. This means the Empire-builders will be way ahead of the game and well positioned for the 21st century.

We're Doing Both and It Seems to Be Working Fine

Some of you now may be using both approaches simultaneously. And that's not only okay, but really great! You can build an Empire and also protect your Fortress at the same time. But problems likely will arise. The first of these problems is most evident when considering the marketing perspective.

Remember that when you sell to your Empire market, you need to be selling competence, experience, specialized knowledge, and understanding. Why? Because the potential clients don't know you and certainly don't trust you. So you need to be offering them (1) a level of competence, (2) in a unique service area, (3) that is important to the client, and (4) is being overlooked or underserved by the Fortress CPA firm. When you sell to the Fortress market, you need to sell how you have helped others. Why? Because the client already trusts and respects you! You don't need to convince them you have unique capabilities. If you say you can provide a service, they will believe you. So the message from a fortress firm needs to focus on letting the clients and referral sources know how you can help them—not just listing various services you sell—but helping them understand how they can utilize your skills and capabilities to benefit them.

Here is a common area where firms often apply the wrong marketing philosophy. Consider a traditional firm newsletter. It is common for newsletters to dedicate 70 percent or more of the available space to technical matters (which your clients often could care less about because you handle those problems for them). This type of newsletter conveys that you are a quality service provider. A message such as this isn't necessary to deliver to your clients and referral sources. Hopefully, they already believe you are a quality service provider so your newsletter is not augmenting their current thinking.

However, demonstrating competence is important if you want to interest people who are unfamiliar with your work. Therefore, when you send out the standard newsletter described above to both your Fortress clients (those who already know, like, and trust you) and Empire prospects (those who don't know and don't care about you), your marketing effort is compromised and is only marginally effective at motivating either audience.

For the Fortress, 80 percent or more of the newsletter should describe, in nonaccounting terms, the many ways you can and have helped your clients. For the Empire, 80 percent or more of the newsletter should focus on convincing the audience that your firm has the background, experience, and specialized knowledge to add value to their organization. The point is messages that will motivate the Fortress marketplace are completely different from those necessary to motivate the Empire marketplace. So when you use both strategies in your firm, it is easy to get sloppy about how you communicate to each group. The net result of trying to optimize your marketing dollar by creating a one-approach-fits-all campaign often converts to wasted money and poor results.

A problem easily can arise when you don't distinguish between which is your primary and secondary approach (Fortress or Empire). That problem likely will be dissatisfied clients. There is nothing wrong with utilizing both approaches. For example, you might utilize a Fortress approach with your current clients and an empire approach with a new niche service. But you still need to make a clear distinction about which one is primary and constantly work on the messaging and actions that need to support each. Here is an example of how confusion about these two approaches can go wrong. Let's say that a firm has three CPAs. One primarily does tax work, another audit, and the third financial statement preparation. When these three services represent 98 percent of those demanded by their clients, everything is fine. But as client demand changes and as each partner creates new niche areas of expertise, it will become harder for them to also maintain their command over the traditional services. Their time will simply be spread too thin. Because so much energy and emphasis has to be given to establishing new niche areas, existing clients often are ignored in an effort to sustain the viability of these services. Clients easily can be lost to a competitive firm reaching out to satisfy unfulfilled needs.

You see, if the preceding firm had recognized that its primary focus was the Fortress, they would have paid close attention to the changing needs of the client base and tried to satisfy those needs using their own skill, their professional network, or through referral. Regardless, they would have stayed involved and taken their job of account control very seriously. While they might have wanted to launch some Empire services to expand their marketplace, they would have done this in a way that did not compromise their first priority, which was to take care of their client base.

You need to know your strategy and use these approaches to guide your implementation. Is your organization's focus to take care of and grow the services delivered to the existing client base (fortress)? Or does the firm plan on making its mark by providing a few super-quality niche services (Empire)? It is our contention that, in the foreseeable future, many firms will choose the Empire strategy and become niche service providers to other small and middle-market CPA firms who have committed to maintaining their Fortresses. We have seen this with audit, forensic accounting, business valuation, wealth management, technology, and many other commonly found services offered by larger CPA firms. Strategic alliances basically will allow both Fortress and Empire firms to operate with most of the same advantages that large firms enjoy today. They can have offices with Fortress mentalities and, when appropriate, deliver unique niche expertise (Empire) from people and organizations that are scattered throughout the country.

Don't Get Complacent

Competition can change a marketplace overnight. As an example, today you may be comfortable referring all fraud detection work to outside vendors. This approach works as long as your accounting peers don't expand into the forensic and fraud arenas. Once a direct competitor builds strength in one of your weak areas, they can and most likely will use it to infiltrate your client base and eventually take away other work you provide. So even though a middle-of-the-road strategy works now, it may not work for much longer. As a matter of fact, in many markets, the competition has already restructured their priorities, and you may soon feel an almost overnight impact as the results of their last year or two's work come to fruition. Dramatic change in your market may not be imminent, but rest assured, change will occur. Don't be caught off guard.

Stay on Top of Your Marketing Focus

If you are building a Fortress, then the marketing effort must be focused at your current clients. If you are not directing your marketing efforts where they belong, you're walking on the edge of disaster. You will miss opportunities because, at some point in the future, your clients' requirements will either shift or not be satisfied by current efforts. New opportunities for service will arise, and if you are unaware of these new demanded services, you are opening the door to poaching from competitive CPA firms. And the best technique we can give you is the one this book is focused on: live the role of being your clients' MTBA. This will keep you in touch and build the right foundation for maintaining and expanding your Fortress.

If you are expanding your Empire, an aggressive, consistent campaign promoting your services needs to extend well beyond the current client-base boundaries. Again, a poorly defined marketing strategy will doom your endeavor to build an Empire. Remember: don't be lulled to sleep regarding the importance of marketing in this strategy just because early on, you enjoy an initial wave of interest (typically generated by current clients and from referrals from those clients).

In order to be successful, you need to be able to

- quickly adjust to <u>current</u> client demand (the Fortress strategy), or
- continue to expand into new territories where the market for your super-quality services is untapped (the Empire strategy).

Because both strategies require planning and preparation, the earlier your approach is identified, the better. We offer this analogy:

> In sports, whether it is football, basketball, golf, tennis, or racing for example, those winning the gold follow some kind of game plan. Their strategy may take either an offensive or defensive flavor. The objectives, talents, and current conditions determine which tactics should be utilized, what kind of talent they should acquire, and how they should develop as an organization. The player or team with the best game plan is the one most often found in the winner's circle.

The same planning and preparation is required when implementing a firm-wide nontraditional service, consulting philosophy, or niche consulting package: you need to follow a plan. If you want to posture your firm defensively, then the Fortress is an approach to consider. If you view nontraditional services or niche consulting packages as an offensive weapon for expansion, then follow the Empire strategy. If you want to adopt both strategies, then planning becomes even more essential because sloppy vacillation between them is a risky alternative to chose.

A Summary of the Differences

The following bullet points recap the differences between the Fortress and the Empire as discussed earlier in the chapter. Although this may seem redundant, we know through experience that it is easy to get confused with these approaches. To many of you, this chapter may seem insignificant. However, by the time you fill out all the worksheets in this book, as you begin to develop your firm strategy and formalize your marketing plan, you most likely will be rereading this chapter over and over. Determining what primary strategy best suits your organization is critical if you want to maximize your scarce personnel and financial resources.

- Where the Fortress aggressively pursues almost every MTBA opportunity and most consulting opportunities with existing clients, the Empire seeks out only those opportunities consistent with the CPA firm's long-range plan.
- The Fortress is centered on client-base protection. The target of the Empire is new client-acquisition. Although you can easily achieve growth through both strategies, one leverages your client relationships, (through service extension and referrals), whereas the other leverages clients accessible through strategic alliances, industry specific target markets, networking with complementary product or service providers, and the like.
- The Fortress is primarily a defensive approach; the Empire is mostly an offensive one. The Fortress expands by taking care of the changing needs of its clients whereas the Empire takes business away from less specialized service providers.
- The Empire takes a great deal more time and money to implement than does the Fortress. The cost of marketing and commitment to personnel training and overhead is far more substantial with the Empire than that required by the Fortress.
- Due to a larger overhead and a predictable revenue shortfall (during the interim between skimming off the demand from your current client base to that time when you have built a marketing engine that can sustain lead generation from new prospects), the Empire is a higher cost alternative and, therefore, riskier than the Fortress.
- The services offered by the Empire remain fairly consistent over time because they are based on the CPA firm's long-term strategic plan. The services provided by the Fortress reshape more often as they are based on the ever-evolving needs of the client base.
- As long as client-demanded services are consistent with the CPA firm's *long-range* strategy, the variation between these two approaches is strictly in the marketing effort. The Empire will direct its efforts towards generating new clients, whereas the Fortress will attempt to build on and expand service delivery to the ones it already has.
- The Fortress will deemphasize past services that are not a priority to the current client base. The Empire's service offering is not dependent on the demands of the current client base but rather supporting the niche specialty it is developing or has developed.
- Because the Fortress emphasizes building a wall of services with minimal overhead, working with your professional network (a select group of subcontractors) or forming a number of strategic alliances with Empire (complementary) firms, or both, is common. The Fortress firm stays involved as the General Contractor in the project regardless of who actually is performing the detailed work. Under the Empire, requests that do not fall within the long-term plan are normally referred to other firms, especially if there is an alliance with a Fortress firm. The Empire firm normally will *not* stay involved if the services are outside of their niche offerings.

It's Time to Make the Determination

Both MTBA services and consulting packages are services that are education and experience intensive, the highest and best use of both. These kinds of services are directed at helping our clients solve today's problems and take advantage of tomorrow's opportunities. The challenge is to support our clients in a manner that allows them to more profitably manage their businesses, financial affairs, estates, and so on.

We believe that the future of our profession lies in our ability to expand our offerings through the MTBA Framework into areas that help businesses survive and thrive. We also believe that CPAs are uniquely qualified for this job. Some of our current bread and butter compliance work, such as tax and bookkeeping, already has been eroded through technology and other non-license-holding competitors. Experience and sound business judgment will become our most distinguishable and marketable characteristics. And, because MTBA assistance and consulting packages require both the theoretical and practical application of knowledge, these nontraditional services are our edge for competing in the 21st century. Understanding whether your firm is a Fortress, Empire, or some combination of both is critical if you want to maximize your firm's potential in the most cost effective way. By incorporating and utilizing the strategy best suited to your firm's objectives, you should be able to

- improve your ability to plan because each strategy has nuances and market reactions you can anticipate.
- better respond to your marketplace with appropriate services.
- more consistently send messages that will motivate your clients and prospects to action.
- significantly improve your odds for success when launching new services.
- enhance client satisfaction and loyalty.
- accomplish all of the above more efficiently and less costly than evolving without the use of these methodologies.

Before We Move On

We have been working through the exercises at the end of this chapter with firms for two decades or longer. They were created to force everyone to think about the skills they possess. As with any organization, it is critical that you take advantage of what you do well. It is also essential that you leverage what you enjoy doing. After everyone fills out the Skills Inventory worksheet (exercise 11-1), you begin to get a better understanding of what you and your people have to offer. You also can gain some of this same insight by utilizing more formal tools, such as personality profiles, skills inventory assessments, 360-degree feedback instruments, competency frameworks, and more. But for now, we have provided some simple forms for your utilization.

After you finish the Skills Inventory exercise, move on and begin completing the Requested Services List (exercise 11-2). This form was created so that you would compose a list of all the services you personally have heard one of your clients or prospects request in the last 12 months. Notice the phrase "personally have heard." The next form, Anticipated or Upcoming Requests (exercise 11-3), is included so you can jot down those services you think will be important in the next few years, even though they may not be in demand now. This becomes a "services watch list." After you have finished working through these, as a warm-up exercise, using the techniques covered in this book, go out and talk to a few of your top clients and listen to what they have to say regarding their needs. This should help verify if you are on track or not. If you are, great! Keep going. If you are not, then have numerous people in your firm schedule visits to clients in the near-term and redo the exercises again once everyone has completed their research assignment.

Each of these lists should prove helpful as you begin to think through whether your firm should adopt a Fortress or Empire primary strategy. Once that decision is made, then once again, these lists should provide assistance in laying out a service delivery strategy. In other words, answer questions like the following:

- What services should you offer?
- What services should you build capability for internally?
- What services should you develop relationships to deliver?

Remember: you can utilize both strategies. For example, many firms have a fortress primary strategy, with some key services being Fortress services and others being Empire services. As you make these determinations, it will give you insight into how to market them and expand the revenue they generate. Next, it's time to create a marketing plan to ensure your marketplace is aware of what you have to offer, which is the subject of our next chapter. However, first, let's get started working through the forms.

Exercise 11-1

Skills Inventory Worksheet

Take an inventory of the skills you feel you have to offer. Keep in mind these are not services, but personal skills you possess. Although there is some similarity, (for example, tax knowledge would logically manifest itself as a tax service), other skills like speaking skills, being a good communicator, or knowing a foreign language might not be as directly attributable to a current service offering. If there is more than one of you in your firm, have every key person in your office fill out this form. Then call a meeting to share this information and discuss how your firm can put this new information to use.

1) _____
2) _____
3) _____
4) _____
5) _____
6) _____
7) _____
8) _____
9) _____
10) _____
11) _____
12) _____
13) _____
14) _____
15) _____

Exercise 11-2

Requested Services List

Prepare a list of all the services you personally have heard one of your clients or prospects request in the last 12 months. Remember, this list is based on personal experience only.

Description:

✓ _____
✓ _____
✓ _____
✓ _____
✓ _____
✓ _____
✓ _____
✓ _____
✓ _____
✓ _____
✓ _____
✓ _____
✓ _____
✓ _____
✓ _____
✓ _____
✓ _____
✓ _____
✓ _____
✓ _____
✓ _____
✓ _____
✓ _____

Exercise 11-3

Anticipated or Upcoming Requests

Prepare a list of all the services you believe will become important to your clients in the upcoming 18 months to 3 years, even though they may show little interest at this time. You are completing this list as an exercise to keep you thinking ahead of your clients' needs. Then this becomes your "services watch list."

Description:

✓ _____
✓ _____
✓ _____
✓ _____
✓ _____
✓ _____
✓ _____
✓ _____
✓ _____
✓ _____
✓ _____
✓ _____
✓ _____
✓ _____
✓ _____
✓ _____
✓ _____
✓ _____
✓ _____
✓ _____
✓ _____

Marketing Your Firm and Your Services[*]

"Marketing is too important to be left to the marketing department."

~ DAVID PACKARD

---

[*] This chapter is co-authored by Michaelle Cameron, Ph.D., Marketing Professor for Saint Edwards University in Austin, Texas

People are too busy, too distracted, and generally too focused on their own problems or opportunities to be very observant of all the messages that are being presented around them. Therefore, if you want to get their attention, you have to develop a marketing strategy that will be delivered with enough frequency that it becomes hard to ignore, rather than hard to catch.

In order to accomplish this, you need to design a marketing program that covers at least a year's horizon, and 18 months is even better. It also should be designed to best utilize your firm's skills and resources. A marketing plan not only manages tools like advertising but every method and technique your organizations use for obtaining new clients. Consider organizations you and your firm belong to, your network of friends, your compensation plan, the sales and communication training that is provided to everyone in the firm, or the internal structure of your organization. These are only a few of the factors that have to be considered when developing a quality marketing plan.

We are not referring to a three-pound document which takes months to create; we're talking about an informal action plan that lays out issues such as the following:

- Actions planned
- How often you plan on making something happen
- Who you are attempting to reach
- What you expect your audience to do in response to each effort
- What each step will cost
- How you will know if what you did was effective

In our profession, the level of commitment required to pull this together rarely is found. Most marketing plans are vapor-ware. A simple test to determine how your organization feels about marketing is to answer this series of questions:

- When you conduct your firm's planning sessions, where is marketing on your agenda? Is it after the "real" issues have been covered or somewhere on the front page towards the top of the agenda?
- Is marketing considered by the partners to be essential or optional?
- Is marketing considered something you do when business is down or an integral part of everyday business?

If marketing is not positioned in an important place on your agenda, then marketing most likely is not considered a core part of your business. Think of it this way: when you reflect on other aspects of your business—from management, to training, to service delivery, to quality control—these functions all generate costs. Only marketing has as its purpose the generation of income. Yet, unfortunately, it often is not even considered a core part of the business to monitor and manage.

Because today's efforts generate next month's or next year's opportunities, a good marketing plan is imperative if you want to remain successful as a firm, and especially if you want to compete effectively as a most trusted business advisor (MTBA) or in the nontraditional service marketplace. Otherwise, your results will be inconsistent. When you consider that the demand for advisory and consulting services is time- and situation-sensitive to begin with, a sloppy marketing effort will only make matters worse.

Here's one more reason why marketing should be a focal point within your firm:

You have to continually attract new clients in order to survive.

The explanation is simple. Some percentage of your current clients won't request your services next year. Their reasons for leaving will be varied, from moving out of town, to being dissatisfied with your products or services, to no longer requiring outside assistance, to death, or to simply closing up shop. Many of their reasons will have nothing to do with you or your firm; they just reflect changes in the clients' lives. So attracting new clients is not just a growth issue; it also is necessary in order to maintain the status quo.

If you still are not motivated to concentrate on marketing, reconsider something we pointed out previously in this book: in spite of demographic issues associated with the number of young entrants into the profession, competition among CPA firms will continue to increase. More competition translates into more firms fighting over the opportunities that exist. Your marketing plan is your strongest tool to help your clients differentiate your firm from all the rest.

Developing a Marketing Strategy

A good marketing strategy needs to take each of the following into account:

- Products and services offered
- Clients
- Competition
- Management team
- Financial resources and limitations

This analysis is likely to require some research, focus groups, surveys, interviews, and numerous brainstorming sessions. Otherwise, you will be attempting to select the best approach for selling something that hasn't been identified. What makes this kind of planning confusing is that effective marketing is difficult to identify. What works for one CPA firm may prove to be worthless to another. Think of your organization's marketing plan as a suit of clothes. Even though two suits visually may appear to be the same, each most likely has been altered to fit the individual wearing it.

So where do you start if you are not sure how to tailor your suit? From a simplistic viewpoint, any good strategy must

- reflect an understanding of the potential clients.
- identify their hot buttons.
- revolve around pushing those hot buttons.

The remaining sections of this chapter will discuss in detail how to accomplish this.

Developing Your Marketing Plan

Putting together a quality marketing plan doesn't have to be expensive. It doesn't have to take an inordinate amount of time either. But make no mistake about it, creating a marketing plan, especially for the first time, is not an effort to take frivolously. Numerous steps are involved. The good news is that once you have gone through the process, the next time around is substantially easier and quicker.

Here are the steps you should take and, generally, the order in which to take them:

1. Understand your market
2. Understand what you are selling
3. Determine your objectives
4. Establish a budget
5. Fine tune your target audience
6. Fine tune your message
7. Choose which exposure vehicles are best for your organization
8. Monitor the results

Understand Your Market

As we covered in earlier chapters, our business is changing. CPAs are offering services to smaller and smaller organizations, clients are demanding more for their money every day, and the needs of the marketplace are moving away from compliance (just to name a few). We are being asked to offer more services that affect our clients' future success rather than just report on their past performance. Although CPAs in public practice tend to know the multitude of services our professionals can deliver, our marketplace does not have this same understanding.

Over a decade ago, a survey conducted by the AICPA regarding their then national advertising campaign provided some interesting information. The survey included 500 key decision makers, including CEOs, COOs, CFOs, chairmen, presidents, owners, partners, treasurers, trustees, principals, vice presidents of finance and controllers. (even though many of these job titles are predominantly held by CPAs, no CPAs were included in this survey). A different set of 500 key decision makers were surveyed both before and after the advertising campaign. Basically, it worked like this: various messages were imbedded in advertisements; we believe it encompassed five print ads, five radio ads, and one TV advertisement. The survey respondents were basically asked whether they agreed with the message contained in each ad. We found the results interesting.

Although they were not CPAs, the people in this survey certainly should have been aware of a CPA's capabilities. Yet only 47 percent of those surveyed after the ad (image) campaign felt, CPAs could help individuals and businesses plan for the future. Only 44 percent agreed that CPAs see more than the numbers, they see opportunities. As a profession in general, CPAs should not blame the ad campaign for these results. We need to take a hard look at ourselves. We have done a *horrible* job letting our clients know what we are capable of doing. It would be one thing if only 44percent agreed that CPAs were the premier provider of automation solutions, but that wasn't the topic. This question asked clients if they think we can "see beyond the numbers," and their answer was frightening. Clearly, not only do we not understand our market, but our market didn't and still doesn't understand us. Although we believe that the market's understanding of what CPAs do has improved somewhat over the last 10–12 years, it still has a long, long way to go. Because each of us, especially in relation to our own clients, is to blame for this, we each can fix this with respect to our own client base.

So what does our market want? Obviously that varies from area to area, industry to industry, time to time, and client to client. But when you consider some of the examples shared previously in this book, helping companies find ways to survive and thrive is way up there. Consider the services identified each year by one of the AICPA's Technology Committees (The Top 10 Technologies). Now there's a list of technologies that organizations around the country are struggling to implement. The point is that there are numerous places to look. However, we think your best source of information is in your own backyard. Survey your clients, talk to them, or conduct focus groups with them on a regular basis. They are the ones whose opinions you should care about. They are the ones you should know about. They are the ones that you should understand.

Before we leave this topic, we want to reiterate a point made earlier, in the first section of this text. It is our belief that:

> The single largest purchaser of CPA services in the 21st century is likely to be the CPA working in industry, government, and education.

Why? Because more and more, the controller's job, the vice president of finance's job, and the role of related positions, is to manage all operational and informational issues. This change in role redefines these traditional accounting jobs to now encompass only about 20 per cent to 30 percent accounting. The remaining 70 percent to 80 percent includes a multitude of other operational issues. Therefore, when you match the expanded scope of services we are suggesting for public CPAs (MTBA services and consulting packages), it mimics very well the scope of control that our counterparts in industry are managing. And guess what? Our counterparts in industry are screaming for assistance. How do we know this? Because we conduct classes for controllers around the country and have done so for years. We have had the privilege to be in front of thousands of controllers in discussion settings and have heard the same story year after year—they want and need our help—assuming we take the time to approach them about it. The opportunities have never been greater for our profession, assuming we take the time to understand our marketplace.

Understand What You Are Selling

We've spent a great deal of time on this subject in earlier chapters. Remember the Feature, Benefit, Result technique? One example used was a burglar alarm: the contacts, horns, and infrared devices are features; notifying you that someone has entered your home uninvited is the benefit; protecting your family is the result. And people buy results. This is one angle.

Consider your answers to the following questions as you think about what you offer clients. You need to understand exactly what it is you are selling.

- Is it expertise, piece of mind, a long-term relationship, improved odds of success, or a higher level of confidence?
- Are you selling a product (like a tax return) or a service (billing purely for your time, however, the client determines how to use it)?
- Specifically, what services do you offer?
- More important, what are the logical outcomes a company can expect when buying each of your services?

You will know you have accomplished the step of "understand what you are selling" when you can give a series of "pop quizzes" to everyone in your organization, asking questions about what it is your firm does and why people do business with you, and hear similar responses. For example, ask the simple question, "Who do you work for?" If you get the answer, "I work for a CPA firm," you're not even close to where you need to be. We will cover this in more depth later in this chapter.

Determine Your Objectives

Why are you spending your valuable resources (time and money) on marketing? What are you trying to accomplish? Why now? These are the kinds of questions this section is supposed to answer. If you are marketing just because you think you should, don't do it. If you are marketing to retain your current clients, make a note of that. If you are trying to build more referrals, make another note. If you force yourself to sit down and answer the few simple questions that started this paragraph, you'll be 90 percent there. After you go through this exercise, let a day or so pass, and then review the questions and your answers again. Don't be surprised if you add another reason or two or more sharply define those you have already written down.

Establish a Budget

This is something you know how to do in your sleep. We have included a simple form at the end of this chapter that we use to identify each exposure alternative, when we plan to use it, how many people we are targeting, and what it is going to cost. It's nothing special, just a simple form we put together to help us look at the combination of alternatives we have selected so we can make sure we try to get the most from each one as it relates to everything else in the plan. The last, and most imperative, item that is addressed on this form, is determining what results you expect from the exposure campaign. List and quantify your reasonable expectations before you leave this step, such as the number of new clients, growth in total revenues, or new projects delivering a particular niche specialty, for example.

> You should be aware of a common costly error regarding the budget:
> Spending an entire year's exposure budget on a week-long comprehensive advertising campaign.

This kind of blitz mentality typically is very ineffective. The success of a blitz campaign is based on the premise that you have a product or service that is so unique and so much in demand that people will beat your door down to obtain it once they know your organization exists. It also assumes that your audience will be so enamored by your product and service that they will remember you forever. This phenomenon virtually never occurs. The normal result of blitz exposure is that it draws a more significant number of prospects during the blitz period than would a normal advertising effort. The problem is in order to justify this financial outlay of cash, it would have to generate a year's worth of traffic during the blitz period because minimal funds will be available for marketing after the event is over. The reality usually is that three or four normal exposure efforts will have a greater cumulative impact than the blitz effort.

This is not to say that blitz campaigns are ineffective. Organizations use this kind of exposure method all the time. The key is that the money expended for the blitz effort is still just a small percentage of the overall exposure budget. This way, a great deal of attention is drawn to the product or service in a short period of time, and then that visibility is maintained on a month-in, month-out basis by the normal, planned exposure itinerary.

So the trick is to put together an exposure campaign that can be implemented in small increments over a long period of time. Why? Because visibility and exposure need to emulate a dripping water faucet. Even though each drop of water may be insignificant by itself, as these droplets constantly continue, they make a greater and greater impact. You have to persistently chip away the various distractions surrounding your existing and potential clients. Then, in that fleeting moment when you have their attention, your message quickly must motivate them into action. Consider being able to emulate this dripping water faucet when you allocate money to your marketing budget.

Fine Tune Your Target Audience

The first issue is to think through how the Fortress and Empire strategies (discussed in the previous chapter) might apply to your objectives. Here's a quick review of how each can affect your marketing approach.

The Fortress

By choosing the Fortress, your target market is your existing client base. The Fort Worth office of the firm where Bill practiced public accounting followed this strategy. Because it had been operating for many years as a traditional practice, a sizable client base had been established. Therefore, client base protection was a primary focus.

To accomplish the Fortress objective, all marketing efforts are directed towards building client loyalty. One way to do this is to promote a wide range of services, so Bill and his partners put together a list of services for the Fort Worth office (created during several brainstorming sessions) that became the primary wall of services that surrounded the Fort Worth client base. By promoting these services, the firm subtly reminded its clients that it could take care of a wide variety of their needs. This list consisted of the following services:

- Negotiation and arbitration of operational, financial, and personnel issues
- Tax planning/minimizing

- Management and leadership training
- Help in obtaining financing
- Acquiring and selling businesses
- Managing audits and reviews
- Accounting and reporting assistance
- Business planning and budgeting
- Advice on how to improve internal controls and procedures
- Computer hardware and software consultation and training
- Cost reduction analysis
- Cash management assistance
- Marketing and advertising strategy
- Prebankruptcy and bankruptcy support

How did they create this list? After completing the Skills Inventory worksheet (found at the end of chapter 11), interviewing a group of their clients, and composing the Requested Services worksheet, they came up with a list of service offerings that they felt fit the needs of their client base at the time.

If a client was in need of a service outside this list, the firm either referred them or satisfied their need through the use of the firm's professional network and subcontractors. The decision regarding which way to go was easy to make. If the service desired was performed by a competing CPA firm, then Bill's firm was going to maintain account control and most likely take on the General Contractor role and utilize his firm's professional network.

Remember, the idea behind the Fortress is client base protection. We don't want anyone making inroads with our clients that might threaten their loyalty to us. So we only refer when we believe no such threat exists.

To keep our clients' attention, we have to continually remind them that we are their CPA firm, and that we offer an exciting variety of services. The good news is it's easy to accomplish this with Fortress-style marketing. Why? Because we know our clients by name, where they work, where they live, what they do, and so on.

Due to the availability of this information, the cost of communicating the details about various new services is relatively low. By utilizing monthly or quarterly newsletters, workshops, direct mail, or even a firm open house, you can stay in touch (we cover these in more detail later). This regular communication is an essential element of building loyalty.

The primary requirement of a Fortress marketing campaign is that you consistently and regularly expose the firm's various services. Response to this campaign is not as important as its visibility. Even when you don't achieve additional direct revenues from the services promoted, the main objective will still have been met. That is, you have reminded your clients that you care about them, that you always are looking for new ways to keep them satisfied, and that you provide much more than traditional CPA services.

This constant barrage of information also tells them that something exciting is always going on at your office. As a result, they will want to stay in contact with you. By creating these positive and recurring images, your clients should always think of you first for help.

And that's a critical marketing objective of the Fortress. It reinforces your position in the market place.

The Empire

If you select the Empire, your target market is much broader than your existing client base. Typically, this approach is selected by those firms

- with an inadequate number of clients (for example, a recently opened office or an established firm with a desire for more growth opportunities than the existing client base offers), or
- desiring a change in stimulation, such as a group of CPAs who are tired of performing daily tax work and have decided it would be more rewarding to build a litigation support practice.

In both of these cases, new clients have to be actively solicited. The first question we want to address regarding this subject is, "Are CPAs allowed, by our code of professional conduct, to actively solicit uninvited prospects?" The level of flexibility in this area varies from state to state, and the AICPA's Code of Professional Conduct, as amended January 14, 1992, states under Rule 501, *Acts Discreditable* (AICPA, *Professional Standards*, vol. 2), "A member shall not commit an act discreditable to the profession." Rule 502, *Advertising and Other Forms of Solicitation* (AICPA, *Professional Standards*, vol. 2), states, "A member in public practice shall not seek to obtain clients by advertising or other forms of solicitation in a manner that is false, misleading, or deceptive. Solicitation by the use of coercion, over-reaching, or harassing conduct is prohibited."

Clearly, this is one area that has undergone significant change in the last couple of decades. It doesn't seem like all that long ago when a CPA needed to be invited before a personal contact could be made. Today, it's really just a test of ensuring that you are not utilizing deceptive advertising practices. Obviously, this is an easy requirement to meet.

In order to be effective, the empire requires that you devise a marketing approach that defines a fairly narrow market segment. This allows you to promote a unique product or service that is enticing and valuable. As an example, consider the broad range of services we defined earlier for the Fort Worth office. This list, although proving valuable for the Fort Worth office, was too broad for the Austin location. Because the Austin office had only been in operation for a few years at that time, its client base wasn't large enough to support its two principals. Expansion was necessary. Therefore, the Empire approach was adopted for that office. The services were then refined to suit a more targeted audience. For example, the Austin office promoted the following:

- Business and marketing planning
- Help in obtaining financing
- Negotiation and arbitration of operational, financial, and personnel issues
- Advice on how to improve internal controls and procedures

Even though they provided other services, the Austin office publicized those services that impacted small business profitability (because that was the unique spin they wanted to put on all of their offerings—helping small businesses, not individuals, make money and be successful). Some of the vehicles utilized to communicate and demonstrate this concentration included:

- Publishing a weekly column on management issues for local newspapers
- Presenting lectures to various business organizations
- Producing a television series called, *You and Your Money*, which was aired by a local CBS affiliate
- Writing several publications for the Small Business Division of the Texas Department of Commerce

This kind of exposure helped build a business expert image in the local community. From there, Bill branched out on a national basis through a variety of nationally published articles, video and live television networks and public speaking engagements.

The Empire strategy is designed to sell niche specialty services (a few unique services) to a broader marketplace (the more specialized your service, the wider the marketing net you have to throw in order to find enough clients to sustain the business given the uniqueness of the services). Although the Fortress is designed to sell a broad set of services to a concentrated marketplace (when almost everyone has a need for one of the offered services), a smaller marketing net is ample to capture enough potential clients to sustain a business. Regardless of your approach, in order to fine tune your marketing plan, you should consider how these strategies fit your organization. Once you have made that determination, the strategy itself will begin to dictate certain alternatives to consider.

Marketing Segmentation

The next issue that has to be addressed in order to fine tune your marketing is market segmentation. *Market segmentation* is simply the process of breaking your market into relatively homogeneous and identifiable groups.

According to the second edition of, *Principles of Marketing* by Lamb, Hair & McDaniel, some basics you need to know are:

> The term *market* means different things to different people. First, they are composed of people and/or organizations. Second, these people and/or organization have wants and needs that can be satisfied by particular products and/or services. Third, they have the ability to buy the products and/or services they seek. Fourth, they are willing to exchange their resources, usually money or credit, for the desired products and/or services.
>
> "Within a market, a market segment is a subgroup of people and/or organizations sharing one or more characteristics that cause them to have similar product and/or service needs." For example, at one extreme, you can define every client you have as a separate market segment. On the other extreme, every business in the world can be defined as a market segment.

"The process of dividing a market into meaningful, relatively similar, and identifiable segments or groups is called *market segmentation*. Segmentation can follow a variety of directions. Common bases are Geographic (by city, region, country, etc.), Demographic (by age, gender, income, etc.), Psychographic (personality, motives, lifestyles, etc.), Benefit (according to the benefits they seek from a product or service) or Usage (divides a market by the amount of products or services consumed)."

For our profession, markets are often segmented by industries or portions of industries (or benefits) that make up the customer or client base. The point of all of this is that in order to put together an effective marketing plan, you have to pinpoint your market. The better job you do defining each market segment you are targeting, the better enabled you are to create meaningful "action enticing" messages for that segment.

Notice the Market Segmentation worksheet at the end of this chapter. It contains a picture of a box. Above the box are some categories such as clients, nonclients, business clients, individual clients, top 15 percent , bottom 85 percent, and specialized industries. Looking at the top row of the box, let's pretend that it represents all potential clients. The next section below that subdivides "all potential clients" into "current clients" and "nonclients." Current clients can be subdivided numerous ways. In this example, we chose "business clients" and "individuals." Business clients can be subdivided into even more categories, such as by specialized industries and so on. The reason you should try to look at your marketplace this way before you put together your final exposure campaign is because the more "relatively homogeneous and identifiable group" you can find, the less expensive and more powerful the advertising message is likely to be, not to mention the less expensive the medium you choose to reach them (for example, advertising in the National Asphalt Paving Association's HMAT magazine (an industry specialty medium) to reach highway construction heavy contractors versus advertising in a number of newspapers (a general marketplace medium) to reach that same audience).

On the other hand, consider this interesting twist. Sometimes you might include your niche clients and referral sources in your broader messaging too. For example, if you only market to the highway contractors we previously mentioned with niche-specific messages, then you might be limiting the universe of referrals those clients will provide. In other words, contractors have many friends, associates, and family that are not contractors. So, when these same loyal contractors are asked for a referral to help them in dealing with their business problems, that contractor may refer another firm because he or she thinks you only specialize in their industry. So while you want to clearly market specifically to your niche groups with messages that will entice them to call you, you occasionally will include them in some of your general marketing pieces to remind them that you also can help their friends and family outside of their unique industry (like sending your niche audience your general newsletters, seminar invitations, postcards, and so forth, which we will touch more on later in this chapter).

Here is one final idea in this area. Because professional service marketing is as much about generating referrals as it is about selling new services to existing clients, every single client and referral source needs to be included in your marketing plan's contact plan. Don't be surprised when that simple 1040 client sends you a great business client because the two have been friends since high school. Because your marketing made your small "C" client aware of the many services you offer, even though that client would never personally need those services, he or she still can generate excellent referrals for your firm.

Managing Price Per Contact

Managing price per contact is more difficult than it sounds. This is the process of determining the specific exposure vehicles that will do the best job of getting the attention of your target audience. One extreme would be television advertising, where you could pay from several hundred to thousands of dollars for a 30-second spot during the local evening news. Another extreme would be a coupon inserted in a package of coupons for literally a few cents per thousand mailed. Paying the least money possible per contact is not the objective. Making contact with your target audience in a way that motivates them to view your message for the least money is the objective.

The following scenario should shed some light on the complexity of this issue:

> Let's say your firm, in Austin, Texas, creates a newspaper advertisement announcing several new, specialized services. Let's assume that you want to purchase a half-page ad to be run for one day during the week for $7,000. If the newspaper is delivered to a quarter of a million people, then your cost per contact is only $2.80 per hundred. This is an excellent price per contact. However, this assumes that you are selling a product or service that all 250,000 subscribers are likely to be interested in. In the accounting business, this just isn't even close to reality. So, in order to make this more realistic, let's say you are targeting general contractors. After a little research, you find out that there are only 200 general contractor organizations that subscribe to the newspaper. Now your price per contact is $35.00, which is a fairly costly price per contact, but still within reason if you knew the 200 contractors always read the newspaper. So in order to increase the odds of being seen, you put the ad in the paper for five days straight. Now, your price per contact, assuming some volume discount for advertising, would be about $122 per contact. As you can see, it doesn't take long for this to get out-of-hand.

> Consider this. Instead of taking out a half-page ad in the newspaper, how about buying a full-page color ad on the back of the Associated General Contractors of Texas's bimonthly magazine? Let's say this has an average circulation of 1,600 copies, and, for the sake of this example, is subscribed to by your 200 general contractor target audience. This ad would cost about $2,000. Your price per contact is now $10.00 for full color exposure on the back of the magazine (which has a theoretical shelf life of several months). With this alternative, you also are getting to the other out-of-market (but still viable) 1,400 general contractors for free. If the back cover proved effective, you could advertise for a year (in all 6 issues) and still only be paying $60.00 per contact ($2,000 per issue × 6 issues / 200 local general contractors = $60.00 per contact).

Defaulting to mass media advertising to sell highly specialized products or services usually is taking the lazy way out. The fact is that it is easier and quicker to spend extra money than to try to identify the more cost-effective alternatives for contacting an audience. We know we are beating this idea to death, but it's important to understand that the most common mistake regarding exposure is

> Spending money on media targeted to a much more general audience than you are trying to reach.

Who knows which medium is better to advertise in? All we are trying to point out here is that you have to balance your cost per contact with finding the best way to get the attention of your target market. Obviously, segmentation becomes a key factor in helping you manage this complex issue.

Fine Tune Your Message

One of marketing's worst enemies is disorganization. Too often, marketing is done on a haphazard basis with little thought given to the following:

- Overall theme
- Creation of a consistent message
- Achievement of a specific objective

This leads us to a question of paramount importance:

> What is in your exposure proposition that will create enough urgency to prod your potential client into action?

If the urgency generated by your proposition is lukewarm, then the results most likely will be marginal. Creating a message that motivates your client to action is what marketing is all about. Unfortunately, no magic formula exists to achieve this reaction, but there are some guidelines. Each message you send must be

- *simple*, so it is easy to understand; being subtle here is wasted money.
- *concise*. You probably get less than a second to get their attention, so net it out.
- *clear*. Don't assume too much. Be clear about what you have to offer. You have a great deal invested to get someone's attention, so don't let them walk away wondering what you were selling.
- *consistent*. Your messages shouldn't change dramatically from one contact to the next. Although you certainly can point out different features, services, and so forth, you should provide a consistent message about who you are and what your organization is all about.
- *repetitive*. Marketing has often been referred to as a contact sport. It takes numerous contacts to make any impact at all.

Make sure that your exposure messages meet these criteria. And by the way, be careful not to describe your services in jargon or "accountant's" terms. A common mistake we encounter is firms using short descriptors in their advertising, for example:

> Below are some of the services we perform. If any of these are of interest, please contact us. We do
> Strategic Planning
> Succession Planning
> Personal Financial Planning

Well, these descriptors are fine for communicating to another accountant, but they hardly deliver the kind of message or sense of urgency that's worthy of our advertising dollar. Business owners don't need

- *Strategic Planning*, but they might need someone to help them figure out how to double revenues in two years.
- *Succession Planning*, but they might need to improve the communications among family members and make sure that the younger generation is ready to take over the business when the time comes.
- *Personal Financial Planning*, but they might want to make sure they have set aside enough money to pay for their children's college education.

Yes, you and I know that these are either one-and-the-same or a component of the service mentioned. However, although the heading "Strategic Planning" is concise, it does not meet the criteria of simple or clear (because this service can be broadly interpreted regarding scope, price, involvement required, time requirements, and output expected).

The Role of Exposure

Even if your work is unsurpassed in creating the best messages, keep a perspective about the role exposure plays in this process. Exposure is like a quarterback. When the team wins, he gets too much credit. When the team loses, he is handed more than his share of the blame. Exposure by itself doesn't accomplish anything: your products and services have to be in demand; the clients have to be ready and able to buy; the exposure vehicles have to be seen or heard; and much more. This is one of the main reasons you have to be visible month after month. Exposure relies on the timing of all of these factors coming together. Even if all of this works as planned, the best you can hope for is an opportunity to sell. If you are not prepared to capitalize on this opportunity, then the time and money involved in implementing your exposure plans are wasted.

Similarly, good marketing, advertising, and exposure practices can speed up the demise of a poorly managed business. By this we mean that, if you are having problems with consistent service delivery or resolving other chronic internal shortcomings, adding a bunch of new business while you are simultaneously running off existing business will only accelerate or accentuate a negative reputation or internal culture. Just remember, disappointed clients will tell far more people about their negative experiences than your satisfied clients will brag to about their positive outcomes. Make sure you keep your house in order as you are growing so you can capitalize on your clients' goodwill as well as on the opportunities your ads and other marketing efforts produce for you.

Exposure doesn't have to be expensive to be good. However, it does have to be well thought out to be effective. Consider that creating an effective exposure plan is far from a science. The more facts you have, the more likely your efforts will result in profit rather than just another expense. With this in mind, let's take a look at the various exposure alternatives.

 Keep In Mind

Disappointed clients will tell far more people about their negative experiences than your satisfied clients will brag to about their positive outcomes.

Choose Which Exposure Vehicles Are Best for Your Organization

Now that we've been through an overview of some marketing basics, it's time to move from theory to practical application. This section of the chapter takes a look at alternatives for gaining firm exposure.

The first issue deals with the definition of the term *exposure*. We use this as a catch-all word to define any and all communication that gives your firm visibility. It is the portion of the marketing plan that lays out the who, what, where, when, why, and how of gaining visibility for the CPA firm.

Generally, exposure fits into two categories: institutional and promotional.

Institutional exposure focuses on image and perception. This type of visibility sells features such as quality, competence, experience, and uniqueness; but, it rarely creates a sense of urgency. In other words, people become aware of your firm and the services provided, but you have given them no more reason to call you today than tomorrow. This type of exposure is often referred to as enhancing your brand identity. The results of your efforts likely will not provide identifiable value for years because it is all about building a reputation or awareness, not about creating a call-to-action. This is a common exposure approach used by CPA firms.

The other type of exposure is *promotional*. This approach is built around an immediate response to some event, item, or call-to-action such as a sale, a workshop, or a coupon. If immediate action isn't taken, then the offer expires. This alternative is utilized less often within the CPA profession, but perhaps it is one that should be given further consideration.

With this in mind, let's look at our various exposure alternatives and consider how each might be used.

Networking

The most obvious form of promotion, and always one of the best, involves the circle of people you work with or know. Most people call this networking. Webster's defines *networking* as "the exchange of information or services among individuals, groups or institutions."

Networking may include participation in professional or trade associations, charitable organizations, specifically designated peer groups, loose associations with other professionals, and many other variations. It also includes using technology for social networking, which is extremely prevalent today (more on that in a minute). The objective behind networking is to establish contacts that will

- provide access to additional or unique resources.
- provide access to people and organizations through existing connections.
- refer opportunities or potential clients, or both.
- augment your knowledge through the sharing of ideas.

Whether you have chosen the Fortress or the Empire strategy, networking in some form should be the cornerstone of your exposure plan. With the Fortress, your primary network is your client base, referral sources, and your professional network because its primary focus is client base protection with growth through additional work with existing clients and referrals. Although you certainly want to tap your clients, other professionals, and friends for help, the Empire approach is more about creating reach through a strong marketing plan to specific targeted audiences, through industry organizations, and the like because normally, the client base is neither substantial enough or centered around the desired type of services. Its focus is on new client acquisition, often outside of the current client base and often promoting services of limited interest to the existing client base.

As an Empire operation, the Austin office of Bill's CPA firm tended to focus its networking energy on professionals (such as CPAs both in public and industry around the country, attorneys, bankers, insurance agents) and a few professional associations. he Fort Worth office, utilizing a Fortress strategy, concentrated its primary energy on the client base and because of a litigation support specialty—attorneys.

One down side of networking is that it often is hard to quantify the results of your promotional efforts. But here's a motivational factor that sometimes eases this frustration:

> Every time you make someone aware of why your firm is special, you create an outside salesperson.

Not only can this salesperson freely introduce your firm to people you don't know, he or she does this without becoming a part of your firm's overhead. This situation is almost too good to be legal. Therefore, be sure that your exposure plan pays attention to the expansion of its network sales force.

A common obstacle that hinders the effectiveness of networking is ego block. *Ego block* occurs when the CPA performing the networking function doesn't want to appear too anxious to obtain new business. So he or she doesn't do much selling. Comments may be made regarding firm size or current projects, but the network is never really informed about the skills and services that can be provided by the firm. This aloofness is ridiculous! But it also is very common within our profession. It is almost as if there is an unwritten rule that says When a CPA shows interest in obtaining new clients, then he or she openly admits to a lack of success. If you think this rule doesn't exist, then ask yourself this question: Has anyone ever asked if you were interested in taking on another client? You're guilty, aren't you? What benefit can be obtained, except for some ego stroking, from sending the message that you have all the business you want? Remember, the point of networking is to obtain new clients. Everyone knows that. So don't kid yourself. The next time you or one of your staff members participates in a networking function, make sure some selling takes place.

To be clear, there are times and places for different levels of selling activity that you engage in during your discussions with others. Sharing fun or interesting projects you're working on when someone asks how things are going or what's new is always safe at a trade association, for example. Making a call to welcome a new member to a trade association as part of your duties of being on the board is not the time to try to sell them something. Use your judgment, but don't be afraid to explain what nifty results your clients have had from the projects you've helped them with or what some of your offerings are when the time is right.

Social Networking

We mentioned social networking previously, but we thought we would dedicate a few paragraphs to it because it is such a new and marginally understood marketing phenomenon.

At this time, no discussion of marketing would be complete without at least touching on social networking. Although we don't consider ourselves experts in social networking, we believe that most readers will recognize what we are talking about, and we suspect that many are currently involved in social networking for personal or business reasons. Social networking includes membership in LinkedIn, Facebook, "tweeting" on Twitter, and using weblogs, or "blogs," and mediums the general market commonly interfaces with like YouTube. All of these involve networking Web sites that allow people to connect with others who have similar interests and share information and experiences. Based on anecdotal evidence, it seems the younger the professional, the more likely they are actively using social networking. At the other end of the spectrum, with some exceptions, we're finding that many boomers, at this time, are not making as much use of social networking. In fact, in our firm, Bill avoided it for the longest time (but he's now doing it too) while Dom was the early adopter. Neither approach is right or wrong—it depends on your preferences.

Should you use social networking for your practice? Some would say that you absolutely must be using social networking to stay in the marketing mainstream. For one thing, those who encourage it cite the advantages of "viral" marketing (no—we're not talking about flu-type viruses.) The notion here is that the more you and your firm are mentioned out in cyberspace through social networking and other means, the more you will continue to be mentioned and noticed, giving you a growing presence in the marketplace. It's like creating an upward-growing spiral of attention and influence. Others who are less enamored with some of this will question the necessity of it, if only from a time management perspective, inasmuch as it typically adds to the amount of time you will spend on e-mail and related activities. So, should you use it? We believe it certainly can't hurt. It can help you maintain an appearance of relevance in the marketplace, and in some cases, actually could help you generate business.

Social networking also can be used as a way to understand more about your client or customer. For example, sites have evolved for many major products and services where consumers complain about a service or product, its quality, or any number of other issues. Consider the Web site www.ihatedell.net. It is clear by the name that this Web site is not supportive of Dell products and services, but rather is a place for people to vent and share their frustrations. Rather than pretending this Web site does not exist, Dell has someone review it constantly and try to intervene to help those who have had negative experiences. But besides helping a few customers resolve their problems, this has a great value to Dell: it is competitive intelligence. Here is a Web site where Dell customers freely share their experiences, although they are negative ones, which turns out to be a great resource for the product giant to identify and uncover systemic problems or weaknesses in its customer experience. Consider another example recently on YouTube—the video "United Breaks Guitars." Here was an example of a customer who was poorly treated by the bureaucracy of the airline giant. When no resolution was offered, the customer created a video sharing his negative experience with the world. At the time we last listened to the song, which is a really catchy tune, there had been over 7 million viewings. Rumor has it that Taylor, the manufacturer of the guitar that was broken in transit, quickly replaced the customer's guitar when they heard the story (partially due to the positive advertising the video gave their company). The customer has gained incredible visibility for his music, and United offered to make this right if the video is removed. But for United, it was too little, too late. Had they been monitoring such media early on, someone in United might have been able to resolve this $3,500 claim before it turned into a "7 million viewings and growing" negative ad campaign. The point is social media can be a great source for understanding your customers' and clients' experiences.

A word of warning about social media too: be careful what you and your people put out in cyberspace. If you ask your employees, they will tell you what they do on their own time is their business. First, we would challenge that interfacing with social media is all done on the employee's own time. (Our experience is that many interactions are done throughout the day, during work time.) What we are trying to bring up is realize that what employees put out in cyberspace is for everyone to see and can't be taken back. So if one of your people is flaunting behavior or personal choices that are contrary to your firm's values, recognize that your clients and customers could be viewing this and deciding not to work with you because of it. So remind your people that what is shared in cyberspace has a far more reaching effect than they may be considering and to be careful and conservative in what they post.

Which type or types of social networking should you use? Again, it's up to you. Although we know of some people and business groups using Facebook for business purposes, we've seen more *personal* use of Facebook, with relatively more *business* use of LinkedIn. LinkedIn allows you to "recommend" others and obtain recommendations from others. These recommendations get published so viewers of your public profile can see who's recommending you and why. This process essentially creates online testimonials from satisfied clients, and that is always a good thing in your overall marketing plan. Twitter has its limits. Your "tweets," or messages, can't exceed 140 characters, but you can use it to keep your name out there and, for example, refer to your blog posts. Speaking of blogs, using a blog allows you to post comments, position papers, and the like and engage others in a running, online discussion on topics of importance to you and your clients. They are easy enough to set up, but maintenance and refreshing them takes time. Here again, they represent an opportunity for you to be recognized for your writing and expertise in a certain area, and they can enhance your online reputation, perhaps leading to more clients and work. As social networking continues to evolve, we predict that it will become ubiquitous and more refined, with a better-defined value proposition for users. But even more important, if your clients and customers are using it, you should at least be looking at it.

Referrals

Referrals are the result of effective networking and client satisfaction. As we discussed previously, referrals are generated through the use of your network: your client base, employees, friends, family, your professional network, and the like.

After surveying thousands of CPAs participating in our training, we have learned that most firms credit referrals for more than 80 percent (often more than 90 percent) of all new business. Based on this response, it's obvious that the most effective marketing tool used by our profession is first-class client service. By keeping your current clients as happy as possible, you build loyalty. The marketing part comes in when these loyal clients become part of your network sales force and tell their friends about how pleased they are with your work.

Due to the success of this marketing alternative, it makes sense that your exposure plan should be built primarily around leveraging this resource. In other words, spend much of your exposure resources subtly educating and reminding those people most likely to refer you for the different ways you can help. Why? Because most of the time, when someone asks for help, the cry isn't "Hey Sue, do you know of anyone who can help me with some mundane accounting work?" Instead, the comment will more likely be "Sue, I'm trying to put together a financial package for my bank and need a little help. Do you know of anyone I can call?"

When people ask for help, they usually are requesting a specific skill or expertise. And while Sue may be your greatest supporter, she probably thinks of your organization from a narrow perspective, those services to which her organization subscribes. She most likely has no idea about the numerous other unique services you offer. So when someone is requesting help in an area in which she has no first-hand knowledge of your firm's skills, even if she has the confidence to refer you, the referral most likely will be weak (maybe to the point of being ineffective). For example: "I think the CPA firm of Jones and Smith has done that sort of work."

The point is that your network of outside salespeople needs to know a few details regarding your operation. We are not suggesting that you immediately start pulling people aside to make a sales pitch. We are proposing that a sales pitch be made through a designed exposure campaign and whenever a suitable opportunity presents itself. Consider this approach when you do:

> Describe your services by telling a story that lets others know about a specific service, such as estate planning. Even if the story isn't an exact match with the discussion topic, it may lead to something. Example: If Bob, one of your clients, starts talking about the fact that he is uncomfortable about who might replace him upon retirement, you might say, "I recently prepared a plan for a doctor who was worried about the very same issue. He decided to sell his practice over a five-year period to his partner. While we looked at a variety of alternatives, here were some of the reasons ..."

This makes it clear that you know something about the subject and that you have experience in such matters. Using this technique, you've informed them in a way that is clear and easy to understand. Many CPAs would respond with something far more obscure like, "Our firm does succession planning all the time. We should get together and talk about that sometime." Note: People love stories. You don't have to give away any secrets to tell these stories either. And if you think your prospect or client might recognize the company you are talking about, change the facts, such as using a different industry, or change the family members from a father and two sons to a father and three daughters. Whatever you do, when you sell yourself in these networking situations, try to deliver your message through stories so that it is interesting to the listener and easy for them to follow. By the way, the same is true when utilizing advertising techniques too, like using newsletters or taking out ads. Tell a short story, don't just list services you offer. Stories make it real. Make what you do jump to life.

The second issue surrounding referrals is recognition. When members of your network refer business to you, what have they done? The most important factor is that your network was willing to risk something for your gain. Each time a referral is made, that individual has put his or her good name and reputation on the line in order to put money in your pocket. What happens if your firm does sloppy work, gives bad advice, or charges more than expected? One thing you can count on: whoever made the recommendation will hear about it.

So what do these people gain by going out on a limb like this? The overwhelming majority of CPAs we polled commented "We <u>try</u> to send them a thank you letter." Our immediate response is, "You *try* or you *do*?" The most common rebuttal: "We send a letter most of the time."

Let's pause here for a moment and review what we've covered so far.

Eighty percent or more of most CPA firms' new business comes from a source that might receive a thank you letter for their high-risk, low-reward effort.

What's really odd about this is the fact that many firms will spend thousands of dollars developing a brochure, thousands again on various advertisements, thousands to sponsor events, and yet the one resource that clearly generates the most new business *might* receive a thank you letter.

Every firm should rethink its position on this matter. We have. In many business relationships, the best way to thank someone for a referral is to reciprocate. However, because this is not always possible, our solution was to make an arrangement with one of our clients who manufactures candy. We identified a variety of products (of different size and cost), presented them with our credit card, and set up a procedure for anyone in our firm to call in and initiate a referral package with an attached card. By the way, our thank you is not conditioned on whether the referred client does business with us because whoever made the referral took the risk as soon as he or she mentioned our name.

Hundreds, even thousands, of ways exist to inexpensively thank those who are partly responsible for the growth of your business. So choose one that best suits your situation. You can have some very high quality note cards printed up with your name on them, and send a handwritten note to the referral source. The fact that you took the time to hand write a note on a nice quality card says that you really, personally appreciate their thoughtfulness. You can get these cards from any number of places, from your local printer, to nationally recognized stationery companies. As an alternative, you might send a novelty item (pens, hats, shirts cups, for example), movie passes, or a gift certificate. Whenever possible, use a client's product or service for this thank you because it not only sends a great message, it supports an organization that is already doing business with you. It's not what you send that matters, but that you clearly say, "Thank you—your referral means a great deal to us." The gift demonstrates a little extra effort on your part to show how much you care.

Note: Many advertising specialty agencies can provide you with some interesting novelty items. For those people that refer business to you and work on an ongoing basis with organizations within your target market, buy them something particularly nice that is likely to remain visible in their offices. By taking this route, you can print your firm name and logo inconspicuously on the item. Then when other people see and comment on it, a discussion about your firm is sure to follow.

Community Relations

This also is a form of networking. Typically, this kind of exposure is gained through involvement with civic organizations and charitable activities. Because the focus of these events is other than business-building, you have to be more low key about selling. If it appears the only reason you are involved is so you can hawk your services, you are likely to do more damage than good. However, this doesn't mean that you should refuse conversation about your firm when asked.

By the way, it's easy to get someone to ask about your firm. The best way is to ask questions about your conversation partner's livelihood. After enough interested inquiries on your part, most people will respond appropriately and ask about your background as well. Yes, this sounds a little manipulative. However, chances are that people have been doing this to you all your life, and you just didn't know it. So learn to use techniques like this one that will help you better control and manage your communication environment.

And don't forget that your civic involvement through, for example, nonprofits, is an opportunity to showcase your personal likability as well as your problem-solving (MTBA) prowess. Don't blow it by being one of those board members who has to be asked to either stick to their commitment or resign because they have been missing so many meetings. Once you make a commitment, stick to it and do an outstanding job—get actively involved and really make a difference. It will come back to you in a big way over time.

This leads us to still more factors for you to consider. If you agree with our premise that you should be very actively involved if you do serve as a board member of a community organization, ask yourself if the organization's mission is something that you are passionate about. Is it something that you personally believe will make a difference? Does it get you excited every time you tell someone about what the organization's programs are? And what about the rest of the board—are they the type of people you want to hang out with and are comfortable spending some time with? Let's consider an example of what we're talking about. If you agree to sit on a board for an organization that has a mission that's a bore for you, and you really don't believe in its cause, your term on the board will play out more like a sentence and, as an added bonus, your lack of passion likely will turn more people off than on. So while it is flattering to be asked to serve on a board, especially when people tell you how much you are needed, you have a limited amount of time, so use it where you can do the most good for the organization you are volunteering for, as well as your firm.

In a similar vein, consider how well-organized or capable of being organized the nonprofit is, along with how well it appears to be doing in conducting its business. Does the nonprofit have the appropriate level of formality and process to ensure that internal controls are in place to protect the organization? Does it take care of business day to day, like keeping up with transmitting its payroll taxes on time? For that matter, does the board hold the executive director accountable, or does he or she lead the board around by their noses? You, as a professional and an "expert" CPA, can incur some liability in your role as a board member. This is all the more reason to conduct some due diligence before you sign up for such a job. Interestingly enough, in a community that had a big media uproar over alleged board conflicts of interests at one nonprofit, another nonprofit asked one of us to serve on its board. The executive director of this organization was one of the most vocal critics of the board at the other organization. Imagine our shock when, during our due diligence before accepting the position, that executive director informed us of his plan to immediately create what would have amounted to an inappropriate conflict of interest on his board! Sometimes, those who shout the loudest are the people covering up their very similar, abusive behavior. Remember that when you serve on one of these community boards, any of their dysfunctional and egregious actions shared publically will taint your reputation and that of your firm simply by association.

Finally, think about your total time commitment to volunteer organizations and what they really need in a commitment from you. Dom serves on the board of the associate member group of an industry trade association. As chair of that subgroup, he was a member of the major board of directors, so he had a minimum of two board meetings to attend every month, plus occasional task force, committee, and membership meetings as well. If you travel a lot, as we do, make sure your seat on the board doesn't require you to attend more meetings than you can schedule around your business travel. Don't underestimate how much time being actively involved can take for one of these positions.

Personal Sales Calls

Personal sales calls are the most effective method of selling. That's why we have spent a good portion of this book discussing ways to improve the skills used in this area. But personal sales calls also are the most costly to make. One reason why this alternative is so expensive is because the most limited resource of a CPA firm is the time of its senior people, so each minute needs to be used wisely. Time thrown away selling in situations that don't warrant such a resource allocation can be very costly to the firm's overall success and profit. This lost time is exacerbated by the fact that selling time is hard to leverage; we normally make personal sales calls one at a time, and they are very time-consuming (when you consider the appointment time, travel time and preparation time.) Because of the high costs associated with this alternative, you only want to use it when you have identified potential clients who are interested, qualified, and ready to buy.

Research and Development Approach

This approach is like selling on-the-job-training. We call it the Research and Development (R&D), or the "earn while you learn" approach because you know you are capable of doing the work, but you haven't actually performed the exact job the client is requesting. Therefore, although your existing experience is adequate to help you navigate successfully through the project, you know there will be times when you will have to do some extra reading, research problems, develop procedures, and much more. Although almost every project requires some of this creation and exploration, because of your inexperience, you are likely to spend a disproportionate amount of time working through these kinds of issues. So in order to make the client feel more comfortable with your inexperience, you either *give away a piece of the job, or perform the job at reduced rates.*

R&D is an excellent technique to use when attempting to provide new services. Enticing an existing client to allow you to perform work at a bargain price in exchange for a reference is a great deal for everyone involved. Why? Because it's hard to obtain new clients with a sales pitch like this: *"Well, we've never done this kind of work before … but we've always wanted to. You would be a great organization to cut our teeth on."*

The R&D approach gives you a track record and confidence, which are both essential to selling consulting services.

Client Seminars and Workshops

The client seminar or workshop is an excellent vehicle. It allows you to sell by offering education. Whether you are promoting new services or reviewing old ones, teaching is marketing.

One of the requirements for success is that you offer something worthwhile. In other words, each seminar or workshop should be organized in a self-help fashion. If you put on a show that is clearly centered on creating new business, it most likely will backfire on you.

The fact is, when you teach someone how to do something, you sell yourself. Some will ask you to merely act as their consultant while they attempt to do the work. Others will get excited about the idea, but hire you to perform the work because they are too busy to do it themselves. And yes, a few will actually use the new-found skills you helped them develop on their own. But don't be afraid of giving away information for fear that the participants will be able to handle the tasks without your involvement. Most problems are complex. Therefore, regardless of your thoroughness, you will not be able to address all the issues in sufficient detail to enable your clients to figure everything out on their own. In fact, it is typically a plus if they *do* attempt to proceed without you. This means your information was valuable to them. And when they inevitably hit a snag, they'll call you for assistance.

Everyone wins. By teaching a skill or identifying how to better use a tool, you gain two things:

• Enhanced client-base loyalty
• Additional opportunities

Either of these is enough to make client seminars and workshops a worthwhile effort. In a recent survey of CPA firm clients, Bay Street Group, LLC found that the clients placed a little more importance on having seminars than the CPAs who were surveyed placed on conducting them, so they are worth looking at as part of your overall marketing strategy. Even if your clients do not take advantage of a value-added service offer such as a seminar, by inviting them, they are reminded of your existence and informed of your capability to perform that service. For those who do not attend, consider following-up after the event by offering the handout materials. This gives you one more contact. And as we said before, marketing is a contact sport.

Finally, you may be pleasantly surprised to find some of the seminar participants wanting to hire you to help them soon after the seminar. On the other hand, you may not have very much apparent uptake after a seminar. Don't be discouraged if you don't have people storming the stage to set up appointments right after the seminar. The seminar helps position you and your firm as an expert in the subject matter. It plants a seed or waters the seed to keep them thinking about you so when a need arises, you are at the top of mind. We've had people contact us up to 18 months after a seminar to have us do a project for them. Sometimes it just takes a while for those seeds to germinate.

Joint Seminars and Workshops

These can create the same positive results as do client seminars and workshops, with the added value of exponentially expanding your audience.

Joint seminars, in our opinion, are one of the most productive marketing vehicles used by professionals. You find lawyers, stockbrokers, insurance agents, psychologists, bankers, CPAs, and others forming strong alliances. These alliances are made in order to take advantage of the referral network and share client bases. So instead of randomly referring business to anyone, most opportunities are referred to those within the group.

These loose associations create two advantages. The first is that each firm has some access to the clients of the other through formal presentations, newsletters, and so forth. This literally can double or triple the size of your available audience overnight. This temporary merging of client bases also gives you direct access to a great many people who would otherwise be difficult to contact. The second advantage is that these alliances form a kind of umbrella of professional services. The combination of these services forms a protective wall (a Fortress) that enhances client loyalty and satisfaction.

Joint seminars and workshops can be used by both Fortress- and Empire-minded firms because this vehicle facilitates both protection and expansion. Because those in attendance already have demonstrated an interest, marketing is not only easy but inexpensive as well. Even though this task may be time consuming, the potential benefits of establishing this association are fantastic. The trick is to find the right professionals with whom to associate. And this is important. We were approached once by an insurance broker we really didn't know. However, he was the son of a client who was a long-time client and friend of the firm, so we agreed to do a joint seminar. As it turns out, we were the only ones marketing the seminar because he simply wanted access to our clients. So make sure you clarify with your copresenters the duties of each organization, agree to check points for each of you to verify progress, and have each party included in the other's exposure vehicle so you can all see the end product delivered, how it looks, and the timing of delivery.

Writing

When we talk about writing, we include everything from position papers to published articles to books. Although writing rarely brings potential clients to your doors immediately, it does, again, help position you and your firm in the minds of clients and prospects, and keeps you in front of them.

Position Papers

Position papers, sometimes referred to as white papers, are essentially unpublished articles that give you a pulpit, albeit in print or electronic media, to use in making a point. The point you are going to make is usually something of interest to you that your target audience also may find interesting, which shows that you have knowledge and experience with that topic. It doesn't have to be long. When we write these, they normally run from about one and one-half to three or four pages of single-spaced, size 12, Times New Roman font. How long should it take to write a position paper of this length? Once you get into the groove, it usually doesn't take more than two to four hours, including a little time to edit and clean it up. Having these position papers available to take with you to meetings with qualified prospects, or for download from your Web site, helps strengthen your brand and differentiation. They also can serve as collateral marketing materials for you.

If you are using the Fortress approach, writing and distributing position papers to existing clients, referral sources, and friends on topics such as services you have added that would be of interest to them, can help dig your moat deeper or add some height to the fortress walls, so to speak. It keeps your clients in touch with what you're doing. Also, because you are telling stories, it helps your clients and referral sources become more effective members of your network sales force. If you are using the Empire approach, position papers are even more fundamental to the approach, as well as powerful because they allow you to set yourself up as having special knowledge, expertise, and insight, which are the drivers for motivating a potential client to leave their existing provider to become your new current client.

Articles

Articles are simply published position papers. Look around to see what publications address your client base (Fortress) or your targeted prospects (Empire) and take a look at what the articles by outside contributors look like and cover. The publication may be a print publication, or it may be one of a burgeoning number of electronic newsletters. Either way, the publishers often are looking for something of interest to their readers. In all but the most prestigious journals, you may be pleasantly surprised at how easily you get a well-written article published. You normally don't get paid, but the payback is seeing your name in the byline (and more importantly, your marketplace seeing your name in the byline).

To increase your odds of being published, visit the Web sites or call and talk to someone about their author guidelines for articles. This document will explain who the audience is, the preferred length, and other requirements for getting published. Talking to the editor is also helpful. Usually, the larger publications will want a bullet point summary of the key issues you intend to cover, who it's for, and what they'll get out of it before they agree to talk with you about an article. Published articles are good resume builders and create even more collateral marketing materials. They also get your name and expertise out to a broader base of people (Empire), reaffirm what your clients already know, or educate your clients as to what they don't know about what you know (Fortress).

As for the marketing value of writing articles, this channel creates much more interest when the topics discussed are specific in nature and targeted toward a small group (for example, addressing theft control for retailers). When you write specific pieces, you can expect them to generate more opportunities than general ones. Why? Because the more specific you are, the more detail you can cover and insight you can give. This allows you to showcase your expertise. A lot of people can wax eloquent about a topic in general, but it takes a real expert to identify a problem and then give specific, practical, and simple suggestions on ways to address it. This is the kind of advice that motivates people to call you—people are looking for professionals that understand their problems, and someone who has the "in-the-trenches" experience to find ways to resolve them.

Obviously, just being published isn't the key. But rather, issues such as who publishes your work, size of circulation, and target market all become central to determining whether your article-writing efforts will impress prospects.

Books

Books are an entirely different topic. Writing a book that someone will pick up and legitimately publish takes a great deal of time. We've already done this, and we're the first to tell you that it's a classic case of mixed emotions while you're going through the process, as well as a big relief when you get through it. However, when a successful book does come along, being published helps create a brand that differentiates you from your competition. We estimate that we close more than 80 percent of the prospective clients we talk to partially due to the perceived value created by exposure vehicles such as writing, be it position papers, articles, or books. An even greater value offered by this medium is that most of the people who call us in the first place already have read something we have written, they feel like they already know a great deal about us through their reading, and the fact that they contacted us usually means that they agreed, at least in part, with what we had to say.

Should you self-publish or hold out to have unrelated party publish you? An increasing number of self-published books and publishing companies have been established to help people publish their own works. Certainly, if it's done properly, a self-published work can be helpful in a marketing sense. However, books published by an unrelated party are where the increased visibility and strongest positioning come from. Real books published by real companies provide you with better differentiation than self-publishing will.

Writing, in general, obviously is an exposure vehicle in which we believe. An effort made in this area should pay off over time. Writing books, and to a lesser extent, publishing articles, most often is selected as part of an Empire-building plan.

Public Speaking

Public speaking, like writing, has a long-term payoff. Although it's geared more toward an Empire philosophy, speaking can help educate your clients in a Fortress approach (that is, talking at local service clubs or presenting at one of your seminars comes to mind). However, getting out on the speaking trail and talking to industry and professional associations clearly is an Empire-building tool, and it is a unique avenue to demonstrate your knowledge.

Speaking on general business topics allows you access to large audiences. The benefit here is the expansion of your network. Covering topics in specialized areas creates more immediate opportunities. However, in either case, if your speech is merely a sales pitch, you will not only insult your audience, but you will lose their confidence as well.

One other issue you face with public speaking is that you are taking on the role of expert, so be well prepared and have a good presentation. Unlike writing, your audience can challenge immediately any comment you make. For some people, there is nothing more exciting than trying to stump or embarrass the expert. How you handle these potentially hostile situations often is more important than the speech itself.

Publicity

Used to promote image and brand, publicity is both an Empire and Fortress alternative. However, the Empire relies on this visibility much more than does the Fortress.

Publicity can come in many forms. The most common is through news releases. Every time your firm decides to offer a unique service or makes a contribution to the local community, a news release should be sent to all major television and radio stations and newspapers. The format of a news release is simple. The AICPA is a great source for this. Just look in the front of the materials of any seminar you attend. A short press release has been inserted for your use announcing the fact that you have gained new knowledge in a unique area. At a minimum, you can follow the format introduced to create press releases of your own announcing different accomplishments. Don't be discouraged if the press does not respond to your press releases—just keep sending them. Their interest is less a function of what you did and more a function of the topics they are covering at the time or the amount of news activity percolating at the moment.

Additionally, there are many other ways to achieve free exposure. In an example that we mentioned earlier, we contacted a local television station, a CBS affiliate, and sold the idea of our firm providing advice in a business tip series called *You and Your Money*. It appeared every weekend during the 6 p.m. news for over a year. This gave us excellent exposure, great credibility, but no short-term results. That's why this type of visibility belongs more in an Empire strategy.

Along these same lines, several years earlier, we did the same thing with the local newspaper. We proposed a weekly column on small business. It was approved after about nine months of negotiation.

The point is that you have to be creative and find free ways to promote your business. Publicity not only gives your firm exposure but enhances your credibility and image too. A word of warning though: alternatives like the television series or the weekly column are very time-consuming. Therefore, even though this visibility had no out-of-pocket costs, it was still expensive in unbilled time. For any benefit to accrue, this type of exposure should occur over a long period of time. So if you can't see yourself making that long of a commitment without direct results, then it is probably not the right vehicle for you to pursue.

The good news is that publicity is free (except for your time). Therefore, something as simple as a news release should be incorporated into everyone's operation and used extensively. Consider this: being covered as part of the news gives you much more visibility than does a paid advertisement. So start a program right away to take advantage of all the free exposure you can get.

Cross-Selling

This channel of exposure has been used widely to generate business for CPA firms in the past. Because it is client-base focused, cross-selling is predominantly a Fortress strategy. *Cross-selling* is the act of selling one service while providing another. For example, while performing tax or accounting services, you can drop a few premeditated hints about other expertise within your firm that could be of benefit. This is an effective technique because the best time to sell future services is while you are solving current problems.

It's important to note that the best chance we have for cross-selling is when we are in front of our clients. Tax practitioners have an enormous window of opportunity each year—Tax Time! During these few months, we have face-to-face meetings with a high percentage of our clients. Make sure you have a game plan for blending in a few sales messages during your client conferences. Look for occasions during these conversations to mention some of the other services your firm offers. You are not really trying to sell them now, but rather plant the seeds for a follow-up later. When you consider how difficult it is to communicate with your clients using other marketing methods (such as direct mail, newsletters, or seminars), you simply can't afford to let this window of opportunity slip by.

Another important point that needs to be made is that effective cross-selling requires the creation of a client service plan for your major clients (at least the top 15 percent to 20 percent, those whom we've referred to earlier in this text as your "A" and high "B" clients). This plan should identify the services you have or are delivering, as well as those you intend to deliver. The services you intend to deliver should be prioritized and scheduled on a time-line. The client service plan is a reminder for all within the firm to see what concepts are important to sell to each client, which in turn, generates a smooth flow of opportunities. Your messages are consistent about what the client should focus on because it's easy for members of your organization to stay tuned in to the client's current situation. This plan should have a horizon of a couple of years and is essential to maximizing your ability to cross-sell. A sample of a client service plan is included in the forms section at the end of this chapter.

If you are currently not aware of a client's additional needs, consider having one of those lunch meetings to ask questions and listen, while keeping track of branches for MTBA services. This commitment of time is justified easily for a firm's larger or more financially significant clients. Regarding your other clients and referral sources, preparing occasional surveys or newsletters that solicit this kind of information can be a time-effective alternative, especially given the ease of doing this electronically.

Newsletters

Because we have mentioned newsletters several times previously, we would like to take this time to make a few points about them. We have already covered how the content and focus of the newsletter should change based on whether it is being published for a Fortress or Empire marketplace, so here are a couple of other points.

First, newsletters are an excellent marketing and exposure vehicle. However, they have to be prepared with marketing in mind. Preprinted (canned) newsletters that just have your firm's name stamped on them don't sell. They do educate, which is good, but they don't tell your clients who you are or why you are special. Our rule of exposure is:

> **Don't send out any material or information that doesn't sell.**

Don't just send out any newsletter; send out a selling newsletter. This can demand a great deal of work if you create it yourself. So consider incorporating some combination of canned and personal information into each issue. For instance, besides a few canned articles, discuss the benefits one of your clients has reported from a new service you provide, or introduce a new person you have hired and highlight one of his or her unique skills you want to showcase. Additionally, don't get bogged down in how elegantly this information is presented. Instead, make sure it always sells your firm and is sent out on a regular basis.

Brochures, Firm Resumes, and Other Collateral Materials

These are image-building or branding alternatives. Although most firms develop them, too many spend an inordinate amount of money doing so. The objective of these promotional pieces is to allow you to leave something tangible with a potential client that will act as an inside salesperson.

Brochures, firm resumes, and other collateral materials are almost like business cards. They rarely generate business but are expected. We feel they are important and should be presented in a professional manner. We also feel that many firms place too much emphasis and spend too much money on vehicles such as these that do not generate new business opportunities. If you are going to create these documents or revise some you already have, get some design help from a good graphic designer so they don't look like a bunch of technicians just sweated them out. As well, rather than go to the expense of printing them professionally, create them in a good looking professional PDF for download. You can always print them out on your wonderful color printer, but rather than just leave these behind after you meeting, always try to motivate your client to visit your Web site to access this information and much more. When they visit, you have captured their undivided attention, at a time convenient to the client, for them to sell themselves on why you are the right firm and learn more about the breadth of services you have to offer.

You also send one other subtle message using this approach. The message is that your firm is effectively using cutting edge tools to market its services. This is a message the client likely is going to want to mimic. When the client sees you as a good advisor and a good business person, they see you as having much more to offer them.

Major Advertising Media

These include media like television, newspaper, radio, and general audience magazines. Although these alternatives can be expensive, at times, they may be your best logical alternative. The real decision about whether you should utilize mass media to promote your services lies in the answer to these questions:

- Can you obtain information that will narrow your target market?
- If so, are there exposure vehicles more targeted toward the audience you are after?

If the answers are "No," then using general media is probably your best choice. However, you should make an immediate effort to start collecting demographic information about your clients and potential clients in order to find some common thread that can be used to better segment your market. Even these general media have various alternatives they will suggest (placement, time, specific events) once they understand the demographic audience you are trying to reach.

In an earlier discussion on mass media, we alluded to the fact that this channel often is a choice of convenience. For some firms, money is in greater supply than time. This makes the mass media alternatives very attractive. This is fine. But recognize that if you opt for convenience, when you analyze the cost benefit of your exposure campaign, your price per real contact most likely is much higher than it needs to be.

Direct Mail

This is a great alternative for both the Empire and the Fortress. However, it is much more cost-effective and productive when generating interest for the Fortress. Even though this form of exposure is impersonal, it is still likely to be reviewed because your client will recognize who sent it.

Direct mail typically is used to promote an event or some special offering. Seminars would be an example of this. But don't limit yourself. Think of ways to create urgency other than by seminars—like sending money. That's right, money! As an example, if you are promoting a new consulting service, send out a hundred dollars of play money. This money can then be used as payment against your newly offered service. Make sure your money offer has an expiration date of six weeks or less, or it won't be as effective at generating immediate response. Remember, the objective is to create some urgency for the client to call.

The idea of sending "funny money" or coupons accomplishes a number of things. Besides creating urgency and calling attention to your new service, it does so without discounting it. Sometimes, when you discount a service, you create an impression that the service is not worth the full price. By sending "money," this issue is less prominent. Besides, you would spend that same amount or more going out and making a marketing call anyway.

Try to be creative and think of ways to take more advantage of direct mail. One CPA firm told us that they had an excellent response from sending out a series of postcards (one each month for about six months), which dissected and discussed the firm's mission statement. Another idea is to create a series of postcards or letters that sell your various services, send them out one at a time, and then send something out once every six weeks all year long. It is a matter of being consistent and repetitive. Remember: marketing is a contact sport, and the intent of campaigns like this is to keep you top-of-mind and to educate your audience. Your payoff will come, just stick with it. And when it comes, it simply might be a referral you would have never received except for the fact that you increased the selling ability of your network sales force because of the slow-drip postcard campaign that allowed your client or referral source to better understand what you have to offer.

As far as direct mail is concerned for the Empire, you have to be persistent. If you are not willing to mail at least four pieces to the same audience, then direct mail is a waste of time in our opinion. The Empire audience is not intimately aware of your firm, at least not like your clients are. So your first mailing most likely will be tossed into the trash. The second might be held for a few seconds before the "file 13" decision is made. By the time the third or fourth mailers arrive, your prospective clients should at least start wondering who you are. They also should start recognizing your name. So with consistency and repetition, the odds begin to swing in your favor that your promotional piece will be reviewed carefully.

Another issue regarding direct mail is timing. People don't have good memories. Therefore, even when your mailers are read, if the prospective clients are not in need of your services at that time, the promotion or announcement won't produce any results. You have to mail to a group of people over and over again. When your message to provide help arrives at a time when your clients or prospective clients perceive they need help, that's when the payoff comes. But because you'll rarely know exactly when that will happen, you have to remain visible month after month. Because of the requirement to remain constantly visible and to present a meaningful message, you want to segment your audience as much as possible before you start a campaign like this. This way, the impact of your investment in your exposure campaign is significantly greater due to targeted messages to a select audience.

One more thought on this. If the intent of a great deal of the marketing pieces you distribute are to stay top-of-mind and educate, which we feel they are, make sure your campaign considers times when your clients, referral sources, or prospective clients are likely to mingle with their network, such as right before holidays, early in tax season, or around local activities like big college sports events. Touching your network with timely messages allows an expanded reach because you will be top-of-mind as they interact with their network.

Trade Related

This vehicle includes media such as magazines, other publications and convention booths and exhibits. When you are targeting an industry or trade, look for opportunities like these that specifically focus on your target audience. By utilizing them, you can more easily get the attention of those who would be most interested in your products or services. This type of exposure is Empire-oriented because it attempts to expand into a specialized area.

A note of warning: any form of promotion needs to be exciting. Even though trade vehicles are addressing an interested niche market, your promotional material, trade show booth, or exhibit need to stand out. Regardless of how, when, or where you publicize your firm, your potential clients always will be distracted by the thousands of other companies also trying to get their attention.

Signage

This channel includes billboards and exterior or interior promotional displays. As far as billboards are concerned, this is more like the mass media we discussed earlier. It is expensive because it is geared towards reaching a general audience. However, if your firm concentrates on an area like manufacturing and your city has a manufacturing district, then this general media could become more targeted with careful placement. Even though billboard presentations can be expensive, when they are targeted, they can be an excellent alternative to help you expand your Empire. We certainly see large CPA firms and consulting organizations leverage this medium all the time.

Regarding exterior and interior promotional displays, you should use them to promote more than just your firm name. Although these need to be tastefully done, interior signs, plaques, and awards should help promote the kind of work performed by members of your firm. In other words, more selling emphasis should be given to the workplace, especially in the waiting and conference areas. A spin-off of this idea is to use one of your computers in the waiting area to display firm propaganda through a presentation software package or video. This way, you can tastefully let your captive audience better understand your firm's capabilities. Make sure you have your propaganda—brochures, mini-brochures, flyers, article reproductions, and position papers available in the waiting area as well.

Whether you're doing external signage, such as a sign on your office building, internal signage, or printed media of any kind, take the time to ensure your image is consistent, and that the fonts and colors used are consistent. This makes a big difference in how you're perceived institutionally. If you have one partner handing out his old business cards (didn't want to throw them away and be wasteful) with block type fonts and an old logo or no logo at all, while everyone else is using the updated logo and fonts, you have the makings of a public image problem. This should be pretty manageable, but everyone in the firm needs to know what styles of font are okay to use for which purpose. Here again, consider engaging a talented designer to help put together your image and branding in your own style guide. At the very least, get rid of old, superseded materials that do not match current designs.

Telemarketing

Telemarketing is one of our industry's fastest growing methods for identifying prospects. Firms all over the country are finding this to be a profitable and productive vehicle. In the past, many organizations found themselves frustrated because the leads generated using this technique were much harder to convert into new business than those referred by clients. However, in the last few years, telemarketing has evolved into one of the tools of choice for middle-market and large firms. Why? Because even though the cost of setting up a telemarketing program is too expensive for most small firms, for larger organizations, this vehicle can generate a waiting list of prospects at a very reasonable price. But even more important, instead of relying completely on the more passive approach of generating leads through client referral, telemarketing is proactive.

Some firms have used a combination of telemarketing plus a giveaway to get in the door. For example, one firm calls up likely prospects (businesses in selected industries) and gives away a quick onsite review of previously filed excise tax returns. They then provide a written report of their findings. For those organizations that have overpaid their excise taxes, which include most of these targeted businesses, they also offer a variety of fee options to file the necessary amended returns. This is an example of a telemarketing giveaway that is turning out to be a great way to open doors and provide immediate value for this particular CPA firm.

Telemarketing also is an excellent method to maximize participation in some event. For example, by following a seminar invitation with telemarketing, your attendance should improve dramatically. As well, many organizations are using this technique to gather essential information like conducting client, market, and competitive surveys. Other common offerings that are used to entice telephone prospects into opening their doors to an outsider are free tax reviews, a free hour of consulting, a free booklet (self-help on a specific topic), or free software.

Regardless, telemarketing is a lead generation vehicle. Don't expect telemarketing to sell anything for you. Their job is to find leads, that is, people or companies that have an interest in your product or service, with an invitation for follow-up. It is then up to your people to convert this lead into something valuable, like new business.

Monitor the Results

Once you have developed an exposure campaign that defines your target markets and delivers appropriate, consistent, and repetitive messages to those markets through cost-effective exposure vehicles, it's time to monitor what you have done. This is the step most often ignored by those firms that actually do create marketing plans. Monitoring the results is something everyone agrees is important, but a task that rarely receives much attention. A plan is significantly more effective if it also is monitored. So what does monitoring mean? Basically, you need to track the results of each exposure or promotion. Make notes about what you did and whether it generated any phone calls or comments, or if any new business resulted from it. Note the time of year, day of the week, and any other information that could prove pertinent (for instance, your biggest competitor staged a free workshop at the same time you offered your for-fee seminar).

We suggest that you create an exposure notebook to record this information. This notebook should contain a calendar upon which the exposure schedule is written. The notebook also should include everything your firm does to create visibility, from mass media (like newspaper, and radio) to lectures, to networking meetings, to publicity, to articles published.

Over time, this information will help you identify what works for you. Also, note that expressions of interest or inquiries are a better indication about the effectiveness of exposure than are new clients or revenues. Remember, the objective of exposure is to prompt your potential client into action to contact you not to buy from you. The "buy from you" part of this transaction is not the responsibility of the marketing plan, but rather your internal sales skills and plan. If you judge your exposure plan by statistics, such as new clients, then you are assuming that your firm is able to convert 100 percent of the interest generated into requests for services. That assumption is not only invalid, but it may lead you to alter an effective exposure plan when the real problem may be the firm's sales and communication skills.

The real benefit to monitoring results is that it keeps everyone focused on fine tuning the marketing effort. For example, let's say your organization pays a 10 percent commission based on the first year's billings to anyone bringing in a new client. Let's also say that your firm is proud of this commitment to marketing. However, the partner group is very dissatisfied with the number of new clients brought in by the junior partners. Rather than just assume that the 10 percent commission is in line, and that you have ineffective junior partners, monitoring requires that you take a much closer look at the system in place. What you may find is that the only people that ever make any real money under this system are the senior partners. Are they just better marketers? They might be. They also have a great many more contacts than do the junior partners. Therefore, by just playing the numbers game alone, the odds of a senior partner bringing in new business is far greater than the odds of a junior partner doing the same. Maybe what you really want to track with the junior partners is the effort they are making to stay in contact with their existing clients and referral sources, as well as the number of networking meetings and events they are attending, rather than simply the amount of sales.

Another factor to consider is that when many business owners call a CPA firm, they ask for one of the named or senior partners. This is because owners have found out over the years that they almost always are better served by working with whoever has the most influence. We bring this up because compensation systems are a definite part of the marketing plan. On numerous occasions, we have found that the compensation system is rewarding the exact opposite behavior that the firm desires. Take this junior partner and new business issue, for example. What we have found several times is that the compensation system is structured in a way that it is far more rewarding for the junior partners to bill work in-house than to find new business. If the firm wants junior partners to make the effort to gain more community contacts, then maybe junior partners should get an additional 10 percent (or 20 percent of the first year's billings) for all new business brought in. Or you might set a sales threshold for the junior partners to be much lower than that of the senior partners, which triggers compensation accelerators (that is, extra compensation for all business over a certain hurdle amount, like 10 percent for the first $50,000 in new business, but 15 percent for business above $50,000 in a given year). Why? Because, once again, junior partners typically have to work two to three times harder to grow their contact network as compared to senior partners. So you want your compensation system to provide the greatest incentive for the behavior you are really looking to obtain.

Every aspect of your marketing plan has to be challenged as time tests it. If it is accomplishing what the firm desires, great! If not, change it. Regardless, note the details of what you are doing so that later, when you analyze what has happened, you have a better chance of determining what worked, what didn't, and maybe even why.

Don't Let Marketing Get Out Of Hand

A word of warning on this subject: marketing is like a bed of roses; it contains beautiful flowers and prickly thorns. One major thorn is that you can spend an endless amount of money performing the marketing function, much of which easily can prove to be of no value. You create twice the problem when you add the fact that the time you take to market is mostly nonbillable. These two issues make it easy to see why the abstract world of marketing often gets out of hand.

Keep In Mind

Marketing is like a bed of roses: it contains beautiful flowers and prickly thorns.

A good first step to help keep things under control is to be honest about which resources are expended as part of your marketing strategy and which are expended just for fun. This is a critical distinction because often you find CPAs talking marketing when they are really just playing. As an example, a golf outing with a client is only marketing when the firm can reasonably expect this time to deliver some increased benefit to the firm. That benefit should be identifiable before the meeting takes place. The next issue is could that same benefit just as easily have been achieved through a less time intensive activity? For instance,

> If you are working on an extended project with a client, then the marketing benefit of playing golf may be the maintenance of ongoing rapport. If that client makes a substantial contribution to your yearly revenues, then spending the time and money to reinforce rapport is certainly valid and justified.
>
> When the possibility exists that a client may retain you to perform some additional work, then once again, golf may be a productive use of time. However, the time involved should be commensurate with the potential reward. Spending $500 in unbilled time to take on a $300 project is playing!

The point is not to limit golf or any other activity, but to label these activities for what they really are. If you don't, then when you analyze the commitment to marketing versus its return, you'll quickly conclude that marketing just doesn't pay. And nothing could be further from the truth, especially if you do the right kind of marketing.

Financially, it's a great idea to mix pleasure and business whenever possible. So if you or some members of your staff enjoy sailing, for example, then arrange an outing with an interested client. This kind of arrangement is not only good public relations for the firm, but a perk for you or the employee. Just remember to label it as such.

Manage Your Marketing Time

Because marketing, at times, is like a black hole, you easily can get sloppy with your time. We are not referring to lack of effort, but to misguided effort. To minimize this waste, everyone involved in marketing within your organization (which should be everyone) needs to undergo a crash course in time management. An old, but good book on this subject was written by Alan Lakein, called *How to Get Control of Your Time and Your Life*. We make a special effort to practice many of the techniques set forth in that publication. However, one particular technique that comes to mind is simple, easy to implement, and effective. When it comes to marketing, just ask yourself:

Is this the best use of my time right now?

This question has several nuances. For example, it spawns the question, "Will the marketing effort I am making right now provide the firm with the greatest benefit?" For many, their answer would be something like, "No, but the things I can do that would have significantly greater leverage take more time than I have right now. So this is at least something positive." It's this kind of thinking that allows marketing to get out of hand fast. If you only have an hour, then spend it working on the high leverage functions. Don't just attend a luncheon; work on that direct mail piece you committed to send out. The problem is the best use of your time is often something less appealing than what you are (or plan to be) doing. All of us are subject to being sidetracked by unimportant, time-consuming projects that have little or no impact on our goals. When this occurs, we need to quickly identify what is happening and stop it. Remember, time does not discriminate. Everyone, regardless of race, color, creed, wealth, sex, height, or foot size, has the same 24-hour day. Learning to make the best use of your time has always been important. But as far as marketing is concerned, good time management is essential. Therefore, some extracurricular reading may be in order, especially for those most involved in marketing.

Marketing Must Be Planned

One reason why the MTBA Framework or more formalized consulting services have been difficult for CPAs implement is due to our lack of internal planning. Consulting must be marketed. When the marketing effort isn't properly planned, it is not only very costly—but even worse—ineffective.

Many ways to attract the attention of both your current and future clients are available. We have covered only a few. Selecting the best combination of alternatives is not something to take lightly because marketing costs can quickly get out of hand. To ensure that your exposure impact is high but manageable financially, creating a marketing plan is essential.

By becoming proficient at gaining visibility for your firm, you will be able to differentiate your services from those offered by the competition. This should translate into an abundance of new opportunities for you and your firm in the upcoming years, especially in the field of consulting.

Everyone Has to Be Accountable to Someone for Marketing to Work

The title of this segment is definitely worth repeating. Everyone has to be accountable to someone for marketing to work. If you are a large enough firm to have a marketing director, great, then this is an easy call as to whose job it is to manage this function and hold people accountable then this is an easy call. By the way, the managing partner is the person who stands behind the marketing director to hold the partners accountable. However, if you don't have a marketing director, then you need someone to fill this role. Generally, this job falls to the managing partner in smaller firms because he or she is responsible for firm wide issues like growth and profitability.

Once the marketing plan is complete, much of the marketing implementation, such as the following, can be delegated to administrative staff:

- Managing the development of the collateral material or promotional pieces
- Working with a graphic artist to draft the first round of content and messaging
- Getting the various partners to give the necessary approvals
- Mailing or distributing information based on the promotion schedule or supporting a specific event

This is all critical work, but it shouldn't be done by a partner. As we have said many times in this chapter, marketing is a contact sport, and you need someone responsible for ensuring that the firm maintains the integrity of the promotion schedule.

In addition to implementing the various promotion pieces (which might include direct mail, newsletters, seminars, and workshops), this person also needs to hold the partners accountable for staying in close contact with their top clients. A key marketing role is to get with every partner, director, or anyone else in the firm that has client management responsibility and accomplish the following:

1. Go over their client list with them to verify who they plan to visit
2. Determine the frequency of those visits (in other words, put them on a calendar)
3. Determine information to find out during those visits
4. Clarify report responsibility after those visits are complete
5. Review the report with the partner to brainstorm about the client, possible ways the firm can help the client, as well as resources the firm might want to engage with that client.

Without steps 4 and 5, the value of steps 1–3 are very suspect. A big part of this accountability process is that a report needs to be filled out, and then someone in the marketing role needs to sit and brainstorm with the partner about how the firm can best serve the client. The reason this rarely happens in the vast majority of firms is because the partner believes the client is his or hers and he or she is not responsible to anyone about how to perform the client service role. However, for a firm to reach its potential for success and profitability, partners need to understand that although they might manage a particular client relationship, they don't own it. The firm owns the client relationship and, therefore, the partner needs to manage that client not in the way that is best for the partner, but in a way that is best for the firm and the client.

If partners are unwilling to conduct their scheduled interviews with clients, if they are unwilling to report the information requested, if they are unwilling to brainstorm about how to best serve the client, then it begs the question as to whether that person should be allowed to remain a partner of the firm.

To conclude, someone specific needs to be charged with overseeing that the promotional material is being distributed according to the marketing plan; that events are being held according to the marketing plan; and that those with client service responsibility are in front of the firm's key clients on a scheduled basis, interacting with those clients in an organized and formalized manner. If the person with this assignment does not have the status to hold partners accountable, then the full force of the managing partner needs to back this person. And the compensation plan needs to be designed as the hammer for those unwilling to play their role in executing the marketing plan. In other words, people should be rewarded for doing a good job, and penalized for not choosing to follow the program, and the right compensation plan can help you with this.

Customer Relationship Management

CRM is short for customer relationship management. Consider the reporting to which we previously referred. We have a client service plan form for your use to plan your client interactions, and CRM is that, on steroids. For example, CRM would start with a database of all of your clients. That same system would

- earmark the appointments each person should be making to visit their clients.
- notate when specific marketing materials were sent to each client.
- contain the notes from each meeting anyone has had with that client.
- include services that client currently takes advantage of, as well as those the firm feels like the client should subscribe to in the next 12–18 months.
- remind everyone when to follow-up on previous contacts and ongoing opportunities.
- keep track of some personal information about that client so when anyone talks to that client or referral source, they have a reminder that he or she is married, his or her spouse's name, his or her kids names and ages, and similar useful information.
- allow you to maintain a pipeline of potential future work volume, as well as when it might convert into new business, and so much more.

The point of a CRM system is to offer a technology that allows all of this critical marketing information about a client to be maintained in one centralized place and available to everyone who has contact with that client. It allows the firm to create a knowledge base of all of the ongoing conversations so that not only can the firm do a better job of consistent messaging and recommending, but everyone quickly can be caught up to date before a meeting with a client.

By having everyone use and constantly update their client interactions and planning on a CRM system, it allows the marketing director (or the person charged with that role) to do a much better job of managing the marketing process, and even more important, of holding them accountable to it.

You can start a CRM system by using Outlook for a small firm with only one or two partners. When you are ready to step up to something that was built for this function, you can access software products like GoldMine, or you can consider cloud computing enterprise-wide solutions like www.SalesForce.com (one of the industry leaders in this field). Every day it seems like there are new vendors offering exciting solutions in this area. Although CRM has been around for a long time, and it has taken hold in various industry sectors, utilizing this technology is not commonplace within our profession. But rest assured that software (1) built to allow a higher level of customized service to clients while (2) simultaneously helping a firm grow through better prospect and client-base opportunity management will become ubiquitous soon.

Where Your Firm Is in Its Life Cycle Matters Too

From time to time in our work consulting to CPA firms, we are asked to help develop a marketing plan for a firm. In some firms, this is fairly easy to accomplish. In other firms, it can be impossible to implement a plan, no matter how expertly crafted or elegantly designed. Why would it be impossible to build or implement an effective marketing plan for a CPA firm? In our experience, we find that the looser the aggregation of the group of CPAs who make up the owners' group, the less possible it is to create a firm-wide marketing plan that will be effective or makes sense. On the other hand, the more tightly a group operates as one firm, rather than as a group of sole proprietors sharing space and staff, the more easily the firm can implement and reap the benefits of a firm-wide marketing plan.

Typically when a firm starts out, it functions under an "Eat What You Kill" (EWYK) business model, where individual owners are paid based on book, or managed revenue, size, individual production, realization, and charge hours. Over time, as the firm evolves, at some point, often between $5,000,000 and $10,000,000 in annual volume, the owners either split up and create multiple new firms, or they start making the switch to a "One Firm" business model where the firm is operated more like a corporation with a board, a CEO with authority to hold owners accountable, and where owners are paid based on other metrics in addition to or in lieu of managed revenues. These other metrics might include factors such as staff training and development, delegation, supporting the firm's strategic plan, cross-selling, and performing MTBA services, for example. Under the One Firm model, we no longer have "my book" and "your book." It's "our book"—the firm's book of client relationships—and we do whatever it takes to make the firm better, rather than creating stronger fiefdoms for individual owners. We are truly joined at the hip in this operating environment, with a shared vision for the future and shared commitment to actions required to achieve the vision.

Under the EWYK business model, there usually is little common strategic direction other than to work together and make money inasmuch as each owner is doing his or her own thing for the most part. Because of this, there usually is no firm policy on client acceptance and retention, and even if there is, because of the way this type of firm usually is governed, the policy is not likely enforced. The reason it is not enforced is because people get paid based on their book of business and managed revenues, so if a partner wants to add a marginal client, that is his or her choice to make, even though that marginal client might utilize critical staff that should be working on more highly profitable work in the firm. Even when firm policies on issues like this exist, no compensation carrot and stick is available to hold anyone accountable to following firm policies and procedures as they should. Thus, the firm typically has grown with each owner having built a book of clients particular to his or her own specific interests, referrals, and so on. So who is the firm? What does it stand for? What types of work does it offer? To whom does it offer the services? You can see that these questions could be difficult to answer for an EWYK business model because everyone is doing their own thing, and one owner's approach may not mesh well with the other's. Because of this, it can be difficult to get anyone's commitment to spending much time and money on a marketing plan, and even if a plan is created, it's difficult to impossible to enforce compliance with it under an EWYK business model.

So what if someone is an owner in a firm that uses the EWYK model, and they want to embrace a more robust marketing approach? To be fair, as an owner in an EWYK firm, you have at least three options you can pursue:

- Attempt to create support within the firm for moving to a business model, such as the One Firm business model, that will allow the firm to be operated more as a corporate-style business, where it is not dependent on the personalities of each owner, and where each owner agrees to be held accountable for furthering the interests of the firm. This can be an easier idea to sell if you are a senior partner with a larger ownership interest or otherwise have significant personal influence over the other owners. It can be difficult to impossible to pull off if you are a more junior partner with a lower ownership percentage and have little personal influence over the other owners.
- Create a marketing plan for you and your part of the practice under which you define what you do, what your clients need, who your target client is, and pursue an overall marketing strategy for your portion of the practice that is consistent with your strategic plan. This would allow you to grow your practice in a more orderly manner.
- Consider striking out on your own now and creating the type of firm you want through the marketing plan you design. Even if you have penalties for leaving where you are now, the net effect of the penalties most likely will be less now than they will be if you stay and grow your practice in an environment that is hostile to supporting firm-wide initiatives and partner accountability.

There are other options or variations of the preceding three concepts, but you get the idea. Marketing plans take time, money, and hard work to bring to fruition. Make sure the resources you devote to yours aren't for naught. If you believe you ought to be practicing in a much different manner than your partners subscribe to, you might all be happier if you did practice in a totally different fashion. Life is short—make the most of it and have fun while you do so. (You can find out much more about the EWYK model, One Firm model, how to go about making the change, and much more in our two-book series *Securing the Future* offered through the AICPA.)

Before You Move On

Now that you have completed this chapter, it's time to put it all together. You are now positioned to decide on a strategy for implementing the growth of all your services, including MTBA and consulting services in your firm. There is a great deal of work left to do, and it starts with requiring a significant amount of thinking time on your part. The following series of explanations and forms (exercises 12-1–12-6) were created to walk you through a step-by-step process for creating your own marketing plan. So, let the marketing plan creation begin!

Exercise 12-1

Stage 1: The Creation of Your Marketing Plan: Creating a Consistent, Effective, and Inexpensive Marketing Plan

The following three strategies can be used in your marketing:

- Passive marketing to your clients and referral sources
- Passive marketing to targeted, segmented, or niche nonclients
- Active marketing in addition to your passive marketing to all A and B clients through personal contact.

The preceding three strategies create the foundation of a marketing approach we call "the drip system." The purpose of this approach is to keep your firm top-of-mind with your clients and referral sources. To do this, you simply have to devise ways to stay in touch with your targeted audiences about once a month to once every six weeks. Do not expect a flood of responses by using this system. Expect the same result you would as if water was dripping out of a faucet. In the beginning, the drip from the water has very little cumulative effect. But after hours, days, months, and years, the accumulation of water becomes substantial and begins having an impact. The same is true with this marketing approach. A constant drip of contact from your firm to your targeted audiences will build a greater awareness of the services you offer, a higher chance of referral from that same audience (top-of-mind versus out of sight), and increase the likelihood that your audience will contact you to help assist them.

Now let's discuss the distinction between the terms *passive* and *active* marketing as used in this document. *Passive marketing* refers to the way we contact the targeted, segmented, or niche audience. For example, typical passive media include client letters, postcards, e-mails, and trade-specific advertising (that is, an industry-specific magazine). We call it a passive strategy because partners and managers don't have to be involved in the day-to-day implementation of this approach. This strategy is really an administrative function once the various messages, media, and timeframes are decided upon.

On the other hand, *active marketing* efforts revolve around face-to-face contact and logically centers on one-on-one interaction. This approach is considered active because all of those who have client account management and referral source relationship responsibilities will be asked to actively and proactively create, maintain, and report back on how their regularly scheduled personal visits and discussions are progressing. This high-touch strategy is by far the most effective technique for attracting new business and maintaining client loyalty for existing business.

So if active marketing is so effective, then why wouldn't all of your marketing efforts be focused on this? Several reasons follow:

- If everyone in your organization made personal visits with all of your clients, you would likely go broke due to nonbillable time.
- You want to be "top-of-mind" throughout the year with your clients and referral sources, not just on occasion. Creating a marketing engine that runs all of the time will pay dividends, especially when augmented by personal visits.
- Not all of your clients are worthy (return on investment worthy) of a personal visit. It doesn't make sense to tie up a $200 per hour person to spend a couple of free hours talking to a $300-a-year client opportunity.
- If your CPAs wanted to spend all of their time selling, they would have chosen a different career.

As with most businesses, there is a generalized 80/20 rule. Although these percentages may vary for your firm, the philosophy behind it most likely will apply. This rule states that about 20 percent of your clients generate about 80 percent of your total fees. For you, it might be 15 percent of your clients generate 70 percent of your fees, but the point is still the same. If you made personal visits on the 80 percent of your clients that generate 20 percent of your fees, your charge hours and profitability would tank, and the amount of business gained overall would be minimal.

While this marketing document has tried to make it clear that you should utilize both marketing mechanisms (passive and active) to create an effective campaign, your foundation is the "top-of-mind" objective. If you devote all of your resources to making personal contact, then you won't be able to cycle through all of your clients fast enough to stay "top-of-mind." For example, you might visit a specific client in May, but they are asked by a friend for a reference in December. Your visit in May is hardly memorable, and most likely, even that discussion was about areas that client was interested in talking about, not the vast scope of services you offer. So in this case, you are not only unlikely to fulfill the top-of-mind objective because of infrequency, but you also are unlikely to be discussing the correct mix of services during your short visit. Your objective is to be educating your marketplace about what you have to offer them all of the time.

Think about an automobile dealership. They don't spend all of their advertising dollars making a big splash in 1 or 2 months; they spread out their messages throughout the year. Why? Because they want to be visible to you when you have an interest in buying their product. For example, if you are very happy with your car, the likelihood of your looking at various automobile promotional ads is minimal. However, if your car was totaled while parked on the street overnight, your interest in looking at alternatives for replacement skyrockets. The point is that you want to be visible to your targeted audience all the time because you never know when their interest in what you offer may peak.

Finally, spending time talking to clients and referral sources is stressful for our professionals. The only way to change this dynamic is to make the event shift from one of selling to providing desired assistance. The best way to accomplish this is to "spend time with the clients and referral sources with the greatest potential." In this situation, you are talking with people who trust you, believe in you, and have more problems and opportunities than they have time to resolve and leverage. The conversation will not be about selling, but rather about providing professional guidance and assistance. This is a role our professionals gravitate to, not run away from—it is the MTBA role.

Now given that you want to remain profitable, you want to develop more business, you want to maintain a top-of-mind strategy, and you want your people to be comfortable and effective, this means that you will reserve the active component of your marketing strategy to focus on regularly being in front of the 20 percent of your clients that make up 70 percent to 80 percent of your revenues. We define *regularly* as once a quarter (with tax season counting as the contact for that quarter). Additionally, you want to target a variety of referral sources into your active contact strategy. Then, the passive marketing strategy is used to augment the personal marketing efforts as well as support your top-of-mind objective with the remaining 80 percent of your clients.

A common way firms approach this targeting of clients is to segment them into classifications. For simplicity, we have used some common categories (A, B, C, D) and created some generic definitions for you to start from (for a quick refresher on this, skip back to chapter 3 where we cover this segmentation in detail). Passive marketing applies to all categories of clients and referral sources. Active marketing is targeted for all "A" clients and referral sources, and if there is personal marketing bandwidth left, start down the high "B" (the "B" clients with the most potential) client and referral list.

To provide a little more definition to these classifications, if a CPA firm only had "C" clients, this is not a bad thing. In this situation, the firm's client base could be described as having a bunch of small clients that pay them timely and are fun to work with. If this is the case, then passive marketing may be all you need to do. But in order to grow the organization and replace the natural attrition that will occur, your passive marketing approach needs to be in full gear all the time. On the other hand, some firms have moved to a more boutique style of firm where they are very hands on with their clients, have a big share of each client's professional services wallet, and staff that is made up predominantly of managers and partners. It may be, in this case, that all the clients fit into an "A" or "B" classification. Therefore, with few clients and a great deal of frequent personal contact and support provided to each, active marketing alone will generate the necessary new business and referrals.

The fundamental questions are

1. Do your clients know what your firm can do to help them?
2. Do you know what is keeping your clients awake at night (the concerns and opportunities they are trying to address at this time)?
3. Do your clients know what your firm's total service capability is so they can request your help when appropriate, and do they have enough knowledge about what you can do to refer you to friends, associates, and family?

For "A" and "high B" clients, the answers to the preceding questions 1 and 2 should be identified through regularly scheduled contact (active marketing campaign). Question 3 should get an affirmative answer from your clients and referral sources because of your firm's passive marketing campaign.

Now we want to take a moment to make a special point regarding question 2. If the partner or manager in charge of an "A" or "high B" client's account cannot at least articulate what each of these clients' priorities are, you are in jeopardy of losing them. Although this likely won't happen overnight, you can bet that the unserviced priority needs will be supplied by someone. And with each passing day, that broader scope of services is likely to be supplied by another CPA firm competitor.

Preparing Your Client and Referral Base for Marketing

At this time, please do the following to prepare for your marketing:

1. Create an easy way to regularly access all of your clients' and referral sources' names and addresses. Identify those clients that should not be contacted and omit them from the list. (Those that should be omitted might include someone with multiple entities. Although you definitely want this person on your contact list, you probably won't want to send that person three or four pieces of the same marketing materials. Another example would be to omit a young child of a client. Although you prepare that child's simple tax return, you likely wouldn't want to send marketing materials to him or her.) What remains should be a clean marketing list of clients and referral sources that can be mailed or e-mailed as a normal part of the marketing plan implementation.

   This process is usually a difficult one and will take you several months (often six or more) to truly clean up. But until you do, you don't have a starting place that makes sense. The partners and managers will complain because they will have to go through their client base lists several times. The key is you want to get it right so that the mailing and e-mailing task for the monthly pieces can be done by administration without partner and manager approval each time. Recognize that partners and managers also will want to omit certain clients and referral sources from certain mailings. This should be part of the clean-up process to identify these exceptions. For example, you might want to omit several of your bankers or broker referral sources when you are marketing your wealth management services. This way, with each mailing and e-mailing, administration will take note of the marketing message being sent out and modify the distribution list accordingly.

2. Go through your clean marketing list and classify clients as "A", "B", "C" or "D."

    If a client is classified as a "D" client, then you need to list a strategy to try to make them a "C" client. That strategy could be as simple as "we will bill them at 90 percent of standard rates this year and see if they want to remain a client," or as drastic as, "the partner needs to call this client and tell them that we need their account paid current and kept that way or they need to find another accountant to service them." Use the simple worksheet that follows to capture that information and evaluate all of the "D" clients at a specified later time to see if they should be reclassified, if more work needs to be done, or whether they should no longer be a client.

    If the client is an "A" or "B" client, then review the second and third worksheets that follow to consider what action plan you are willing to put in place to provide them with regular contact and a higher level of service. The second worksheet is the client service plan, which you would fill out for every "A" and "B" client in order to create a strategy as to how you plan to best serve them. The third worksheet is just a simple contact calendar that you can use to map out dates for when you plan to schedule your personal visits.

Note: These worksheets are simple and provide you with an example. Obviously, once you decide what you want to do and how you want to manage it, you should create more automated, customized tools to manage and monitor these processes more efficiently.

"D" Client Exercise

Partner/Manager Name:

Client Name:

   Action to be taken:

   _____

   Date Action Taken:_____ Follow-up Date:

   Result Expected:

   _____

Client Name:

   Action to be taken:

   _____

   Date Action Taken:_____ Follow-up Date:

   Result Expected:

   _____

Client Name:

   Action to be taken:

   _____

   Date Action Taken:_____ Follow-up Date:

   Result Expected:

   _____

Client Name:

   Action to be taken:

   _____

   Date Action Taken:_____ Follow-up Date:

   Result Expected:

   _____

Client Service Plan

Fill out one of these for each client who represents a major client (top 15% to 20%) for your firm. It is important that you have a strategy tailored to each of these clients that outlines: What services are to be provided, when, for how much, and how you plan to make it happen.

Client Name: _____

Client Address: _____

Contact Name:_____   Day Phone #: _____

Evening Phone #: _____   Fax #: _____

Mobile Phone #:_____   E-mail: _____

Services Currently/Past Performed	Frequency	Revenue
_____	_____	_____
_____	_____	_____
_____	_____	_____
_____	_____	_____
_____	_____	_____

Future Services to Perform	Quantification Amount	Expected Revenue	Time Frame
1. _____	_____	_____	_____
2. _____	_____	_____	_____
3. _____	_____	_____	_____

Strategy underway which will create the desire within the client to hire you.

1. _____

_____

2. _____

_____

3. _____

_____

_____

Client/Referral Source Contact Plan

Partner/Manager: _____   Date of Plan: _____

Client/Referral Source Name	Class	Jan	Feb	Mar	Apr	May	Jun	Jul	Aug	Sep	Oct	Nov	Dec	Actual Dates of Contact

Class = Classification (A=A client, B=B client, R=referral source). Place an X in planned months for contact. Note actual dates of contact. Results and perceptions of each contact should be reflected in each client's "Client Service Plan."

Exercise 12-2

Stage 2: Inventory of Services and Skills

Now that we have covered some of our general philosophies about CPA firm marketing, the partner group or marketing team or committee needs to identify the menu of services that the firm wants to highlight.

As you know, you already have done the work on this part when you worked through the forms at the end of the previous chapter. So, at this time, insert into this process the work you already have done preparing your "Skills Inventory," "Requested Services List," and "Anticipated or Upcoming Requests" worksheets. Next, we will add one more service list to the mix. It is the "Current Services List," which is a list of services you currently offer your clients (the form follows below). Here, instead of just referring to "attest" work, you might break down the list a little further by recording audit, internal control review, fraud investigation, various offered special procedures, and so on.

All of these worksheets are provided for brainstorming and getting you in a good marketing frame of mind. However, if you know what services you want to market and what message will resonate with your audience, then just skip ahead to the next section.

Current Services List

Prepare a list of services currently being offered to your present clients. The list provided below is just to spark ideas. It is not meant as a list to choose from or an exhaustive list. You should put into your own words what it is you do for your clients.

To the right of each Service, under the column titled "Percent," estimate the contribution each service listed makes to your total revenue stream. Once complete, this should total 100 percent.

To the right of each Service, under the column "Competition," note whether this service is being delivered by your competition. Use the following categories.

C. Our competition in this area is from other CPA firms.

O. Our competition in this area is from other than CPA firms.

N. We have virtually no competition in this area today.

Services:

- Accounting/reporting assistance
- Acquiring/selling businesses
- Auditing
- Budgeting services
- Business valuation services
- Cash management assistance
- Cost reduction analysis
- Employee benefit plans, administration, and *services*
- Estate planning and administration services
- Financial planning
- Financial Statement and reporting analysis
- Financial statement preparation
- Forensic accounting
- Fraud detection services
- Help in obtaining financing
- Internal control review
- Litigation support services
- Marketing strategy
- Merger and acquisition services
- Negotiation and arbitration of operational, financial, and personnel *issues*
- Outsourcing of technology infrastructure
- Prebankruptcy and bankruptcy support
- Software implementation and support services
- Special assurance projects
- Staffing and career placement *services*
- Strategic planning services
- Succession planning services
- Tax planning/minimizing
- Tax return preparation
- Technology consulting
- Technology implementation & support service
- Wealth management services

Current Services List

Description	Percent	Competition
Total		

Exercise 12-3

Stage 3: Creating Your Services-for-Promotion List

Now that you have worked through the preceding exercises, it is time for you to build a list of services that you either are offering or want to offer. This list of services will become the foundation from which your marketing messages and target audiences will emerge.

Using the form that follows, build your list of services and the component parts of each. For example, you might have something like this:

Information Technology Services

- Technology strategy
- Custom programming
- Networking
- Technology troubleshooting
- Technology outsourcing
- Software support and installation

This example shows a broad classification of the service offered, and then breaks it down into services that are being delivered under that classification. Understand that a service does not have to have any breakdown of subservices if component parts of the service are not bought by themselves. For example, business valuation may stand alone because the firm would not sell the various subcomponent services as stand-alone offerings.

Now it is your turn to do the same. Just copy as many of these forms as necessary to complete your analysis.

Services Worksheet for Promotion

Service Category: _____

    Subservices: _____

    _____

    _____

    _____

    _____

Service Category: _____

    Subservices: _____

    _____

    _____

    _____

    _____

Service Category: _____

    Subservices: _____

    _____

    _____

    _____

    _____

Service Category: _____

    Subservices: _____

    _____

    _____

    _____

    _____

Exercise 12-4

Stage 4: Marketing Training and Skills Development

With any change of expectation in what you or your people do, there is the responsibility to provide training to assist your people in their personal development and growth. As you move through the creation of your marketing plan, consider new skills you are expecting your people to demonstrate and then try to identify the training that would facilitate those changes.

We would be remiss if we did not at least mention the Trusted Business Advisor Workshops put on by the AICPA's Private Company Practice Section throughout the country as a logical source of training.

Marketing Skills Enhancement Worksheet

Name: _____ Year: _____

Current Skills Needed	Type of Training	Month	Budget $s

Total Budget: _____

Name: _____ Year: _____

Current Skills Needed	Type of Training	Month	Budget $s

Total Budget: _____

Exercise 12-5

Stage 5: Developing Your Passive Marketing Strategy

Because you now have identified your "A" and "B" clients, and everyone has a personal schedule of contacts to make, it is time for the partner group or marketing team or committee to put together your passive marketing campaign. The first campaign should be to your clients and referral sources. This campaign should optimally identify one mechanism or medium per month that will educate your client and referral base about a service you offer. If you can't afford one contact per month, then minimally try to make eight contacts per year. To develop your marketing campaign, you need to answer these questions for each contact:

- What medium do you want to use for each contact of your target audience (letter, postcard, seminar, or newsletter, for example)? Refer to earlier in this chapter for ideas on exposure vehicles)
- What is the service and message you want to send?
- When do you want this message to arrive?

Note: Look to your "Services Worksheet for Promotion" for ideas on what services or subservices to promote and what timing for visibility would be best for each one.

Now, once you have defined and priced your foundation marketing effort (your monthly or eight annual contacts mentioned previously), if you still have money left in your budget, you should consider developing one or more niche industry or service campaigns. These campaigns should have a minimum of three to four contacts in fairly rapid succession (over three to four months or something about every three weeks). Because these niche campaigns are likely targeted to nonclients and prospects, you want to feature a unique service that will catch the attention with the narrowly segmented audience you select. And you want your promotion piece to be interesting enough to catch their eye too, so bring in a graphics artist to help you come up with something that really pops. For example, we put together a letter, a couple of postcards, and a telemarketing script promoting R&D credits for one of our clients who purchased a list of local manufacturing prospects. We sent a postcard, followed by the letter, followed by another postcard, with the final contact of this campaign being from a telemarketing call. All four contacts occurred in about 3 months. Using another approach, with this one supporting a contact about every 6 weeks, we devised a list of 10 services and brought in a graphic designer to create a postcard for each one using the same theme. In this case, all 10 service postcards were based around a "game" theme with messages like this:

Service: **Estate Planning**
- Game: Chess
- Theme: Don't play games with your financial future—Play to Win

Service: **Litigation Support**
- Game: Cards
- Theme: Don't Gamble with important legal issues—Play to Win—We're your Ace in the hole

Service: **Cash Flow Forecasting**
- Game: Dice
- Theme: Don't leave your future success to the roll of the dice—Play to Win

Now it's time for you to consider what services you want to promote and start putting together your exposure campaign. For example, if this were August, your plan for the remainder of the year might be as follows:

Postcard	Year-end tax planning & gifting	10/15/2010	Client/Referral base
Letter	Client letter thanking them for their loyalty & asking for referrals	11/10/2010	Client/Referral base
Postcard	Financial Planning and Investment Advisory Services	12/10/2010	Client/Referral base

Obviously, with each of the preceding pieces, you would have to craft the proper message. In addition, your actual plan, rather than this example, needs to be developed for a entire year to 18 months. Should a niche campaign or two be sprinkled in this, you would notice the last column would identify that specific target audience rather than the Fortress default of "client/referral base."

Marketing Schedule
(Use as many sheets as necessary to lay out your campaign)

Campaign: _____

Target Audience: _____ Responsible Party: _____

Date	Medium	Topic

Message (craft about a 200 word message regarding your topic)

Date	Medium	Topic

Message (craft about a 200 word message regarding your topic)

Date	Medium	Topic

Message (craft about a 200 word message regarding your topic)

Exercise 12-6

Stage 6: Establishing Your Marketing Plan Budget

Finally, the partner group or marketing team or committee should prepare and monitor a budget for this marketing plan. This budget should outline the direct costs required to fulfill the plan defined previously. It also should outline expectations of your marketing plan, like increase in gross revenue, contacts from prospects, referrals from referral sources, new clients, and new projects with existing clients. It is up to the partner group or marketing team or committee to define the metrics, which will be used to judge the success of the marketing plan. Remember that the marketing plan requires that both the active and passive approaches are utilized. Additionally, marketing campaigns require time to take hold. If you are going to test this for a few months, don't waste your time and money. The effects of marketing in the first 6 months will be revealed over the following 6–12 months. Remember: we call this the "drip system" because it is based on small, consistent, repetitive, and inexpensive efforts that over time have a huge positive impact on the firm's bottom line.

Generally speaking, the annual marketing plan budget should be considered as a percentage of sales. It is common to see number from 3 percent to 5 percent of sales for professional service firms. However, if you are just beginning your efforts in this arena, you likely will need to invest more than that in the first few years because you have to develop more processes, skills, and systems that will support and monitor your marketing program. On an ongoing basis, the 3 percent to 5 percent number is a good one, but it is just a little low for a start-up effort.

Marketing Budget

Medium (postcard, letter, etc.)	Month	Contact #s	Budget $s

Total   Contacts: _____ Budget: _____

Expected Results

_____ By _____

_____ By _____

_____ By _____

_____ By _____

_____ By _____

_____ By _____

_____ By _____

Section 5

Putting It All Together

Facilitating Your Clients' Meetings

"The leader is a teacher who succeeds without taking credit. And, because credit is not taken, credit is received."

~ LAO TZU

We picked the opening quote to this chapter because it really distills the essence of the most trusted business advisor's (MTBA's) role as a facilitative advisor. A CPA's role in helping clients and their teams of owners and managers really is about helping them succeed and learn something at the same time. It is *not* about the CPA taking on the mantle of the expert and telling them, in a group setting, what they need to do.

Of all the value-added services a CPA can offer, helping a client with meetings—whether the meetings are for the purpose of problem definition, decision analysis, or implementation planning—is where the MTBA skill set all comes together for maximum impact.

Our Role in Meeting Facilitation

Most owners of small to midsized companies relish the thought of having someone come along side of them to help them sort through issues, identify root causes of problems, and determine which of the top potential actions to try in an effort to make improvements. And it's even better when that someone is their CPA, and the CPA can help them have a productive meeting that gets results.

Facilitating meetings simply involves providing the structure for the meetings, keeping everyone on track, and seeing that they are moving toward achievement of their meeting objectives. In fact, the following are some bullet points we often use to clarify our role at the start of meetings we facilitate:

- Stay neutral—do not take sides
- Manage the process
- Help the group stick to its guidelines
- Help stay on track and keep moving along
- Ensure all are heard
- Provide concepts and comments when useful
- Suggest procedures

We want to point out here that the meetings we're talking about you facilitating often are going to be somewhat informal, with two to six people in attendance, and lasting from one to four hours. The meetings will take place for the express purpose of looking into one or more of the various issues you've uncovered through your past one-on-one discussions with the owner or CEO of the company. So you can RELAX—we're not talking about putting you in front of a group of two-dozen opinionated executives for a formal, two-day session (although some of you may already be doing that kind of work). As our starting point, let's take a look at each of the bullet points above and how they define our role as a facilitator:

Stay Neutral—Do Not Take Sides

The role of the facilitator is to be the independent, outside, objective person who makes sure that all sides are heard. If you're seen as one person's hired gun, your effectiveness will be diminished. Yes, we know the CEO brought you in, but you owe it to him or her to let them know upfront that you will be most effective at the meeting if you are walking the neutral line throughout the discussions.

This point of staying neutral can be confusing and difficult at times because sometimes when you are running client meetings, although your primary role might be to serve as a facilitator, the group might want you to take on a secondary role as expert on certain topics. So you are likely to have to wear two different hats during these meetings. That is okay, but we specifically bring up the hat metaphor because when you shift to responding as an expert, we want you to think about putting on your expert hat so that as soon as you have made your point or shared your ideas, you will remember to take it off. We get in trouble when we don't treat these roles as uniquely different and recognize when we are playing each role and respond accordingly. The biggest danger comes from keeping your expert hat on for too long. It is a hard one to take off because our ego gets stroked a lot while we are wearing it. But before long, in expert mode, you start dominating the meeting, pushing your ideas, and destroying the major benefit for the gathering in the first place, which is to get the best ideas from the group, not just your best ideas. We will cover more on this in a few paragraphs.

Manage the Process

To be effective, meetings need to have a process, and the process needs to be managed properly. The process typically includes the following:

- Identify the purpose and objectives of the meeting
- Set an agenda for the meeting
- Develop an approach for the meeting or meeting segments, if applicable
- Clarify and get agreement on your role as facilitator
- Identify the role of participants (such as participate fully, share all relevant info
- Develop group meeting guidelines
- Keep everyone from becoming too judgmental about spontaneous ideas to avoid the group being stifled for fear of ridicule
- Facilitate action plan development
- Facilitate the creation of a communication plan
- Conduct wrap-up and identify next steps

We'll cover the meeting process in more detail later in this chapter.

Help the Group Stick to Its Guidelines

What guidelines? Well, every meeting—and we want to emphasize that *every* is the operative term here—needs to have some guidelines that set expectations for behavior to allow the group to function effectively. You can create this from scratch by asking participants first to think of meetings they've attended that didn't go as well as they could have in the past, and what ground rules, if they had been in place, would have made the meetings better. Another alternative is to provide them with a suggested list, such as the list that follows this paragraph. Yet another alternative is to throw out a couple of suggestions from a list like the one that follows, and ask them to add to it. It depends on the size of the group and the amount of time you wish to take for this process. If you generate the list from scratch with a small group of three or four people, count on this only taking you about 5–10 minutes. Use whatever title fits best with your group. We've suggested 3 different captions for the list: Group Meeting Guidelines, Meeting Norms, or Rules of Engagement

- Nothing is personal; critique ideas, not people.
- Don't take things personally.
- Be respectful and tactful.
- Keep an open mind.
- Don't interrupt.
- Listen for the real meaning and understanding.
- Test your assumptions with questions.
- Accept responsibility for your own actions.
- Don't pull rank.
- Stay on task.
- What's discussed among this group stays among this group—speak with one voice afterward.
- It's your meeting; you have to commit to the outcomes.
- A "critical issues list" will track issues we can't work through here.

Help Stay on Track and Keep Moving Along

You will add tremendous value if you achieve nothing more than keeping the group on track and moving along toward its objectives. Many meetings, without good facilitation, disintegrate into various tangential discussions, getting far too granular for the topic at hand and jumping into "how to" discussions before determining the "what" and the "why." As facilitator, you can gently nudge them back on track when the meeting participants choose to stray from the path.

Ensure All Are Heard

In some meetings where the participants are all assertive and opinionated, making sure everyone is heard looks more like acting as the communication traffic cop, allowing everyone to share their opinions while the rest of the group stops talking and listens. At the other end of the spectrum, often where multiple levels of people are involved (a boss and his or her direct reports, for example), part of the facilitator's role requires you to create a safe environment as well as to structure discussions and processes that solicit comments from each individual without fear of being bullied, embarrassed, or having someone pulling rank on them.

Provide Concepts and Comments When Useful

This part of the facilitator's role can range all the way from putting on your "expert" hat (as we talked about previously) and addressing something that the group has asked about, to providing objective comments about what you see and hear going on in the group. In the former case, be sure you signal to the group that you're stepping out of your role as facilitator to address the estate tax question they've asked you in your role as an expert, for example. Similarly, if you do human resources (HR) consulting and you're asked about overtime pay for exempt people in the context of a facilitated meeting, let them know that you're opining on their issue as an expert and have temporarily stepped out of the facilitator role.

As far as providing objective comments about your observations of the group goes, it's not uncommon for a facilitator to use his or her skills of listening and observation to help the group tune up its meeting processes or to overcome a stalemate and work toward agreement on a disputed issue.

An example of that might be when there is seemingly a disagreement over an issue, and the facilitator can help clarify the issue and positions being taken:

> "If I could step in at this point in the conversation, I'd like to make an observation. I've heard Jack saying that he and Joe just can't find any common ground on this problem. I've heard Joe saying that they are miles apart as well. But what I also heard was that Jack wants outcome A and Joe's desired outcome is not that far apart from Jack's. It seems that you might be closer than you think. I'd like for us to explore that for a moment."

Suggest Procedures

As the facilitator, you may need to suggest processes and procedures during the meeting to address issues and get people to participate fully and actively. Take for instance the situation where you have some very loud, assertive individuals meeting with one or two quiet or even timid individuals. Assuming that everyone at the meeting is there for a good reason (which is another topic we will cover later), you might suggest that each person individually write down their key thoughts and post them for observation as a way to start off a discussion, for example. Small group versus large group discussions are another area where you might suggest one approach or another. We'll be covering specific facilitation tips in more detail later in this chapter.

The Bottom Line About Our Role

It is very helpful to have an objective outsider involved in critical or sensitive meetings because the outsider (in this case, the MTBA) often can help the client get more out of the group's time together. So don't be surprised when you are asked to assist by providing the process and structure for the meeting as well as offering subject matter expertise, when appropriate, to help your clients address their challenges and opportunities. The facilitator can add a great deal of value by keeping them focused and letting them know when they've taken a step backward as well as how to resume their forward momentum.

Types of Meetings

For the purpose of this discussion, we've identified three different types of meetings you might become involved in with your clients:

- Problem definition
- Decision analysis
- Implementation planning

The preceding list excludes a type of meeting you probably have heard of and perhaps have participated in—the strategy or strategic planning meeting. We've left this meeting off the short list for a reason: it is a much more formal endeavor, and although it is a part of the types of services and assistance that MTBAs provide to their clients, it is beyond the scope of discussion of this text. The meetings we are covering in this chapter are, in our view, not much of a stretch for MTBAs, and they represent a natural extension of everything we've covered thus far. So let's talk briefly about each of the types of routine meetings you might be involved in with your clients as a result of your previous discussions with them on what's keeping them awake at night.

Problem Definition Meetings

These meetings are convened for the purpose of trying to figure out what the real issue is that the client should be addressing, that is, separating out the root causes of problems from their symptoms. Typically, you will be helping the group collectively answer questions such as the following:

- What outcomes are we seeing now versus what should the outcomes be? (This is to isolate the deviation from expected outcomes.)
  — Example: Production defects in the plant have been running at 5 percent rather than the previous 1.5 percent rate of production.
- When is it happening?
  — Example: We need to isolate the problem by type of product being produced, shift and time of day, crew, and so forth, to get more specific if possible.
- How long has this been going on?
  — Example: We've noticed that the problem first showed up in reports for the month ended June 30, 20XX.
- What are possible causes?
  — Example: Consider brainstorming the possible causes, visiting with people at the front line to get more information or other applicable means.
- What is or are the most likely cause(s), and how can we confirm that this is the case?
  — Example: What can the group do to test their assumptions?

As you can see from the list of questions, some of these meetings end up requiring advance work, as well as interim steps in between the first meeting and follow-up meetings.

To the extent that you can prepare the client management team for the first meeting by asking them to come prepared to discuss the preceding questions, it can cut down on the time and number of meetings required to get to an answer.

A key factor to note here is that this meeting, as previously defined, is not about finding solutions. It's focused instead on understanding the issue and finding causes of variances between what you expect and what is occurring. Unless you do this properly to begin with, your client can end up wasting time and resources solving the wrong problem. However, this is not to say that if you quickly come up with some causes, you can't move to the next phase within the same meeting.

Decision Analysis Meetings

These meetings are designed to help pick the best of the potentially many solutions to employ in addressing the root causes previously identified. For situations that present opportunities instead of challenges or problems, this type of meeting is used to identify the best way to proceed in taking advantage of the opportunity presented to the enterprise.

For situations where your client is trying to solve a problem or improve some sort of performance, consider asking the following questions first:

- What has worked in the past?
- What should work, but seems to be less effective than anticipated?
- What does your competition do that seems to work?
- What have you thought about doing but have yet to try?
- What do you see as being your biggest downside risk if you stay your present course?

Also consider the following questions for any decision you are going to make, whether it's a decision about fixing a problem or a decision about expanding the business or some other opportunity:

- What specifically are we trying to accomplish here?
- What criteria does any solution need to meet for us to be happy with it?
  - Example: The solution should take advantage of our existing distribution channels to the extent possible.
- What does success look like, and how will we measure it?
  - Example: If we're going to "the land of milk and honey," what kind of milk (whole milk, 2 percent fat content, 1 percent , lactose free, condensed milk, or evaporated milk?) and how much?
- Which solutions meet our criteria better than others?

At this type of meeting, we are not crafting implementation plans. Rather, we are identifying what solution to implement. Implementation planning is a separate process that may or may not be conducted in the same meeting, depending on time available.

For more information on problem definition and decision analysis, we recommend *The New Rational Manager* by Charles Higgins Kepner and Benjamin B. Tregoe and *The Thinking Manager's Toolbox* by William J. Altier. Another interesting text on problem solving in general is *The Art of Problem Solving* by Russell L. Ackoff.

Implementation Planning Meetings

This type of meeting, we believe, is the bread and butter of the MTBA offerings. No matter how well you identify the problem or opportunity or how elegant your selected approach to deal with it, your client must be able to implement whatever change is required for ultimate success. Great plans and ideas are mere pipe dreams without implementation. This is where consultative CPAs can add immense value to their clients. We recall a study reported in the news some years ago that cited a finding that something like 90 percent of managers are considered to be good at planning, but only about 10 percent of them are equally as good at implementation. The actual percentages are not important, but the fact that chronic implementation issues are so common is the key point. With your assistance, clients will find that implementation is actually possible.

By the time you've come to implementation planning, your client already should have identified performance metrics to track successful implementation through achievement of desired outcomes. If they have not, take some time to help them do so before getting into action planning. For example, if your client wants to grow the business, what does successful growth look like, not only at the end of, say three years, but at interim points along the way? Are there goals in place such as those illustrated in the following table?

Metric	12 mos.	24 mos.	36 mos.
Growth in annual sales per year by	$2MM	$4MM	$6MM
Gross margin on sales	25%	27%	29%
Return on sales	5%	6%	8%

Once your client has set some measurable, tangible goals to let them know if what they are doing is working, it's time to help them work through the process of implementation planning.

Implementation planning, or action planning, can take place at a couple of broad levels. High-level implementation planning identifies the major tasks required to get some traction on an initiative, with overall responsibility assignments for the broad actions. At a more granular level, detailed implementation planning breaks the major tasks down into more detailed steps with accountability assigned for each detailed step.

Senior-level executives normally only focus on high-level plans, if at all, because implementation plans should be crafted by those who will be responsible for doing the implementing! Unless the people in the room during your meeting actually are going to be doing the implementation, you should only cover high-level implementation planning, if it is applicable. Afterwards, you can be of value to the client by facilitating roll-out meetings involving the people at the next level or two down the organization chart, who actually will be in charge of making the initiatives happen.

A key point: Action plans, to be truly actionable, must identify due dates for each action, with single point accountability assigned for each action.

Accountability must be single-point accountability; if everyone is in charge, then in actuality, no one is in charge. If you have a task force or team, whether there are 2 members or 20 members assigned to some action steps, that's okay, but the leader of the team or task force is ultimately responsible for completion of the steps specified.

Table 13-1 is an example of a high-level action plan developed to deal with some HR issues by a client. You can see some high-level tasks that need to be done by certain dates, with the initials of the person responsible for each step. When more than one initial occurs, the first person is the lead on the task, and the others are supporting him or her on it.

A similar grid could be constructed for more detailed action plans with finer cuts made of shorter timeframes, with detailed activities and accountability assignments listed for each.

The process you will use in this type of meeting is pretty straightforward. You'll be facilitating their thinking process to allow the client participants to identify what steps are required in what order, by when and whom, to achieve their previously identified goals. Questions such as the following can be helpful:

- Where do you need to start with this initiative's implementation?
- What is the first step that needs to be taken to kick off this program or initiative?

Table 13-1: **Sample High-Level Action Plan**

5/31/2009	6/30/2009	7/31/2009	8/31/2009	9/30/2009	12/31/2009	3/31/2010	6/30/2010
Determine qual.'s & job desc. BA	Advertise for HR person BA			Orient HR person BA, PM			
		Review applications BA		Review current HR systems HR			Develop perform. reward system HR, PM
		Hire best candidate BA			Implement new hiring policy HR		
					Implement new drug policy HR		
				Develop long range training plan HR, BA	Implement training plan HR		

- When should that step be completed by?
- Who should be in charge of doing it?
- What's the next step?

From a facilitation point of view, you can make this process easier by drawing column separator lines down a flip chart sheet and heading up the columns with dates of quarter-ends or month-ends. The participants can use Post-it notepads and fine point markers to write actions and responsibility assignments (initials of who's doing the action). They can post these under the column with the appropriate timeframe for the action to be completed by. This approach allows the participants to constantly add or delete action items and to move them around as to due dates and sequence. By avoiding writing something down that can't be moved easily, you make it easier for them to be flexible in their thinking and to consider various options to make their implementation process more successful.

> Another key point: it's not uncommon for many clients to get caught up in the positive energy from these meetings and create totally unattainable action plans based on unrealistic estimates of time required for implementation.

As the outside facilitator, you may need to rein in your client group and have them rethink the speed of implementation, depending on their capacity and everything else going on at their business. One of the worst things that can be done is to leave with unrealistic expectations of accomplishment across a broad number of initiatives. The implementation will be doomed from the start, and chronically missed deadlines will take a toll on enthusiasm and motivation for change.

Process Facilitation: Facilitating Your Clients' Meetings

CPAs naturally struggle between when to exercise content skills versus process skills. Content skills also are called "expert skills," and process skills also are referred to as "facilitation skills" (which we covered in some detail in an earlier section). In this section, we are going to cover a few issues that affect your ability to facilitate. We'll review the following:

- When to exercise content and when to exercise process skills
- Getting agreement on your role
- Getting everyone on the same page
- Keeping everyone on the same page
- A few other issues

Here are some questions that will give you some guidance about when to exercise content skills versus process skills. The key to coming up with the right answer is working hard to make sure you give the client credit for what they do know and can do and not giving yourself credit for what you don't know and can't do. Given this introduction, answer these questions: Does your client

- sufficiently understand the issue?
- understand the impact or effect of taking or not taking action?
- seem to maintain a reasonably high level of objectivity over the issue?
- have the time and ability to gather relevant information?
- have access to all of the information you believe is relevant?

 Keep In Mind

The key to coming up with the right answer is working hard to make sure you give the client credit for what they do know and can do and not giving yourself credit for what you don't know and can't do.

If you answer "Yes" to all of the preceding questions, then you probably should be operating as a process expert. You do this by facilitating discussions to work through various issues. The client has a good idea about what the answers are, but you create a framework that allows them to not only reach a conclusion, but to decide on what action steps to begin taking.

If you answer "No" to any of the preceding questions, you might have to step in, at least temporarily, as a content expert for specific issues, or find someone who can. For example, consider that a client has a misunderstanding of the benefits of updated IT in managing their business. If a discussion is initiated on this topic, you might provide your client with your insight about what the current landscape of options typically provides to help them better assess the actions they might want to take. When doing so, as we have said before and will likely say again, you should be careful to inform the client that you're temporarily switching roles from process facilitator to content expert, and when you are done, let them know when you're back in the facilitative mode again. Notice that we did not say you should provide your client insight so they could follow your recommendations. Your role is to help the client find solutions through *their* knowledge.

The next issue is to get agreement on the purpose of the meeting, related logistics, and your role in the meeting. Get agreement with your client in advance of the meeting about the purpose and objectives of the meeting, the timing and duration of the meeting, participants required, and any advance work necessary for the meeting. Make sure you are on the same page about what your role and the participants' roles will be at the meeting. You can achieve this understanding in a brief e-mail with your client, using bullet points to cover the items suggested. Depending on the size, complexity, and risk of the project, you can make it more formal by issuing an engagement letter. In our opinion, long, formal engagement letters for half-day meetings are a waste of productive time if you can achieve the same understanding through a brief e-mail, however.

Note that if a work product is to come out of the meeting, it is both the creation of and the responsibility of the client. Your job is not to be the note taker and report writer, but the person who helps everyone clearly see the gaps. Your meeting with your client's team is not an administrative project, and it is not a writing project. It's an enlightenment project. It's not the glitz of a report that matters, but the objective insight you can provide. Having said all that, we recognize the fact that you likely will be writing some points on flip charts throughout the meeting. It's not uncommon to have those notes typed up for the client's use and distribution after the meeting. But unless the client requests that a report is part of the agreed-to scope of your deliverables upfront, let your client know that the best use of your time (and, therefore, their resources) is for you to act as a facilitator, not a stenographer. The real benefit to the client comes from the thinking and discussion processes you help with, not from some 100-page report after the fact. On top of that, it is hard to take good notes and stay in the "now" enough to manage the meeting.

When you act as a facilitator, inform all of the participants what you will and will not be doing. Earlier in this chapter, we presented you with a list that we use to define our role as a facilitator when we are kicking off a meeting. You may want to modify, cut back, or expand it to fit your needs. For example, you might want to include something like, "Make sure the real issues are not overlooked, even though in some cases the subject matter may be difficult or tense to address."

Gaining a Shared Understanding of Objectives, Agenda, and Approach

Normally, you get everyone in the meeting sharing a common focus for the meeting by

- making sure all critical decision makers are involved upfront.
- providing the facilitation participants with a sample agenda and advance materials if required (push them to read this advance material).
- reviewing with the group the objectives, methodology, and agenda as you start the session.
- periodically recapping where the group has been in its discussion, where it is now, and what remains to be covered.

Expectations and Concerns

In some situations, we've used this activity at the opening of the meeting to surface any issues that might be lingering among the participants about the meeting and its possible outcomes. We conduct this piece by

- asking each person to make a note about their expectations, concerns, and what they can do about them with regard to the session.
- having each participant read that note aloud as you make it visible to everyone by writing it on a flip chart.
- reviewing, after this expectation information has been gathered, what is reasonable to expect and what will likely be follow-on items, covered in another venue.

• ensuring that everyone participates in this expectation exercise if you use it. (Our experience is that when a person passes on this, they often end up being the person who will present us with some problem behaviors later on in the meeting.)

Keeping Everyone Focused on the Matters at Hand

To keep everyone on the same page during a facilitated session, you need to

- review the "meeting guidelines," a sample of which we provided earlier in this chapter, that are to guide everyone's behavior during the session.
- post these guidelines on a flip chart so they are visible throughout the meeting, if the situation is expected to be tense or if there are warring factions.
- ask the group to help by self-policing these policies.
- interject when discussions seem to go off-target. An example might be:
  "You were talking about strategy, but now it sounds as though you are discussing action plans or solutions. Those topics are scheduled to be discussed later. I recommend we get back to the topic of _____ unless the group feels like this discussion is too important to leave at this time. What do you think?
- use a flip chart to take notes, illustrate points, and keep participants focused on the discussion at hand.

Processes to Help Your Group Be Productive

You can do a variety of things to get the best thinking out of the meeting participants and help them have a successful meeting.

- Large group discussion
  — This is a discussion by the group as a whole. If the group is small to begin with (2–4 people, for example), almost all of your work will likely be done in "large group" (or the whole group) discussions. When a group gets to about 10 people or more, you will probably need to create smaller break-out groups to maximize discussion and creativity. For group sizes in the middle, you can go either way.
- Break-out or table group discussion
  — We suggest breaking up larger groups to minimize monopolization by one talkative, assertive person and to create more discussion among the quieter, more reserved members. With larger groups, the existing personality dynamics and hierarchy stimulate a more traditional meeting dialogue, which stifles the brainstorming or think-tank environment we often desire to create. As a side note, even if there are only three people in a meeting, some exercises would be done together; but for some of them, we would break into one group of two, and the facilitator would join the one to brainstorm various ideas. Or we'd ask each individual to privately write his or her thoughts out, and then we'd share them in the full group discussion.

— Depending on the topic and number of people involved, we let the table group discussion go from 15–50 minutes or so. If, at the end of the first allotted time segment, groups need a little more time, we would extend the time a bit.

— Upon completion of table group discussions, we have each group present a flip chart of their ideas on the matter under discussion. (This can take from a few to 10 minutes or more per group.)

— Depending on the matter under discussion, we may then go to a large group discussion, move on to another topic or activity, or utilize another round of break-outs groups to drill down even deeper after one of the table group presentations.

• Individual ideation

— This is what we call the process of having individuals write out their ideas about something individually before sharing it with the rest of the group.

— Depending on the topic and number of people involved, we typically let individual thinking time go from 5–15 minutes or more, if the topic requires it. If, at the end of the first allotted time segment, people need a little more time, we extend the time a bit.

— Upon completion of individual thinking and writing, we have each person present their ideas on the matter under discussion and then hand in their written notes to the facilitator. Sometimes we go around the room and ask each person to list the idea they felt was most important. We do this several more times until we get all of the items out in the open. This way, everyone gets a chance to talk and feel like they got to share an important idea (this can take from a few minutes to several minutes per person for each round.)

— Depending on the matter under discussion, we may then go to table groups, a large group discussion, or to another topic or activity after these presentations.

• Why flip charts from the groups and individuals?

— We insist that ideas almost always be written down on flip charts when in groups. We do this for numerous reasons. First, it forces participants to commit to their own ideas. Second, flip charts allow you to write large enough so that everyone can see whatever each group has decided to share. Third, and most important, once written, it is difficult to pretend a belief, issue, or problem doesn't exist. Often, if we don't use flip charts for individuals, we ask them to hand in their notes page as part of exercise completion, so it serves the same purpose. The whole point of these meetings is to address critical issues and help the organization improve, so you need to get all of the issues out on the table for discussion.

— After the clock runs out on a break-out exercise, we have each group present their winning ideas to the rest of the management team. This update requirement keeps everyone honest and allows each group a chance to sell their vision of the corporate future. Once again, committing ideas to the flip chart, or for some individual exercises, on paper to hand in, is critical to this process. Why? Well, here's what happens when a group's thoughts are just written down on someone's notepad or on their computer without the required audit trail. When it comes time for group reporting because no one but the group spokesperson can see all of the points identified, issues that are confrontational or challenging often are skipped over. And common spokesperson statements are made like, "we came up with the same ideas as did the last group except one. It was …" If you allow this level of noncommittal sharing, you're wasting people's lives. Think about it this way: as the facilitator, what can you do with information this vague? Did group two really agree with everything group one said? Or did they just agree with some of the ideas group one shared? There is a big difference about how much weight an idea has if four groups came up with it independently versus just one. And more importantly, what about those ideas that were discussed that challenged the status quo? Because many of them won't be shared because you didn't insist that each group's ideas be committed to flip charts before the reporting begins, the process loses a significant amount of power.

- Group size advantages and disadvantages
  - Advantages: The biggest advantage of a large or whole group discussion is that everyone hears the entire conversation and gets to listen to a wide variety of suggestions and discussion. The biggest advantage of a break-out group discussion is that everyone talks and gets engaged in smaller groups. As well, if multiple groups come up with the same exact ideas, it gives you, the facilitator a real insight about synergy or mind-share between the individuals.
  - Disadvantages: The biggest disadvantage with large group or whole group discussions is that they often allow people to become wall flowers, listening in, not contributing, and then objecting to issues after the meeting rather than during it because large group discussions can be far more intimidating. Large group meetings provide more opportunity for getting sidetracked than smaller break-out group meetings. The biggest disadvantage of break-out groups is that the process normally takes more time. As well, sometimes a small group will be ill-equipped to address a certain issue; however, this can lead to some interesting discussion and ideas as well.

Dealing With Difficult Behavior

Although it probably will be rare in the informal meetings you will be facilitating for your clients, occasionally problem behaviors pop up among participants, so it's good to think about how you can deal with them once they do arise. The reasons why people misbehave are many and varied. Most often it involves someone feeling challenged, threatened, disrespected, insecure, or simply not wanting to go along with whatever decision the group is considering because of some personal interest that is at stake. It doesn't matter so much why it happens, but what you do to address it is critically important. You truly earn your pay every time an outbreak occurs because this is the time for you to make sure the group addresses the issue rather than running from the inappropriate behavior. Following are some tips on dealing with difficult participants' behaviors:

- Stay calm; be as assertive (*not* the same as aggressive) because you need to be to keep the group on task.

- Use active listening techniques, such as the following:
  — *Paraphrase.* "What I think you just said was that you are frustrated because you asked for help last month, and you felt you received embarrassingly inadequate assistance."
  — *Summarize.* "So to summarize, it sounds as though you are in general agreement with the overall plan, but you are concerned about this one step of implementation."
- Refer to the ground rules, agenda, and desired outcomes. Point out how what the group is doing is not in alignment with one or more of these.
- Use descriptive statements, such as the following:
  — "Here's what I am observing: Whenever Joe raises a point, Sam, you automatically begin to analyze and criticize it, before he's had a chance to fully explain it. Has anyone else noticed this?"
  — "When this happens, it is frustrating because we all agreed that we wanted to finish our task today, and this makes it very hard to do that."
- Take a break and meet one-on-one with the person who is causing the problem and discuss it privately with him or her.
- Use a "parking lot" flip chart to record topics or critical issues that may be irrelevant for now but that you can come back to later in this meeting or at another date.
- Similarly, use this "parking lot" to post miscellaneous action items that come up and need to be done but that are outside the scope of the agenda.

Note that just because someone becomes anxious or loses control, it does not make him or her a bad person. You just need to know you are hitting a nerve, and emotion is running high. However, just because one person has less self-control or less emotional intelligence than another, it does not mean their disruptive action should crown them winner of the debate either (which it often does when we, as facilitators, are not around). Most people run from conflict, especially dramatic outbursts from friends and family. It becomes your job to get them settled down and back talking to each other as soon as possible. Although you might call for a 20-minute break, don't just default to calling it a day. In our experience, the longer this dispute goes without reconciliation or talking it through, the greater the emotional damage on all sides that will set in. Although there are occasions when this is appropriate, letting everyone cool off overnight often will only (1) teach people that blowing up is a powerful manipulation tool; (2) make the people that remained at the table ready to talk through it mad; and (3) waste everyone's time because the day is blown with virtually no resolution. Get everyone back to the table as soon as possible and then work through the issues, focusing on the issue, not the individual, and bringing clarity to the task, not critiquing a person.

One more thought on this. Sometimes, out of a group, one or two people are very comfortable with confrontation, whereas the rest of the group isn't. Once again, these people are not bad, but they will use this technique to put everyone off-balance while they push one of their agenda items through. In this case, as the facilitator, you need to recognize this for what it is—a bullying technique—and quickly change the tone and stifle the action. Usually, simply mentioning that you feel like a bullying technique is being used is enough to curtail it.

By following these simple techniques, you will find everyone working cooperatively towards the same objectives. The key here is that you are providing them with an opportunity to structure their interactions. This means that, for the most part, they will "control" themselves. Without this structure, facilitating becomes more exciting than necessary for the facilitator. When they get off track, bring them back together. At times, you may just need to deviate because the "off topic" discussion may be more important than the planned topic.

Remember, in a facilitated discussion

- you are not the answer person, but the process person.
- have a plan and constantly reevaluate your plan.
- if the plan is working, keep everyone on track.
- if the plan is not working, abandon the plan.
- be flexible.
- *listen* to both what is being said and not said.
- *watch* how the participants react in general and to each other. For that matter, you should be watching the facial expressions and body language of the rest of the group when one of them is speaking, rather than just watching the speaker, so you can *observe* how group is reacting to the speaker's statement or comments.

If you trust yourself, trust the group, relax, and enjoy this process, you will find that you are not only creative, but a true value to the organizations you serve.

Meeting Management

We go from process facilitation to a primer on meeting management, just to be sure everyone keeps a few basic tips in mind to assure that any meeting can be a success. Why is it that business people dislike business meetings? John Kenneth Galbraith, a noted economist, was quoted as saying, "Meetings are indispensable when you don't want to do anything." In his book *The Effective Executive*, Dr. Peter Drucker sarcastically comments, "One either meets or one works. One cannot do both at the same time."

If there is such a genuine belief that meetings are a waste of time, why do we keep conducting them? In the book *How to Run Better Business Meetings,* authored by the 3M Meeting Management Team, several important issues were addressed. We have summarized and paraphrased many of the book's concepts in the subsequent paragraphs that we believe need to be essential knowledge to facilitating group discussions. As a facilitator, it is imperative that our skills are exemplary in this area because much of our time is spent in meetings with our clients. This section identifies what it takes to run a productive and effective meeting.

First, Dr. Drucker says, "We meet because people holding different jobs have to cooperate to get a specific task done." In today's fast paced environment, decisions have to be made quickly and then communicated even quicker. Meetings, which can be held for all kinds of reasons, are an effective way to gather, decide on, and disseminate important information. The trick is to make sure that every time you meet, you have an identifiable and appropriate reason for the gathering.

In 3M's book, 13 "good reasons" were cited for calling a meeting. We will elaborate on three that are common to the advisory function that are consistent with our experience. You should call a meeting when you need to

- *reach a group judgment or decision.* This is the kind of meeting called when the participants are expected to express opinions regarding a subject or action in order to reach a consensus about direction. However, many people call these meetings, when in reality, the decision has been made. Therefore, not only is the meeting a waste of time, but it is an insult to those attending.
- *analyze or solve a problem.* Group dialogue regarding problem resolution not only brings unique insight and experience to the table, but simultaneously instills solution commitment and ownership. Yet with many companies, problem solving meetings are really witch hunts in disguise. In the typical meeting, it's not as important to fix the problem as it is to find someone to blame it on. Obviously, this meeting type is often mismanaged.
- *ensure that everyone has the same understanding of the information.* It is so easy for management's seemingly straight-forward actions to be misinterpreted to mean so much more. As an example, let's say an employee is quickly let go due to unique circumstances. By the end of the week, the masses are expecting a company-wide layoff. Timely informational meetings are a good way to keep the negative impact of the grapevine in check.

Informational meetings like this need to be concise and to the point. All too often, people either aren't prepared to simply or clearly explain the issues, or they arrive with a week's worth of charts unwilling to skip over a single one.

Meetings are an important tool to help facilitate organizational success, so it is important to not only know when to call them, but how to run them as well. Unfortunately, meetings with legitimate purposes become disasters because they are run so ineptly. This happens because there are entire corporate cultures that rarely conduct a good meeting. So those employees climbing the rungs of the success ladder continually learn their meeting management skills from people who never knew how in the first place. This brings us to the next point. What are the characteristics of a well-run meeting?

- A purpose, one that everyone knows and understands
- Occurs at the right time and place
- Should be called only when other less expensive, less time-intensive alternatives won't provide a satisfactory solution

One of the points that really hit home from the 3M book was that, "The real issue isn't that meetings are a waste of time. It's just that too much time is wasted in meetings." Assuming there is a legitimate reason to have one, several issues regarding conducting a productive and effective meeting need to be considered. The first is who should attend. In order to make a contribution, attendees should have one or more of the following:

- A working knowledge of the business to be discussed
- Power to make a decision or approve an agreed-to action
- Responsibility for project continuation or implementation
- Responsibility to a group that will be effected by any meeting decisions
- A need to know the information presented

The bottom line is never invite anyone to a meeting who doesn't need to be there. This leads us to an important discussion on decision making in organizations that you, as an MTBA, must be aware of.

Utilizing the Minimum Decision Resource to Make Decisions: Who Should Be Making the Decision?

When facilitating a discussion in an organization, it is important to have the right person or persons involved in the discussion. In some firms, it is not clear which decisions are made by whom. This is a common affliction of many smaller companies. It is especially true for family businesses and professional service businesses where multiple owners are all highly involved in the running of the business. It's not as much of an issue with larger businesses because as businesses grow, they embrace a more formal corporate model and try to build clear distinctions between the roles of the board of directors and management. An even more critical factor is that these board members of larger organizations normally are not active in the day to day business, so they are not trying to influence their daily work environment. Rather, they take on a fiduciary and advisory role to protect the corporate entity itself.

So let's get back to the smaller company that has several to many active owners in the business. In this situation, it's likely that there is no clear delineation between management and the board of directors. Therefore, it's also likely that the board (or at least some of the board members) probably will take on a much more active role in management. In these cases, you have to avoid meeting overload. If you are not careful, your firm and your clients will find themselves meeting about everything, with the meetings getting out of hand time-wise. The more you tie up these talented people in administrative matters, the less time they have to fulfill their day-to-day duties in their roles as key personnel.

To limit the administrative burden, the owners need to embrace a decision model that constantly looks for the minimum resources required for the level of decision that needs to be made. For example, let's say the CEO needs approval for a decision he or she wants to make that is outside of the budget and outside of his or her personal approval limit (let's say the CEO has a $25,000 a year personal budget that can be used for unbudgeted or over-budget expenditures). Here is what this decision tree might look like:

- *CEO decision.* The CEO can make decisions without additional board approval as long as they have been budgeted, and the decision is within the budgeted amount.
- *CEO decision within personal budget.* The CEO can make decisions without additional board approval if the amount is in excess of the budgeted amount, or even unbudgeted, as long as the total of these excess expenditures is within the personal budget of the CEO (in this case, that amount would be a running total for the year of $25,000 or less of independent approvals of the CEO.)
- *CEO decision or board decision.* Let's assume that we have a situation where the decision before the CEO is one he or she can make if the personal, budgeted amount is used, but the CEO doesn't want to use those funds. In this case, the least resources that can be activated to approve this would be the CEO sending out an e-mail to the board members with a short analysis of the issue and a recommendation with a request for approval. In this case, the CEO opts to get the board approval to keep his or her personal budget open for other future issues. This same technique can be used for issues that are outside of the personal budget of the CEO.
- *Board Decision with advance, limited discussion.* The next level of resource would be to use an e-mail with a short analysis of the issue and a recommendation with a request for approval. However, in this case, the CEO might involve a board member or two in a quick discussion and include their opinions and vote as part of the recommendation.
- *Board decision using board task force.* The next level of resource would be, in our opinion, the CEO's creation of a task force of board members or of key management, or both, to research the issue and come up with their findings. At this point, the CEO, using e-mail again, would provide a short analysis of the issue, share the report of the task force, and make a recommendation with a request for approval.
- *Board decision using board conference call.* The next level of resource would be, a conference with the board (which is very close to that required in the preceding item. In this case, the CEO would provide a short analysis of the issue, a list of possible solutions, and a recommendation if he or she has one, with an expectation of a decision at the end of the phone call.
- *Board decision using in-person board meeting.* The highest level of decision resource is a meeting of the board. When all of the decision levels below this response level are perceived as not appropriate for the nature of decision or resources being requested, then a physical meeting of the board members would be called.

Although this discussion and example may seem to be a bit of overkill, the point of going through it is simply to emphasize that you should not just default to getting *everyone* together for *every decision.* Face-to-face meetings require the greatest amount of resources and are the easiest way to waste time if they are not needed or if all invitees really don't need to be involved.

Similarly, if you are not prepared, skilled, and organized to run the face-to-face meeting effectively, you will be wasting valuable time. If you are going to have a face-to-face meeting, start it on time, run it well, keep it moving forward, keep it on subject, stay with the agenda, and end it as soon as you have covered the agenda items. A common mistake is to set up a meeting for an hour and let it go for an hour regardless of the topics being discussed. Or an even worse mistake is setting up a meeting for an hour, poorly managing it, and then letting it stretch out for two to three hours. Unfortunately, the participants of face-to-face meetings often default to the mentality of "oh well, we are here anyway, so we might as well also talk about ...." When you let meetings run long, you lose meeting integrity and, from that time forward, no one will know how to schedule their time for a meeting you are holding.

If an agenda item gets out of hand, is more complex than expected, or creates an emotion chasm you can't easily cross, set up a task force or a specific group to look into it and come back with a recommendation. But don't make the most common mistake of all and let your decision meeting turn into a brainstorming meeting. These two meetings are not one and the same, and they need to be run differently. Although it is okay to let a group brainstorm for about 10 minutes to see if an easy and logical solution avails itself, as the meeting facilitator, it is your job to keep close tabs on the time and cut it off if a solution is not readily coming forward.

The decision resource tree previously described is just an illustration. Make one up that suits your firm or your client's business. And by the way, this resource tree doesn't just apply to CEO versus board meeting decisions but all kinds of meetings whether they are task forces, committees, or special projects. Use the least amount of resources possible for the task and decision at hand. A conference call takes far less time and resources than conducting a meeting (first, because people don't like to stay on the phone for extended periods of time, and second, because the phone doesn't normally promote the same kind of off-topic discussions that in-person meetings do). An e-mail takes far less time than a conference call, and more important, is less disruptive because everyone can respond as their schedule permits (although you miss the real time interaction and collaboration when using e-mails, which can run into serial discussions that take on a life of their own at times).

One more point to note: the decision tree example previously provided is not intended only to describe when the CEO should kick discussions up a level to the board. It's also intended to provide a guideline for when the board should move an issue down to the CEO, a task force, or a committee, and it can be used at the task force or committee level as well. In other words, if a committee chair sends a recommendation that one of the committee members disagrees with, rather than having the objection default to a requirement for a face-to-face meeting automatically, the objecting committee member should request what he or she thinks is the right level of resources required for resolution.

For example, a committee member might not really have a problem with the chair's recommendation but knows that a specific committee member is very experienced in the area being discussed and simply wants (1) the recommendation run by that committee member, and (2) to know the opinion of that committee member before voting. The objecting committee member sharing this view easily could save the company a great deal of resources by proactively not letting his or her objection default to a face-to-face meeting of the entire committee in this situation.

The Bottom Line

Our discussion about the least amount and best usage of decision resources is being shared to empower people in various roles to

- make the logical decisions on their own that are commensurate with those roles.
- highlight the need for each of us to avoid the default of scheduling face-to-face meetings when less expensive, less resource-intensive and equally effective alternatives are available to us.

If you keep this in mind when working with your clients, you will be an even more effective MTBA. Similarly, if you apply this type of thinking to your own firm, you will have a more effective governance process in place, which allows everyone to optimize their time and create appropriate focal points to address what really matters.

The Right People, the Right Number, and the Right Climate

After the right people have been included in the meeting, the next question is how many should come to the meeting. Keep in mind that *too many people* is the easiest way to ensure that an otherwise quality meeting ends up in disaster. For example, experts suggest the following:

- Five or fewer participants for decision making and problem solving
- 10 or fewer for problem identification
- Less than 30 for informational meetings (in order to maximize a sense of intimacy and, therefore, promote personal participation)
- 15 or fewer for training

In our experience, these numbers are definitely conservative. However, they at least give you an idea about where to start. We believe you can have many more than 15 in attendance for training, but then, this partially depends on the kind of training you are providing.

More people can be accommodated than the numbers previously suggested, but it requires higher levels of facilitative skills, more time, cofacilitators, or some combination of these. Use whatever numbers you are comfortable with. This gives you a couple of different perspectives to consider. Depending on the objective of the meeting, the optimal and maximum number of participants changes. And by using techniques like break-out groups, you can counter-balance an inappropriate size and still have an effective meeting. Several years ago, we held a planning session for over 200 board members. Obviously, this represented an inappropriate size. By using break-out sessions, involving the organization's staff to monitor various groups; fine-tuning the discussion questions to narrowly focus the dialogue within each break-out; doing more advance preparation work than typically required in order to accommodate the large volume of people; and determining an efficient way to consolidate the findings of each group without requiring each group to publically report, the board members were pleased with the event, and the planning session came off without a hitch.

Once you have invited the right people and have an appropriate number in attendance, setting a positive climate is the next critical area for good meeting management. A couple of key considerations that ensure a positive climate are as follows:

- If key people can't attend, cancel the meeting. Many don't follow this policy because they feel it is a slap in the face to those that can come. Don't kid yourself. The biggest slap in the face is wasting the time of those that do come because you decided to conduct a futile meeting.
- Start and end meetings on time. You have an obligation to honor those who work with you by ensuring that their time is not wasted due to poor meeting management.
- Regarding levity, humor can be an asset in establishing a positive work environment. However, if it becomes too pervasive, it easily could undermine and derail the meeting.
- As identified by the 3M Meeting Management Team to be their primary meeting commandment, NEVER begin any meeting without a written agenda. Regardless of the informality, every meeting should attempt to accomplish something within a specific period of time. An agenda formalizes that objective. If you don't have an agenda, cancel the meeting.

Finally, how often and for how long should the breaks be when you are conducting meetings? Well, if your meeting is less than -one and one-half hours, breaks are not essential. But for every minute you push beyond this hour and a half window without a break, the likelihood of losing someone goes up exponentially. Also, studies have shown that beyond this timeframe, productivity starts to decline, exponentially eroding as you surpass the two-hour mark. In all-day meetings, try to break every hour in the afternoon if you want to maintain the group's energy and interest.

As for the length of the breaks, they should last about 10-15 minutes. Remember that we are talking about breaks relative to hour and hour and a half sessions. For example, breaking on the hour with a 10-minute break works well. But because you are breaking so often, you need to be diligent about getting people back together and continuing your sessions on schedule. You want to keep breaks less than 20 minutes because with this kind of time, people will get involved in other activities. If the breaks are too short, like 5 minutes or so, there is not enough time for your participants to get refreshed and reenergized.

There is a great deal to consider if you want to run productive and effective meetings. It requires planning, organization, and effort. Without all three, you've just joined the group of people who run poor meetings and waste your firm's or your client's most scarce resource: management's time.

Effective Group Presentation Techniques

When providing MTBA services or consulting updates, often the meetings consist of one or two CPAs and several members of the client's organization. This kind of setting, although still being somewhat informal, usually is more formal than a one-on-one or very small group dialogue. Therefore, parts of this discussion might resemble a presentation more than a conversation. In addition to using some of the facilitation tips we've provided earlier, you easily can expand your comfort zone in this situation, as well as increasing your odds of success by considering the tips we have in this section called presentation techniques.

Some of the skills required to conduct or facilitate the informal client meetings we're talking about are similar to those used in public speaking. In fact, as scary as it may sound, this environment is actually public speaking, but it's a much smaller audience than you would normally think about when you hear the term *public speaking*. Therefore, in order for you to better prepare for these occurrences, we have included a few important group communication techniques. With just a little practice, you quickly should become more comfortable in larger group settings and as effective as you are in one-on-many dialogues. The following ideas and techniques were developed by Communispond, Inc., a Dallas, Texas company that focuses on communication training.

Control Your Eyes

Controlling your eyes is the act of focusing on and talking to only one person at a time. At the end of each thought (usually about five seconds), find someone else to address. Controlling your eyes helps you avoid brain overload, a condition that usually results in

- losing your train of thought.
- appearing nervous.
- repeating yourself.

Brain overload occurs because your brain receives too much simultaneous stimulation (like looking at five people, the room, and trying to come up with an intelligent thought within the same three to four second period). Focusing your eyes on one person at a time seems too simple to be the answer, but it is. A side benefit is that this direct eye contact works well in the more formal group setting because it gives your words a personal touch.

Mastering this technique is imperative; it is the foundation for group speaking. Even though it may be uncomfortable at first, you'll get used to it within a short period of time.

Along the same line, but with a slightly different twist, controlling your eyes has another meaning to us. We alluded to it in chapter 5 regarding communication skills. It is your job as the MTBA or consultant to look at everyone in the meeting and make inclusive eye contact. One of the exercises we conduct with firms (again using three or four people per group), focuses on this issue. In each group, one person is chosen to represent the MTBA, another is identified as the key client contact, and the remaining one or two are considered involved members of the client's organization. An interview is conducted between the MTBA and the key client contact. Even though the majority of the conversation will occur between these two individuals, the trick is for the consultant to include the observers in the conversation by maintaining occasional, but regular, eye contact. This is one of the most poorly performed exercises that we conduct. Why? Because CPAs tend to focus on the decision maker or the person with the highest authority. This causes them to fixate on one person and exclude everyone else. Although this conversational style doesn't seem to have a significantly negative impact on highly technical matters, when it comes to management-related issues, it is a catastrophe waiting to happen. Virtually an unlimited number of stories exist about one CPA firm being chosen over another because an apparent observer in a conversation was a powerful influencer who felt disregarded and disrespected due to the lack of inclusion. An equal number of stories exist about quality ideas that were covertly sabotaged for this same reason. In the facilitation, persuasion, and consensus building business activities of the MTBA, it is essential to be aware of inclusive eye contact and develop it as an instinctive skill.

Be Aware of Your Posture

Stand squarely facing the group with your arms relaxed at your side. This is called the neutral position. It gives the appearance of confidence and sincerity. However, if you're like most people, the neutral position will feel horribly awkward.

Most of us naturally either put our hands in our pockets, behind our backs, or in front of us (also known as the "fig leaf position").

Additionally, we often stand with one foot in front of the other. Any of these combinations of hands and feet look bad. As a matter of fact, almost every position besides the neutral position is displeasing to the eye. If you don't believe us, videotape yourself and witness the effect of these different stances on camera.

Use Gestures to Give Emphasis and Avoid Appearing Stiff

As we have mentioned before, gestures are important to conversation. Gestures should be in line with the group size. As an example, when you are conversing with one or two people sitting at a table, using gestures in front of you at table top height are very appropriate. However, to a group of seven or eight, these gestures need to be exaggerated to have the same impact. For example, you might stand up and use gestures that extend beyond the frame of your body. And when you talk to a very large group, consider gesturing to the side of your body. Gestures made in front of you to groups of 50 or more can be affected negatively by the depth perception of your audience.

Also, don't abuse gestures by over using them. If you do, people will get distracted and tired from watching you. The best tip we can provide is before you start talking, take a second or two and muster some excitement about your topic. Then, just let your natural energy flow into gestures. Don't try to confine that energy, use it to your advantage.

Project Your Voice

In communication studies, speaking with a strong voice has been rated as the single most important ingredient to appearing confident.

You want to talk loudly enough for people to hear what you're saying. Generally, if you project your voice at a level you think is appropriate, it isn't. The right volume often is a notch or two above your instincts. In groups of 15 or more, the appropriate level may be about the point you feel you are screaming. Don't worry, you're not.

The reason you should go to all of this effort of monitoring your volume, besides appearing confident, is very simple. Your clients shouldn't have to struggle to hear what you are saying. They are paying good money for your time and talents; allow them painless and easy access to your knowledge.

Clear Your Visual Aids

When a visual aid (for example, flip charts, PowerPoint slides, or marker boards) is first shown, the reaction of your audience will be to read it from top to bottom. During this time, you momentarily have lost control. In order to regain everyone's attention, mention each point shown on the visual aid with only a brief comment (this technique is called clearing your visual aid). This satisfies the curiosity of your audience and allows them to refocus their attention back to you. At this time, you can return to the first point and begin elaborating in more detail, one point after the other, until you have fully discussed the references on the visual aid.

Also, avoid using the "peek-a-boo" technique. You know, the one where you use a flip chart or an overhead and cover up the part you don't want the audience to see just yet. This can be very distracting. Your audience is likely to spend more time wondering what's being covered up and why than paying attention to what you are saying. At best, it's awkward for the speaker to try to manage the "cover-up:" covering up too much, not enough, *"oops they saw something they weren't supposed to see,"* and so forth. The good news is that this issue has pretty much gone away with the ubiquitous presence of the data projector, laptop and PowerPoint, or other presentation tools because the clumsiness of the "peek-a-boo" technique has been replaced by simple transitions and effects that you use to reveal your information exactly on time and as planned.

Using PowerPoint or Other Presentation Packages

With the increased use of laptops and projectors, we find an increased misuse of presentation packages. It's fairly easy now to crank out a PowerPoint presentation for just about any meeting. At times, you really should not rely on presentation software, but would be better served to use a marker board or flip charts. What we are referring to here is the more informal meeting of a few people to kick some ideas around, or for the purpose of your walking through a five- or six-point bullet list to update management on a project's status. You can do an effective job of communicating without any slides in many of these situations. As a matter of fact, the meeting covered by the sample agenda we've provided (at the end of this chapter) included nearly 20 people. The presenters, except for a couple of spots in the meeting, simply used oral reports to update everyone about the status of various issues.

On the other hand, when the use of a laptop and projector are warranted, make sure that the technology works before you start the meeting and have an alternate plan ready to go to if you end up with technical difficulties. Keep in mind that most slides will take, on average, from two to three minutes each to cover, so if you have a 15-minute presentation and you have more than five to seven slides, you are in trouble from the outset.

Regarding slide content, we've seen it all. When the slides also serve as the written support, we'll see more text on a slide, (most of the time, more than should be used) because the presenters are asking for a dual purpose from the slides (both for presentation and report or collateral material). Usually, less words per bullet point, with only a few bullet points per slide, provides you with a more elegant look along with the ability to maintain the best control of the audience (because they are not trying to read a significant amount of text while you are speaking). The font size used on your slides generally should not be smaller than 20, and be sure that your background and font colors make for legible reading in the room where you meet. Regarding colors, don't use too many. Stay with your company's color scheme and limit each slide to just a couple of colors. When your slides have text with three colors or more, from our experience, it is not as clear to the audience what you are trying to highlight because the text starts to compete with itself. It is also preferable to go with highly contrasting background and font colors than to have to turn off the lights. If your meeting is meant to be a working meeting, the room should be well lit. Finally, given the advancing age of the population as a whole, consider printing out your slides in a two-per-page format, rather than a smaller, three-per-page format with notes. For many people, it's just too difficult to read the tiny print resulting from a three-per-page handout format.

Look, Then Turn and Speak

The proper way to clear your visual aid is to first look and point to the item with a full hand, not just a pointed finger. Then, turn toward your group ... and finally ... speak. This tip is to remind you to speak to your audience, not to your visual aids. Look at your chart, but before you say a word, turn to your audience. By doing this, you keep everyone involved, you are easier to hear, and you maintain better control of your group.

This is especially important in small group meetings. In large group meetings, the presenter is likely to be wearing a microphone, so when he or she turns and reads from the screen, everyone can still hear. However, in small groups, when the presenter turns and speaks to the front of the room when everyone is sitting behind, a large portion of what the presenter has to say will never be heard. This is partially true because most presenters talk too quietly in the first place, so when you couple speaking in a lower than optimal volume with facing away from the audience, you likely will end up with a group that has *not* been engaged and thinks poorly of your message, partially because they couldn't hear it all.

Silence Is Powerful

What often seems like an eternity in front of a group is really only a few seconds. If you are not sure of what to say next, look at your notes or flip through some of your paperwork. The interesting thing is sometimes when you just stop and stare at your audience while you think of what you want to say next simply emphasizes the last point you were making. But whatever you do, don't stand in front of your audience saying "uh" a zillion times as a nervous response to maintain sound. Although we know it is hard to get rid of that ugly sounding noise altogether, you *can* minimize its use, especially when you embrace the power of a pause or no sound at all.

The preceding ideas are only a few tips that promote effective public speaking. With just a little practice, your speaking capabilities should improve dramatically. But even if you have mastered them, you're not out of the woods yet. How you handle questions is the next area that can make or break your entire presentation. Communispond, Inc. has some suggestions to help simplify this process too.

Handling Questions

Effective question and answer sessions easily can be achieved by focusing on the following rules:

- Never lose control of your session.
- Always show absolute confidence.
- Be courteous—even if someone in your audience is out of line.

Maintaining control of your audience is the key to a strong, positive finish. The following ideas should help.

After you finish your talk, make the statement, "What are your questions," and raise your hand. This subtly demonstrates the etiquette expected for asking questions. And yes, this can be used effectively in small groups as well.

If your audience doesn't respond, be prepared to ask a transitional question, such as, "Raise your hand if you're ready to start using videoconferencing at your office." Now you can call on someone and ask why they do or don't see videoconferencing in their near future. Regardless of whether meeting participants raise their hands or not, they are now involved. And that's the trick: because once involved, talking is the next natural step. However, this creates a whole new set of problems, which leads us to our next topic.

Dealing With Questioners

If you are asked a question and don't know the answer—say so! You can always tell the questioner that you'll find out and get back to him or her later. On the positive side, saying that you don't know something gives added credibility to the issues you do address.

If a question is asked that is outside the scope of your discussion (for example, too technical for the rest of the group, of such narrow interest that it likely only applies to the person asking it, or it's seemingly been covered to some extent through questions already), make the comment, "If you don't mind, I would like to table that answer and talk to you one-on-one after this session." This treats the questioner with respect, but doesn't allow the conversation to get side tracked on unimportant, confusing, or inappropriate topics.

Speaking Out of Turn

Let's say someone speaks out of turn. How do you stop that? One technique is to hold up one hand, palm towards the interrupter, as if you are stopping traffic. Then point with the other (*pointing* in this context refers to using a full hand, never just a finger) to someone that has their hand raised. Follow this by saying something like, "Excuse me, the gentleman in the corner had his hand up first, and then I will come to you." This politely, but firmly says that you are in control and reemphasizes the proper question-asking etiquette. However, if the top dog of your client's organization speaks out of turn, well, that's a different story. Although we don't want anyone to be cut off when they have used the proper technique to take the floor, cutting off the CEO after he or she has interrupted an employee can carry a high price tag too. However, when this happens, and it will, just remember who was interrupted and as soon as possible, go back and say something like, "I believe you had something else to say on this subject. Would you mind sharing that with us now?" If the issue has been addressed, or the participant no longer wants to make a statement, he or she will just comment as such.

Call Everyone by Name or No One by Name

This is a common mistake. Don't recognize a questioner by name unless you can do so with everyone in the group. Why? Because the person whose name you call aloud feels special, but those you don't know feel left out. Alienating part of your audience is not an effective communication technique. If you feel it is important to call people by name, then use name tags or name cards so you can treat everyone the same. By the way, when you are conducting a meeting (especially the small group meetings we were talking about with a few to several participants), *it is always your job to learn everyone's name*. Use whatever techniques work for you, but make sure that by the end of the meeting, you have personalized your conversation by being able to address everyone individually.

A technique that we use at the start of a meeting is to draw a simple chart of the table set-up and write down everyone's name in the position they are sitting. If you didn't do this right away, get the names down on paper as soon as possible. Listen as the other meeting participants call each other by name, and once you hear a name, make a note of it. While it may be embarrassing 15 minutes into a conversation saying, "I'm sorry, what's your name again," that's not nearly as bad as asking that same question as the meeting is wrapping up or while at dinner, after spending several hours together. After you have written down the names, try to incorporate them into a couple of your directed comments early on to help you memorize them.

Finally, Other Issues About Questions and Answers

Let's assume a question has been asked that you plan to answer. What's next? First, paraphrase it back to your audience. Here's an example:

Questioner:	Do you feel preprinted newsletters are an effective marketing tool?
CPA:	Are preprinted newsletters an effective marketing tool? Well, we believe...

This technique buys you time to think and keeps everyone involved. However, don't start off with, "That's a good question." This comment subtly categorizes every other question as being a bad question. Also, you normally don't need to say, "The question is," because a well-executed rephrase makes it clear to the audience that you are repeating the question.

Here's a technique that can save your entire presentation and make you look like a hero to your peers. If the question is antagonistic, then paraphrase it to restate it more positively, then answer it. For instance:

> Questioner: Our firm has been using preprinted newsletters for years, and it works for us. I don't think you know what you're talking about.
>
> CPA: Why are we so adamant about personalizing your newsletters? Well, our experience has been ...

This takes practice to do really well, but it is an exceptional tool for controlling your audience. *You should never verbally attack a questioner*, no matter how far he or she is out of line. You don't want to become the bad guy. Using your power as the group leader to embarrass someone is a good way to become an instant villain. Some of the people who trusted you and felt comfortable talking in your group will now think, "I wonder if I should share my thought because he may attack me next?" Others will take the position that, "I know this character is a pain in the neck, but he's *our* pain in the neck, so just who do you think you are, Mr. or Ms. Speaker, to slam him like that!?!"

What do you do if one person is monopolizing the question-and-answer phase of your talk? That's easy. During the first part of your answer, look at the questioner. Then turn and look at someone else and give the remainder of the answer. This break in eye contact from the original questioner allows you the chance to call on someone new.

Finally, when you're about ready to wrap up, or more importantly, out of time, say "We have time for one more question." Take the question, answer it, and quit, and then either end the session or turn it back over to whoever is in charge of the meeting. You do this as a meeting management technique. Obviously, there are many times when you want to keep answering questions as long as the client is interested in asking. However, when you have asked a group of managers for 45 minutes, and they stated upfront that they have minimal time flexibility, make sure the meeting is over on time by controlling the questioning phase. Otherwise, you may find it much more difficult to get on their calendar for the next meeting.

Practice Creates a Path to Comfort

The techniques discussed in this chapter form the basics of successful one-on-one and group meetings and presentation management. As an MTBA, or in the field of consulting, your success depends on your ability to communicate to both individuals and groups. Therefore, a little work in this area should go a long way towards developing your client base and then keeping them satisfied.

In order to become more comfortable with public speaking, consider examining the numerous books and courses available. However, nothing is as effective as practice. You might consider Toastmasters International (www.toastmasters.org) as a good forum for improving your skills. Another suggestion is role playing between you and a peer, one acting as client and the other as consultant. Take advantage of the opportunity to practice in front of your colleagues at work by running staff meetings or making presentations on technical topics. Consider getting out and getting involved in running meetings or making presentations to nonprofit boards or service clubs with whom you're involved.

If these concepts are already familiar to you, then we hope the material has served as a refresher. However, if this information is new, then you are not alone if you feel a little overwhelmed by the complexity of what seems to be a simple task. Regardless of your current level of expertise in this area, improving these skills should be a part of your itinerary to better prepare you to compete more successfully in the future.

Before We Move On

Giving presentations to a group, especially to your peers, has to be one of the most stressful situations you can imagine. But as consultants, this is an imperative skill to develop in order to facilitate the level of change our clients are demanding. Therefore, a role play exercise is in order (exercise 13-1).

This is an exercise for everyone in your group, one at a time. Take about 10 minutes and think of a story you enjoy telling about yourself, a member of your family, or a friend. This story should be less than three minutes in length. You are provided a note sheet to help you outline your ideas.

Observers, or put another way, those awaiting their turn to make a speech, should take out a sheet of paper and take notes on each lecturing MTBA and consultant. For each person giving a speech, notice how he or she controls his or her posture, uses gestures, projects voice, uses silence, uses visual aids (if used) and "looks, turns and speaks" (if appropriate). Remember, we are looking for constructive criticism.

As always, we've included a self-assessment exercise (exercise 13-2). No doubt this exercise will elicit plenty of areas you feel need work. So let the presentations begin!

Exercise 13-1

Group Presentations

Presenter's Role

Relate a story you enjoy telling about yourself, a member of your family, or a friend. This story should be less than three minutes.

Be aware of the issues we covered earlier:

- Control your eyes
- Be aware of posture
- Use gestures to give emphasis
- Project your voice

Notes/Outline for talk:

_____

_____

_____

_____

_____

_____

_____

_____

_____

_____

_____

_____

_____

_____

_____

Exercise 13-2

Self-Assessment Timeline

Based on the materials covered in this chapter, please take a few moments and assess your weaknesses. Then, using the form that follows, make note of any skills you plan to work on as well as a timeframe to reassess your progress. In addition, if there are activities or exercises, or both, you plan on attempting, jot them down and note your intended completion date. This form is provided solely as a self-improvement tool.

Name: _____

The following are skills I plan to improve:

- _____ By when: _____
- _____ By when: _____
- _____ By when: _____
- _____ By when: _____
- _____ By when: _____
- _____ By when: _____
- _____ By when: _____
- _____ By when: _____
- _____ By when: _____

The following are activities I plan to improve:

- _____ By when: _____
- _____ By when: _____
- _____ By when: _____
- _____ By when: _____
- _____ By when: _____
- _____ By when: _____
- _____ By when: _____
- _____ By when: _____

Conclusion

"Time sneaks up on you like a windshield on a bug."

~ JOHN LITHGOW

It seems fitting that our last words complete the full circle and take us back to the beginning of our book. As we mentioned in the beginning of this book, Anne Drozd's article published in *CAMagazine* listed seven key skills all consultants should have. They are as follows:

1. Ability to learn quickly
2. Proficiency in asking questions
3. Ability to patiently listen and observe
4. Possession of people skills
5. Adeptness at analyzing information and situations and drawing conclusions
6. Creativity
7. Competence as a communicator

It is our contention that as a CPA, before you even opened this book, at a minimum, you possessed the first skill, had an implementation of the second, and more than enough of the fifth and sixth skills. This book was focused on providing you with a different approach to asking questions relative to being a better most trusted business advisor (MTBA) and consultant. Traditional services, in order to be proficient, force us to develop skills in asking questions that rule out information. As an MTBA, our questions need to help us find and uncover new information—sometimes even helping our clients open their eyes to the reality of their situations. And often, it is the way we ask those questions that helps our clients uncover and realize, what is *really* bothering them or keeping them awake at night. We talked a great deal about the importance of improving listening and observing patience, for both you and your client. As far as possession of people skills is concerned, CPAs have always been people who care about other people. However, many times we ignore those little communication techniques that convey just how much we really do care. All of these factors combine to contribute heavily to our competence as communicators. We hope our book has provided value in these areas.

Another key to the success of serving as your clients' MTBA or consultant is proficiently obtaining, managing, and executing the engagements in a manner best suited to your clients' needs. We discussed numerous techniques to help with this, from project estimation to billing, from selling to specific implementation techniques, from meeting management to presentation skills and more. Once again, we hope the ideas we have shared will prove helpful.

With any firm, organizing and administering the practice plays a large role in the profitability of service delivery. We hope our topics like marketing, our Fortress/Empire methodologies, and how to formalize the MTBA focus, as well as nontraditional services within your firm gave you some new ideas about how to refine what you are doing.

One would agree that much of this book is basic stuff. However, our experience is that when you want to improve a process, profitability or delivery, or almost anything, a back-to-the-basics review is the best place to start. So as a parting comment, if there is anything else we can share here, it is to go back and complete all of the forms and exercises in this text. The forms themselves are not the key, but the fact that you take the time to think about all of the issues this book raises is. And don't forget the exercises. Many of them require the involvement of others. It's worth the effort to get together with a couple of your peers (even if they are from other firms) and experience the process. You likely will find that you can revisit these exercises every year and build on the efforts of the past. If you do all of this, you will find that the entire experience will not only help you create a vision of what your firm should look like three or four years from now, but what you should start working on now to facilitate your desired transition.

If you want to beef up your MTBA processes or skills or make some other changes in your practice or the way you serve your clients, there is no time like the present to start. It's never too late to make some changes or strive for more improvement. The clock is ticking. Start now, and you will not be disappointed when you look back at what you have accomplished!

And as a final word: thank you for the time you have given us, and we wish you the best of luck in the future!

Appendix A: Sample Timed Agenda

Date	January 30, 2010
Time	11:00 am–3:00 pm
Location	XYZ Project Site Office
Purpose	Quarterly status review of project
Objectives	• Shared understanding of status and progress to date on project • Discussion, decision making on relevant issues
Special Instructions	None

Agenda Item	Time	Objective	Responsible	Duration
Opening comments	11:00 am	Set a positive tone	Jack and Jim	5 min
Introduction	11:05 am	Information sharing: • Objectives • Agenda • Introductions • Norms • Admin. Issues	Dom	10 min
Safety update	11:15 am	Information sharing: • Review of quarterly safety metrics	Jim	5 min
Lunch break	11:20 am			30 min
Design update	11:50 am	Information sharing: • Review of design activities, milestones reached, status, upcoming activities	Pat and possibly Matt Jones	15 min
Construction update	12:05 pm	Information sharing: • Review of construction activities, milestones reached, status, upcoming activities • Discuss lane closures and switch	Ralph, Bob, and Charles	60 min
Break	01:05 pm			15 min
Quality update	01:20 pm	Information sharing: • Review of quarterly quality metrics	Jack with input from Bill	30 min
Other updates	01:50 pm	Information sharing: • Review of other, relevant quarterly metrics/information	Jim and Jack	10 min

(continued)

Agenda Item	Time	Objective	Responsible	Duration
Action items	02:05 pm	Information sharing • Review of status of action items from prior meetings to the extent they haven't already been covered under other update segments	Jim and Jack	15 min
Process evaluation report	02:20 pm	Information sharing: • Review of quarterly survey results	Dom	20 min.
Update on issues	02:40 pm	Information sharing: • Review of outstanding issues, issues resolved	Jim and Jack	20 min
Materials issue	03:00 pm	Information sharing and decision	Executive Team	20 min
Adjournment			Dom	-----

Appendix B: Food for Thought for CPAs Regarding Facilitating Client Meetings*

Some CPAs have begun to seize the opportunity to help their clients conduct a variety of meetings. These meetings may involve anywhere from a few to several dozen people, taking up hours and hours of valuable time. Many of our clients are coming to the realization that they need to get broad input and involvement for major organizational decisions. Yet, merely assembling a group of managers for dialogue around an agenda will not guarantee a useful end product. Successful meetings require significant forethought on the part of the CPA facilitator and the client.

> **Example:** Recently, an executive we work with told us that his organization had hired a facilitator several years ago to help run a meeting. The session was a disaster, so the organization proceeded to conduct its meetings without any outside assistance for a few years. But something was missing—the meetings were not as effective as they should be. The group has many intelligent, outspoken members, with strong opinions and a great deal of confidence in their own opinions. The meetings often degenerated into tangential discussions dominated by the loudest members. In spite of their best efforts, most meetings were perceived as a lot of wasted time.

What could they have done to improve the quality of their meetings? Following are some tips that will be of benefit to CPA facilitators and their clients.

Planning Is Not Just for the Facilitator

Successful meetings do not just happen. They require rigorous advance planning to make the most of everyone's time. CPAs need to work with their clients to educate them to the fact that managers *cannot* delegate the entire responsibility to meeting facilitators. Even if a manager engages a CPA facilitator, the manager needs to devote some serious time and effort to plan for a successful outcome. By posing the following questions, CPAs can collaborate with their clients to plan successful meetings.

---

* Adapted from Dominic Cingoranelli, "Successful Meetings," *The CPA Journal* 58, (2001). Reprinted from *The CPA Journal*, January, 2001, copyright 2001, with permission from the New York State Society of Certified Public Accountants.

1. What does the client want to take away from this meeting as a deliverable end product?

This may seem trite, but it is the foundation on which you build the rest of the meeting. Will there be a training component to the meeting, or is it solely group decision work? All participants must be clear about why they are at the meeting. There is no room for ambiguity regarding the purpose of the meeting. In a book by the 3M Meeting Management Team on meeting management, their number one rule is NEVER start a meeting without an agenda.

> **Example:** A meeting to clarify roles and expectations among different work groups will require a totally different approach than one required for development of a mission, vision, and objectives for the total group.

2. Based on the purpose of the meeting, who should attend it?

Whose input is vital to the issue? Who has the knowledge essential to dealing with the problem? Whose involvement afterward is critical to implementation?

> **Example:** If a project management team is meeting to develop a partnering charter, who are the key stakeholders in the project? Who from the stakeholders can commit their organizations to supporting the charter?

> **Example:** If you are conducting a strategic thinking or planning retreat, who should attend? How far down in the organization does top management wish to go for the participant list? This is a tough decision. If the meeting has too many people, it could easily bog down ... if it has too few, you could limit the creativity of the sessions. At times, we suggest a multitiered meeting. For the creative part, we go further down the organizational chart to include more people. And then for a later part of the meeting, we excuse everyone (depending on the size of the firm) but the executive group, partners, or partners and key managers to establish a small decision making group.

3. How much time can and will the client devote to the meeting?

Help your clients be reasonable in their expectations. Many managers underestimate the amount of time required to deal effectively with the issues they want to address in the meeting.

> **Example:** A nonprofit organization wished to involve its senior staff and board of directors in a planning meeting. Management initially proposed two half-days for the meeting, trying to cut down on expense and time away from the office. Many directors were new to the board. Some of them were relatively inexperienced in serving as policy makers. They needed education both in their responsibilities and in the background and purpose of the organization. Two half-days would not allow the level of planning necessary. They could begin to get at some strategic issues, but would need more time to develop plans for the future of their agency. Therefore, they ended up spending about 50 percent more time and

money than they needed to because they had to have two meetings to accomplish what they should have done in one meeting that ran just a bit longer.

4. When will the meeting be conducted?

What time of the year, month, and week is the best time for the participants? Is there a seasonal "slow time" that is more conducive to meeting? What day(s) of the week should they meet?

Example: One CEO initially planned to kick off a meeting for his executive team on a Friday evening. Meeting at the end of the week, after a full week of work, would not necessarily result in high-energy, creative discussions. What made this worse was the CEO, trying to cram as much as possible into as little time as possible, continued the meeting all day Saturday, from 8:00 am until 9:00 pm. This resulted in a waste of time, bad attitudes, and misleading information.

Group meetings take energy and effort. They require participants to be fresh. It's fine to start meetings on a Friday, but not Friday evening after working all day. It was especially unproductive to push all day on Saturday. By Saturday afternoon, people stopped trying to deal with real issues or come up with acceptable solutions for organizational problems. The focus of the participants was to come to an agreement so they could move on to the next topic. Although this might sound productive, as soon as everyone was back at work the next week, people were sabotaging the directives of the meeting. Why? Because they didn't really agree, they were just beaten down into not caring at that time. Some meeting participants retaliated by outwardly opposing various initiatives, whereas others accomplished the same thing by displaying passive-aggressive behavior and simply ignoring the initiatives.

The point here is that trying to stuff a lot of work into a little amount of time may seem productive, but that efficiency will cost the organization significantly more as the ideas are attempted to be implemented because they most likely were not as well thought out or vetted as they should have been. If you are going to have a meeting over the weekend, consider half-day meetings with partial play activities scheduled in to allow people to re-energize.

Example: A firm recently held their retreat at a nice resort a couple hours away from the office. The organization conducted one and one-half days of meeting time in three half-day sessions. All of the participants agreed that they did some of their best work at this meeting. Limiting the sessions to four hours each avoided the mental fatigue of an all-day meeting, and they had an opportunity to recharge in between each session.

5. What must be prepared in advance of the meeting?

Effective planning usually requires advance development of background information and fact-finding. What does the facilitator need to find out in advance in order to help the client? Who will perform what parts of any data collection? How long will it take? Should someone survey or interview people? What sort of workbook should you (or your client) provide to participants before or at the meeting? Effective decision-making requires good information, not just opinions and feelings.

6. Who will conduct the meeting?

Although someone within your client's firm is likely to have the skills and experience to effectively conduct meetings, your clients can still benefit from hiring you to run certain meetings because of the sensitivity of the subject matter or politics, or both. It can be difficult for a person from inside the organization to run certain meetings without stumbling over his or her own viewpoints and biases. Using you as an outsider will help avoid this problem. Use these concepts to help sell your facilitation services. Effective meeting planning and facilitation requires skills in managing group processes.

7. What processes might be used in the meeting?

Many different vehicles can be used to get to the end product. Does your client understand the processes, exercises, and discussions that you propose to use at this meeting? How do they seem to fit the group involved? Are the materials appropriate for the level of participants? What is the objective of each segment or process planned for the meeting? How do they all fit together to achieve the end product? Make sure that the agenda makes sense and that you allow adequate time to cover agenda items. Be certain that your client truly understands what you will be doing during the meeting.

> **Example:** Recently, we worked with a client to plan a meeting for the purpose of developing a project mission statement and charter. We suggested a format that we commonly use for this particular type of workshop for partnered projects. The executive in charge at our client organization suggested that we switch the order of a couple of items on the agenda to mesh with his organization's approach to problem solving. We worked together to modify the agenda for the meeting to make it fit his situation.

8. What critical logistics should you consider for the meeting?

Where will you hold the meeting? Even if your client has adequate facilities in house, you may want to consider holding the meeting off-site to minimize distractions. Will the meeting room accommodate the number of people expected? How should it be set up for the meeting (table groups, classroom style, horseshoe-shaped table, or hollow square for example)? Each of these setups has pros and cons, so you want to choose the one that best fits the meeting you are about to conduct. Can you hang flip chart pages on the walls? Has someone from your firm or your client's organization actually been to the facility and seen the meeting room?

Consider also how you will capture and process the work notes of the meeting. Given the widespread use of laptops, it is relatively common now to have someone at the meeting transcribing the notes during the meeting. Can someone from your client's firm do the transcription? Distribution of notes can occur during or immediately after the meeting. Does the facility have the technical equipment and support you will need for the meeting?

Example: A recent meeting of two dozen managers required real time transcription and distribution of notes throughout the day-long meeting. Unfortunately, the hotel's word processing equipment was outdated. This caused unnecessary aggravation and effort for our assistant to produce and distribute the written output in a timely manner.

9. What should we plan for meals and breaks?

Don't forget about factors like meals, breaks, snacks, and refreshments. A common complaint of ours is that meeting rooms often lack sufficient quantities of ice water and other beverages to keep people adequately hydrated throughout the course of the meeting. Menus and their impact on group work also are often overlooked.

Example: We recommend that meals served at group meetings avoid heavy carbohydrates, such as pasta, as well as turkey. Both of these foods have a tendency to create lethargy in participants. Carbohydrates require our bodies to work harder to assimilate them, and turkey contains tryptophan, a chemical that activates endorphins to make us too relaxed for the work at hand. Strike these items from your meeting menu!

10. What sort of social activities should we plan?

Should your client have a group dinner the evening before the meetings begin? Should they have a breakfast together the morning the meeting begins? How about group recreational activities, or a celebratory dinner or cocktails at the end of the meeting? The facilitator can help clients capitalize on the opportunity to let participants have some fun together outside of the meeting. Giving people the chance to get to know one another, or rekindle their relationships on a personal level will result in better working relationships, yielding even greater long-term payoffs.

Example: Many retreat and meeting-seasoned executives have learned the importance of carefully planning executive sessions. They have learned that there is more to the meeting than just coming to consensus about various current issues. If this more formal meeting is well thought-out and properly conducted, they know that consensus will be far easier to achieve numerous times throughout the year for more informal impromptu discussions. This means you need to pay attention to include after-hours socialization, grouping the individuals in ways to maximize the development of individual working relationships, and take time to structure golf, fishing, or other activities that allow people to get to know one another on a more personal basis.

Conclusion

CPA facilitators easily can add value to their clients' meetings. At times, it may appear to your clients that you, the facilitator, simply walk in, ask a few questions, the participants discuss them, and the group has a successful planning workshop. Nothing could be further from the truth. The most effective meetings require advance planning and discussion. Successful facilitators help their clients understand this and work with them to proactively design their meetings for success.